The Campaigns of Sargon II, King of Assyria, 721–705 B.C.

THE CAMPAIGNS OF SARGON II, KING OF ASSYRIA, 721–705 B.C.

SARAH C. MELVILLE

UNIVERSITY OF OKLAHOMA PRESS | NORMAN

This book is published with the generous assistance of The McCasland Foundation, Duncan, Oklahoma.

All illustrations reproduced by kind permission of Pauline Albenda from her book *The Palace of Sargon II: Monumental Wall Reliefs at Dur-Sharrukin, from Original Drawings Made at the Time of Their Discovery in 1843–1844 by Botta and Flandin* (Paris: Éditions Recherche sur la Civilisations, 1986). The illustrations reproduce original drawings made by Eugène Flandin in the nineteenth century. The drawings are now in the Bibliothèque de l'Institut de France in Paris.

Library of Congress Cataloging-in-Publication Data

Names: Melville, Sarah C. (Sarah Chamberlin), author.
Title: The campaigns of Sargon II, King of Assyria, 721–705 B.C. / Sarah C. Melville.
Description: Norman, Oklahoma : University of Oklahoma Press, 2016. |
Series: Campaigns and commanders ; volume 55 | Includes bibliographical
    references and index.
Identifiers: LCCN 2015047732 | ISBN 978-0-8061-5403-9 (hardcover : alk. paper)
Subjects: LCSH: Sargon II, King of Assyria, –705 B.C.—Military leadership. |
    Assyria—History, Military.
Classification: LCC DS73.8 .M45 2016 | DDC 935/.03—dc23
LC record available at http://lccn.loc.gov/2015047732

The Campaigns of Sargon II, King of Assyria, 721–705 B.C. is Volume 55 in the Campaigns and Commanders series.

The paper in this book meets the guidelines for permanence and durability of the Committee on Production Guidelines for Book Longevity of the Council on Library Resources, Inc. ∞

2 3 4 5 6 7 8 9 10

Interior layout and composition: Alcorn Publication Design

To my beloved family:
Be watchful; stand firm in your faith; be courageous, be strong.
Do everything with love.
(1 Corinthians 16:13–14)

Contents

Illustrations

Figures

Table

Maps

Acknowledgments

I got started on this project after an inspiring breakfast meeting with the OU series editor, Greg Urwin, and the editor-in-chief, Chuck Rankin. Letting my enthusiasm blind me to the magnitude of the undertaking, I assured them that I could finish the book in two years. Now that more than five have passed, I can only thank them for their patience and offer my deep gratitude for their unflagging encouragement, help, and advice. I owe similar debts to many others. My friend and brilliant colleague, Lou Ann Lange, provided constant moral support and read multiple drafts with a true historian's eye for substance and detail. Her insightful suggestions improved the final version immeasurably. I thank my husband, Duncan, who endured my lengthy disquisitions on Assyrian chronology, kept me calm, and plied me with wine at strategic intervals. You are indeed a helpmate. I am grateful to Ben Foster, Ulla Kasten, Seth Richardson, Eckart Frahm, and Alice Slotsky, who generously answered questions and shared resources and who always inspire. Pauline Albenda graciously gave permission for use of the illustrations in this volume, for which I am sincerely grateful. I am especially beholden to the anonymous readers who evaluated the manuscript and made so many valuable recommendations and corrections.

This project would not have been possible at all without ready access to vital cuneiform sources that are scattered across the world in museums and private collections. I owe profound thanks to many scholars, particularly Assyriologists Andreas Fuchs, Simo Parpola, Giovanni B. Lanfranchi, Frederick Mario Fales, and Mikko Luukko, who have published editions of Sargon's royal inscriptions and correspondence. Naturally, any errors this book contains are my own.

In addition, I would like to thank those who have worked so tirelessly behind the scenes: Stephanie Evans, assistant managing editor; Chris Dodge, eagle-eyed copy editor; and Ben Pease, cartographer. I am also grateful to Barb Osgood and the interlibrary loan staff at Clarkson University for their ingenuity in tracking down obscure sources, and to friends in the Department of Humanities and Social Sciences for their untiring support.

Finally, I would be nothing without my wonderful boys, Duncan, James, Chris, and Tim, and my dear siblings, Chris and Katie. You make everything worthwhile.

Conventions

Proper Names

Until the decipherment of cuneiform in the 1840s, Assyrian names were known primarily as they appeared in the Bible. The use of these Hebraized spellings has persisted despite the discovery of the original name forms. This volume follows convention by referring to Assyrian and Babylonian kings by their normalized names (e.g., Sargon, Tiglath-pileser, Shalmaneser, or Merodach-Baladan). All other names are rendered in their original form, although special characters and diacritics have been simplified: sh replaces š; t stands for ṭ; h for ḫ. I have retained ṣ (as in Muṣaṣir), because inserting a t to capture the ts sound of ṣ often results in awkward English spelling (Mutsatsir). There was no "w" consonant in Akkadian, which captured the sound with "u" when necessary. To avoid confusing spellings like Uaush, Uaisi, and Uishdish, I have replaced "u" with "w": Waush, Waisi, Wishdish. Since there is no one right way in English to spell most Akkadian names, readers who consult other sources may find alternate spellings. For example, while I use the spelling Ashur, elsewhere it may appear Assur or Aššur.

Geographical Names

Many place names that appear in ancient texts have yet to be matched to actual locations. Places mentioned in the book that do not appear on the maps are listed in Appendix A, section II ("Unlocated Place Names"). Some of the map locations are provisional. In the scholarly literature (and in the ancient texts), spellings of geographical names vary a great deal.

Translations

When quoting a passage from an ancient text, the convention is to mark breaks or unreadable portions with square brackets. For example, the brackets in the phrase "[sco]uts of the palace herald" indicate that only half of the word "scouts" is legible, whereas [. . .] means that entire words are missing. Words added to ease readers' understanding or make the English translation smoother appear in parentheses: "those (gods) whose temples you have built." Words that cannot be translated into English appear in *italics*. "PN" denotes "personal name" and "GN" denotes "geographical name."

Ancient Words

Transliterated Akkadian words are rendered in italics (*šarru*), while Sumerian logograms appear in small caps with periods between signs (DINGIR.MEŠ). Diacritics and special characters are included when citing the original language.

Chronology of Sargon's Reign

722	Death of Shalmaneser V—Sargon crowned king in Assyria; Merodach-Baladan II seizes the throne in Babylon
721	Ilu-bi'di of Hamath and allies rebel; Sargon secures the Assyrian throne
720	Battle of Der against the Elamites; campaign in Syria-Palestine
719	Campaign in Mannea
718	Punitive campaign against Kiakki of Shinuhtu in Anatolia
717	Conquest of Carchemish; foundation of Dur-Sharrukin
716	Assyrians establish trade center on Egyptian border; campaign in Zagros Mountains
715	Campaign in Zagros Mountains
714	Campaign against Urartu and victory at Waush; looting of Muṣaṣir
713	Campaign to Tabal; Karalla and Ellipi rebel
712	Campaign in Melid
711	Sargon stays in Assyria; the *turtān* puts down a rebellion in Ashdod, takes Gath and Ashdod-yam, and campaigns in Gurgum
710	Invasion of Babylonia
709	Sargon crowned king in Babylon
708	Siege of Dur-Iakin; Magnates campaign in Ellipi and Kummuh
707	Sargon leaves Babylon, enters Dur-Sharrukin; Egyptians extradite Iamani to Assyria

706   Magnates campaign in Karalla

705   Sargon is killed in battle in Tabal; Sennacherib
          crowned king in Assyria

THE CAMPAIGNS OF SARGON II, KING OF ASSYRIA, 721–705 B.C.

INTRODUCTION

During the early part of the first millennium B.C., the Assyrian state grew from a modest kingdom on the Tigris River to a vast, well-organized empire. Arguably the greatest warrior-king of this period, Sargon II (721–705 B.C.) ranks among the most illustrious ancient military minds. Scholars call the final, greatest phase of Assyrian expansion the Sargonid period after him, yet today his accomplishments are little known outside specialist circles. Indeed, most studies of ancient warfare that discuss the Neo-Assyrian Empire do so in general terms, conflating the discrete developments and political nuances of more than two hundred years into a uniform narrative of brutal conquest. In this vein, Sargon is remembered chiefly for his war against Urartu and for deporting the hapless Israelites. In fact, his campaigns not only changed the geopolitical dynamics in the Near East but also made Assyria into a world power, inspired a period of outstanding cultural florescence, and helped pave the way for the empires of Persia and Alexander.

Sargon's achievements stand out all the more when we consider the world in which he lived. Sun-drenched and wind-blown, Assyria received enough rain (in a good year) to dry-farm its crops, though a secure food supply required irrigation and careful water management. The specter of drought, blight, locusts, and floods haunted farmers. Theirs was an unpredictable and precarious world of contrasts. Villages of mud-brick hovels nestled close to magnificent cities, whose massive fortifications and lush pleasure parks spoke of privilege and plenty. Elites lived in huge, beautifully furnished mansions, in which servants catered to their every need. Colossal temples rivaled the palace in complexity and financial organization, but their mission was to please the gods, rather than to benefit the poor or proselytize. Remote, cryptic, and seemingly capricious, Sargon's gods communicated with humans through divination or natural phenomena, such as earthquakes and pestilence. Pregnant with hidden meaning, the natural environment required constant interpretation. The king, in particular, had to attend to ominous events, for he was responsible for his people's well-being. His was a world in flux and perennially at war. Rulers vied with each other for supremacy, armies clashed, and might made right. Politics proved to be as complex, theatrical, and brutal as warfare. Slow communication afforded political players time to process, brood upon, and react to their opponent's intentions, but the high stakes made the game particularly deadly. One slip could spell death, and rulers frequently paid with their lives for errors of judgment. In this unforgiving environment, Sargon established a new world order in which Assyria reigned supreme.

This study investigates Sargon's military achievements within the context of Assyria's transformation from hegemonic state to a primarily territorial empire, complete with a provincial system, standing army, and central administration.[1] A far cry from the raider-kings of the early empire, Sargon had the resources to take a more sophisticated approach to imperial rule. He could apply force selectively, with deliberate economy, and as only one of several possible ways to deal with external threat or to exploit opportunity. What had begun as annual extortion raids had progressed, by the late eighth century, into carefully planned conquests carried out by experienced regulars and temporary levies. With the capacity to supply the army and the disciplinary means to exert control over it, Sargon could apply military force with a precision few other states could match. Knowing that Assyrian supremacy depended as much on creating a credible impression of power (through spectacle and diplomacy) as on tangible evidence (material riches and the use of force), Sargon became adept at managing both. Given the circumstances, Assyria's survival depended on it.

In the Near East's harsh physical environment, in which water, basic raw materials, and arable land were in perilously short supply, the quest for survival and security did not leave much room for sentimentality. The critical need to control strategic locations, transportation, and trade routes created an unstable geopolitical situation and a nearly constant state of war. As a result, the peoples of the ancient world viewed violence and warfare as legitimate and even natural ways to achieve their objectives. The deprivations of war raised few qualms, at least among those who stood to benefit most. For ordinary people, it remained an unavoidable evil that they had to endure in order to survive. But if defeat brought despair and death, the rewards of victory proved transitory at best. Peace was impermanent because it represented combatants' exhaustion rather than the actual resolution of their differences. No matter how great a leader or his army, power remained contingent and ephemeral. The effort to secure resources and political advantage over surrounding competitors naturally inclined Assyria to develop as an expansionary state.

Imperial growth proved to be a complex, difficult process. In addition to sustained human effort, expansion required an immense outlay of the very resources that it aimed to secure. The attendant, unpredictable political and economic problems put tremendous pressure on the state, its leadership, and the army. For every solved problem, several new ones emerged. Even the removal of plunder consumed human and material resources, while conquest burned through men and matériel. Losses required replenishment, which in turn fueled the need for further expansion. Always fragile and conditional, the imperial system required constant, thorough oversight and planning. As it turned out, Sargon had exactly the qualities necessary for Assyria to thrive. An intelligent leader, he united the Assyrian elite to his purpose and maintained their support for over fifteen years. His methods—both violent and peaceful—were no different from those of his contemporaries, or from those of other storied leaders such as Alexander or Caesar. Although conquest often started on the bloody battlefield, Sargon did not campaign for sport or from some perverse love of destruction. Nor did subjugation lead inevitably to resource exploitation and population deprivation. The king understood that the economic development of conquered lands would lead to a higher standard of living and increased political stability throughout the empire. While deportation also served as an effective pacification measure, the goal was a secure and prosperous environment for everyone in the empire. The best way to create a sustainable flow of goods to the Assyrian core was to encourage trade and production on the periphery. Consequently, where new lands would not repay investment, they were abandoned and their people moved to areas with greater economic potential.

Commercial interests were nothing new to the Assyrians. By the eighth century, trade and conquest had become inextricably linked, and even royal trade agents (*tamkāru/tamkārānû*) were involved in military operations.[2] Knowing that his predecessors' territorial acquisitions had provided him with the military means and wealth to control Near Eastern trade, Sargon made this one of his primary objectives.[3] Naturally, economic goals dovetailed with other strategic aims, including imperial security, dominance over rivals, and internal stability. While there is no doubt that Sargon's actions contributed to the deaths of tens of thousands, he also spared many people, for he understood the utility of clemency and made a point of showing mercy when it suited his purposes. Rare cases of extreme violence (flaying or impalement) were considered earned punishment and inflicted at the will of the king. Every practical royal decision also resonated within the spiritual plane.

Unlike our society, which scrupulously separates the religious and secular spheres, ancient Near Eastern societies did not recognize a distinction but considered the earthly realm a reflection of the divine one and the king the link between the two. To put it another way, the ancients understood that "the world of appearance and the world of essence" were the same.[4] This outlook infused every act— especially royal ones—with latent meaning that required discovery and explication. The most successful kings always explained what they did in ideological terms that imbued even the most calculated practical action with symbolic significance. Violence and subjugation became "more than simply stratagems of power, they [were] right, good, beautiful, desirable, and sublime in their accordance of the particular individual with the course of the universe."[5] Thus, like his contemporaries, Sargon recorded every important undertaking—from executions, banquets, and building projects, to gift exchange, rituals, and battlefield victories—in ways that not only helped to fulfill ideological imperatives but also simultaneously bolstered his reputation and realized his strategic goals. Military operations must be understood within this dualistic setting.

If hindsight clarifies many of Sargon's goals, it cannot completely unmask his strategy for achieving them or reveal the personality behind his deeds. Precious little personal information about him has survived. Time has obliterated the names of all but a handful of those closest to him. Nevertheless, we know that the king made use of those he trusted: he made his brother grand vizier; married off his daughter for political purposes; sent the magnates to campaign on his behalf; and when he traveled, he left his son, Sennacherib, in charge. Of court life we know chiefly that the royal palaces were sumptuous, the administrative organization large and complex, and that the king preferred to appoint eunuchs to top positions, presumably because they were more loyal and less inclined to intrigue than married men seeking advantage for their families. Sargon's character remains opaque, although his nearly constant campaigning suggests that he was a man of action who preferred life with the army to a more sedentary, comfortable existence at court. Likewise, his accomplishments demonstrate that he was a decisive leader, an excellent judge of human nature, and a savvy politician, one able to attract a capable coterie of supporters and maintain their loyalty. Above all, Sargon proved adept at the Near East's unique brand of power politics, which involved an equal measure of prestige-making spectacle and Realpolitik. For all we know about Sargon's world, there is much more that remains obscure, chiefly because the evidence is cryptic, chronologically diffuse, and fragmentary.

Although only a fraction of what once existed has survived, Sargon II's reign is the best recorded of any Assyrian king. Letters, royal inscriptions, administrative documents, chronographic sources, ritual texts, literary works, sculptured reliefs, architectural remains, and artifacts are what allow scholars entrée into a remote world of politics, intrigue, and war. Most of the written sources have now been published (or republished) in up-to-date transliterations and translations in two main series: the Helsinki-based State Archives of Assyria (SAA) and the Philadelphia-based Royal Inscriptions of the Neo-Assyrian Period (RINAP), which continues the work of Toronto's now-defunct Royal Inscriptions of Mesopotamia: Assyrian periods (RIMA). All of the SAA volumes and most of the RINAP material (though not yet Sargon's inscriptions) are currently available online in fully searchable formats.[6] Additionally, Andreas Fuchs has published Sargon's royal inscriptions from Dur-Sharrukin (*ISK*) and his Nineveh Annals (*AJ 711*) in score transliterations that reveal significant variations among the numerous texts and copies. Helsinki's multivolume *Prosopography of the Neo-Assyrian Empire* (PNA) helps us to reconstruct the social network of Assyrian officialdom under Sargon, while Parpola and Porter's *The Helsinki Atlas of the Near East in Neo-Assyrian Period* and Google Earth have contributed significantly to our knowledge of terrain and the geopolitical environment. Without access to all of these resources, completion of this project would have been attenuated, if not impossible. Nevertheless, many questions about the chronology of this period lack definitive answers. In some cases, the best we can do is to piece together an interpretation based on a critical reading of the sources and a well-developed understanding of their purpose, historical context, audience, and cultural and ideological milieu. The following introduces readers unfamiliar with Assyriology to the most important types of evidence and the problems involved in their interpretation.

Written Sources

The Assyrians spoke Akkadian, a Semitic language, of which Assyrian and Babylonian were the main dialects. Using a reed stylus, scribes impressed cuneiform (wedge-shaped) signs onto clay tablets without including spaces between words, paragraph breaks, or punctuation of any kind. Each sign of this syllabic and polyvalent writing system could represent several different syllables, and one syllable could be written with numerous signs. For example, there were sixteen different ways to write the vowel "u," while the sign we know as *tar* had more than twenty additional readings, some more common than others. For some reason unknown to us, scribes almost always wrote common nouns, such as king (*šarru*), country (*mātu*), or god (*ilu*), with a Sumerian logogram (LUGAL, KUR, and DINGIR, respectively) instead of spelling them out syllabically. Despite its complexity, cuneiform proved so versatile that several non-Akkadian-speaking peoples, including the Urartians, Hurrians, Hittites, Elamites, and Persians, adapted it to write their own languages. Other groups developed their own writing systems, but everyone viewed writing itself as a vector for communicating with the gods. Anything written down, particularly royal records, acquired the potential to influence reality.

Of increasing importance during the eighth century was the West Semitic language Aramaic, which eventually became the lingua franca of the Near East, although cuneiform persisted into the second century A.D. in some areas. Scribes wrote Aramaic in an alphabetic script on cloth, leather, lead strips, potsherds, and wax-covered writing boards. Assyrian sculptured reliefs depict pairs of scribes, one writing on a board and one inscribing Akkadian on a clay tablet.[7] Although most Assyrians probably spoke both languages, under Sargon the royal court conducted official business strictly in Akkadian. Sargon himself famously answered a query about the use of Aramaic by insisting, "Why would you not write and send me messages in Akkadian? Really, the message that you write in it (the dispatch) must be drawn up in this very manner— this is a permanent regulation!"[8] However particular Sargon was about royal correspondence, the Assyrian empire confronted and was influenced by a wide range of ethnic groups and their associated languages, including Elamite, Urartian, Luwian, Phrygian, Phoenician, Hebrew, Egyptian, Greek, and the Indo-Hurrian and early Iranian dialects of the Zagros Mountain dwellers. Most of the written sources referred to in this volume—whatever their original language—offer the advantage of having been composed as the events they describe unfolded, or soon thereafter.

According to long-established tradition, each Assyrian king produced a body of texts that celebrated his most glorious military, religious, and civic accomplishments. Royal inscriptions took a variety of forms: some were inscribed on freestanding steles or natural rock formations; some on the walls, doors, thresholds, and bull colossi of palaces; some on prism- or cylinder-shaped clay tablets dedicated in temples; and others on small gold, silver, copper, lead, or lapis lazuli tablets buried in the foundations of important buildings. The intended audience for these texts varied accordingly.[9] Although the public could see (if not read) most large-scale monuments, only courtiers, noble visitors, and perhaps some military personnel could view palace inscriptions, whereas texts dedicated in temples, buried in the foundations, or otherwise hidden from view were meant for the gods and future kings who might find them during building renovations. Even though they recorded real events, royal inscriptions combined "different levels of discourse, including heroic presentation, literary elaboration, traditional definitions of space and peoples, programmatic views of dominion and of conquered and conquerable territories."[10] In other words, the king's narrative texts served a number of social, ideological, and political purposes. Conceptually, those steles and rock reliefs that the king erected to mark the limits of the ordered Assyrian world (limits that he created) harmonized with those that he put in his palace at the heart of the empire.[11] A chief feature of these texts was the report of military campaigns arranged according to regnal year (palû), eponym (limu), or geographical area. Some kings used more than one organizing principle in different sets of inscriptions so that the order of events given in one text appeared out of sequence in another. Since text production continued throughout the king's reign, as scribes composed updated editions, they often revised accounts of earlier events to reflect the most recent political and military developments. Once-celebrated incidents were sometimes altered or omitted if their relevance had declined over time.[12] By the same token, later editions sometimes included information not found in earlier versions. Scribes varied content according to present circumstances, the intended audience, and the display location of the text.

Royal inscriptions focused exclusively on the king and adhered to certain conventions in order to prove his legitimacy, the gods' approbation, and Assyria's might. Campaign accounts were narrated in the first person by the king, who took credit for every endeavor whether or not he had personally participated. These texts rarely, if ever, related grand strategy, diplomatic and military objectives, or battlefield tactics, and they only tangentially recorded the personal experiences of anyone other than the king. All military campaigns, although they might entail hardship, were ultimately successful: the king triumphed and the army suffered few, if any, casualties and never suffered defeat, though it was sometimes implied. By contrast, the enemy was always perfidious, illegitimate, poorly prepared, and unsuccessful. Despite their formulaic style, the popular and oft-repeated view that these texts were the product of "gross exaggeration and a degree of spin verging on outright fabrication" both misses the point and oversimplifies.[13] Scribes chose wording with precision, making subtle distinctions between types of engagement, size of enemy settlements, the relative power of enemy leaders (ranging from city lords to kings), and even the significance of campaigns.[14] While authors did omit unfavorable events and embellish for dramatic effect, they did so within strict parameters that had developed over a long time in accord with core cultural and religious beliefs. They could not lie outright. The present challenge lies in discerning the limits of their equivocation. By paying careful attention to actual wording, by being attentive to omissions, and by finding corroborating or supplemental evidence in outside sources whenever possible, we can extract valuable historical information from royal inscriptions. By using all the evidence at our disposal, we may also determine how these texts (and images) functioned within the society as a whole.

Together, text and image (narrative reliefs and royal statues) effectively shaped and canonized cultural memory. At the very least, they tell us how the Assyrian king wanted people, the gods, and posterity to view the events of his reign. More than disingenuous royal propaganda, these works mediated between what Egyptologist Jan Assman terms communicative memory and cultural memory.[15] As Niven and Berger explain, communicative memory develops over time and "is linked to personal experience and social interaction," whereas cultural memory "takes a set form embodied in, for instance, texts, images and rituals through which societies and groups celebrate and commemorate defining moments."[16] As part of a centuries-old tradition—therefore an organ of cultural memory—the Assyrian royal inscriptions also helped shape communicative memory. For example, the Letter to Ashur, composed immediately after Sargon's campaign against Urartu in 714 and probably read aloud to the people of Ashur at a ceremony in the same year, clearly served to influence the way people understood and remembered what had just happened. In this way, the king could establish a connection between his own interests and those of the public. Both the memory of a shared past and the Assyrian collective identity coalesced in the person of the king. In turn, the king used his symbolic place within cultural memory to manipulate communicative memory and so retain power.

In addition to the complexities the genre itself offers, Sargon's inscriptions present the modern interpreter with a variety of difficulties, and it is useful to review the salient features of his text corpus here. Before Sargon took up residence in his new city, Dur-Sharrukin, in 706, he governed from Calah (Nimrud) where he renovated the palace of Ashurnaṣirpal II (883–859) and added his own twenty-two-line text above that of his predecessor on a couple of door jambs. The Calah inscription summarized the campaigns and building activities of the first eight years of Sargon's reign.[17] Prism fragments, also from Calah, recapped Sargon's accomplishments through at least 709.[18] Additional text fragments from Nineveh and Ashur are generally dated to 711 on internal grounds.[19] For Sargon's new capital, Dur-Sharrukin, royal scribes created several different texts categorized today as "Summary Inscriptions," "Display Inscriptions," and "Annals," the contents of which were arranged in different ways. For example, the Summary Inscriptions on the bull colossi of the palace at Dur-Sharrukin organized Sargon's campaigns geographically, starting with operations in western Iran, moving counter-clockwise around the empire's periphery, and ending in Babylonia.[20] Every one of the stone thresholds recovered from Sargon's palace had one of five different Summary Inscriptions carved into its reverse side, and many of the wall reliefs also had similarly brief texts carved on the back where no one would ever see them.[21] A continuous inscribed band divided the two registers of sculptured narrative reliefs with one of two texts: Annals reporting Sargon's first fourteen campaigns arranged according to regnal year, and the Display Inscription, a geographically organized summary account similar to the text on the bull colossi.[22] Unfortunately, these have survived in very poor condition.

A further complication arises from the fact that the chronological arrangement of campaigns in Sargon's inscriptions is inconsistent. Some texts—the poorly preserved Nineveh prism, a tablet fragment probably also from Nineveh, and Ashur prism fragments—dated all the campaigns one year earlier than the Dur-Sharrukin Annals. The numbering discrepancy seems to represent scribal efforts to gloss over the brevity of Sargon's two-and-a-half-month "accession year" (722) by ignoring it, or to disguise the military inactivity of his first full year (721) and his ninth year (712), during which the king stayed home.[23] This explanation resolves most of these chronological problems and conforms to Assyrian ideology, which emphasized military accomplishments and presumed that the king would campaign annually. In order to avoid confusion, modern scholars follow this chronology and date the start of Sargon's reign to 721.

In addition to the inscriptions that Sargon distributed throughout Assyria proper, several steles and monumental rock reliefs marked the empire's borders and commemorated conquests. These monuments did not copy Sargon's domestic inscriptions but tailored content to local conditions and so supplement the longer texts. For example, the Borowski Stele, which was erected in the vicinity of Hamath in Syria in circa 708, and its probable contemporary, the Cyprus Stele, found at Larnaka, both include statements that Sargon deported 6,300 Assyrian "criminals" to Hamath, a claim that so far has not appeared in any of his domestic inscriptions.[24] Similar monuments have been discovered in western Iran, northern Syria, and southern Palestine near the Egyptian border.[25]

Some texts served a more specialized purpose. A very large, beautifully inscribed tablet, the Letter to Ashur, found in the private house of an exorcist in the city of Ashur, contains a stunning literary account of Sargon's eighth campaign against Urartu in 714. While this text offers the most detailed record of any ancient Near Eastern military campaign, and although a dated colophon proves that it was composed immediately after the events it describes, it is by no means a straightforward campaign history. The Letter to Ashur is a masterwork full of literary references, figurative language, poetic cadences, puns, and other wordplay.[26] It also includes (uncharacteristically) a wealth of ethnographic and geographical information about the peoples and places the Assyrians encountered.

Another unusual tablet, the Ashur Charter, records the exemptions awarded to certain cities and temples as a reward for their support during the king's first, uncertain months on the throne.[27] The text also reveals Sargon's contempt for his brother and predecessor, Shalmaneser V, whom it characterizes as a criminal heretic.

In addition to this large array of official texts, a significant corpus of epistolary material has survived. About 1,200 letters and letter fragments from Sargon's reign amount to "the most extensive political correspondence of a major ruler extant from ancient Mesopotamia and probably from ancient times altogether."[28] Despite their quantity, these texts resist straightforward reading. In Assyria, the social conventions governing communication with the king prohibited invoking him by name. The standard greeting formula read, "To the king, my lord, your servant, [Personal Name]. May it be well with the king, my lord," and although some letters refer to the day or month, none name the eponym or regnal year. Letters rarely mention foreign rulers by name but refer to them instead with a place-of-origin designator such as "the Urartian" or "the Ukkean." Since writers assumed the reader's familiarity with the subject matter, they seldom included background information or explanations of context. As a result, the only way to attribute a particular letter to Sargon's reign or assign a relative date is through painstaking prosopographical analysis (the study of the relationships between people who belong to the same group) and the cross-referencing of subject matter, both within the correspondence and externally with other categories of text.[29] Unless a letter mentions events also known from royal inscriptions or foreign texts (and is thus datable), prosopography offers the best means of dating.

Dating and attribution problems notwithstanding, the letter corpus contains a wealth of detail about military and intelligence operations throughout the empire. Only a few letters authored by Sargon himself have survived, and the bulk of the correspondence comprises reports that officials or the crown prince, Sennacherib, sent to him. The fact that many letters quote the king's or some other correspondent's previous messages helps to reconstruct the topical context. The royal correspondence also reveals a great deal about Assyrian diplomacy, military operations, politics, and administrative hierarchy. Governors and officials on the frontiers of Assyria sent out spies and gathered information about enemy activity, which they then reported to the crown and to each other.[30] Because communication was not only vertical (from informant to governor to king) but also horizontal (between officials), almost all information could be corroborated and its accuracy checked. The habit of quoting previous letters provided additional means of verification. Though royal inscriptions and correspondence are the most valuable written sources for Sargon's reign, coordinating them with each other has proved extremely difficult.

Thus far, most attempts to match letters to specific events in the royal inscriptions have proved inconclusive, because the two genres differed sharply in focus and purpose. Each one represented a different source of royal power—what one scholar famously termed "prestige and interest."[31] The ideologically charged royal inscriptions dealt retrospectively with the king's activities for the chief purpose of establishing his reputation and legitimacy, thus his prestige. As official documents, they tell us how the king wanted his various audiences to think about what happened. By contrast, the correspondence reported daily events in order to inform the king about his interests—that is, what had transpired outside of his immediate presence. Royal inscriptions focused on conventional military operations: the king and his army on campaign, fighting battles, and undertaking sieges. Letters informed the king about almost everything else, including espionage, diplomacy, intelligence findings, covert operations, criminal activity, and resistance. The inscriptions commemorated past events (usually) in chronological order; the letters recorded events as they unfolded out of chronological context. Likewise, the inscriptions included only those events deemed worth celebrating, whereas letters reported anything of note. In other words, the contents of the two genres tended to be mutually exclusive.

The result is that, while the inscriptions have produced a relatively certain chronology of Sargon's campaigns, we cannot be sure exactly how the letters fit into that chronology. Rather than adopt a false certainty about my dating of the letters, I prefer to acknowledge the problems as well as draw the reader's attention to alternative interpretations in the endnotes. A case in point is the especially problematic group of dispatches concerning Assyria's chief enemy, Urartu, located to the north of Assyria. Well over fifty tablets and tablet fragments report Urartian activities during Sargon's reign.[32] Those that describe an important Cimmerian victory over Urartu group together fairly easily, but many others, such as those tracking

the Urartian king's movements, offer no clues about whether they
belong to the Cimmerian sequence or stand alone. Nor do they identify the Urartian king by name. As a result, scholars have proposed
several competing interpretations, none of which resolve all the
problems associated with the letters. The highly contested case of
Urartian/Assyrian/Cimmerian chronological concordance merits a
separate discussion in an appendix (appendix B), because the resolution that I propose greatly affects the arrangement of this book, not
to say the final assessment of Sargon's reign.

Although Assyrian sources provide the bulk of the written evidence for the period under investigation, many of the peoples con-
fronting Assyria produced their own records, and these survive in
numerous languages and forms. Like their Assyrian counterparts,
foreign texts were subject to conventions and served the multifari-
ous purposes of the individuals who produced them. Assyrian kings
were not alone in creating self-aggrandizing monuments, although
they did so in vastly greater numbers and with more detail and
sophistication than neighboring rivals. The Urartians borrowed
from Assyria both the cuneiform writing system and the practices
of composing annals and erecting inscribed monuments. Sargon's
contemporaries, Rusa, son of Sarduri (ca. 730–714 B.C.) and Argishti
II (ca. 713–685), left inscriptions that, with one or two exceptions,
did not include information about Urartian politics or Urartian-
Assyrian relations. So far, excavations at Urartian sites have not produced the quantity or variety of texts found in Assyria.

To the east of Assyria, many of the small tells (ruin mounds) of
the Zagros Mountain polities have been mapped by archaeologists,
but scattered excavations have produced very little writing of any
kind. One exception, a stele found near Bukan in West Azerbaijan,
Iran, bears a fragmentary inscription in nonnative Aramaic, while
recent excavations at nearby Rabat Tepe have uncovered several
cuneiform brick inscriptions that await full publication.[33] Virtually
all of the area's tells remain unidentified. Only circumstantial evidence (such as size and location along a main route) allows us to
associate a given site with one named in the royal inscriptions, a
fact that inhibits the reconstruction of campaign routes. The situation in Syria-Palestine is much more positive, although not without
similar problems. The biblical books Isaiah, First and Second Kings,
and Chronicles trace the Israelites' mixed experiences with different Assyrian kings, among whom Sargon receives less attention

than some of his fellows. No other contemporary foreign texts refer directly to Sargon, though a wide variety of fragmentary inscriptions in Luwian, Phrygian, Aramaic, and Phoenician bear witness to the fortunes of local kingdoms, such as Tyre, Patina/Unqi, Sam'al, and Carchemish in Syria, and the principalities of Quwê, Tabal, Melid, and Gurgum in Anatolia.[34] Narrative art that is sometimes used to corroborate or supplement texts must also be interpreted critically.

Palace Reliefs

After Ashurnaṣirpal II decorated the walls of his palace at Calah with sculptured bas reliefs, it became the practice for all of the most successful (and therefore rich) Assyrian kings to decorate their royal residences with sculptures commemorating their military deeds, manly pursuits (hunting), and state occasions (banqueting, delivery of tribute, or review of prisoners). At some locations, wall paintings or modeled glazed brick augmented or replaced reliefs.[35] For the first few years of his reign, Sargon resided in Ashurnaṣirpal's palace, which he renovated, although little evidence of his work has survived.[36] In 717, he began building a new city called Dur-Sharrukin (Fort Sargon). Construction continued throughout his reign, and the city was officially dedicated in 706, just a year before the king's death.[37] The site was first excavated by the French in the 1840s and 1850s, followed by the Oriental Institute of the University of Chicago in the 1920s and then briefly by the Iraqi antiquities authority in 1957.[38] Most of the surviving sculptures are now in the Louvre, the University of Chicago's Oriental Institute, and the Iraq Museum, although a few remain on-site or in private collections. The narrative reliefs were arranged in two registers separated by the Display Inscription or Annals. Unfortunately, not only were the reliefs found in a very poor state of preservation, but a large number of those excavated by the French were lost when the ship transporting them sank in the Tigris River. French archaeologists left other sculptures open to the elements at Dur-Sharrukin, where they crumbled away in a matter of decades. Consequently, most of the narrative reliefs survive only in drawings made on-site during excavation. Archaeologists found war scenes in only five rooms. Each room depicted one region and probably even a single campaign: Room I contained fragments of an unidentified eastern campaign; Room II illustrated the Zagros

campaign of 716; Room V was devoted to the 720 invasion of Syria-
Palestine; Room XIII included fragments showing the eighth campaign of 714; and Room XIV depicted the 715 campaign into the
Zagros.[39] The reliefs can only be associated with four campaign
years, and no sculptures illustrating campaigns to Tabal, Babylonia,
or central Anatolia have survived. Hence the harlequin nature of
this book's illustrations.[40]

Depictions of warfare on the palace reliefs have long been used
to supplement the textual material, and while the sculptures provide
a wealth of military detail, their analysis entails many of the same
problems that we associate with royal inscriptions. In focusing on the
king's deeds and Assyrian might, the reliefs functioned as the visual
equivalent of the inscriptions, though the sculptures complement,
rather than reproduce, textual content. Although they illustrate contemporary events and may have been designed by eyewitness artists, the reliefs are not precursors of modern photojournalism but
the highly idealized and stylized interpretation of events. Like the
royal inscriptions, the sculptures helped to shape memory and pro-
mulgate an Assyrian identity (at least among the elite). In order to
glean reliable information from the sculptures, it is necessary briefly
to identify and understand the ideological, cultural, and technical
constraints that governed artistic representation in Assyria.[41]

Foremost among these conventions was the same principle that
dominated the inscriptions, namely that the Assyrians should always
be shown as victorious and negative results omitted. On the reliefs,
soldiers experience just enough hardship (usually involving sieges)
to garner the viewer's admiration, but the result is never in doubt:
Assyria's various enemies fight and are vanquished in turn. The focus
on victory over an ill-prepared, unorganized, less civilized enemy
served not only to improve the morale of the troops and encourage
public support but may also have helped soldiers overcome both the
fear of death and the social proscription against killing.[42] Assuming,
that is, that any of those groups got to view the reliefs.

Other conventions peculiar to artistic narrative were at work
as well. Artists used set behavior and collective stereotypes to distinguish between different groups such as foreigners and units of
the Assyrian army. Thus, all Itu'ean auxiliaries wear short kilts,
have bare chests, and sport headbands; Assyrian heavy infantry
wear mail shirts and conical helmets; Egyptian Kushites are clean-
shaven, have tightly curled, cropped hair, wear tunics, and carry two

javelins; and warriors from the Zagros Mountains wear animal skins and fight using spears and bows.[43] Enemy cavalry and chariotry do not appear on Sargon's reliefs, even though we know from written sources that many, if not all, opposing armies fielded equestrian contingents. Presumably the omission had both an artistic and an actualizing purpose. Showing only Assyrian chariotry and cavalry not only eased viewers' reading of the narrative but also secured a permanent advantage for the Assyrians through a kind of sympathetic magic. In the ancient Near East, the image was thought to embody the essence of the object it depicted and thus achieved a sort of agency.

The best way to transfer a continuous narrative of three-dimensional activities to a two-dimensional surface proved an ongoing challenge for ancient artists, who solved the problem by arranging the sequence of events like a comic strip. Sculptors used narrative devices to represent movement through time and space so that one scene flowed naturally into the next. In the process, a type of artistic shorthand reduced military operations to their most important elements: the march in-country; the battle or siege; and the aftermath, when the king reviewed prisoners. Soldier duos, chariot teams, and cavalry pairs could represent whole contingents; therefore, it is impossible to tell how many troops were involved in a given engagement. By following these guidelines, artists not only fulfilled the precepts of Assyrian ideology but made the narrative easy for viewers to follow.[44] Likewise, while the reliefs seem to represent arms, armor, and equipment accurately and with fine detail, it is important to be aware of their shortcomings. The image of a shield, dagger, or helmet cannot reveal the material from which the actual objects were manufactured. The weave of a tower shield might represent wicker or leather, whereas plate armor and helmets could denote bronze, iron, or even leather. Identifying specific locations is still more problematic. Only a few of Sargon's reliefs carry cuneiform epigraphs that name the cities depicted, and, of these, still fewer have actually been located. On the whole, however, details such as flora, fauna, terrain, enemy costume, and architecture allow us to determine the general region shown. Ideological imperatives notwithstanding, it is clear that both artists and scribes took care to represent warfare as accurately as the confines of convention and the limits of style allowed.[45]

Archaeology

While archaeology has uncovered virtually all of the extant evidence, there is much that even the best, most technologically advanced archaeological methods cannot reveal. Sometimes, even though excavations of large tells indicate that they were once important fortified cities, archaeologists can neither identify their ancient names nor link them with places named in inscriptions.[46] The unsatisfactory result: a host of nameless sites and site-less place names. Even when we can identify a tell, it is seldom possible to match evidence from a particular excavation level to a known historical event or person. For example, while Neo-Assyrian remains are well attested in Syria-Palestine, there is no way to ascribe them to the reign of a particular king without datable material found in situ. The fact that kings often campaigned repeatedly in the same area makes precise dating even less likely. Finally, the tendency for archaeologists to privilege famous historical events over lesser known ones when attempting to interpret evidence has skewed our understanding of the historical and chronological record.[47] Nonetheless, archaeologists have contributed important new insights into Near Eastern political processes, the built environment and the politics of landscape, and the physical manifestations of sovereignty.[48]

The preceding discussion makes it apparent that as a study of war this work differs substantially from those that treat more modern subjects. The type of detailed information available for other periods simply does not exist for the ancient Near East, which has produced no written military theory, no treatises on strategic planning, no soldiers' memoirs, or explanations of logistical organization, tactics, or fighting styles. Today's most popular subjects, such as the gritty war experiences of common soldiers and civilians, did not interest ancient chroniclers, who forbore from recording personal feelings except in stock terms to benefit the king. As for how common folk felt about the decisions of those in power—decisions that often resulted in social upheaval, death, and deprivation—we have only what the texts insinuate, which is precious little. Common soldiers, merchants, farmers, deported families, faceless bureaucrats, and all the rest participate only as extras or in walk-on roles. Moreover, as we have seen, much of the information concerning Sargon is subject to debate. In order to maintain the narrative flow, I omit the kind of lengthy, detailed argumentation found in specialist articles and leave the endnotes to point the reader to corroborating or opposing views. The single exception to this is the discussion of the Urartian/ Assyrian chronology in Appendix B.

In recording their own story as they chose to remember it, the Assyrians captured a meaningful truth, one that reflected their world-view, their values, how they operated, and how they thought about their actions.[49] Within this cultural framework, Sargon applied power in a variety of subtle ways, depending on circumstance and the other actors involved. This book presents a critical interpretation of the currently available sources for Sargon's reign within their military, political, economic, and cultural context in order to shed light on methods of Assyrian imperialism and contemporary geopolitics. Above all, it establishes Sargon II as an exceptional military leader and visionary ruler.

CHAPTER I

Setting the Stage

ASSYRIA AND ITS ARMY

Posterity has long recognized Sargon II as one of the chief archi-
tects of the Neo-Assyrian Empire, the man who transformed
a burgeoning power into the undisputed master of the Near East
by continuously and successfully waging war. Despite the popular image of the Assyrians raping and pillaging their way to power
and ruling through fear, the evidence reveals a complex process that
not only responded to contemporary imperatives but also respected
long-standing tradition. Sargon belonged to a culture more than a
thousand years old, one whose war fighting reflected a common
Near Eastern worldview that made the king responsible to the gods
for everything that happened.

In the ancient Near East, warfare had many functions and
meanings. Kings enacted political decisions through warfare, yet on
another level war was an "ordalic procedure" (a trial by combat)
through which rulers sought to impose order on the universe and
defeat the agents of chaos.[1] It was also a masculine contest between
individual leaders and a chance for elites to prove their worth and
gain status. The fortunes of war fed or depleted economies and
helped the ruling class maintain power over the common people.
Just as war ravaged the countryside and decimated populations, it
led to the intermingling of different ethnic groups, provided opportunities for individual and group advancement, and promoted the
exchange of ideas and technologies across borders and geographic
zones. Then, as now, it had far-reaching consequences, not all of
them negative. The ravages of war also inspired literary works such
as Erra and Ishum that explored the moral implications of violence.[2]
Over time, nearly constant conflict among competing states had a
homogenizing effect so that historical enemies developed similar
cultures of war (rules and expectations) and methods of political

discourse.[3] Conversely, when expansion took armies into distant foreign lands, whose terrain often proved difficult and whose "barbarian" people did not share the same cultural or military practices, violence tended to escalate. In pursuing his interests, Sargon II utilized methods of warfare and imperialism that were as well known to his contemporaries as the theater of war was familiar to the Assyrians (map 1).

From the third millennium the Assyrian heartland comprised the Ashur-Nineveh-Arbela triangle roughly demarcated by the Tigris, its tributary the Lower Zab River, and the northern highlands. Over the following centuries, Assyria's territorial influence expanded and contracted according to its political fortunes and the abilities of its kings. During the late second millennium and then again at the beginning of the first, the Assyrians won large but ephemeral empires that they ruled more through threat and armed robbery than by law and commercial development. By the middle of the eighth century, after a period of decline, they were ready to initiate a new type of empire based on their permanent presence in fully administered provinces. In the decades preceding Sargon, the Assyrians had extended undisputed control west to the Euphrates, north into upper Tigris region and east to the Zagros piedmont. By his first full regnal year, 721, the geographical area in which the Assyrian army regularly campaigned stretched well over a thousand miles, from Anatolia to the borders of Egypt, from Lake Urmia to the Persian Gulf, and from the Mediterranean Sea to Iran. As complex as it was vast, the theater of operations encompassed widely different types of terrain—rich agricultural land, rugged mountain ranges, arid plains, marshland, and unpredictable waterways—filled with a variety of flora, fauna, and natural resources. Joining Assyria in the fierce competition for control of resources and trade routes were a few other powerful states, myriad smaller polities, and various nomadic tribes, whose loyalties shifted according to the dictates of survival and opportunity.

Over the course of centuries, a pattern of interstate competition had developed. By the first millennium, much of the conflict between great powers took place in the buffer zones that separated them. Violence was not the first resort of conflict resolution, and kings often preferred diplomacy, espionage, and armed threat to direct confrontation. Nevertheless, war was endemic in all of its manifestations, including everything from less-frequent, high-intensity sieges and pitched battles to more common, low-intensity raids and skirmishes. Thus, Egypt vied with Assyria for control of Palestine; Phrygia, Assyria, and Urartu struggled over the Taurus polities and Syria; and Urartu challenged Assyria in Anatolia and competed with Assyria, Elam, and occasionally Babylonia for suzerainty over the Zagros piedmont and Median plateau. Occupying the dangerous central position in the geopolitical arena of the Near East, Assyria was surrounded by enemies yet managed through military, economic, and political prowess to extend its sphere of influence over much of the contested territory.

The primary goals of Assyrian expansion were to supply the core with vital resources that it lacked (e.g., metal, wood, and stone) and prevent competitors (other kings) from gaining power. Although ideology mandated that Assyrian kings strive to develop barren lands so that their subjects could "graze in the meadows in plenty and abundance," taxes and a thriving textile trade provided insufficient capital for them to realize this objective.[4] Conquest of new territory seemed to offer a solution. Since the army provided the means to this end, maintaining a military edge became a central concern. As Assyria extended its territory through annexation and by creating clients, its economic potential increased, but so did demands on its military. In response, the state gradually developed a system of governance that maximized both human and material resources.[5] By reducing the need for armed intervention, political spectacle and diplomacy further alleviated the strain that territorial expansion put on the army.

Indeed, at the highest levels the Assyrians did not distinguish between civil and military administrations but operated under a unified system in which a handful of the king's most trusted officials, the magnates, were involved in the whole spectrum of government, from court business, temple administration, and royal construction projects, to provincial management, diplomatic endeavors, and military campaigns.[6] If the system encouraged the king to micromanage, it required his officials to become adept multitaskers. The royal treasurer, for example, besides handling court business, not only administered a province but oversaw the construction of Sargon's new capital city, Dur-Sharrukin. Nevertheless, the imperial administrative structure functioned as a fully integrated, highly flexible organization designed to move resources—animals, metals, stone, wood, and people, especially craftsmen—from the provinces and distribute them among public works projects and the army. This is not to say that the provinces were bled dry. In fact, they retained much of what they produced. This way surpluses could benefit the locals as well as supply the army when it marched through their area. For the most part, it was in Assyria's best interest to encourage the economies of both territories and clients; the more these flourished, the more they could contribute. Thus, Assyrian hegemony actually stimulated production and improved the quality of life in some areas, at least for local elites.[7]

The number and size of imperial provinces fluctuated periodically due to territorial gains and demographic shifts. Under Sargon, there were three standard types: foreign lands annexed through new conquest and governed by royal appointees (e.g., Arpad, Damascus, and Unqi); those strategically vital territories on the northern and northeastern frontiers and in the Syrian Jazirah that the king's magnates governed; and the heartland provinces managed by city governors.[8] Historically the king's magnates were the treasurer (*masennu*), palace herald (*nāgir ekalli*), chief cupbearer (*rab šāqê*), field marshal (*turtānu*), chief eunuch (*rab ša rēši*), chief justice (*sartennu*), and vizier (*sukkallu*).[9] The first four of these—the treasurer, cupbearer, palace herald, and field marshal—governed the strategically important border provinces on the heartland's frontier and thus were instrumental in managing adjacent buffer principalities.[10] The other three—chief eunuch, chief justice, and vizier—did not govern provinces but remained closely tied to the royal court. Table 1 outlines the duties attested for these officials as well as known office holders during Sargon's reign. The groups of magnates had different responsibilities as well as different power bases. Those magnates who administered provinces were responsible for border security, public order, management of resources and personnel, tax collection, gathering and reporting of intelligence, building and garrisoning of forts, and construction and maintenance of dams, levies, aqueducts, and roads, as well as mustering troops and leading them on campaign.[11] The magnates also had their own household troops—in effect small, private armies—and thus the king had always to keep these men in check.

Since land ownership paved the way to wealth and individual power, the king had to be careful lest any of his governors gain control of enough territory (and thereby resources) to challenge his authority. To this end, he made sure that their estates were scattered

$$\text{TABLE I.I. The Magnates}$$

Office	Name	Province	Additional nonmilitary duties	Military duties
Treasurer— *masennu*	Tab-shar-Ashur	On the northern frontier with Urartu	In charge of construction of Dur-Sharrukin and other building projects; orator	Involved in collecting horses; campaigned against Urartu
Palace herald— *nāgir ekalli*	Gabbu-ana-Ashur	On northeastern frontier, adjacent to treasurer's province	Responsible for transportation of bull colossi for Dur-Sharrukin	Commander against Urartu
Chief cupbearer— *rab šāqê*	Na'id-ilu	On northern frontier to east or west of treasurer's province	Dealt with deportees; on assignment to cut timber	Commander against Urartu
Chief eunuch— *rab ša rēši*	Unknown	No province	Duties as assigned by king	Head of standing army; in charge of collecting and distributing horses
Vizier— *sukkallu*	Uncertain. Maybe Nabu-belu-ka''in	Represented the king in Babylonia; no province	Judicial	Took part in campaigns against Urartu and against Babylonia
Grand vizier— *sukkalmah*	Sin-ah-uṣur, the king's brother	No province; residence at Ashur, then Dur-Sharrukin	Honorary title?	Headed king's personal cavalry guard; campaigned in Urartu and elsewhere
Chief justice— *sartennu*	unknown	No province	Judicial	Campaigned against Urartu
Commander— *turtānu*	unknown	Governed the Harran region		Campaigned with king or in his place; active in Babylonia and the Levant
Commander of the left— *turtān bēt šumēli*	unknown	Governed Kummuh and Melid		Position established around 708

Source: Dezsö, "Army of Sargon."

among several provinces rather than held as a single estate within their own provinces. For example, letters demonstrate that the chief justice, the vizier, and the governor of Calah all held land in Arzuhina province.[12] This practice not only helped to curtail elite ambitions but also, as Raija Mattila notes, "established a network of interlocking economic interests within the provinces and tied the personal interests of the major land owners to the fate and welfare of the entire empire."[13] Landownership dispersal also went a long way toward solving one of the weaknesses inherent in a system whose central administration competed with an entrenched aristocracy, many of whose members had ties (and thus claims) to the throne. A further function of widespread landholding was, in effect, prebendary, as the magnates were under obligation to the crown to share key materials such as wood and stone, precious metals, and horses. In return for services and loyalty, the king bestowed grants of land and a portion of audience gifts and campaign plunder.[14] Together the magnates' provinces and those of the heartland comprised "Assyria proper," and it was from these core territories that the crown enlisted the main chariotry, cavalry, and heavy infantry units of the standing army. All of the provinces provided levies for temporary duty.[15]

Individually and as a group the magnates were vital to Assyria's military effectiveness, but it was up to the king to direct their activities toward the fulfillment of his strategic goals. In particular, war and the conduct of war played a pivotal role in creating bonds between the king and the Assyrian elite. All of Sargon's top officials not only benefited materially from Assyria's wars but also were responsible for supplying and leading portions of the army on campaign. Members of the nobility traditionally formed part of the king's chariotry and cavalry, and it is probably safe to assume that many of the army's highest-ranking officers—among them a large number of eunuchs—belonged to the upper echelons as well.[16] This system created a symbiotic relationship between the king and the affluent classes on the one hand and between the economy and the military on the other. Warfare played an important role in sustaining the imperial system, but it was the standing army that made it possible to rule a territorial empire of closely administered provinces, as opposed to hegemonic empire, in which the king held sway over semi-independent, tribute-paying clients. In fact, although the king managed a vast provincial system, in some areas—where strategic considerations or rough terrain made it expedient—he maintained the old hegemonic system.

During the reign of Tiglath-pileser III (745–727 B.C.), the king's personal guard transformed into a standing army, the royal cohort (*kiṣir šarruti*), that consisted of chariot and cavalry units (including foreign elements recruited into the army after being defeated), Assyrian infantry, and auxiliary light infantry. Up until this point, economic and demographic restrictions had generally limited military operations to yearly raids aimed at collecting plunder and forcing targeted polities into paying tribute. In order to annex new territory and incorporate it into the provincial system, the army had to be capable both of extended campaigning far from the Assyrian heartland and of occupying conquered territory. For this reason and to balance the power of provincial governors, who levied and led troops for the crown, Assyria needed a fairly large force under permanent royal control. By institutionalizing the related practices of deportation and colonization, Tiglath-pileser was able to populate areas selected for agricultural or trade development and also control newly conquered peoples. Likewise, by incorporating selected units from defeated armies into his standing army, he could augment his own forces with experienced specialist units, while simultaneously crippling the ability of defeated peoples to rebel.[17] Finally, the crown forged long-term agreements with a number of Aramaean tribes (Itu'eans and Gurreans), who provided auxiliary infantry for the standing army.[18] Since auxiliaries and deportee troops depended on the crown for their livelihood and security, and since they had no stake in Assyrian court politics, they tended to be both reliable and loyal to the king. Thus, the allegiance of a large number of non-Assyrian troops increased the king's power over his own officials.

Sargon's Army

Although Sargon mainly adhered to the model established by his father, the size and organization of his army varied according to economic and political circumstances, military objectives, and the will of the king.[19] Ancient Near Eastern societies produced no written corpus of military doctrine but carried out military operations pragmatically in accord with tradition, to meet necessity, and to exploit opportunity. What we know about the organization of Sargon's army inevitably depends on the available sources, which in this case consist of horse inventories and personnel lists from Fort Shalmaneser (the review palace at Calah) as well as letters and a few miscellaneous administrative documents found at other sites. All of these texts lack the context that could explain their purpose and shed light on the plethora of ranks and administrative titles mentioned in them. Much of the terminology seems to be used interchangeably, and it is often impossible to detect distinctions between ranks or establish the full chain of command, hence the finer nuances of the ranking system remain stubbornly unavailable. Another oft-cited source, the sculptured palace reliefs, depicts arms and armor realistically, but offers limited insight into military organization and hierarchy.[20] A detailed consideration of all the evidence is not within the scope of this work, and even the most thorough studies fall short of definitive answers; the sources are simply too ambiguous and fragmentary.[21] Given the number of unresolved questions involving the structure of the Assyrian army, much of the following is necessarily provisional. Readers should refer to the illustration gallery for pictorial examples of the arms, armor, and tactics discussed here.

Under Sargon, the standing army consisted of the royal guards, equestrian forces (cavalry and chariotry), heavy infantry, and some units of auxiliary infantry comprised of Itu'ean archers, Gurrean spearmen, and occasionally other tribal peoples. The Assyrians did not hire mercenaries, although they did maintain a special relationship with certain tribal groups, who served the military in an auxiliary capacity.[22] How long and under what terms permanent troops served we do not know. Nor is it clear whether these men usually lived in barracks, with their own families, or sometimes billeted among locals. The living situation probably depended on where the troops were stationed. To augment the standing army, provincial governors could levy a large temporary force, "king's men" (ṣāb šarri), from those liable for compulsory state service (ilku). The Assyrians also required clients to provide troops when called upon to do so. The king ultimately made all major military decisions. Directly subordinate to him were the chief eunuch, who administered the standing army, and the field marshal, who commanded a sizeable force of his own and sometimes led the magnates on campaign on the king's behalf. As mentioned earlier, the magnates and provincial governors raised and commanded troops—their own permanent household guards and temporary levies. A precise chain of command cannot be reconstructed fully from the large number of attested officer titles, but the basic infantry organization (using modern terminology for unit types) went something like this:

Divisions of five thousand to ten thousand men commanded by
   a high official (magnate or provincial governor)
Brigades of one thousand men commanded by a rab 1-lim
   (chiliarch)
Battalions of five hundred men commanded by a rab 5-me-at
   (commander of five hundred)
Companies of one hundred to two hundred men commanded by
   rab 2-me-at (commander of two hundred), rab 1-me-at (commander of one hundred), or rab kiṣri (cohort commander)
Platoons of fifty men commanded by a rab ḫanšê (commander
   of fifty)[23]

Squad-level units of ten—essentially the number of men that could fit around a campfire—are sometimes attested in later texts but not so far in those of Sargon. The equestrian divisions used additional ranks such as team commander (rab urâte) and chariot or cavalry commander (rab mūgi), whose position in the chain of command eludes us. Some of the highest-ranking Assyrian officials and officers were eunuchs, but otherwise eunuchs do not appear to have been associated with any one particular military arm or unit.[24] On the sculptured palace reliefs eunuchs intermingle with bearded Assyrians at sieges, and they never appear as a segregated corps.[25] Specialized ranks and offices are discussed below within their specific military branches.

The Standing Army's Equestrian Units

The chief eunuch was in charge of the core equestrian divisions of the standing army, including the king's military entourage, the horse and chariot guards, foreigners recruited from conquered armies, and the "city units" (cavalry and chariot troops raised from the Assyrian heartland).[26] There were at least two categories of royal bodyguards—the ša šēpi (literally meaning "at the feet") and ša qurbūti ("close by")—both of which included chariotry and cavalry. These elite guards, probably recruited from the nobility, worked closely together.[27] Of Sargon's guards, the most prestigious corps was the one-thousand-strong cavalry troop (*pēthal qurubti*) that always accompanied Sargon and which his brother, the grand vizier, Sin-ah-uṣur, commanded.[28] That the king put his brother in charge of this elite outfit was a signal honor and a public display of trust. From a political standpoint it served to keep a potential rival at hand and content with his lot.

The *ša qurbūti* guards were regularly seconded to other units or sent on special-duty assignments. They occasionally oversaw the relocation of troops or operated as the king's plenipotentiaries in the provinces.[29] These troops acted with the full weight of royal authority, and there are several letters from governors and other high-ranking officials requesting that the king send one of these officers to resolve a dispute, evidently because a royal representative could get better results than local administrators.[30] Certainly the presence of the king's envoy would have helped speed up diplomatic and administrative processes that might otherwise have foundered due to communication delays. Aside from the guard units, which were something of a special case, chariots represented the most prestigious combat arm.

Chariotry had been the dominant, elite force in Near Eastern armies up until the introduction of cavalry in the ninth century.[31] The fact that chariot contingents are always listed before cavalry and infantry in Neo-Assyrian royal inscriptions and administrative documents provides further evidence of the high status of this combat arm. Over time, war chariots became steadily larger and heavier, and by the mid-eighth century Assyrian chariots required teams of up to four horses and boasted eight-spoked wooden wheels reinforced with iron hobnails.[32] There were several distinct chariot units in the army: the palace chariotry (GIŠ.GIGIR É.GAL); bodyguard chariotry (GIŠ.GIGIR *qurbūte*), the *ša šēpi* guard chariotry (GIŠ.GIGIR *ša šēpi*), the "city units," and some foreign contingents recruited after conquest.[33] Each chariot normally had a three-man team: the warrior/knight (*mār damqi*), the driver (*mukīl appāti*), and a "third man" or shield bearer (*tašlīšu*).[34] Chariot teams were organized into units of fifty, each with its own commander (*rab ḫanšê*). Each contingent organized its men according to their function on the chariot; hence we find officers of the rank "chief third man" (*tašlīšu dannu*), "deputy third man" (*tašlīšu šaniu*), and "cohort commander of the knights" (*rab kiṣir ša mār damqa*).[35] This arrangement mirrored both social ranking and the specialized duties of the different chariot personnel. Various other official titles get mentioned in letters and administrative documents, but the context rarely (if ever) reveals the holder's position in the hierarchy. The offices of the commander of chariotry (rab mūgi ša GIŠ.GIGIR.MEŠ), chariot supervisor (ša pān GIŠ.GIGIR), and overseer (?) of chariots (ša GIŠ.GIGIR) thus remain something of a mystery.

While chariots were still important during Sargon's reign, their prominence decreased as the army undertook more campaigns in mountainous territory where the use of wheeled vehicles became problematic. Nonetheless, chariots remained a valuable military asset in the more hospitable terrain of Syria-Palestine and Babylonia. When conquest delivered competent chariot troops into his hands, Sargon incorporated them into his own army. In his first regnal year he recruited fifty chariot teams (150 men) from Samaria. After his conquest of Hamath in 720, he took two hundred chariots (six hundred men), and after the conquest of Carchemish in 716, he acquired fifty chariots (150 men).[36] Presumably, these men, like their Assyrian counterparts, belonged to the upper stratum of their respective city-states. By incorporating conquered elites into his army, Sargon not only allowed them to save face after defeat, but he also encouraged their assimilation into the empire. Sargon even permitted some foreigners, such as the Samarians or Chaldeans, to retain their national character and officers.[37] Others were absorbed into the deportee (šaglûte) units and commanded by Assyrian officers.

According to the sculptured reliefs from Sargon's palace, chariot personnel wore no armor other than the standard Assyrian pointed helmet, and they sometimes eschewed protective gear altogether. Aside from a whip, drivers did not wield weapons, and, although chariot fighters carried swords, they are only depicted shooting bows in battle. The chariot's "third man" defended his compatriots with one or two shields. Some chariots carried spears and extra shields hung across the back to provide additional protection to those in the cab or to be detached for use in ground combat.[38] The slight variations between chariot teams depicted on the reliefs do not allow us to distinguish between unit types (e.g., ša šēpi or qurbūte chariotry) or national origins (Assyrians, Samarians, or Chaldeans). The same may be said of the cavalry.

In addition to the horse guards already discussed, a regular cavalry (pēthallu) also served in the standing army. These troopers belonged in the city units recruited from the main centers of the Assyrian heartland, including Ashur, Arbela, Arzuhina, Arrapha, and "Aramaea" (a broader, regional designator).[39] As in the case of foreign chariotry, Sargon recruited conquered horsemen into the deportee regiments on several occasions: six hundred from the defeated army of Hamath, two hundred cavalrymen from Carchemish after that city's defeat, and another six hundred from Babylonia after 710.[40] As mentioned earlier, this policy allowed the king not only to augment his own cavalry force but also to foster compliance among conquered peoples, who were simultaneously prevented from fomenting rebellion in their home territories.

During Sargon's reign, the importance of cavalry increased a great deal due to the army's growing need for mobility over the rough terrain north along the upper Tigris and in the Taurus regions, and east into the Zagros Mountains. Horse soldiers wore robes (hiked up in front for ease of movement), leggings, and boots, but no armor other than a standard conical Assyrian helmet of iron or bronze. At this time, riders carried lances, short swords, and bows.[41] Although the Assyrians had neither saddles with girth straps nor stirrups, they developed a good bridle-and-rein system that allowed horsemen to fight at the gallop without losing control of their mounts.[42] Before the invention of the rein holder, bareback riders lacked the ability to discharge a bow without dropping their reins.[43] In the ninth century the Assyrians solved this problem by having cavalry operate in pairs, with one rider to hold the reins of both horses, while the other shot his bow. By the late eighth century, horsemen rode singly. Nevertheless, while Sargon's cavalry are depicted on the reliefs carrying encased bows, they never appear shooting while galloping. It seems likely, therefore, that Sargon's reign marked a period of transition for the cavalry.[44]

Since the mounted divisions were essential to maintaining Assyria's military edge, the acquisition and care of horses and mules were top priorities. The Assyrian army needed several different types of horses. Large and hardy, Kushite horses from Egypt made excellent chariot teams, whereas smaller horses from the Taurus and Zagros pasturage were especially desirable as cavalry mounts.[45] Horses acquired through trade, tribute, and war fell under the purview of the chief eunuch, as did control of the system based on the regular tax collection scheme that assembled them for military use.[46] In the off-season, the army distributed mounts to their riders, who would pasture and attend to them, while the recruitment officers (*mušarkisāni*) oversaw the process and made sure that the horses received fodder and the men remained battle-ready.[47] At muster time in each province, two of these officers together with a subordinate team commander (*rab urâte*) or cavalry prefect (*šaknu ša pēṭhalli*) organized both horses and soldiers for the mounted units of the standing army.[48] Recruitment officers delegated horses to the cavalry and chariotry, put some out to pasture in reserve, or occasionally assigned them to work as draft horses in public building projects.[49] Another class of high official, the stable overseers (*šaknûte ša ma'āssi*), was in charge of horse care for all equestrian units on campaign.[50] In addition to this system—perhaps for emergency needs—larger herds of horses were kept on estates in the provinces under the care of provincial governors and probably in special state-run pasturage in the heartland.[51]

The central government put a lot of effort into making sure the army had an adequate supply of horses and pack animals (mules and sometimes camels), but the job was not an easy one. The royal correspondence attests that sometimes people had to be coerced into contributing their assigned allocation. For example, in answer to Sargon's query about the availability of a particular kind of horse, one provincial official replied: "I sent the servants of the king, my lord, to the town, Kibatki. They became frightened and they put people to the iron sword. After terrorizing Kibatki, they got afraid and wrote to me, and I set a deadline for them."[52] In another case the palace instructed several officials assembling cavalry under emergency conditions: "Get together your officers plus the h[orses] of your cavalry contingents immediately! Whoever is late will be impaled in the middle of his own house, and whoever changes the [. . .] of the city will also be impaled in the middle of his house and his sons and daughters will be slaughtered by his order. Do not hold back; leave your work, come right away!"[53] Given how rarely this type of threat appears in the royal correspondence, it is likely that Sargon included it to emphasize the urgency of the situation, though clearly the king expected immediate results and felt able to threaten his subordinates as necessary.

The availability of food and fodder for the equestrian divisions was also a frequent subject for complaint in letters to the king, as provincial governors had difficulty providing enough for the army without inflicting shortages on their own men. Lower-ranked officers met similar problems as they tried to supply their men and mounts. One letter, written to Sargon from the governor of Ṣupat (in Syria), recounts a conflict over fodder:

> The king, my lord, ordered [me to] give bread to the grooms. Now [PN] came (and) I told him [. . .] but he said: "The king has given orders to me and I will take two [. . .] of each (provision)." I did not agree; I did not give it to him, so he went into one of my villages, opened a silo, brought in his measurers and piled up (grain) for [x] healthy men. I went and spoke with him, saying: "Why did you by yourself, [with]out the deputy, open the king's granaries?" He would not look me in the eye [but said]: "In the month of Nisan my fodder (supply) fell, and the horses are collapsing (before) me; I [can]not [manage]."[54]

Another official, while waiting for king's men to muster in the northern Habur region, noted, "The horses of the king, my lord, had grown weak, so I let them go up the mountain and graze there."[55] In a world subject to every vicissitude of nature, the management of food and fodder for large numbers of people and animals presented a serious challenge. Facing similar obstacles, the regular infantry formed the backbone of the king's army.

The Standing Army: Infantry

Armored spearmen and archers recruited from the home provinces and men recruited from the elite infantry of certain conquered states (e.g., Shinuhtu and Samaria), made up the Assyrian heavy infantry of the standing army.[56] These soldiers wore the standard conical helmet and metal or leather scale armor over a knee-length tunic.[57] Officers often carried a mace as a symbol of office and for coercive purposes, albeit probably not as a battlefield weapon. The reliefs do not show any Assyrian using a mace in battle. Additionally, archers and spearmen carried short swords or daggers, but for obvious reasons only the latter carried shields. There is no evidence for slingers during Sargon's time, although they became prominent in the army later.[58]

Auxiliaries made up the standing army's light infantry divisions, each with its own distinctive costume and weaponry. The light archers, the Itu', represented an Aramaean tribe that inhabited central Mesopotamia. After Tiglath-pileser III finally pacified them around 738, members of the tribe formed a permanent corps of the Assyrian army. Text references show that under Sargon other Aramaean tribes such as the Hallatu, Rihiqu, Litanu, and Iadaqu sometimes served as auxiliary archers as well, though only the Itu' served continuously.[59] On the palace reliefs, auxiliary archers always appear bare-chested and barefoot, dressed in short kilts, and wearing headbands to control their long hair. Though primarily serving as archers, they are occasionally shown using a dagger to dispatch an enemy in the aftermath of battle.[60] Commanded by an Assyrian officer (*šaknu*), the Itu'ean auxiliaries nonetheless retained some tribal organization under the subordinate leadership of chiefs and village headmen.[61] The Gurrean auxiliaries fulfilled somewhat different tasks.

So far it has been impossible to identify the Gurreans' place of origin, but based on their distinctive crested helmet and light armor it is generally agreed that they hailed from a wide area along the northern and northwestern frontier of Assyria; that is, northern Syria and central Anatolia. The term "Gurrean" seems to have been used broadly as an ethnonym and military designation rather than a specific tribal name, and texts suggest that these soldiers served under the sole command of Assyrian officers. In battle each wore a crested helmet, a small chest plate (sometimes referred to by the Greek term *kardio-phylax*), a knee-length tunic, and usually boots. They carried spears (their weapon of preference, judged to have been about eight to nine feet long), short swords, and round bucklers made of woven wicker or leather.[62]

As part of the standing army, the auxiliaries owed loyalty only to the king, who often allocated them for duty in the provinces. Auxiliary troops—especially the Itu'ean archers—were in high demand as a kind of mobile military police to help with internal security and peacekeeping, border patrol, and intelligence gathering.[63] The governor of Ashur, for example, once wrote to Sargon asking for Itu'eans to oversee some workers in his absence: "The governor of Arrapha has 100 Itu'eans standing guard in the town of Sibtu. Let them write to the delegate of Sibtu and let 50 (of those) troops come and stand with the carpenters until I return."[64] Both types of auxiliaries made up a significant portion of the army on campaign.[65] On the Dur-Sharrukin reliefs, Itu'eans and Gurreans appear in nearly every combat or siege scene, and it is clear that they were an integral part of Sargon's standing army.

The Provincial Army: Levies

In Assyria all adult males were eligible for annual temporary service (*ilku*) in the army or to do work for the crown. If there were any formal criteria for eligibility, such as age and physical condition, they are not known, though texts reveal that even very young boys sometimes served, probably as substitutes for older family members or richer men who bought themselves out.[66] Presumably, the local village headman along with the recruitment officer decided whether individuals were fit for duty, though how strict they were about it probably depended on the quota they had to fill. Levies served as infantry, cavalry, and possibly as chariot drivers and "third men." Among those who apparently counted as king's men and mustered for seasonal service was an ambiguous group called *kallāpu* (plural *kallāpāni*) that appears to have formed in the eighth century after the adoption of a rein-holding device obviated the need for cavalry to ride in pairs, with one to fight and one to hold the reins. Having been made redundant, the former rein-holders became a new unit called *kallāpāni* that functioned as lancers or as a type of dragoon (mounted infantry).[67] These troops performed a wide variety of duties, including serving as the army's vanguard or rearguard (or both), reconnaissance men, foragers, sappers, MPs (to keep levies in line), and guards for royal messengers.[68] As the lowest-ranking soldiers, seasonal levies receive relatively little attention in Sargon's texts and sculptured reliefs.

Notes on Arms and Armor

Excavated examples of arms and armor dating to the late Assyrian period reveal a great variety in materials and construction and little uniformity, though certain trends emerge. As we have seen, the main weapons of the Assyrian army were spears and bows, and since both were made almost entirely of perishable materials, few traces of which have survived, analysis rests on the interpretation of blades and metal points. Despite being more expensive than bronze, harder to work, and requiring a long process of carburization, hammering, and quenching, iron was the preferred metal for swords and daggers, probably because it was strong and could be sharpened and re-sharpened easily.[69] Iron did not entirely eclipse the use of bronze for the manufacture of military equipment, however.

Lighter weight than iron, bronze was suitable as shield covering and for helmets, and, because it could be recast repeatedly, it proved particularly appropriate for the speedy production of arrowheads and spear points.[70] Scale armor made of bronze, iron, or perhaps leather provided body protection.[71]

Bows depicted on the reliefs appear to have been a composite, recurve type constructed of wood, bone, and sinew strips glued together.[72] Estimations based on the length of surviving spear points suggest that shafts were about nine feet long and that both infantry and cavalry used them for close-quarter combat rather than for throwing. Judging from the reliefs and the size of the extant examples of swords and daggers, which are all quite short—no sword exceeds forty-five centimeters in length—the Assyrian soldiers used the double-edged blades should their primary weapon fail or to finish off defeated enemies in the aftermath of battle.[73] Short swords, daggers, and spears, used for stabbing rather than slashing, delivered killing blows more effectively, penetrating stab wounds invariably being more deadly than most surface cuts. These blades also functioned as handy tools comparable to the modern marine's KA-BAR knife or a Gurkha's kukri, both of which are famous for their versatility as murderous weapons, entrenching tools, and path-breaking implements. Indeed, on Assyrian reliefs, sappers are often shown using their blades to undermine the walls of besieged towns, while on at least one occasion soldiers use their daggers to butcher animals.[74]

Since few datable examples of shields have survived, most information comes from the reliefs, according to which Sargon's army utilized a number of shield types fashioned from various materials: large, round shields made of bronze or possibly wood reinforced with bronze bands; smaller round and rectangular combat bucklers, probably made of densely woven wicker or leather; and full-length tower shields curved at the top and composed of the same woven material. All shields had one central handgrip. The material evidence, such as it is, suggests that Sargon's army was as well equipped as possible at the time. On campaign, accompanying craftsmen replaced or repaired the equipment that they could, while plundering soldiers carefully fieldstripped weapons and armor from dead enemies for reuse. The arms and armor plundered from captured cities that the king did not dedicate at a temple or award to the magnates filled the storerooms of a review palace (ēkal māšarti) for future use.

The Army on Campaign

The Assyrian army has often been portrayed as a mercilessly efficient fighting machine capable of overwhelming any obstacle, but
the reality was much more commonplace and involved a great deal
of human effort, effective planning, and strenuous physical labor.
Warfare was seasonal, with the likelihood of good travel weather and
the availability of food and water determining the duration of campaigns as well as campaign route. After careful planning throughout
the winter, campaign season began in late spring or early summer
with the annual muster, which could take a month or more to complete.[75] A complicated process, the muster involved constant communication between governors, officials overseeing troop movements
and logistical arrangements, and the king. A recruitment officer or
cohort commander collected the enlisted men in the area assigned
to him and then decided which recruits were fit to serve and which
should stay in reserve.[76] Once he had gathered his troops, he delivered them to his immediate superior, a prefect or a provincial governor, who marched them to a review palace (armory) or a destination
closer to the area of operations.[77] The Assyrians used the review
palace "to maintain the camp (and) to keep thoroughbreds, mules,
chariots, military equipment, implements of war, and the plunder
of . . . enemies; . . . to have the horses show their mettle (and) to
train with chariots."[78] These large, fortified complexes at Calah and
Dur-Sharrukin could board three thousand or more horses.[79] At the
muster point, troops trained before being outfitted with such items
as armor, packs or saddle bags, cloaks, tunics, water skins, sandals,
and reserve food rations, according to the requirements of their specific units.[80]

   Much of the time, assembly went smoothly, as evidenced in
a report from an official on the northeastern frontier, who calmly
assured the king that "I will assign my king's men, chariots and cavalry as the king wrote to me, and I will be in the [ki]ng my lord's
presence in Arbela with my king's men and troops by the [dea]dline
that the king, my lord, set."[81] Fulfillment of manpower obligations
could be onerous for the officials involved, however. Several letters complain about the quality of recruits and indicate that the
crown's demands sometimes met with resistance at the local level.
In a report to Sargon, for example, one official protested, "I wrote to
the king, my lord, but only obtained [2]60 horses and [x number] of

little boys. [2]67 horses and 28 men—I have 527 horses and 28 men altogether. I keep writing to where there are king's men, but they have not come."[82] Other officers grumbled about men being late for a muster or avoiding duty completely. One frustrated official confessed, "My chariot fighter [cal]led Abu-[. . .]—for the second year [. . .] has not g[one on] campaign with me."[83] A similar dispatch, in which an official testified that "[120] king's men who did not go on campaign with the king are in the presence of the governor of Arbela; he does not agree to give them to me," suggests that high-ranking officers were sometimes loathe to turn their troops over to someone else, especially someone who might be regarded as a competitor.[84]

The Assyrians obliged clients and allies to send men on campaign when required. Here too calls for troops were sometimes greeted with passive resistance. For example, Sharru-emurani, the governor of the Assyrian province Zamua, in the Zagros foothills, wrote to Sargon: "Last year the son of Bel-iddina did not go with me on campaign but kept the men at home and sent with me young boys only. Now may the king send me a deportation officer (literally "mule-stable man") and make him come forth and go with me. Otherwise, he will (again) rebel, 'fall sick,' shirk, and not [go] with me, but will send only l[ittle] boys with me (and) hold back [the best men]."[85] Foreign contingents or mercenaries could be difficult for Assyrian officers to control, and there are several letters regarding unruly soldiers. One officer, writing from Arbela, protested that "the Philistines whom the king, my lord, organized into a unit and gave me, do not agree to stay with me," while another official indignantly reported troops "loitering in the center of Calah with their mounts like [. . .] common thugs and drunkards."[86] Unsurprisingly, most of the letters saved in the permanent archives were those that reported problems rather than those that merely confirmed positive results, and we should be cautious about reading too much into them. Nonetheless, complaints of shirking, delay, dereliction of duty, and occasionally overt resistance to imperial authority evince themselves with striking regularity.

Since muster lists are incomplete and no text explicitly states how many men went on a given campaign, it is impossible to determine the size of Sargon's army accurately. Based on ration information given in a couple of letters, one scholar tentatively reckons that the Assyrians could have raised an army of thirty-five thousand to forty thousand for large operations.[87] Muster lists dating to the period 710–708 tally more than twenty-five thousand men available for active duty or held in reserve, thus indicating the minimum size of the force during that time.[88] Given the logistical constraints under which the army operated, it seems most likely that it seldom exceeded thirty-five thousand and more commonly amounted to fewer than twenty thousand men. Scattered epistolary evidence suggests that the Assyrians experienced chronic manpower shortages, especially when soldiers had to be removed from garrison duty to go on campaign. In one instance an unidentified author explained that he could not send two thousand men to the royal delegate at Der as requested, because "the men from here do not suffice (even) for the fortresses! Whence should I take the men to send to him?"[89] Moreover, the construction of the new royal capital, Dur-Sharrukin, drained manpower and material resources from the provinces to the point that governors had a difficult time fulfilling work quotas while maintaining provincial security and military readiness.[90] With mounting frustration the palace herald, Gabbu-ana-Ashur, wrote to Sargon protesting that "all the straw in my land is reserved for Dur-Sharrukin (to make mud bricks) and my recruitment officers are now running after me; there is no straw for the pack animals." He went on to demand irritably, "Now what does the king, my lord, say?"[91] The conquest of new territories, while theoretically expanding the recruit pool, inevitably put additional stress on the standing army, though the real problems arose after the army left the muster area.

Care and Feeding of the Army

Few studies of ancient military campaigns get into the nitty-gritty of logistics, partly because so little factual information has survived about how armies dealt with supply and partly because combat is generally considered more interesting. But those who confronted the reality of ancient warfare understood implicitly the principle that "supply is the basis of strategy and tactics" or their armies suffered the consequences.[92] In the harsh and unpredictable climate of the ancient Near East, it had always been the case that logistical requirements—particularly the need for water—dictated routes of march as much as tactical considerations. For this reason, successful military operations depended on control of travel routes, river fords, and mountain passes. Accordingly, the Assyrian Empire spread not as a "stain" but along communication lines, which sometimes meant that Assyrian-held territory was not fully contiguous. When moving into a new area, the Assyrians first took over travel corridors and key cities that they secured with networks of forts.[93] Rather than attempting to occupy entire conquered territories, the Assyrians left unproductive tracts of countryside alone and depopulated trouble zones.

Supplying troops and animals during the muster period posed a challenge, but provisioning a large army on the march over difficult terrain in hostile territory took months of careful preparation and organization. It is generally agreed that active duty soldiers require a minimum of three thousand calories a day plus two quarts or more of water, although the average Assyrian soldier, who was shorter, slighter, and more used to heavy labor than his modern counterpart, probably managed well on fewer calories. Horses and pack animals needed roughly eight gallons a day of water and ten pounds of straw or chaff plus another ten pounds of grain to be supplemented by pasturage when available.[94] For an army of any size, carrying sufficient supplies for an entire campaign quickly became impossible, since sufficient food and fodder became too heavy for men and pack animals to carry. To mitigate this problem, the Assyrians created forward supply depots as part of their provincial system, while carefully choosing the route outside their territory to maximize client aid and the availability of forage.[95] At the outset soldiers received small amounts of barley and oil to be held in reserve as "iron rations," but the troops prepared their own victuals. There was neither a food service nor a central mess in the Assyrian army.[96]

When traveling through the client states bordering Assyria's outer provinces, the army could expect to be provided with necessities. In his Letter to Ashur, for example, Sargon reports approvingly of his Mannean client: "Like one of my own eunuch governors of the land of Assyria, he made provisions of grain and wine to feed my army."[97] The real test began when the army crossed into enemy territory, where it was sometimes impossible to find potable water and provisions. Under such circumstances, relief came only with the capture of enemy food sources. Thus, after Sargon swept through the district of Wishdish in northwestern Iran, he could celebrate only after he opened "their innumerable granaries and fe[d] my troops on immense quantities of grain."[98] As long as they timed things right, this type of warfare offered the Assyrians great benefit for minimal risk. Captured granaries fed Assyrian troops and deprived the enemy of food, while the application of overwhelming force terrorized locals into submission and served as an example to neighboring polities that often capitulated without a fight. From the Assyrian point of view, this sort of operation was the most cost-effective form of warfare. Hence, food became a weapon. If the king could control access to it, he could supply his own men and deprive his enemy, who might well face starvation as a result.

In addition to food, providing soldiers with clothes, equipment, weapons, and mounts was a tremendously difficult task, involving a high level of organization and numerous specialized support personnel: craftsmen to create replacement parts for arms, armor, and vehicles; engineers for bridges and siege engines; grooms; and mule drivers. The royal campaign retinue also included scribes, domestics (cupbearers, bakers, confectioners, body servants, and cooks for the king's household), scouts, messengers, and scholars to read the omens and advise the king.[99] The magnates and other high-ranking officers brought their own household personnel along with them. Except under extraordinary circumstances—even Sargon had to walk on occasion—the elites traveled in relative comfort, riding in chariots or on horseback during the day and spending nights in camps with large, fully outfitted tents where servants prepared meals and cared for equipment.[100] By contrast, the average Assyrian soldier walked all day and then constructed a fortified camp, erected a tent, built a campfire if that was possible, fed himself, and probably looked to his equipment before turning in for the night. The unlucky ones pulled guard duty.

Very little information has survived regarding the common soldier's experience of war, but given the circumstances under which he served, it was sure to have been taxing. Assyrian soldiers faced many hazards in the course of their service: disease; the physical and mental stresses of campaigning; combat injuries; capture; and death. Close-quarter living, indifferent hygiene, and bad food and water almost certainly caused outbreaks of those epidemic diseases—typhus, typhoid, dysentery, cholera, influenza, and diphtheria—that plagued all premodern armies. There was not an official medical corps in the Assyrian army, though the king and other elites traveled with their own personal healers (*asû* and *āšipu*), some of whom might have treated lower ranks when the need arose. The Assyrian medical literature deals with both disease and wound treatment, but it contains little (if any) specific reference to military personnel. Interestingly, the curse formula of a Neo-Assyrian treaty contains some hint of normal wound treatment: "When your enemy stabs you, may there be a dearth of honey, oil, ginger, and cedar resin to put on your stab wounds."[101] As honey and cedar resin are natural antiseptics, the wound victim would have stood some chance of recovery. Normally, regular soldiers probably had to treat each other with whatever medicaments they carried, without the aid of an expert.

Travel in the ancient Near East was grueling under the best of circumstances, and several letters attest to unforgiving road conditions even within Assyria. For example, the governor of Ashur, Tab-ṣil-esharra, warned Sargon to send his officer via an alternate route because "the [roa]d through the province of Arrapha is very choked; there are gullies permanently filled with reed and it is *getting* (worse)."[102] Another dispatch reported that a proposed campaign itinerary to the east was not feasible because "the ground is difficult; it lies between the mountains, the waters are high and the current is strong, not fit for launching either wineskins or keleks (to cross). The king, my lord, knows that the troops are unskilled (in swimming)."[103] Similar messages spoke of travel hindered by swollen rivers, storms, and the devastating impact of snow. In order to explain his continued absence from court, the magnate Nabu-belu-ka"in wrote, "We are clearing the roads, but snow is filling them up. There is very much snow. . . . The year before last, there was snow like this, the rivers were frozen and the men and horses with me died in the snow."[104] By contrast, the Near East's extremely hot summer temperatures proved no impediment to the hardy, well-acclimatized Assyrians, who apparently took it for granted. Debilitating heat did not get mentioned in letters or inscriptions, though the effects of drought figured periodically.

Sargon's Letter to Ashur, the account of his campaign against Urartu in 714, offers one of the most eloquent descriptions of the rigors of mountain travel:

> As for Mount Simirriu, a lofty peak that thrusts up sharp as a spear point and whose summit, the dwelling of the goddess, Belet-ili, rises over the mountains, whose topmost summits, indeed, reach to the very sky, whose roots below thrust down to the depths of the netherworld, and which, like the back of a fish, offers no way to pass on either flank, and the ascent of which, from front to back, is exceedingly difficult, on the sides of which yawn chasms

and mountain ravines, a fearsome spectacle to behold, discouraging to the ascent of chariotry and to the high spirits of steeds, the worst possible going for the ascent of infantry . . . I provided my engineers with heavy copper picks, so they broke up the sharp peak of the mountain into fragments as if it was limestone, and made good going.[105]

Even in modern times, the Zagros Mountains present a formidable challenge to nomads. For example, the documentary film *People of the Wind* records the annual Bakhtiari tribe's migration to upland pasture during the 1960s. Of particular relevance are the sections that show the crossing of mountain rivers via inflated goat skins, the recutting of a path after a winter washout, and an enforced halt after rain has rendered waterlogged woolen tents too heavy for the pack mules to carry.[106] Each of these problems—and indeed their solutions—would have been familiar to the Assyrians.

The Order of March and Battle

Those soldiers who survived the march had to face the rigors of combat. Campaign season usually began sometime in Nisan (March–April) after the celebration of the New Year's festival and lasted until it was time for the fall planting or, more rarely, until the advent of winter precluded further action. Expeditions to the Zagros Mountains might start later, since snow could block passes as late as July.[107] On campaign, the standing army marched in unit order under the chariot standards of prominent deities such as Nergal, Adad, Ashur, Ishtar, Sin, and Shamash. Tradition associated particular regiments with certain gods, as in the case of the royal cavalry guard and the Arbela city unit, whose patron was Ishtar of Arbela.[108] In royal inscriptions when the king made statements such as "I prepared the yoke of Nergal and Adad, whose standards march ahead of me," he not only referred literally to divine standards (*urigallu*) but tacitly indicated which divisions took the lead position.[109] The order of march, although seldom mentioned in royal inscriptions, undoubtedly changed to meet the exigencies of war, weather, and terrain, but it was probably also contingent upon the presence of magnates, who had the right by privilege of birth, social status, or the king's favor to travel and fight near him. While ascending a very steep mountain, for example, Sargon claimed, "I took the lead position before my army,

I made the chariotry, cavalry, and my combat troops fly over it like valiant eagles, I brought after them the support troops and *kallāpāni*, the camels and pack mules frolicked over its peak, one after another, like mountain goats bred in the hills. I brought the surging flood of Assyrian troops easily over its arduous crest and made camp right on top of the mountain."[110] Recognizing the possibility of ambush and harassment attacks as they marched through enemy territory, the king placed himself with the best troops in the vanguard, put vulnerable baggage and noncombatants in the well-protected center of the column, and brought up the rear with the expendables.

Over the course of nearly constant campaigning, the Assyrians had developed a tripartite offensive strategy of devastation, battle, and siege. When they entered enemy territory, if an opposing army did not meet them in battle immediately, then the Assyrians would typically go for easy targets—small, poorly defended villages and towns—that they would wreck, ruin, and plunder with devastating efficiency. This technique served several purposes. First of all it was the easiest way to secure supplies, acquire plunder, and deny the enemy vital resources. Second, by terrorizing the countryside, the Assyrians could isolate and then bypass bigger settlements and cities that might otherwise prove too costly to besiege.[111] Finally, devastation put pressure on the enemy leader(s) to fight or surrender. If opponents did not acquiesce quickly enough, then battle or siege would ensue. As we have seen, the Assyrian army typically consisted of chariot units, cavalry, archers, and heavy-armed spearmen, but just how they were deployed in battle is not well known. Sargon's inscriptions emphasize sieges and mention only those battles that were particularly significant, omitting smaller or indecisive engagements. Moreover, the palace reliefs offer little insight into the experience of battle. They limit the scene to the moment of victory, when the elite chariots or cavalry trample fallen enemies and chase down those fleeing the field, as professional infantry dispatch the wounded and round up prisoners. There are good reasons to suppose that full-scale pitched battles were not a common occurrence and that most contests—even ones involving substantial forces—were generally of short duration.[112]

The disposition of Assyrian troops on the battlefield and the tactics employed would naturally have depended on a number of circumstances: the morale and fitness of Assyrian troops; terrain and weather; the size of the enemy army and the unit types it employed;

and the assessed quality of enemy troops and leadership, to name only the most obvious. The strict social hierarchy in Assyria probably also determined the battle array as the magnates and their troops claimed field positions by right of rank and tradition. The king in his chariot, accompanied by his brother's elite cavalry, took the center, but just how the other magnates arranged themselves is not clear. The chariot's function in battle is still much debated; however, by the late eighth century it had traded much of its mobility for the added security of heavier construction, and this in turn may have relegated it to a reserve or command position on the battlefield.[113] There is no reason to doubt, however, that Sargon and his nobles actually fought. Recent attempts to reconstruct Neo-Assyrian battle tactics have had mixed results, although texts indicate that the army was capable of executing standard maneuvers such as flanking and envelopment.[114]

Thanks to the detailed depiction of sieges on the palace reliefs and some fruitful archaeological excavations, we know a great deal more about how the Assyrians conducted siege operations than we know about how they fought battles. In the Near East all sizeable cities and towns boasted some sort of defensive system, though smaller settlements had only simple mud-brick curtain walls and perhaps a towered gateway. For large cities, however, defenses could include a sophisticated combination of double walls, moats, glacis, and towered gates from which defenders could provide enfilading fire. With stone foundations and mud-brick superstructure, city walls commonly achieved heights of thirty to forty feet and could be extremely thick—Calah's wall was 120 feet (thirty-seven meters) deep in places.[115] Fortification walls extended for miles in circumference, making full blockade or circumvallation highly problematic for a besieging army. In all regions of the Near East from at least the middle of the second millennium B.C., armies practiced standard siege tactics that included ruse, blockade, escalade, mining, sapping, and frontal assault using siege engines equipped with battering rams. Common counter-measures included sorties, the undermining of ramps with tunnels, and the construction of secondary walls.[116] By the eighth century, the Assyrians had honed their siege craft to the highest standard, but because sieges could be time-consuming and result in high casualties, they did not undertake large-scale operations lightly. For attacking soldiers, a siege promised plenty of hard work, physical privation, danger, and the more attractive prospect of loot. Before committing to a siege, the Assyrians encouraged surrender or attempted to take the city by subterfuge; frontal assault was not usually the first course of action. In one letter, for example, an official writing from northeastern Babylonia reported being approached by a local faction plotting to betray their city to the Assyrians.[117] Another letter writer suggested capturing a town by tunneling through the mud-brick wall of a house and bringing the soldiers through the breach secretly at night. One of Sargon's siege reliefs depicts an official delivering surrender terms to the defenders from a siege tower (see figure 11).[118] Sometimes, however, the army had to take a city the hard way.

Siege operations varied in scale and intensity from fast and dirty frontal assaults to protracted affairs that required ingenuity and a great deal of coordinated effort. Since most fortified cities were also located on heights, soldiers had to attack uphill over formidable obstacles. Typically, large contingents of Assyrian archers provided cover for smaller units—the Assyrian equivalent of the forlorn hope—who would leapfrog forward to attack the defenses at multiple points in preparation for a concerted assault. Assyrian spearmen with tower shields or lighter, more maneuverable bucklers protected long-range archers from counterfire and enemy sorties. Assault units operated in a variety of groupings: spearmen with shields to protect archers; spearmen together; sappers working alone or in pairs to dig through walls; and archers (usually Itu'eans) shooting without the benefit of cover.[119] Equestrian forces probably patrolled, foraged, or acted as mobile units that could counter enemy attacks. The reliefs also depict dismounted officers and magnates—identifiable by their long robes—discharging arrows from behind covering shields. In the event that the defenses required siege engines, a ramp had to be built to bridge ditches and reach the walls. The construction of a siege ramp was not an easy task, although it did not require advanced engineering expertise or any mathematical calculations as has sometimes been asserted.[120] Basically, soldiers got whatever dirt, rocks, wood, and other handy materials they could find, including building detritus, then piled it all up and tamped it down until they had a surface sufficient to carry the weight of siege engines. The key variables included the size of the ramp, the type and disposition of obstacles, the number of men that could be spared to work, and the abundance of available materials. All of this occurred under enemy fire, and it is likely that unburied corpses soon made the killing zone distinctly unpleasant and unhealthy. Disease posed one of the greatest risks of extended siege work.

If unfavorable circumstances (e.g., high casualties or lack of food) prevented the Assyrians from taking a city, they could choose the economical alternative, which was to ravage the countryside, cut down fruit trees, wreck irrigation canals, and destroy fields in order to cause the enemy to suffer hardship and prohibit his ability to wage war. Besides the collection of supplies, one of the main reasons to devastate small cities and towns within a target area was to reduce the enemy's resources so that he could not field a retaliatory army for the foreseeable future.[121] Without the means to rebel against the Assyrians, many polities had no choice but to submit. Nor did the Assyrians raze every city they besieged successfully. The fate of a captured city and its inhabitants depended on a variety of military, political, and strategic factors. Although looting was inevitable (even necessary), the Assyrians reserved burning buildings and dismantling defenses for certain circumstances. Strict attention to the wording of royal inscriptions and the details of relief sculpture reveals that a lot less violence occurred than is often assumed. Sometimes the appearance of the army inspired immediate capitulation, thus saving lives on both sides. As will become apparent in the following chapters, ancient warfare was not simply about killing as many of the enemy as possible. The Assyrians did not blindly rape, pillage, and obliterate but followed whichever course of action (including clemency) allowed them to achieve their objectives with the least cost to themselves. Whatever they did, however, they imbued with meaning expressed through religious observation.

Military Ritual

Ritual pervaded every aspect of life in Assyria (and indeed the ancient Near East in general), including military activities. Soldiers affirmed their loyalty to the king by swearing allegiance before the gods, while the king reassured his followers of divine support through constant public acts of piety (e.g., temple-building and religious festivals), and naturally everyone attempted to secure divine approval for risky undertakings such as war. Prognosticating and prophylactic rituals played a prominent part in all military endeavors. Several sculptured reliefs, for example, depict religious performance in army camps.[122] Phrases such as "at the command of the god, Ashur, I mustered my chariots," so common in royal inscriptions, testified to the king's reliance on divination to secure divine approbation. Although all wars were fought in the name of the gods, they were not holy wars in the modern sense. The Assyrians did not attempt to eradicate the worship of foreign gods or impose their own gods on defeated people, though they did encourage assimilation by conflating local cults with some of their own.[123]

Neo-Assyrian rituals dealt with every aspect of warfare. One rite called "so that in battle arrows do not come near a man" helped warriors prepare mentally for approaching combat.[124] A cultic commentary for a ritual to be performed at the camp (madāktu) after a battle describes a ceremony in which the king symbolically defeated his enemy with the aid of the gods Nergal, Adad, and Belet-dunani ("lady of the strong," the warrior aspect of Ishtar).[125] During the course of this elaborate multipart ceremony, officials made sacrifices and rode the sacred chariot, the king carried out a procedure involving his bow and arrows while driving his own chariot, and officials performed a "ritual voodoo-like shooting of an enemy or his image" as onlookers and participants shouted, sang, and chanted the requisite liturgy. Subsequently the king symbolically captured his enemy, the group raised shields, and priests made more sacrifices, after which the entire party processed back to the camp to enjoy a celebratory meal in a portable sanctuary (qersu).[126]

Religious observance informed everything from symbolic declarations of war, the surrender or execution of enemies, and the review of prisoners to the triumphant march home and ensuing celebratory banquet. Sacrifices carried out when armies mustered and before they crossed into enemy territory often alerted watchful enemies to impending attack and thus created the opportunity for legitimate war. The numerous Assyrian intelligence reports informing the king of enemy rituals almost certainly had significance beyond mere surveillance.[127] Likewise, the akītu festivals of particular Assyrian gods have been associated with both pre-campaign ceremonies and post-campaign triumphs. It is likely that after particularly important wars, such as Sargon's victory over Urartu in 714, the king's representative read or recited publicly an account of the campaign in the form of a letter addressed to Ashur and the people of the city. Afterward he dedicated the text at the appropriate temple.[128] Doubtlessly intended to secure victory as well as the king's safety, military rituals served multiple secondary purposes: they promoted the king's legitimacy, signaled political action, helped an ethnically diverse army establish a corporate identity, fostered good morale, and encouraged the public to view the army favorably.

On another level, all public ceremonies promoted the ideology of the Assyrian elite and helped that group maintain its hold on power. That the Assyrians were talented self-promoters is undeniable, but this should not lead us to dismiss them as cynical posturers. In Assyria, as in medieval Japan (and most early modern monarchies), pomp and ceremony were "a visual symbol of the social order and served an important function in vitalizing and renewing the polity. . . . [F]rom the very beginning, court ritual and ceremony *were* politics."[129] This principle also held true for international relations, in which every move a king or his representative made, from gift exchange, dining, and ritual to the mutilation of an enemy, sent a deliberate message to friend and foe alike. In this light, the bloodthirsty rhetoric and brutal visual imagery of Assyrian kings and warfare itself were all part of the political spectacle. Although Sargon wielded formidable military strength (as this chapter has demonstrated), he had to use it wisely. For each campaign that he undertook, he had to manage not only immediate military conditions, but also emerging threats outside the field of operations. The following account of Sargon's campaigns amply illustrates the complex, often refined methods that this king employed in his quest to augment and maintain a great Assyrian empire.

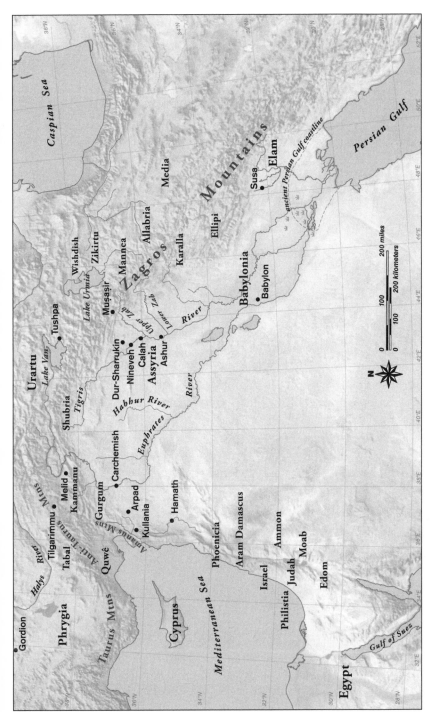

Map 1. The Ancient Near East. Map by Ben Pease. Copyright © 2016 by the University of Oklahoma Press.

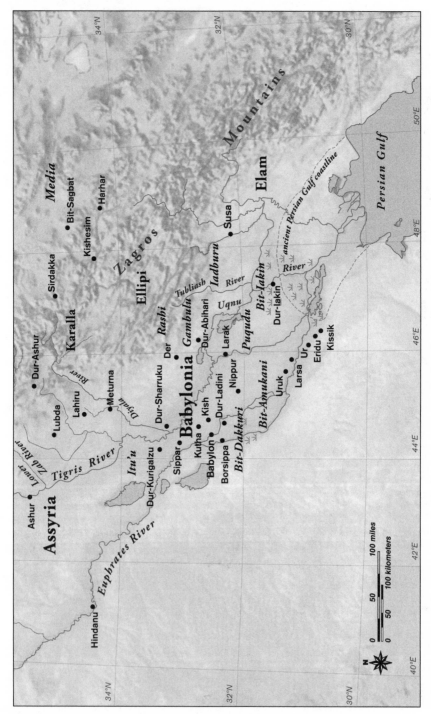

Map 2. Babylonia, Elam, and the Southern Zagros. Map by Ben Pease. Copyright © 2016 by the University of Oklahoma Press.

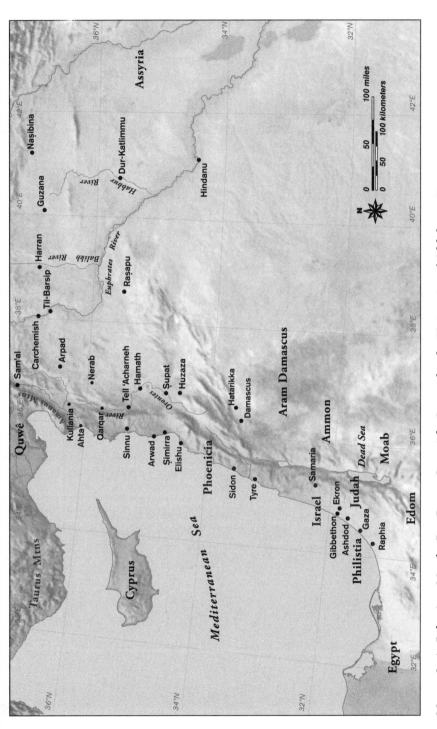

Map 3. Syria-Palestine. Map by Ben Pease. Copyright © 2016 by the University of Oklahoma Press.

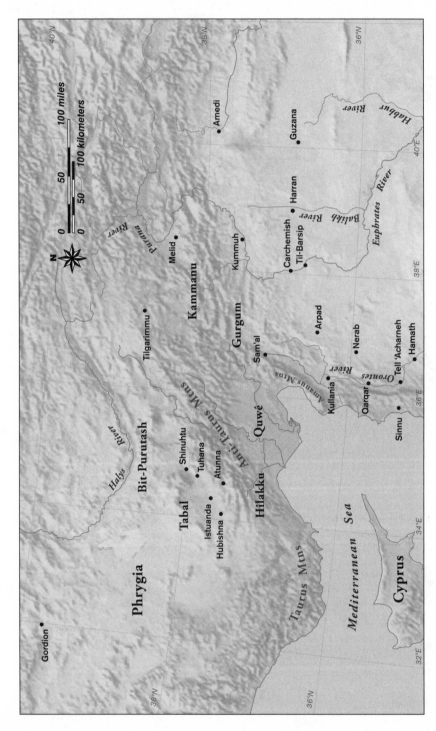

Map 4. Central Anatolia and Northern Syria. Map by Ben Pease. Copyright © 2016 by the University of Oklahoma Press.

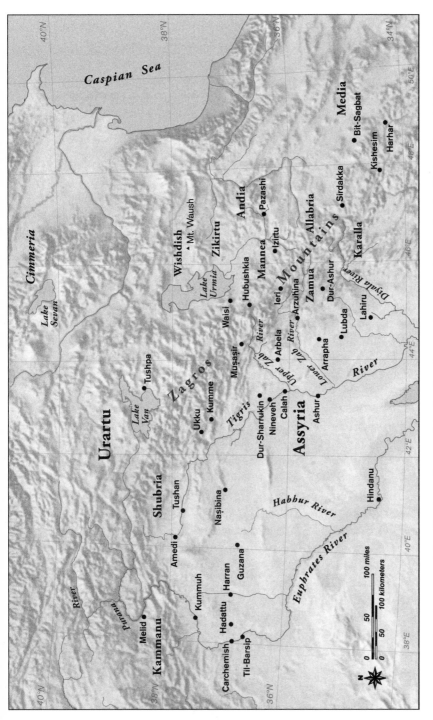

Map 5. Assyria, Urartu, and the Northern Zagros. Map by Ben Pease. Copyright © 2016 by the University of Oklahoma Press.

CHAPTER 2

WINNING THE ASSYRIAN THRONE, 722–720 B.C.

The Accession in Context

Sargon was born around 762 B.C. and grew up during a period of weakness and civil strife in Assyria. Outbreaks of plague and rebellion marked his early childhood during the short and ill-fated reign of Ashur-dan III (772–755).[1] Civil unrest continued under Ashur-nirari V (754–746), who spent his reign in Assyria attempting to maintain his precarious grip on power. Eventually a rebellion broke out in Calah that deposed Ashur-nirari, and in the aftermath Sargon's father, Tiglath-pileser III (745–727), managed to take the throne. Whether Tiglath-pileser, who was Ashur-nirari's younger brother, instigated the revolt or gained the throne by suppressing it is uncertain, but he did not follow a conventional path to kingship.[2] Very little is known about Tiglath-pileser's family beyond the names of one of his wives, Iabâ, and three of his sons: Sargon; Sin-ah-uṣur, and the eldest, Ululaya, who took the throne name Shalmaneser when he succeeded his father. Sargon and Sin-ah-uṣur were full brothers and Ululaya (Shalmaneser) apparently their half-brother.[3] Around the time of his father's accession, Sargon married a woman named Ra'īmâ, with whom he fathered at least three sons, the first two of whom died before the third, Sennacherib, was born.[4] Sometime later Sargon had a daughter, Ahat-abisha, and at least two more sons, whose names are not known. The grave of a second wife, Atalia, was discovered at Calah in the 1980s.[5]

No evidence survives concerning Sargon's activities before he ascended the throne in the last days of 722, but if he learned statecraft as a young man, his father made an excellent role model. During the chaotic mid-century period, Assyrian prestige throughout the Near East had declined dramatically. An energetic and innovative ruler, Tiglath-pileser not only regained all of Assyria's recently lost territory, through expansion and administrative reform, but he also transformed the state into a true territorial empire. In the west Tiglath-pileser annexed powerful kingdoms in Syria, including Arpad, Unqi, and Damascus. Beyond these he created a string of client states from Anatolia right down to the border of Egypt and also imposed tribute on various small frontier polities in Anatolia.[6] The objective of this western expansion was to secure resources, seize control of trade, and put pressure on Assyria's chief rival, Urartu, thereby checking the enemy's further encroachment into Syria and Anatolia.

In the east Tiglath-pileser pursued similar goals, making Mannea, Ellipi, and lesser Zagros polities into clients in order to obstruct growing Urartian influence in that region and procure necessary resources, especially horses. In 743, after successful campaigns in Syria, the Assyrians invaded Urartu itself, penetrating all the way to its capital, Tushpa, which they besieged briefly but did not capture.[7] Two years later, while Tiglath-pileser was campaigning in Syria, a revolt in Babylonia deposed its king, after which Mukin-zeri of the Chaldean tribe Bit-Amukani overthrew the usurper and took the throne for himself. Taking advantage of the discord, Tiglath-pileser intervened and spent the next three years (731–729) conquering Babylonia. A strategy combining covert political operations with conventional military force allowed the Assyrians to carry out a successful and largely bloodless operation there. Over the course of the campaign, Tiglath-pileser managed to conclude treaties with numerous Chaldean and Aramaean tribal leaders, including Balassu of Bit-Dakkuri and Merodach-Baladan of Bit-Iakin, both of whom would play important roles later during Sargon's campaigns in the south.[8] In siding with the Assyrians, Balassu, who was Mukin-zeri's uncle, let self-preservation and ambition overcome kinship obligations.[9] Such expedient behavior characterized interpersonal relations throughout the Near East. After subduing his enemy, Tiglath-pileser formally ascended the throne in Babylon, where he clasped the hands of the god Bel/Marduk to become a legitimate Babylonian king.[10] Over the course of eighteen years of nearly constant warring (745–727), Sargon's father managed to establish Assyria as the supreme military and economic power in Near East. If Tiglath-pileser represented Assyria's bright potential, his son and successor, Shalmaneser V, proved to be something of a disappointment.

After Tiglath-pileser's death, the throne passed without incident to Shalmaneser, who ruled for a scant five years (726–722), during which he held Assyria's newly acquired territory, annexed Sam'al and possibly Quwê, and captured Israelite Samaria after a protracted siege.[11] Shalmaneser died in December 722, and just a few days later Sargon ascended the throne. Whether or not the new king took power after a violent coup is a source of much debate.[12] The Babylonian Chronicle, a seemingly straightforward catalog of major events relating to that region, reported baldly that "Shalmaneser died" (*šimāti*).[13] Since in Akkadian this wording normally indicated death by natural causes and because there was no reason for the authors of the Babylonian Chronicle, which elsewhere included direct reference to assassinations, to gloss over an Assyrian regicide, the accusation of murder against Sargon appears groundless.[14] Nonetheless, in the surviving Assyrian sources there are hints of underlying discord, and Sargon's very name invites doubt about how he acquired his crown. Evidence surrounding his accession, while scanty and ambiguous, reveals a great deal about how the Assyrians explained whatever happened in terms of the prevailing ideology. Hence, it is important to examine it in some detail.

Before Akkadian was deciphered in the nineteenth century, the names of Assyrian and Babylonian kings were known only from the Bible, in which a Hebraized version appeared. Even after the discovery of the original Akkadian name forms, the convention of referring to Mesopotamian kings by their biblical names has continued and is followed here. The original form of "Sargon" was "Sharrukin," which, like most Akkadian names, formed a translatable sentence intended to express an individual's fundamental nature.[15] Sargon received an intriguingly malleable name. In cuneiform, "Sharrukin" could be written and translated in different ways: logographically, LUGAL.GIN, or with a combination of logogram and syllabic signs, as in LUGAL-*kē-nu* and LUGAL-*ú-kīn*. Since "Sharru-kenu" means "true/legitimate king," the assumption has been that only ruling monarchs could use it, therefore Sargon must have adopted it as a (false) declaration of legitimacy when he usurped the throne. The discovery of an official with this name during the reign of Sargon's grandson, Ashurbanipal (669–627), complicates the issue further, although it is still possible that Sargon adopted a throne name.[16] Since Sargon more often spelled his name "Sharru-ukin," meaning "the king has established order," the significance of name choice is even less clear. It now seems likely that "Sharru-ukin" was Sargon's birth name and that it referred to the king who reigned when he was born (Ashur-nirari V), in which case Tiglath-pileser probably chose it as a sign of support for his brother.[17] When scribes wished to emphasize Sargon's divine election or invoke his namesake, Sargon of Akkad, ca. 2334–2279 B.C., one of the greatest rulers of antiquity (and incidentally a usurper), they used the spelling "Sharru-ukin." Whether or not the Assyrian Sargon adopted a throne name, he consciously manipulated the connection to Sargon of Akkad, a point to which we return later. Although there is currently no way to resolve the name problem, it is important to note that no interpretation clearly indicates that Sargon deposed his brother.

Other evidence is equally ambiguous about how he became king. The Ashur Charter, a poorly preserved tablet written a couple of years after Sargon's accession, sheds some light on the issue. In this text Sargon explained that the gods expelled Shalmaneser V because he rescinded the privileges due the people of the cult center Ashur: "But S[halmaneser], who did not fear the king of the totality, whose hands have brought evil to this city, se[t . . .] on his people [he] impo[sed] corvée and bitter labor and paid them like an underclass [. . . .] The Illil of the gods, in the fury of his heart, overthrew his rule, and [appointed] me, Sargon, as king of [Assyria]."[18] On the face of it, the phrase "overthrew his rule" seems as direct a confession of usurpation as a historian could desire. However, the statement could just as easily have been a politically motivated expression of the common Near Eastern belief that a king's fortunes depended on the gods' favor. A successful king signaled divine approval, while ill fortune of any kind revealed divine displeasure. According to this rationale, Shalmaneser's early death indicated that he had somehow affronted the gods. Any successor would naturally dissociate himself from an unlucky or sinful predecessor, as indeed Sargon's heir did after his father's unfortunate death in battle. By a typical Mesopotamian *post hoc ergo propter hoc* (after this, therefore, because of this) argument based on the assumption that humans generally only discovered the gods' will after the fact, Sargon could justify the claim made in the Ashur Charter that it was his destiny to rule Assyria simply because he had become king. The circular argument is typical of Near Eastern royal rhetoric, which could always find a justification for present circumstances in past actions.

The second allegation, that Sargon took the throne unlawfully even if he did not actually kill his brother, rests on the assumption that there was a fixed order of succession by primogeniture in

Assyria. The fact that brothers often succeeded one another—as in the case of Shalmaneser IV, Ashur-nirari V, and Tiglath-pileser III— disproves that notion. All that can be said with certainty about the Assyrian succession is that "rules were fluid and any male belonging to the royal family might attempt to claim the throne if he saw an opportunity."[19] Typically a king chose one of his sons, usually (but not necessarily) the eldest, to be crown prince. Since infant mortality was high and life expectancy for adults equally precarious, the eldest son frequently did not survive to succeed his father.[20] In order to ensure the succession, kings had many children so that at any given time there must have been a significant number of men with some claim to the throne, however tenuous. Essentially, kings always had to risk political stability for the continuance of the royal line. If the crown prince grew to maturity and proved to be capable and if the political situation was stable when the king died, then the succession passed smoothly. Conversely, any perceived royal weakness could spark a violent fight for the throne.[21] Given what we know of the situation, it seems most likely that Shalmaneser, having died of natural causes, left no viable heir and that Sargon, as the king's half-brother and a capable member of the elite, took over as soon as news of the king's death arrived in Ashur. In any case, there is no reason to believe that Sargon did more than crown himself with untoward haste in order to preempt the competition, which, to be sure, may have included one or more of Shalmaneser's children.[22]

Whatever the precise circumstances of Sargon's accession, it did meet with opposition, and it took him a full year (721) to secure the Assyrian heartland. Even so, his most serious challenge did not come from within the regime but from simultaneous rebellions in Syria and Babylonia. In the ancient Near East, a contested succession frequently sparked revolt among subject peoples, whose leaders regarded any hint of instability at the core as an opportunity to break free from unwanted hegemony. There is some question as to whether Sargon, facing campaigns on two fronts in one year, split his forces and sent a separate army to Syria-Palestine under the command of the field marshal or chief eunuch, or personally led both operations consecutively. Each scenario presents problems. On the one hand, given the distances covered, sequential campaigns would have taken at least six months, making for an excessively long campaign season and an overall trip in excess of two thousand miles for anyone who participated in both operations. On the other hand, the crucial importance of these campaigns mitigates the extraordinary effort, and it seems unlikely that a new and vulnerable ruler like Sargon would delegate something so important to a subordinate. I propose a third alternative that accommodates both scenarios and is compatible with the existing evidence, namely that two campaigns began at roughly the same time, that Sargon led the army into Babylonia while his official marched into Syria, and that the king joined the western operation as soon as he concluded the southern one.[23] At this critical juncture Sargon could not have afforded to let someone else earn a military victory in his stead.

Securing the Rear Flank: The Der Campaign, 720 B.C.

About three months after Sargon became king, Merodach-Baladan of Bit-Iakin, the Assyrians' former ally, overthrew their administration in Babylon, declared himself king, and prepared for reprisals by raising an army and purchasing military aid from the Elamite king, Humban-nikash (743–717).[24] At about the same time, Ilu-bi'di, the ruler of Hamath in Syria, incited the kingdoms of Arpad, Ṣimirra, Damascus, Hatarikka, and Samaria to rebel against Assyria.[25] After securing Egyptian support, Hanunu, the king of Gaza, also claimed independence. These rebellions not only posed a security threat to Assyria but also disrupted their control of vital trade networks in Iran and along the Mediterranean coast.[26] Moreover, Assyria's expulsion from the western territories created a power vacuum that opportunistic enemies, Urartu, Phrygia, or Egypt, might have exploited to threaten Assyria's flank while the Babylonians and Elamites menaced from the south. Although weakened by internal strife in the eighth century, Egypt had pursued a vital interest in Palestine since the second millennium, whereas competition between Urartu and Assyria to control the Syro-Hittite kingdoms began in the ninth century and intensified throughout Tiglath-pileser III's reign. The struggle between Assyria, Babylonia, and Elam also had a long history. Caught between these larger powers, the rulers of smaller city-states and tribes shifted loyalties chameleonlike in order to survive.

If allowed to go unchecked, the new rebellions threatened the very fabric of the Assyrian Empire. Nearly all of Tiglath-pileser's hard-won territory had been lost in the course of a few months. This was not the type of blow to prestige that a new king—especially one who had to fight for the throne—would find easy to survive unless he won swift and decisive victories. The concurrent uprisings thus put Sargon in an extremely difficult position. Merodach-Baladan's situation was at first equally precarious. When the Chaldean chief seized the throne, he broke a treaty established with Tiglath-pileser during the Mukin-zeri revolt.[27] Though such agreements seldom outlived the individuals who entered into them, the breach gave Sargon a valid pretext for retaliation. However often Merodach-Baladan declared himself to be the divinely chosen liberator of Babylonia, not everyone supported independence or approved of their self-appointed king.[28] Some tribes and cities had benefited under Assyrian rule, while others did not want to see Bit-Iakin gain power at their expense. During this period, Babylonia was not a homogeneous state but a loose aggregate of diverse polities and social groups nominally united under the aegis of a king based in Babylon, the long-standing seat of kingship (map 2). The Babylonian (Akkadian) population dwelled in the cities, while seminomadic Chaldean and Aramaean tribes occupied the Zagros piedmont, the southern marshes, and the riverine hinterland on the periphery of the settled urban countryside. The inhabitants of the ancient, established cities tended to regard seminomads with suspicion, even as the tribes insinuated themselves into the political and commercial lives of the city-dwellers.[29] Persistent tensions, both among the cities and between cities and tribes, which got rich off the trade routes at the expense of the urban population, exacerbated political fragmentation and prevented Babylonia from coalescing into major international power.[30] In some ways the area was "merely the object of competition between Assyrians, Elamites, and Chaldeans."[31] Forging lasting unity out of these disparate groups would take patience, plenty of wealth, and deft diplomacy, hence Merodach-Baladan's urgent need to secure his throne against Assyrian retaliation. Elamite support helped him intimidate dissenters within Babylonia and effectively prevented Sargon from attempting to retake the entire south in a single campaign. With the western rebels still unchecked, the Assyrians could not undertake the type of extended, complex operation required for the conquest of Babylonia.

An exact timetable cannot be established, but it is clear that at the start of hostilities the Elamite army marched on the Assyrian-held city of Der (near modern Badra) in an effort to take it before the Assyrians could react. Since the tenth century when they first captured Der, the Assyrians had fought with varying success to hold the city, and it was not until the reign of Tiglath-pileser III or Shalmaneser V that the area finally became an Assyrian province.[32] Perched on the edge of the Zagros foothills in northeastern Babylonia, Der controlled the main road between Assyria, Babylonia, and Elam. It also served as a major stop on the east–west trade route.[33] Whoever controlled the city gained an important strategic advantage over his rivals and a solid base for defense of his own territory. Unless Sargon held Der, he could not operate freely elsewhere. The main Elamite and Babylonian objectives were also both defensive and commercial. Humban-nikash and Merodach-Baladan meant to secure their borders with Assyria and reduce their enemy's ability to mount military operations against them. Moreover, they would reap economic benefits if they could regain control of this key trade route into Iran. Since Sargon could not afford to surrender Der without a fight, he had little alternative but to march south and offer battle. The ensuing campaign did not win back Babylonia, but it did fulfill Sargon's immediate objectives to secure Assyria's southern border.

If the Assyrian troops mustered at Calah as was customary, then they took the road southeast through Lubda, Lahiru, and Meturna and along the edge of Zagros foothills to meet the Elamite army, which arrived outside Der ahead of them (map 2). Marching at an average rate of fifteen miles a day with no rest days, the journey of more than 250 miles normally took a little over two weeks. In order to prevent his enemies from joining forces, Sargon had to move quickly. Although supplies were not a problem because the route took him through well-provisioned Assyrian cities, a forced march would tire his men and so put them at a disadvantage on the battlefield. The situation presented Sargon with a difficult choice: he could rest his forces and risk having to take on the combined armies of the enemy, or he could engage the Elamites with road-weary troops in the hopes of achieving a decisive victory before the Babylonians could intervene. Given the urgency of the situation and in light of Sargon's later penchant for swift action, it seems safe to assume that he chose speed over prudence.

The question became moot, however, when the Elamites, preferring to fight fatigued Assyrians (or perhaps because they did not want to share the spoils of victory with the Babylonians), attacked before Merodach-Baladan arrived with his army.[34] None of the details of the battle has survived; there is neither description of the composition or size of the armies involved, nor of the tactics used on the battlefield. Moreover, the sources disagree dramatically about the outcome. In his Annals, Sargon claims succinctly that "in my second regnal year, when I had settled on the royal throne . . . I smashed the forces of Humban-nikash, King of Elam; I defeated him."[35] By contrast, the Babylonian Chronicle states: "In the second year of Merodach-Baladan, King Humban-nikash of Elam fought King Sargon of Assyria in the region of Der; he caused Assyria's retreat and massacred it. Merodach-Baladan and his army, who went to the aid of the King of Elam, did not arrive at the battle (in time) and he turned back."[36] Although he did not participate in the battle, Merodach-Baladan also took credit for the success, claiming in another text to have "prevented them (the Assyrians) from treading on the territory of the land of Akkad (Babylonia)."[37] Far from demonstrating the deceit of royal propagandists, each of these contradictory accounts represents (with some equivocation) the fulfillment of the respective parties' objectives.

The battle was indecisive. The Assyrians held their own against the Elamites, possibly even besting them on the field, until the impending arrival of the Babylonian army prompted Sargon to withdraw, which seems to have been exactly what Merodach-Baladan planned. Unwilling to commit his own forces and thereby reveal their shortcomings to friend and foe alike, Merodach-Baladan adopted a clever alternative; he arrived late, stayed out of the battle, and by proximity alone induced the enemy to retreat. The Elamites could claim victory because they held the field after the Assyrians withdrew.[38] The fact that neither the Elamites nor the tardy Babylonians pursued the enemy or subsequently laid siege to Der, which remained firmly in Assyrian hands, belies the notion that the Assyrians suffered a major defeat there. The Assyrians were not routed but, rather than face a fresh enemy army, executed an orderly tactical withdrawal and afterward settled the situation through diplomacy.

Circumstantial evidence suggests that the three kings concluded a treaty to stabilize the relationship between them.[39] In any case, détente lasted another ten years, at which point favorable conditions in the rest of the empire allowed Sargon to turn his attention to Babylonia once again. Sargon's decade-long absence from the south has often been cited as proof of a disastrous loss at Der, but this view fails to consider both the wider political situation and the military exigencies involved in conquering Babylonia.[40] At this point, Sargon could not afford to become embroiled in the type of extended campaigning that it would take to defeat the Chaldean and Aramaean tribes, let alone take back Babylonia's cities and deal with the Elamite threat. In fact, each of the adversaries accomplished his objectives: Sargon secured his flank and rear and could now move freely against the Syro-Palestinian coalition; Merodach-Baladan consolidated his position in Babylonia without using (or losing) any of his own troops; and Humban-nikash not only established his alliance with Babylonia and made some money out of the enterprise, but may have gained territory south and east of Der as well.[41] While the Battle of Der was not the type of resounding victory that lent itself to lengthy glorification in Assyrian royal inscriptions, neither was it the near throne-toppling disaster for Sargon that it has sometimes been made out to be. Far from sidling home with the tattered remnants of his army, Sargon moved on to Syria. The subsequent string of outstanding Assyrian victories in the west hardly represents the actions of a king who had just been thoroughly beaten.[42]

Suppressing Rebellion: The Syro-Palestinian Campaign, 720 B.C.

In the eighth century, a number of ethnic and cultural groups occupied Syria-Palestine: Neo-Hittite and Aramaean city-states (e.g., Carchemish, Arpad, Damascus, and Hamath); Phoenicia; the Israelite kingdoms, Samaria and Judah; Philistia; and Semitic tribal kingdoms Ammon, Edom, and Moab (map 3).[43] These polities struggled continually among themselves and against more powerful external foes such as Assyria, Urartu, and, to a lesser extent, Egypt. From the ninth century on, Assyrian hegemony gradually spread toward the Mediterranean, but imperial expansion west began in earnest under Tiglath-pileser III, who systematically reduced the area to the status of client or province as a means to seize control of the Mediterranean trade, preempt rivals' efforts to expand, and safeguard his own borders.

First the Assyrians secured the eastern section of the route to the Mediterranean by conquering Arpad, which at the time was allied with Urartu. Then, after the defeat of a Syrian alliance in

738, Tiglath-pileser captured the kingdom of Patina/Unqi, located on the Amuq plain, and from there extended Assyrian suzerainty over coastal Phoenician cities and inland to Hatarikka, which he made an Assyrian province. Judah became a willing client of Assyria when an alliance between Israel and Aram (Damascus) motivated the Judean king, Ahaz, to seek help from Tiglath-pileser.[44] The invitation allowed the Assyrians to attack Philistia, sacking Gaza, its principal commercial center, but subsequently restoring the city and its king, Hanunu, who became a client.[45] Control of Gaza, which thrived on the maritime trade and traffic with the tribes of the Arabian Peninsula, afforded Tiglath-pileser the opportunity to take over a profitable port as well as muscle in on the Arab trade and thwart Egypt's efforts to do the same. He then consolidated his hold on the region by destroying the power of Damascus and the northern kingdom of Israel (Samaria). In 732 Damascus fell and the Assyrians subdued Galilee and Transjordan.[46]

In order to secure the Phoenician end of the trade route, Tiglath-pileser made Tyre a client and subsequently established a series of trading centers (kāru) in Phoenicia and Philistia, in which he settled deportees and Assyrian colonists.[47] From these emporia, the Assyrians could control prices, collect duties, or impose economic sanctions, while forts built along main roads kept communication lines open, provided security for caravans, and acted as way stations for troops and messengers.[48] Since Assyria was a land power and the Assyrians inexperienced sailors, they allowed the maritime centers in Phoenicia and Philistia to retain quasi-independence as clients in return for their naval services. In the wake of Assyrian conquest, it took the city-states Arpad, Damascus, Gaza, Hatarikka, and Ṣimirra over ten years to recover the material means and manpower to challenge Assyria, but eventually the confusion after Shalmaneser V's death provided them the opportunity to take action.

The geopolitical situation in the Levant leading up to the rebellion is not altogether clear. Ilu-bi'di originally came from Qarqar, which since the time of Tiglath-pileser III had belonged to the Assyrian province of Hatarikka, although earlier it had been part of the kingdom of Hamath.[49] At some point, though it is impossible to say exactly when, Ilu-bi'di usurped the throne of Hamath and soon after that began to foment widespread revolt against Assyria. A recently discovered inscription from the beginning of Sargon's reign admits, most unusually, that Ilu-bi'di "killed the citizens of Assyria who were present in [. . .] altogether [and left no one alive (. . .)]."[50] Although violence against Assyrian administrators and soldiers undoubtedly occurred every time rebellion erupted, the Assyrians rarely recorded such negative outcomes lest they reflect poorly on the king or magically induce additional ill fortune. This reticence has skewed modern perceptions, with the result that we often view the Assyrians as constant perpetrators, rather than occasional victims, which of course they must have been. Assyrian kings were duty-bound to avenge administrators, soldiers, and civilian colonists who died at the hands of enemies or rebels. Sargon's response to the western coalition differed dramatically from his reaction to the Babylonian-Elamite alliance. Whereas the Der campaign had been brief and defensive, the Assyrian expedition to the Levant was an entirely offensive operation, and Ilu-bi'di, whom Sargon contemptuously dubbed "a camp follower, with no claim to the throne, an evil Hittite," received the full force of Assyrian vengeance.[51] As much as he wanted revenge, however, Sargon needed to reestablish the Assyrian trade monopoly in the west, and this goal inevitably governed his treatment of the different rebel elements.

The leaders on both sides faced a number of serious challenges. While the Der campaign had been relatively short (four to six weeks, not including time to muster) and easy from a logistical point of view, the Syro-Palestinian campaign was a much more complex undertaking. Distance alone offered a formidable challenge, as the round-trip journey from Calah to the farthest point the Assyrians reached—Raphia on the Sinai border—covered around 1,650 miles.[52] Syria-Palestine also presented a much more varied landscape than the area around Der. In northern Syria, the terrain included densely forested mountains, rain-fed steppe punctuated by oak groves, fertile river valleys, and warm coastal plains where fruit trees flourished. Farther south and east, dense scrubland and terebinth-covered hills gave way to wormwood-studded steppe and finally desert. Bisected by the Jordan rift valley that stretched from the Sea of Galilee to the Red Sea, the drier south encompassed fertile valleys, mountains, and *shephelah* (the low, rolling hills between mountains and valley bottoms), before tapering off into the vast wastes of the Negev Desert. In summer at the height of campaign season, finding good sources of potable water would have been difficult.[53] Although climate and terrain in the west were mild relative to, say, the Zagros Mountains, winters could be cold, wet, and sometimes snowy, making large quantities of food difficult to procure, even by force. The longer the campaign lasted, the greater the risk to the army. Under these circumstances, it would have been unwise to field a massive, slow-moving force or undertake lengthy sieges. Given the overall situation and the length of the campaign, it is likely (as mentioned above) that Sargon sent his field marshal or chief eunuch to command the army until he arrived.

Despite the difficult political situation, military circumstances favored the Assyrian leader, for he commanded well-organized, well-equipped troops via a clear chain of command, something the coalition probably could not claim. As alliance leader, Ilu-bi'di faced the many problems traditionally associated with coalition warfare—namely lack of command cohesion, political in-fighting, cultural differences, and conflicting strategic aims. In the ancient world, multiple polity alliances such as Ilu-bi'di's rarely survived contact with the enemy, even in the event of victory. There were simply too many variables at play for cooperation to last. Long-standing rivalries, old grudges, conflicts of interest, and shifting political affiliations made stable alliances among the Syro-Palestinian states uncommon.[54] Although united in their desire to rid themselves of the Assyrians, coalition members did not share the same long-range goals. We can infer, therefore, that political expedience figured as heavily as military strategy in decisions about the chain of command, logistics, and the positioning of the separate forces on the battlefield. Since he could not expect to hold the coalition together indefinitely, Ilu-bi'di's best—perhaps only—strategic option was to defeat the Assyrians quickly in a decisive battle. But even this decision raised a host of difficulties.

Once Ilu-bi'di knew that the Assyrians were on the march, he had about a month to choose a suitable battleground that could provide the right mix of tactical and logistical advantage. The plain around Qarqar was an obvious choice for it gave Ilu-bi'di the home field advantage over allies and enemies alike. The area also made an excellent battlefield and, indeed, had been the site of an earlier coalition's victory over the Assyrian king, Shalmaneser III, in the ninth century.[55] The decision to fight at Qarqar thus carried moral weight; what their ancestors had accomplished, they could repeat. Perhaps most important, the fertile alluvium of the Orontes valley ensured plentiful food and water for the gathering army, which took time to muster and await the enemy's arrival. Centrally located with regard to the other coalition members, Qarqar was one of the best areas in the region for supplying a large, stationary army over a substantial period. The battle site suited the Assyrians as well, for Sargon would have the chance to scotch the rebellion quickly at its source.

Two main routes led to the battlefield. The more southerly road west would have taken the Assyrians along the Euphrates from Ashur to Dur-Katlimmu and Raṣapu and thence to Hamath and the Orontes River. By approaching Qarqar this way, they could have forced Ilu-bi'di to abandon several key sites, including Hamath and Tell 'Acharneh, which the Assyrians would have looted and burned. This outcome, though costly for Ilu-bi'di, also would have proved to other coalition members the depth of their leader's dedication and forced his followers to commit completely to the upcoming battle. For the Assyrians, it would have brought an easy, morale-boosting success and whatever provisions the inhabitants had left behind. A second route approached Qarqar from the north, following the road from Assyria to Naṣibina, Guzana, Harran, and Til-Barsip, thence from Nerab to Kullania on the Orontes where it flowed into the Assyrian province of Patina/Unqi. This road afforded the Assyrians ample logistical support for the entire journey, so they could march relatively fresh to the battlefield. No text explicitly states which way they went, but the fact that Sargon set up a stele at Kullania to commemorate this campaign, even though that city had not rebelled, strongly suggests that the Assyrians took the northern route.[56] In addition, this choice would have effectively isolated Arpad from its allies.

The opposing armies fielded chariots, cavalry, and infantry, although in what numbers and dispositions we cannot say. According to Sargon's sculptured reliefs, which offer our best—albeit stereo-typed—evidence of contemporary Syro-Palestinian forces, northern coalition members carried curved swords and oval shields and wore metal or leather helms, whereas their southern neighbors wore no armor but donned soft hoods of leather or felt and wielded bows and spears (figures 1 and 2).[57] Of the battle, only Sargon's boastful sum-mation, found on a stele from Tell 'Acharneh, survives: "[They (the troops) inflicted upon th]em a major [defeat], blocked up the river [with their corpses], burned [their cities], (turning them) [into ash] es; they established [devastation in the land] of Hamath."[58] Another text claims that Ilu-bi'di fled into Qarqar, where the Assyrians promptly captured him.[59] As a stark example to others, they sent the rebel leader to Ashur to be flayed publicly after Sargon's triumphant return. Indeed, the punishment was later depicted on the throne room reliefs at Dur-Sharrukin.[60] Since the rebellion had started in the kingdom of Hamath, the Assyrians dealt most harshly with the area, destroying numerous sites and killing or deporting large numbers of people.[61] The extent of the retaliation is well attested archaeologically. At Hamath and Tell 'Acharneh, a large site south of Qarqar on the Orontes River, excavations have revealed widespread destruction.[62] Not content simply to burn the place, Sargon set up a stele at 'Acharneh to commemorate the event. The stele's inscription mentions that he erected similar monuments in three or four other cities, including Hamath and Hatarikka, located less than thirty miles northwest of Damascus.[63] It was probably during the post-battle mopping up that Sargon rejoined the army, if indeed he had not been with them from the start.

With the northern coalition crushed and its survivors in disarray, the army crossed the densely wooded Amanus Mountains to the Phoenician coast in order to secure trade centers such as the island settlement Arwad and punish the cities Ba'il-gazara and Sinnu, presumably for daring to interfere with Assyrian commercial interests.[64] Our only evidence of this action comes from drawings of the Room V reliefs from Dur-Sharrukin that show that the Assyrian assault on Ba'il-gazara required a siege ramp and siege engines. There is no indication that after capturing these towns Sargon destroyed either one. Sinnu, at least, was not razed, for it is mentioned subsequently in letters.[65] The Assyrians then marched south along the coast road past Ṣimirra, which either capitulated without a fight or was bypassed by the Assyrians, who opted to isolate rather than besiege it. If they did not do so willingly, smaller towns along the well-populated coast would have been forced to provide the Assyrians with food and fodder.

Continuing south through friendly Phoenician territory and beyond the Lebanon, the Assyrians penetrated a few miles inland into what had been the northern kingdom of Israel before the Assyrians annexed it. Here Sargon targeted its capital, Samaria, which capitulated very quickly, almost certainly without a proper siege and attendant destruction.[66] According to Sargon's prism inscription, "[The inhabitants of Sam]aria, who agreed [and plotted] with a king (Ilu-bi'di) [hostile to] me, not to endure servitude and not to bring tribute to the god Ashur and who did battle, I fought against them with the power of the great gods, my lords, (and) I counted as spoil 27,280 people, together with their chariots and gods, in which they trusted. I formed a unit with 200 of [their] chariots for my royal army."[67]

The Assyrians singled out Samaria because it was strategically important and, despite being nestled among steep hills, an easy target (having fallen to them previously in 722) that they could take without wasting valuable time and scarce resources on a full-scale siege. Following this campaign, Sargon not only renovated the city and pacified the area by deporting the inhabitants but also enlisted into his army its chariotry as an elite corps led by Samarian rather than Assyrian officers.[68] Wholesale slaughter and devastation were reserved for punishment of particularly heinous crimes (e.g., killing Assyrians as an act of rebellion). It took time to raze a city, and there was little to be gained by destroying what they could exploit. Although Arpad, Damascus, and Ṣimirra had rebelled, Sargon made no mention of attacking them. Both Arpad and Damascus offered formidable defenses that had proved difficult to breach in the past. Tiglath-pileser had besieged Arpad for three years and it took him two successive campaigns to capture Damascus.[69] By circumventing these larger cities and going after more vulnerable towns (e.g., Sinnu and Samaria), Sargon not only maintained the initiative, but also won food, fodder, and plunder with relative ease. This cost-effective strategy saved Assyrian lives and isolated Sargon's more powerful enemies by eroding their spheres of influence, cutting off their resources, and reducing their ability to wage war. This strategy also sent an explicit message that the Assyrians did not need to capture a city in order to inflict long-term suffering on its inhabitants. Just how Sargon recovered control of by-passed city-states is nowhere explained. Presumably, their leaders surrendered after the battle at Qarqar.

Having dealt with the northern rebellion swiftly and efficiently, the Assyrians marched into Philistia, where the road wound through flatter and dryer terrain. Here, according to the Room V reliefs, the auxiliary troops (Itu'ean archers and Gurrean spearmen) attacked Gibbethon and Ekron, located just a few miles apart on the Philistine coastal plain.[70] On the banks of a stream near Gibbethon, Assyrian lancers overwhelmed some lightly armed Egyptian troops, who fought as allies of Hanunu, the king of Gaza (figure 3).[71] The Egyptians, stereotypically depicted as curly-haired Kushites wearing no armor and each wielding a pair of javelins or short spears, were no match for the mounted Assyrians. Although heavily fortified at the time, both Gibbethon and Ekron surrendered quickly, probably without attempting to withstand a siege (figures 3 and 4).[72] The reliefs show fighting outside the city and defenders on the walls shooting arrows or brandishing spears, but at neither location do the Assyrians employ any of the standard siege techniques. Having lost these skirmishes, the Egyptians retreated south. With central Philistia back in Assyrian control, Sargon installed a local dynast, Padi, on the throne of Ekron and then pursued Hanunu and his Egyptian allies south to Raphia.[73]

Of the major actions of this part of campaign, only the battle of Raphia receives much attention in Sargon's inscriptions, which describe the battle as follows:

> He (Pharaoh Osorkon IV) ordered his general (Rē'ē) to go to his (Hanunu's) aid and do battle and fight against me. At the command of the god Ashur, my lord, I defeated them and Rē'ē, like a shepherd whose flock has been stolen, ran off alone and disappeared. Hanunu I seized with my own hand and took him to my city, Ashur, in chains. The city of Raphia I destroyed, I tore down, I burned with fire; 9,033 people, together with their many possessions, I carried off.[74]

The clever pun on the Egyptian general's name—in Akkadian ra'û means shepherd—also parodied the phrase "shepherd of the people," which was normally used as an epithet of kings.[75] Evidently the scribe wished to emphasize the inadequacy of the Egyptian leader. The passage is also noteworthy for the fact that Sargon did not claim to have captured or deported any Egyptians. At this point neither Egypt nor Assyria was prepared to let the situation escalate into war, and Sargon did not attempt to capitalize on his victory, although the thorough destruction of Raphia, which was never rebuilt, gave the Egyptian ruler a good idea of what he could expect if he continued to interfere. As for Hanunu, punishment awaited him after deportation to Assyria, for not only had he set a dangerous precedent by appealing to Egypt, but he had also rebelled against Assyria for a second time (the first time being in 732 against Tiglath-pileser, who generously reinstated him afterward). Those left in Gaza, now fully an Assyrian possession, had learned their lesson, and the city remained submissive for the rest of Sargon's reign.

By now the Assyrian army was no doubt reaching the end of its mission effectiveness, and with the onset of winter fast approaching they needed to head home. On the return journey, the Assyrians marched in triumph through client territories, parading their captives and demanding supplies, although, again, the exact route they took is unclear. The Assyrians fought war on a scale that the smaller city-states of Palestine found difficult to fathom, accustomed as they were to fighting limited engagements among themselves. Faced with such uncompromising Assyrian aggression, there was not much that the kings of Judah, Edom, Ammon, and Moab could do, so they submitted without a fight and reaffirmed their status as tribute-paying clients of the Assyrian king.[76] The Assyrians did not simply march through the Levant to wreak havoc and then leave, however. Administrative provisions and preparations for territorial investment had to be made before they could return home. As was customary, clients ruled on their own with the aid of an Assyrian delegate (*qēpu*), who sent regular reports to the king and kept an eye on his interests.[77] Trouble spots, such as Samaria and Gaza, were simply annexed. As Sargon put it, "People of the lands I had conquered I settled therein, put my eunuch as governor over them, and had them pay tribute and taxes as Assyrians."[78] The laconic remark contains no hint of the sophisticated provincial administration put in place to maintain Assyria's grip on this area. The work involved finding solutions to a complex and continuously evolving set of problems. In the meantime, Sargon had chalked up his first major triumph.

Over the course of this campaign the Assyrians had covered more than 1,600 miles (from Calah to Raphia and back), fought two pitched battles (at Qarqar and Raphia) and innumerable smaller engagements, and captured at least nine cities of varying size and importance. In the process they had reclaimed all of their lost territory while confirming Judah, Edom, Ammon, and Moab as clients. Altogether this was an astonishingly successful campaign, the military and political rewards of which stood in marked contrast to the provisional achievement at Der. Politically the western victory was of immense value to Sargon. Not only had he managed to defeat Ilu-bi'di's coalition decisively, but he had also bested Egyptian troops in battle and established control over all the territory right up to Egypt's border. Even so, the task of securing and governing the newly subdued territories in the west would soak up time, energy, and resources before the payoff could begin to flow in a steady stream to the core. The subjugation of Syria-Palestine would also require additional military intervention and constant attention: whole populations would move, cities would be rebuilt, and constant wearying problems, such as the effects of drought and the destabilizing presence of nomadic Arabs, would have to be addressed. Although Sargon's inscriptions speak only of triumph, the letters reveal that pressure put on the provincial system nearly overburdened it, and the situation in these provinces sometimes became rather desperate.[79] Still, to the consternation of his enemies, the events of 720 had revealed Sargon as a king and commander of exceptional abilities.

The Triumphant Return to Assyria and Political Developments

In a favorable month on a propitious day, as the saying went, Sargon II and his army entered triumphantly into the city of Ashur to celebrate the successful conclusion to the new king's first campaign season. It had not been an easy year, but now that he had proven himself on the battlefield, the king could concentrate on political matters. To this end, Sargon and the army marched their captives to Ashur, where the king awarded appropriately gruesome sentences to the rebels. He had Ilu-bi'di tied spread-eagle to stakes on the ground and flayed, while he himself blinded Hanunu with a spear.[80] Flaying, impalement, and mutilation (blinding or amputation) were the worst Assyrian punishments, and the king reserved them for extraordinary circumstances. Ilu-bi'di had killed Assyrians and dared to incite rebellion against the vulnerable new king. His had been an existential threat and thus called for extreme retribution, whereas Hanunu, a repeat offender, had sought help from Assyria's rival, Egypt.

The harsh punishments were a pointed prelude to what came next. Sargon proceeded to consolidate his power by rewarding his supporters and appointing the best among them to the empire's highest administrative positions. Although he had secured the loyalty of well-trained, experienced troops, he still needed to confirm the backing of the aristocracy and the most powerful priests. Accordingly, "in order to make firm the foundation of the throne and stabilize my rule," Sargon granted the citizens of the important cult centers, Ashur (eponymous city of the god Ashur) and Harran (home to the moon god, Sin), together with "all the temples of Assyria," exemption from taxes and services.[81] Then, in order to demonstrate his piety and additional support of temples, he donated a large silver vessel (roughly twenty pounds in weight) to Ashur, commemorating his beneficence.[82] Sometime thereafter (the exact date is unknown), as another example of his just and merciful nature, Sargon let a large group of "guilty" Assyrians live, though he deported them to Hamath.[83] The miscreants' specific crimes were omitted from inscriptions lest they detract from the message of clemency or magically spread the treason, but they had probably supported rival claimants to the throne.

All of Sargon's actions were designed to show both friends and enemies that he was a legitimate Assyrian king, the true representative of Ashur, and someone who would not hesitate to do whatever it took to protect Ashur's empire. From the very beginning of his reign, Sargon demonstrated a remarkable level of political acuity. He understood that power and prestige depended on a balance between ruthlessness and benevolence; too much of either would leave him vulnerable. The campaigns of Sargon's first year are particularly revealing in this regard, and it is important to look at the composite effect of his actions. Though new to the throne, Sargon had already exhibited the same level of clearheaded calculation that would distinguish the rest of his reign. The decision to make peace with Merodach-Baladan might have made Sargon look weak had it not been followed by the ruthless punishment of Ilu-bi'di and Hanunu, which proved to enemies and subjects alike that he could exact revenge as and when he chose. In retrospect, therefore, violent retribution served several purposes: it showed Assyria's clients and subject lands what they might expect if they rebelled and it proved to the magnates and gods that Sargon was man enough to impose justice in its most extreme forms. In fact, Sargon took great pains to create an image of himself as a just and spectacularly successful king.

In this regard, Sargon deliberately evoked the image of a famously heroic ruler from the distant past, Sargon the Great of Akkad (Agade). Throughout the Assyrian Sargon's reign, scribes would draw parallels between the two kings. For example, a text now known as the Sargon Geography celebrates the conquests of Sargon of Akkad as ruler of the known world. Though the origin and purpose of this text are much debated, the Neo-Assyrian copy was found in a private house at Ashur along with other important tablets dating to Sargon II's reign. According to van de Mieroop, this text offered an "idealized view of a world-empire, indeed ascribed to the third millennium ruler, but intended to reflect on the living Sargon. He is portrayed here as the follower of the great king of the past, Sargon of Agade, who was the paradigm of a successful ruler."[84] In order to promote the correct image, the Assyrian Sargon manipulated people's deep-seated respect for the past, their understanding of the significance of names, and belief in the magical efficacy of association. He was by no means the first king to do so—in fact, he was simply fulfilling expectations—but he proved to be very good at it. There is no reason to believe that Sargon promoted himself in a cynical fashion, however. Like history's other visionary leaders, he undoubtedly bought into his own image.

Over the next few years, Sargon began to implement his plan to improve Assyria's economic situation. In a cylinder inscription, he declared eloquently that he "paid attention to the settlement of the uncultivated steppe (and) set his mind to make high mountains, which before had never grown vegetation, yield produce."[85] In many ways, his goals were the natural continuation of plans set in motion by Tiglath-pileser III, and although Sargon benefited hugely from his father's groundwork, it would take a new approach to political and military affairs to overcome the many challenges facing Assyria. In order to emphasize that his reign represented a new beginning, Sargon omitted his patrimony from nearly all of his royal inscriptions. Yet if he continued his father's expansionist policies, he did so on his own terms with the purpose of creating an empire that did not merely abuse its territories, robbing them of people and resources, but that developed trade and agriculture to the mutual benefit of both core and periphery. Successful fulfillment of these goals would require nearly constant campaigning in every theater of operations.

CHAPTER 3

THE "GREAT GAME" NEAR EASTERN STYLE

MILITARY MANEUVERS, 719–716 B.C.

H aving successfully established himself on the Assyrian throne and demonstrated his ability to lead the army to victory, Sargon was ready to move forward with his plans for economic development, political dominance, and the glorification of the Assyrian core. By the end of 720, the south and west of the empire had been temporarily secured. Elam and Babylonia seemed content with the outcome of the Der campaign, and Egypt, after its defeat at Raphia, presented no immediate military threat. Elsewhere, however, the situation was not so favorable. While Sargon was winning his throne, his two northern rivals, Urartu and relative newcomer Phrygia, were steadily maneuvering against him. For the next few years, Sargon directed his military and political power toward foiling the machinations of his northern adversaries. By neutralizing the military threat they offered and taking over the trade networks on which they relied, Sargon could secure his own financial and military superiority. Formidable enemies, the Urartians would not be easy to defeat, whereas Phrygia represented something of an unknown quantity.

The Phrygian kingdom rose to prominence in central Anatolia during the ninth and eight centuries (map 4). Little is known about Phrygia's political or military organization, although excavations at Gordion and other sites attest to the sophistication of Phrygian construction, fortification techniques, and craftwork in metal, glass, ivory, and textiles.[1] As the Phrygians became wealthy from trade, they forged political connections with the Aegean Islands and mainland Greece as well as the Neo-Hittite (Luwian) city-states of Cilicia, central Anatolia, and Syria. Later classical authors such as Herodotus, Arrian, and Justin ascribed semi-mythical status to the Phrygian king Midas (ca. 738–700 B.C.), he of the fabled golden touch, who dedicated a gilded throne at Delphi and whose capital city housed the famous Gordion knot.[2] Contemporary Assyrian sources paint a more prosaic picture of a talented ruler attempting to improve his country's position in the international political arena chiefly through intrigue and diplomacy. Under Midas, the Phrygians began to extend their sphere of influence east and south in pursuit of commerce and in order to forestall Assyrian expansion into the same areas. Although proximity made it easy for Midas to conspire with weaker rulers seeking an alternative to Assyrian domination, Phrygia was nevertheless no match for Assyrian military power.

By contrast, Assyria's main rival, Urartu, was a complex state whose organization and military industry were similar to those of Assyria (map 5). Geography played an important part in the formation of the Urartian state, which has been aptly described as "a terrestrial archipelago, where settlements and fortresses clustered in pockets of fertile land, more or less cut off from one another by mountains and inhospitable terrain."[3] The mountains in eastern Anatolia often exceed seven thousand feet in height and indeed much of the country lies more than a mile above sea level. To master this rugged environment, Urartian society developed both urban-agrarian and pastoral-transhumant elements, albeit the latter have left little evidence. Arable valleys produced cereal crops such as barley, wheat, rye, and millet, while densely forested uplands provided Scotch pine and European black pine for use in building.[4] During the harsh Urartian winters, snow closed mountain passes and curtailed communication between settlements. A shortened campaign season, therefore, required leaders to pay especially close attention to weather. Though its origins remain obscure, by the ninth century the Urartian state had developed into an imperial power centered at the capital, Tushpa, on the eastern shore of the saltwater Lake Van, extending west to the upper reaches of the Euphrates and southeast into the Urmia basin. In addition to the cuneiform writing system, the Urartians borrowed many of their strategic practices from the Assyrians, including mass deportation, recruitment of defeated troops into the army, hegemonic relationships with clients, and the agricultural and commercial development of conquered lands.[5] They were also famed throughout the Near East for their skill as horse breeders, vintners, and hydraulic engineers.

Sargon's contemporary rival, Rusa (ca. 730–713), was in some ways markedly similar to him. Both kings, though scions of a royal house, had won the throne by unorthodox means and set out to prove their legitimacy by enriching their countries through economic development and expansion.[6] Like Sargon, Rusa undertook major building projects as concrete manifestations of his legitimacy. A worthy opponent, the Urartian king also controlled a standing army that he augmented with troops levied from the provinces. While there is little evidence of Urartian military organization, material remains indicate that the king fielded a well-equipped army of cavalry, chariotry, and infantry. Assyrian intelligence reports describe Urartian unit types with the terminology they apply to their own troops (e.g., *kallāpu* units), suggesting that both countries followed similar organizational practices.[7] Pictorial evidence indicates that the Urartians fielded light cavalry, whose troopers wielded javelins rather than lances, in contrast to Assyria's horsemen, who used lances and bows. At least some Urartian soldiers were permanently under arms at fortresses placed at ten-to-twenty-mile intervals in the highlands, overlooking main communication corridors. These forts protected the roads to Tushpa and facilitated the movement of armies to and from war zones. Like his Assyrian counterpart, the Urartian king went to war under the aegis of his gods: Haldi, Teisheba, and Shiuini, among others.[8] In the late eighth century, Urartu was the single Near Eastern power that the Assyrians had reason to view as an existential threat, although geographical and cultural circumstances and a common understanding of warfare made it highly unlikely that either state intended to destroy the other.

At the beginning of Sargon's reign, as Rusa plotted to subjugate the buffer states to the west and south, Midas of Phrygia began cultivating the support of Assyrian clients in Anatolia and Syria. An alliance between Rusa and Midas would have blocked Assyrian access to the Anatolian trade routes and posed a genuine threat to imperial security. Sargon's counterstrategy was to gain control of these same trade and communication routes in order to isolate his enemies, diminish their military and commercial capacity, and get rich at their expense. Because mountainous terrain proved an effective barrier to outright conquest, and since direct confrontation required a huge commitment of resources, the conflict between the three powers typically proceeded indirectly through the small buffer polities located in the Taurus, Anti-Taurus, and Zagros Mountains that separated the larger states. Everyone involved—great powers and smaller polities alike—employed espionage, diplomacy, bluff, and coercion to achieve their respective goals. Extremely rough terrain also made full annexation of the buffer states impractical, so imperial powers competed to impose hegemony over them.

Little is known about these contested buffer kingdoms other than fragments gleaned from Assyrian sources. Few sites in these areas have been subject to full archaeological investigation, and even fewer have produced any written record. Nor do scarce Phrygian and Urartian inscriptions elucidate matters appreciably. In Anatolia, the Assyrians made a province of Quwê (the Cilician plain), which provided good access to the Mediterranean, whereas Hilakku in the mountains to the north and west of Quwê acted as a barrier against Phrygia. Farther to the north and northeast, the Assyrians competed for hegemony over the Luwian-speaking successors of the earlier Hittite Empire: Tabal (Bit-Purutash), Tuhana, and satellite polities in Cappadocia.[9] Farther east, Gurgum, Melid, Kummuh, and Shubria were still nominally independent at the beginning of Sargon's reign (maps 4 and 5). All of the Anatolian polities shared cultural affinities. The strategic picture among the semi-independent buffer kingdoms farther east looked something like this: the Assyrians claimed control over Kumme, Mannea, Allabria, Karalla, and Ellipi; whereas the Urartians counted on the support of Waisi, Wishdish and the rebellious Mannean sub-districts, Andia and Zikirtu. Ukku, Hubushkia, and Muṣaṣir maintained relations with both sides, though at the beginning of this period Urartu had greater influence over Ukku and Muṣaṣir, while Hubushkia leaned toward Assyria.[10] A host of small semi-independent chiefdoms occupied the Zagros Mountains between Allabria and Ellipi.

Though hard-pressed, petty rulers enjoyed varying degrees of autonomy and pursued their own interests vigorously. In the interest of clarity, I have adopted the terms "patron" and "client" to describe the relationships between the powerful empires (Assyria and Urartu) and weaker polities. But readers should be aware that no such terminology can fully capture the fluid nature of international relations in the ancient Near East. Despite Assyrian and Urartian kings' official claims to sovereignty over their clients, local leaders usually considered themselves allies rather than subjects of the more powerful rulers. Much to the consternation of their self-proclaimed overlords, buffer states doggedly pursued their own interests and switched sides whenever political circumstances made a shift in allegiance expedient. Most of them cultivated relationships with opposing powers simultaneously. Diplomatic double-dealing was the norm, and no one expected otherwise. For example, Assyrian intelligence reports indicate that the kings of Muṣaṣir and Hubushkia maintained cordial relations with both Assyria and Urartu, though Muṣaṣir shared a religious affiliation with Urartu and Hubushkia leaned toward Assyria.[11] In effect, these less powerful rulers acted as intermediaries, facilitating the exchange of information and feeding the rivalry between the great kings, who tolerated blatant duplicity when it suited their interests and because they could cite client disloyalty whenever they needed a pretext for military action. In other words, what we now recognize as classic cold war conditions prevailed. For the rulers of the weaker states, survival required political dexterity, intuition, and a great deal of nerve.

Neither the abstract concept of freedom nor the form of government was at issue as monarchs ruled throughout the Near East, and any change in government simply meant an exchange of leaders. Lesser kings habitually sought the help of those more powerful, knowing full well that in doing so they risked self-determination. A ruler's decision to rebel against Assyria in favor of Urartu (or vice versa) was less an indictment of Assyrian or Urartian hegemony than the result of expedience and opportunism. Limited resources and ever-changing circumstances forced Near Eastern rulers to make decisions based on imminent threat and potential benefit rather than personal preferences or ideology—even though political decisions were always justified retrospectively in ideological terms.[12] When the army of Assyria or Urartu visited one of the buffer kingdoms, its ruler had little choice but to pay up, kowtow, and swear fealty, though oaths and tribute never guaranteed loyalty. The conflict encompassed a diversity of cultures and language groups, but, even so, participants understood their roles, the rules of the game, and how their actions were likely to be interpreted. Reciprocal feasting, gift exchange, information traffic, and mutual promises of military support were always "a polite fiction, formalism, and social deceit," masking "obligation and economic self-interest."[13] All participants understood the political discourse, the calculated ambiguity of which guaranteed leaders deniability and latitude for future action. Only a shrewd judge of character and a politically nimble strategist could hope to frustrate the machinations of his rivals and keep the smaller powers in line. Sargon had an aptitude for political theater and military operations, but he also understood that without good intelligence he would be fighting blind. Then, as now, success favored the side with effective information gathering and the means to act on it.

The Assyrian spy system gave Sargon the edge he needed. A large part of the royal correspondence concerned political and military activities in the border provinces, in contested client states, and even in the Urartian capital, Tushpa.[14] The spymaster Ashur-reṣua, based in Kumme, where he served as the Assyrian delegate to the local government, directed intelligence operations involving Urartu. Ashur-reṣua reported to Sennacherib in Nineveh as well as to the king, wherever he might be.[15] In turn, Sargon received news from the crown prince, the magnates, governors and other officials, spies, foreign emissaries, client rulers, and merchants, each of whom cultivated his own informers. Naturally, Urartu and Phrygia gathered information with equal urgency, if not the same level of efficiency.[16] Although it is impossible to assign most Assyrian letters absolute dates (and sometimes they even defy efforts at relative dating), these documents attest that Sargon could make informed decisions based on a constant flow of detailed information gleaned from multiple, corroborating sources. Thus, when Sargon's royal inscriptions assert that a client king colluded with the enemy or otherwise broke a treaty, it is safe to assume that this information was not wholly invented but derived from intelligence received. When and if Sargon chose to act on that information—whether he punished real infractions or exploited trumped up ones—depended on what best suited his purposes at any given time.

In order to prevail, Sargon needed to obstruct a Phrygian-Urartian alliance, secure his territorial gains in Syria-Palestine, strengthen his ties to client allies everywhere, and build up his economic base in the most cost-effective way possible. For the next few years (roughly 719–715), the Assyrians concentrated on consolidation and containment. Accordingly, Sargon's first three campaigns of this period involved important clients occupying strategic positions on Assyria's northern and eastern flanks.

Backing Up a Client: Aid for Mannea, 719

At this time, Mannea, a region of high mountains, verdant rolling hills, and fertile valleys to the south of Lake Urmia, was home to several polities: a central, dominant kingdom based at Izirtu (modern Qalaichi) and semi-independent peripheral principalities such as Andia and Zikirtu (map 5).[17] Farmers, pastoralists, and famous horse breeders, the people of Mannea were culturally more attuned to Urartu than to Assyria. Indeed, they worshipped the Urartians' primary god, Haldi, among their indigenous pantheon.[18] The cultural barriers were such that the Assyrians had to assign junior officials the task of learning the Mannean language, which was probably of Indo-Hurrian origin and akin to Urartian.[19] Mannea's strategic location, rich grazing land, and abundant supply of horses inevitably drew the interest of Urartu and Assyria, neither of which could stand by while the other gained political traction there. Generally speaking, the Assyrians regarded all mountain dwellers as inferior barbarians, people who wore animal skins, could not write, and did not even speak a civilized language. But they managed to overcome their antipathy in case of the semi-urbanized Manneans, whose cooperation they required.

The struggle over the Urmia basin had been going on intermittently since the ninth century, when Shalmaneser III raided the area in search of horses and loot and in order to counter Urartu's growing influence there. During the first half of the eighth century, Urartian kings persisted in their attempts to establish hegemony over Mannea, aiming to redirect the flow of goods from the east through Urartu and away from Assyria. Urartu's early success meant that the Assyrians lost a key "source for the production of capital" and slowly slid into the period of economic decline that characterized the decades before Tiglath-pileser III.[20] The Assyrians eventually pushed back, and, under the guise of helping the Mannean king resist a Urartian coup, Tiglath-pileser campaigned there in 744 and again in 737 in exchange for Mannean fealty. Rusa reacted by campaigning south along the western shore of Lake Urmia. Local Urartian settlements as well as hegemony over key city-states in this area, Muṣaṣir and Waisi, afforded the Urartians a clear route to Mannea and improved territorial security. Muṣaṣir was of particular strategic importance due to its proximity to Assyria and because it guarded the western end of the Gelishin pass, the best, most direct route between Assyria and Urartu.[21] Perhaps more compelling than Muṣaṣir's strategic value was its status as the cult center of Haldi and the spiritual home of Urartian kingship. No self-respecting Urartian king could let the Assyrians occupy the city, nor could the

Assyrian king easily tolerate a Urartian satellite just fifty miles (as the crow flies) from Arbela and seventy-five from Nineveh. At some point between the last years of Tiglath-pileser III and the early years of Sargon, Assyria and Urartu may have come to an accord regarding the city, for Sargon later accused Rusa of breaking his oath.[22] It is possible that the breach involved a Urartian move to impose hegemony over Muṣaṣir.

Three undated bilingual (Urartian-Akkadian) steles, two of which were erected by Rusa near the head of the Gelishin pass in the vicinity of Muṣaṣir, celebrate his brief occupation of the city.[23] In one of the fragmentary inscriptions, Rusa explains: "Urzana (ruler of Muṣaṣir) closed the temple door in my face and ran away to Assyria. I went to the temple of Haldi, I went there and made sacrifices. I went to Assyria; Urzana arranged the troops for battle. At the command of Haldi, I went to the steep mountain Andarutu, I defeated Urzana, the king of Ardini (Muṣaṣir), I seized him (and) he laid a tribute (before me). . . . 15 days I stayed in Ardini."[24] The same text claims that Rusa exceeded his ancestors in terms of the rich donations he made to the temple of Haldi and the number of sheep he sacrificed there. Nevertheless, with prudence that belied the vaunting inscription, Rusa restored the city's semi-neutrality by retaining Urzana as its ruler. Not mollified, the Assyrians could only view the erection of monuments provocatively close to their territory and boasting in Akkadian as a deliberate challenge. Yet to destroy the steles in response would have been viewed as an overt act of war, and Sargon was not fully prepared for that eventuality.[25] Although he did not react immediately, Sargon would not forget the incident, and when the opportunity arose in 714, he would consciously reverse each of Rusa's claims. In the meantime, the two kings took care to avoid direct conflict, limiting themselves to proxy wars of varying intensity. Sargon could tolerate Urartian visits to Muṣaṣir as long as Urzana maintained communication with Assyria, but he could not allow the Manneans to fall under Urartian influence, for he needed the horses they could supply. Rusa had already begun to woo (or coerce) the rulers of the Mannean districts, Andia and Zikirtu, into joining him, thereby jeopardizing Assyrian interests in the region.

In 719 the situation became critical. After some additional Mannean city rulers, acting on Rusa's orders, joined Mitatti of Zikirtu in a rebellion against their king, Iranzi, Sargon had to respond or lose Mannea and lose face. According to Sargon's Annals, "In my third regnal year the cities Shuandahal and Durdukka, strong cities, plotted to fight Iranzi of Mannea, their lord, who bore my yoke, and they relied on Mitatti of Zikirtu. Mitatti of Zikirtu lent to them his battle troops with their cavalry which was given for their aid. I mustered the massed might of Ashur and I marched forth to vanquish those cities."[26] Since Mannea lay roughly 180 miles into the Zagros Mountains east of Assyria, and the army had to pass through high mountains—some over 5,000 feet—in order to get there, this punitive campaign represented a substantial undertaking.

Mountain travel was always dangerous and unpredictable. Pathways often became obstructed or even obliterated by the effects of winter snows, floods, and avalanches, and food could also be scarce. Several passes cut through the Zagros Mountains, but not all of them were open to the Assyrians. For example, the Gelishin and Gowre Shinke passes in the northeast that gave access to Muṣaṣir, Hubushkia (the area around modern Mahabad), and Urartian settlements southwest of Lake Urmia remained closed to the Assyrian army for obvious reasons.[27] However, they could follow an itinerary from Arbela into the Assyrian client state Habhu south through the mountains to Anisu and Ieri, and then east through a series of passes and valleys to Izirtu.[28] But on the whole, the Assyrians favored a more direct route starting in the province of Zamua and following the Lower Zab drainage system through the mountains to Mannea.[29] Once the Assyrian troops reached Mannea, they could expect its king, Iranzi, to supply them.

Although Sargon accused Mannean city rulers of plotting with Rusa, the Assyrians did not seek battle with the Urartians, nor did Rusa come to the aid of the rebels. Sargon's purpose was to secure the Mannean throne for Iranzi and to retake the rebel strongholds. He could frustrate Rusa's plans perfectly well without attacking Urartu. For his part, Rusa could test Assyrian strength and resolve without having to commit his own military. Even with the help of Mitatti of Zikirtu, the hapless city rulers had little hope of success. In the Annals, Sargon claims that:

> With my strong battering rams I shattered their walls and I razed them to the ground. The people, together with their possessions, I carried off; those cities I demolished, I tore down, I burned in a conflagration. The cities Sukkia, Bala, Abitikna concocted a wicked plan to eradicate the foundation of their land (Mannea) and with Ursa (Rusa), the Urartian, they agreed to become (his) subjects. On

account of the sin they committed, I tore them from their place and caused them to dwell in the lands Hatti and Amurru (Syria).[30]

The Assyrians proved unstoppable as they plundered the rebel towns and then deported their prisoners to northern Syria. The deportations served various purposes. Deportees acted as hostages for the continued good behavior of those left behind, and they helped the Assyrians develop new agricultural lands elsewhere in the empire. Finally, by depleting local populations, the Assyrians might prevent future rebellions. Not incidentally, the ability to move large groups of people around without interference demonstrated Assyrian invincibility.

For the time being, at least, Iranzi retained his throne. In effect this campaign was an Assyrian show of force against Urartu and the Zagros buffer states, as well as a testament to Sargon's commitment to his clients. The Assyrians made no move against Muṣaṣir nor did they go after Waisi, Andia, Zikirtu, or Wishdish; that would come later. It was more important to keep Mannea out of Urartian hands, a feat that Sargon managed with a calculated measure of punishment and reward. Too little violence could make the Assyrians appear weak, while too much would simply turn the Manneans toward Urartu. Despite his finely tuned political stratagems, Sargon had not settled his Mannean problem, and Rusa remained unchastened.

Punishing a Disloyal Client: Kiakki of Shinuhtu, 718

The situation in the east having been dealt with temporarily, Sargon opted to campaign on his extreme northwestern flank to punish the small polity of Shinuhtu (modern Niğde), one of a number of city-states—collectively referred to as Tabal in Assyrian sources—that occupied the region of central Anatolia between the Halys River, Quwê (Cilicia), Phrygia, and the Anti-Taurus mountains (see map 4). Attracted by the area's access to trade routes and abundant natural resources, the Assyrians first ventured there during the ninth century, when Shalmaneser III raided to collect plunder and extort tribute from the local petty kings.[31] During the period of weakness following Shalmaneser's reign, Urartu had in turn exploited these polities, though neither state had been able to occupy territory so distant from its core on a permanent basis.[32] By the eighth century,

the city-states of central Anatolia had coalesced into two main kingdoms, Bit-Purutash (Tabal proper) and Tuhana, plus several semi-independent principalities such as Shinuhtu, Istuanda, Hubishna, and
Atunna.[33] At the beginning of Tiglath-pileser III's reign, the competition between Assyria and Urartu escalated, but eventually a
string of Assyrian victories drove a number of nonbelligerent states,
including the main Tabalian kingdoms, to submit to Assyria.[34] In
about 730, Tiglath-pileser intervened directly in Tabalian affairs by
replacing disobedient client king Uassurme of Bit-Purutash, with a
more tractable commoner, Hulli, "the son of nobody."[35] Assyrian
tribute demands and the economic by-products of interstate rivalry
(gift exchange and bribery) stimulated production in Tabal, which
experienced a period of economic and cultural vitality throughout
the second half of the eighth century. Prosperity inevitably attracted
the attention of avaricious foreign powers.

When Kiakki, the ruler of Shinuhtu, colluded with Midas of
Phrygia, he "forgot (his) oath (before) the great gods and was negligent
in readying his tribute."[36] Sargon then "covered Shinuhtu, his royal
city, like a fog" and "counted him (Kiakki), together with his warriors, 7,350 people, his wife, his sons, his daughters, and the people of
his palace together with his many possessions, as plunder."[37] Booty
from the campaign included "elephant hide, ivory, ebony, boxwood,
multi-colored garments, linen apparel, weapons, implements of battle . . . their flocks (of sheep and goats), herds of horses, (and) donkeys
without number."[38] Exotic luxury items such as these were symbols
of power. Elites exchanged them, wore them, donated them to temples, or adorned their homes with them as visible proof of status.
Moreover, the list of plunder attests to Tabal's position at a commercial crossroads, for materials such as elephant hide and ivory were
not indigenous to Anatolia and had to be acquired through trade,
theft, or gift exchange.[39] Sargon's account of these events strongly
suggests that he and his army simply arrived unopposed at Shinuhtu
(a client city, after all) and took possession ("covered it like a fog")
without undue violence. Despite this show of force, it remained for
Sargon to discourage Midas from further meddling.

The challenge Sargon faced was how to manage his Tabalian clients without alienating them or having to commit military resources
for the long term. The full annexation of this distant region, with its
high mountains and broad valleys, was impractical, so Sargon met
his objectives through political maneuvering.[40] In a strikingly adept

move, he gave Shinuhtu to Kurti, the ruler of Atunna, but balanced the gesture by increasing Kurti's annual tribute of horses, mules, gold, and silver.[41] At the same time, Sargon reinstated Hulli on the throne of Bit-Purutash, from which it seems Shalmaneser V deposed him.[42] These dispensations took advantage of the geographic distribution of the pertinent kingdoms along a relatively direct north–south axis: Bit-Purutash, Shinuhtu, Tuhana, and Atunna. In order to stop any of the Tabalian kingdoms from becoming strong enough to threaten Assyrian hegemony, Sargon redistributed power among them. The gift to Kurti of land not adjacent to Atunna but located on the far side of Tuhana rewarded Kurti's loyalty while limiting the advantage he could gain from the acquisition. At the same time, the insertion of Atunnan territory between Bit-Purutash and Tuhana, together with Hulli's reinvestment, effectively prevented the two most powerful Tabalian kingdoms from uniting and also strengthened ties between loyal clients, Atunna and Bit-Purutash. Within the next year or so, when Hulli's son, Ambaris, succeeded his father as ruler of Bit-Purutash, Sargon showed him special favor by allowing him to marry the Assyrian princess, Sargon's daughter Ahatabisha, and by awarding him Hilakku as her dowry.[43] According to our current understanding of the area's political geography, Hilakku was located in the coastal mountains to the west of Quwê, and thus it was adjacent to an Assyrian province but not to Bit-Purutash, which lay some distance to the northeast.[44] With one bold stroke Sargon honored Ambaris above other Tabalian kings and limited his power, thus signaling that the Assyrians would not allow their clients to pursue their own territorial ambitions.[45]

Sargon managed Tabal without recourse to widespread violence, yet his message to the Tabalian leaders (and to Midas as well) was unambiguous: the Assyrians could remove a subject ruler from his throne at will no matter how distant his kingdom; loyalty could expect reward but disobedience would not be tolerated; resistance was pointless; and rebels could expect to stand alone (neither Midas nor Rusa had aided them). Sargon's skillful political play kept Tabal under Assyrian hegemony, which in turn drove a convenient wedge between Phrygia and Urartu. Nonetheless, though Midas temporarily ceased operations in Tabal, he commenced (or continued) them at Carchemish, Assyria's only remaining client in inland Syria.

Creating Opportunities: The Fall of Carchemish, 717

Located on the western side of the Euphrates River where it enters Anatolia, Carchemish was a prosperous Neo-Hittite city-state, whose king, Pisiri, became a tribute-paying client of Assyria in 738, during the reign of Tiglath-pileser III.[46] The city controlled one of the main Euphrates crossings on the east–west trade route. Though it lost some traffic to the neighboring Assyrian regional center, Til-Barsip (situated about twelve miles to the south on the other side of the river), Carchemish remained both strategically important and attractively wealthy.[47] Although Pisiri had not participated in the revolt against Sargon in 720, the defeat of the Syro-Palestinian coalition left Carchemish the lone client among Assyrian provinces. Nervous about his isolation, Pisiri sought an alternative to Assyrian hegemony with Midas of Phrygia. After discovering this rebellious behavior, Sargon moved quickly and decisively to seize Carchemish.

Sargon's inscriptions take little notice of the campaign against Carchemish other than to vilify Pisiri, who had "sinned against the oath of the great gods and sent (messages of) hostility against Assyria to Mita (Midas) of the land of Muski (Phrygia)."[48] The sources make no mention of war but report laconically that Sargon deported Pisiri, his family, and followers to Assyria, and recruited fifty chariots and two hundred cavalry into the Assyrian army, while incorporating Carchemish into the provincial system and resettling the area with Assyrian colonists. As in the case of Shinuhtu, Sargon appears to have taken Carchemish without a fight. Plunder included "11 talents of gold, [2,1]oo talents of [silver], [x] talents of bronze, tin, iron, elephant hide, ivory, [. . .], (and) battle equipment."[49] Although the seizure of Carchemish looks very much like a cynical money grab, Sargon took care to find some legitimate reason—treason or the rumor of it—to justify the act, even if his own political machinations forced Pisiri's hand. In the ancient Near East, sacking a city or removing its ruler without formal justification—however spurious or rationalized—would have violated age-old notions of just war and betrayed the legal foundation of the patron-client relationship (a treaty sealed by an oath sworn before gods).[50] Phony or not, the suggestion that Pisiri had been in contact with Midas gave Sargon a convenient excuse to complete the annexation of Syria. Just as important and revealing, the city's riches would help fund the construction of Sargon's new capital, Dur-Sharrukin, founded the very same year.[51]

The Jewel of the Empire: Dur-Sharrukin 717

According to the tenets of Assyrian royal ideology, kings were to celebrate success in war by public acts of piety and largesse, usually involving building temples, palaces, irrigation works, and trading centers, as well as by erecting inscribed monuments enumerating their deeds.[52] More victories meant more money, more building, and ever greater claims to supremacy. Soon after his triumph over Ilu-bi'di in 720, if not from the very beginning of his reign, Sargon began to reenvision himself as the founder of a new Assyrian golden age. Although in many ways he followed through on plans that Tiglath-pileser initiated—particularly with regard to economic strategy—Sargon's methods of rule were more clement than those of his father and his vision altogether more grandiose. As mentioned earlier, one of Sargon's first acts was to exempt the inhabitants of the holy cities Ashur and Harran from tax and state service.[53] With the priestly class and elites thus satisfied, he could take steps to enrich and glorify the whole empire, both heartland and outer provinces.

The focal point was to be Dur-Sharrukin, a new city built on virgin soil, where the king could display Assyria's wealth and "provide the wide land of Assyria with food to repletion."[54] The common assumption that Sargon moved his court in an attempt to escape the "active and fierce resistance his rule had met with in the Assyrian heartland" is untenable, given the fact that Sargon's base remained the old capital at Calah until 706, the year before his death.[55] Since Dur-Sharrukin took over ten years to build, it is hardly likely that the king saw it as a means to avoid those who opposed him. More to the point, a king who attempted to escape opposition rather than confront it could not expect to survive for long.

In many respects, Sargon's actions were in line with age-old Mesopotamian concepts of kingship that associated the king and the gods with the capital city that they inhabited together. Since the gods determined Assyria's future, it fell to the king to secure their happiness and support by maintaining their temples.[56] Thus, city building and improvement were among the most important royal prestige activities. A cylinder inscription recovered at Dur-Sharrukin plainly describes Sargon's motivations:

> He (Sargon) turned his attention to the settlement of the abandoned steppe and the opening of the uncultivated land (and) the

planting of orchards; he pondered how to get steep cliffs, which
from antiquity had not brought forth greenery, to sprout crops;
his heart directed him to set furrows in uncultivated waste areas
which had not known a plow under earlier kings, and to cause a
joyful song to reverberate . . . (part omitted) . . . day and night I
(Sargon) planned to build that city.[57]

In other words, Sargon built the city both to demonstrate that he
had something spectacularly different to offer and to improve his
subjects' standard of living, which may have suffered as a result of
Tiglath-pileser's relentless expansion. In bringing abundance to the
previously barren steppe, the new construction would also "evoke
a spatially effective sense of economic prosperity."[58] Moreover, the
accomplishment of a project that required the involvement of nearly
every high-ranking official encouraged cohesion. Ideally, those who
helped build Dur-Sharrukin would grow to identify strongly with
their king and his image.[59]

Although construction projects were among the most significant
royal duties, kings rarely attempted anything quite as ambitious as
a new capital city, and those who did carefully refrained from taking credit for the idea in their inscriptions.[60] The practice had taken
on negative connotations when Tukulti-Ninurta I (1243–1207) was
murdered shortly after founding the eponymous city, Kar-Tukulti-
Ninurta, just a few miles from sacred Ashur.[61] Knowing this, Sargon
carefully avoided any suggestion of hubris. Before beginning work,
he consulted the appropriate deities and received "their clear assent"
through prognostication. He even made sure to pay a "fair price" to
the farmers who owned the land chosen for development.[62] More
than an expression of royal self-confidence, Dur-Sharrukin was a
statement of piety, proof of the gods' endorsement, and a resplen-
dent monument to Assyria's (and by association Sargon's) majesty.
According to a cylinder inscription written in 713, Sargon "made
the measure of its (perimeter) wall 16,283 cubits, my name, and
established the foundation platform upon the bedrock of the high
mountain."[63] The phrase "platform upon the bedrock of the high
mountain" refers not to the construction site, which comprised flat
agricultural land, but to one of Mesopotamia's most important literary and religious texts, the Epic of Creation (Enūma eliš), thus
emphasizing the special significance of the undertaking.[64] Through
the gematria (using the wall length as a cipher for his name), the

fortification wall became the mystical equivalent of the king, the protector of the people.[65] In serving as the cornerstone of the civilized world, Dur-Sharrukin had both a practical and an ideological purpose.

Despite the city's martial designation—in Akkadian *dûru* means fort—neither the site nor the layout offered obvious military advantages.[66] Yet Dur-Sharrukin's location and the establishment of a new province around it had significant political and economic ramifications for the Assyrian heartland. Local waterways made the area particularly fertile and thus able to produce enough food for the inhabitants as well as surplus for export to other heartland cities.[67] Sargon placed his capital just eleven miles north of Nineveh, a very ancient, well-established city that could act as a conduit through which travelers from Dur-Sharrukin would pass to the rest of Assyria. Nineveh naturally benefited from the association, which brought an increase in traffic and goods. So that Nineveh's new importance would not lead to an imbalance in power among the provinces, Sargon took a portion of that city's territory for the province of Dur-Sharrukin. By locating the new city near the old established one, which had become a significant trade hub as the empire expanded westward, Sargon could more readily manage his economic priorities.[68]

Having amassed a great deal of wealth through conquest and having deported large numbers of subject peoples to Assyria, it remained for Sargon to put these assets to good use. Accordingly, he employed deportees—particularly skilled craftsmen—on construction projects, while the influx of money and materials won on campaign helped defray the cost.[69] That is not to say that Sargon kept everything for himself; he distributed a portion of campaign plunder, tribute, and audience gifts among temples, the royal family (consort and crown prince), and the most powerful magnates.[70] Nevertheless, Sargon could not rely solely on these sources of income but had to borrow from moneylenders to finance the construction.[71] The development of trade remained a high priority. Now, more than ever, the king and his magnates would have to divide their attention between domestic matters—especially commercial enterprises—and military operations.

Making a Profit: Campaigns and Commerce in the West, 716

In 716 Sargon (or his representative) led an expedition to the southern border of Palestine in order to establish a trading colony there
and as a demonstration of Assyrian military might (map 3). Although
Tiglath-pileser III had commemorated his advance through Philistia
by setting up a stele at Nahal Muṣri, the Brook of Egypt (probably
modern Wadi el-Arish), it was not until Sargon's sixth year that
the Assyrians managed to exploit the trade advantage that power
over the area afforded them.[72] Now that the main Phoenician and
Philistine cities were Assyrian clients and trading stations had been
established at key ports along the Mediterranean coast—at Ellishu,
Ṣimirra, Ahta, Sidon, and Gaza—Sargon aimed to take over the
Palestinian terminus of both the Egyptian and Arab overland trade.
Accordingly, Sargon "opened the sealed trading station at the 'Brook
of Egypt.' Assyrians and Egyptians I caused to interact and I made
them trade [together]."[73] This endeavor was peaceable. The idea
was to create a mutually beneficial commercial arrangement with
Egypt and the Arab tribes without having to govern this distant area
directly or maintain a strong military presence. To this end, Sargon
appointed a local Arab chief based at Laban (probably located near
Raphia) to oversee trade. He also opened diplomatic relations with
Osorkon IV of Egypt, who sealed the deal a year later with a gift to
Sargon of twelve horses.[74] In fact, Osorkon's present may have been
a bid to "demonstrate his potential value as an ally at a time when
he himself was in need of one" to help him oppose the increasingly
powerful Kushites.[75]

The patron-client arrangement allowed the Assyrians to reap
the benefits of the maritime and overland trade without incurring
the cost: the client did the work and the Assyrians got rich. Each
emporium was run by an Assyrian official, the commerce officer
(rab kāri), who kept an eye on the client, reported to the king, collected taxes and tolls, and, most important, controlled the flow of
resources into and through Assyrian provinces.[76] In addition to creating new opportunities for trade, the relationship with Egypt and
the annual tribute from the Palestinian states provided Assyria with
a vital supply of sturdy Kushite horses, which made especially good
chariot teams.[77] Several letters and administrative documents report
deliveries of horses from western tributaries. For example, a letter
to the king from Marduk-remanni, the governor of Calah, records

horses delivered from "the emissaries from Egypt, Gaza, Judah, Moab and Ammon," while an administrative document attests to the arrival of seventeen horses from Gaza.[78] Thus far, Sargon had achieved his primary military and mercantile goals. Yet, despite careful planning and excellent intelligence, the Assyrians experienced unexpected setbacks, including a succession crisis in Mannea.

From Containment to Attack: Mannea and Beyond, 716–715

Not long after the events described earlier in this chapter, the king of Mannea died, leaving two sons, Aza and Ullusunu, to fill the power vacuum there (map 5). With the support of Assyria, Aza succeeded his father as king of Mannea but soon faced opposition from a Urartian-backed coalition that supported his brother. According to Sargon's Annals: "Ursa (Rusa), the Urartian, sent his rider with lies to tell to Bagdatti of Wishdish and [Mitatti] of Zikirtu, governors of Mannea, and he caused them to rebel against Sargon and Aza, son of their lord, and brought them to his side. On Waush, a steep mountain, they repulsed the Manneans and threw out the corpse of Aza, their lord."[79] The murder of Aza won Rusa the initiative in the Urmia basin. Thus, he not only accomplished one of his most important political objectives—mastery over Mannea—but, even better, insulted Sargon, who had been Aza's patron and protector. In order to foil his enemy and maintain credibility, Sargon's retribution had to be swift and uncompromising.

In preparation for war, the governors of the Assyrian border provinces collected supplies, increased security at frontier forts, and diligently monitored the developing situation. That the Assyrians considered Ullusunu a client even though Rusa had supported his accession is suggested by a letter that the governor of Zamua wrote to Sargon about the upcoming campaign:

> As many days as I have camped on the Mannean border, the son of the widow (Ullusunu) has set his camp opposite me on his side of the border. On the day that Nergal-bel-uṣur came, making me set out, and I entered into Mannea, I sent my third man to him (Ullusunu) saying, "Get going!" He said, "I am sick." I said, "Let your son come!" He said, "He is sick. I will send my brother with my troops." I sent the third man. As of now, he (the brother) has not arrived. The rest of the city lords' troops are with me.[80]

The excuses, meant to postpone Sargon's discovery of Ullusunu's disloyalty, nonetheless alerted the Assyrians, who immediately sent out spies to uncover the truth. One of the Assyrian intelligence agents operating in the area quickly discovered that "Ashur-le['i] is going to Ullusunu and Ullusunu gave five horses to Ashur-le'i," clear evidence that the Mannean king sought to strengthen his position by allying with Ashur-le'i, the ruler of Karalla, a small polity located south of Mannea and east of the Assyrian province of Zamua.[81] Soon after, as Sargon's inscriptions tell it, Ashur-le'i induced Itti, the king of Allabria, a neighboring principality, to join the alliance with Ullusunu.[82] As the canker of rebellion spread and more of Assyria's clients defected, Sargon's forces prepared to retaliate, although they would not risk open war with Urartu. In contrast to recent Assyrian interventions in the west, which were largely peaceful, the Zagros campaign of 716 proved to be both more extensive and much more violent.

Initially Sargon directed his attack against Mannea, where he "devastated the countryside like locusts . . . clapped shut Izirtu, his royal city, like a trap, slaughtered their multitudes, burned Izirtu in a conflagration and conquered the cities Zibia and Amaet."[83] This ruthless demonstration of force got results. Ullusunu and "his land in its totality" surrendered unconditionally. Notably Sargon did not punish the Mannean king but retained him on the throne as an official Assyrian client. Sargon's actions here typify the complexity of cold war political play, for everything Sargon did sent discrete messages to clients and rival powers alike. Sargon acknowledged Ullusunu as the rightful king of Mannea but made it clear that only Assyrian endorsement could legitimize the new ruler. Association with Rusa, by contrast, dragged Ullusunu into disrepute and brought his country to ruin. Earlier, Rusa's treatment of Urzana of Musasir made a similar statement. Nor could Assyrian clients expect to make alliances without first getting approval from their overlord. Thus, Ashur-le'i of Karalla and Itti of Allabria, who were at this point somewhat less important to Assyria than Ullusunu, received harsher punishment. Moving south through rugged mountain valleys into Karalla, the Assyrian army pillaged the countryside into submission, clapped Ashur-le'i in irons, and deported him and his family to Assyria, after which they annexed Karalla and merged it with the Assyrian province of Zamua.[84] Though Itti of Allabria was also deported, Sargon did not simply take over his lands. Instead he appointed a certain Bel-apla-iddina (possibly an Assyrian official) to rule there as a client.[85] Sargon seized Karalla but not Allabria because direct rule of the latter did not fit his policy of dominating main communication arteries and leaving more peripheral areas to clients. In other words, political expedience and the estimated cost-to-benefit-ratio dictated Sargon's treatment of these two areas.

The immediate crisis having been averted, the Assyrian army continued south. During the subsequent hundred-mile journey through a series of valleys into Parsua, the Assyrians raided continually and acquired large numbers of horses, cattle, donkeys, and "small cattle" to serve as remounts, pack animals, and to feed the troops. Here Sargon destroyed a number of fortified towns, including Ganghutu, whose capture is depicted on the Room II reliefs of Sargon's palace at Dur-Sharrukin (figure 5).[86] Located on a steep height, Ganghutu had an outer wall with crenellated towers at intervals, at least two gates, and an inner citadel also protected by a crenellated wall with towers. Since it was not feasible to bring a large siege train into this terrain, the Assyrians did without and took the city by storm. While levies maneuvered in close to set fire to the gates, Itu'ean archers covered the attackers from the surrounding hills and Gurrean spearmen prepared to attack.[87] The defenders, dressed in stereotypical animal skins, apparently did not offer effective resistance, yet, even so, the city's capture cannot have been easy for the Assyrians, who were attacking uphill against a well-fortified position.

After devastating Parsua, the army continued on to Kishesim (modern Najafehabad), which was a prime target because of its location on the Great Khorasan Road, the main southern trade route east through Iran. The city lords of the fortified caravanserais such as Kishesim essentially had a protection racket going. They would guard and support passing caravans for a price or pillage them if they proved unwilling to pay up. Recognizing the profit potential in this lucrative arrangement, the Assyrians sought to take over. In the Zagros, as in parts of Syria-Palestine, Sargon preferred to keep local systems in place under the firm guidance of an Assyrian delegate or governor and thus save resources and ease the transition to Assyrian governance.[88] Although occasionally this policy led to rebellion, enough of these rulers accepted the political and economic benefits that the Assyrians offered to make conquest appear feasible.[89]

Kishesim's ruler, Bel-sharru-uṣur, tried belatedly to placate Sargon with gifts of "horses paired to the yoke, goods, property, gold, silver, multi-colored garments, linen apparel, weapons, (and) combat gear," which he brought to the Assyrian camp. As an example to others, Sargon detained Bel-sharru-uşur and then had him deported to Assyria for spreading calumny among neighboring chiefs.[90] Once again, Sargon justified the removal of a client ruler and the annexation of his city on legal grounds. That is, Bel-sharru-uşur's sedition broke an existing treaty. After the unfortunate leader's arrest, the Assyrians attacked Kishesim, whose capture is depicted on the Room II reliefs (figure 6). Although Kishesim's elaborate fortification system included a triple wall and defensive towers on the outer perimeter, the Assyrians made a straightforward attack, deploying Gurrean spearmen in support of the Assyrian levies, who charged in and set fire to the wooden gates.[91] The frontal assault here and at Ganghutu probably owes as much to the difficulty of the terrain and the need for speed—it would not do to get caught in the mountains when winter set in—as to the quality of the enemy's defense. As usual, the Assyrian levies got the dirty job as the forlorn hope, presumably because they were easier to replace than the regulars. The lack of siege machinery could also indicate that Sargon had not originally intended to campaign in the area but took advantage of the swift achievement of his objectives in Mannea to extend the campaign into new territory. After Kishesim surrendered, Sargon renamed it Kar-Nergal (trading post of the god Nergal) to indicate its status as an Assyrian trade center and the capital of a new province in the charge of an Assyrian eunuch governor.[92] Now that he had subdued Mannea, Karalla, Allabria, and Kishesim, Sargon had only to safeguard his gains to establish direct control over the western section of the Khorasan Road and thereby greatly advance Assyria's commercial interests. With his clients acting as buffers, he could effectively prevent Urartu from interfering in the southern trade. Although the loyalty of subject rulers was always suspect, they could be useful both as sources of information and purveyors of misinformation. Not content with these substantial achievements, the Assyrians pushed on.

For a number of reasons, the nature of the campaign changed at this point, and the Assyrian army became increasingly violent. Sargon's inscriptions claim that the denizens of Harhar (modern Malayer) and the surrounding region had withheld their tribute of horses since overthrowing their pro-Assyrian city lord, Kibaba, four years earlier.[93] Four years in tribute arrears and the (presumed) murder of an Assyrian appointee provoked a ruthless response. It was also the case that the Assyrians were now fighting people with whom they had had limited previous contact and whom they considered savage. The most cost-effective way for Sargon to achieve his goals was, therefore, to fight hard and instill fear in the indigenous population. After he had cowed them, he could treat them with clemency and make concessions to encourage their continued acquiescence. Consequently, the Assyrians burned and battled their way from Kishesim to Harhar, capturing at least three sizeable towns before tackling their main target. The Room II reliefs at Dur-Sharrukin that depict these engagements are particularly instructive about Assyrian field operations. Working together as shock troops, the Assyrian equestrian units fought an engagement near a small fortress called Bit-Bagaia, apparently killing the male inhabitants, stripping and beheading many of the bodies, and burning the town to the ground (figure 7). What became of the women and children is not shown, but they were probably either deported or left to fend for themselves. Led by Sargon in his chariot, the Assyrians then pressed on to the next town, Tikrakka, killing and despoiling enemy warriors who fought on foot. After losing a fight outside their gates, the townspeople surrendered (indicated by mourning figures on the battlements of the city in figure 8). No siege was necessary, and this city, at least, seems to have survived undamaged. Throughout the proceedings, Assyrian cavalry and chariots intermingled, working together.

Notwithstanding the artistic and ideological conventions that required the celebration of the elite over common soldiers, it is likely that the mounted units actually were responsible for fast devastation attacks such as these. The infantry offered support but was primarily reserved for security, drudgework (building camps, dismantling enemy fortifications, and so forth), sieges, and rarer set piece battles. This type of mobile warfare was well suited to mountain terrain as well as to the geographical disposition of the enemy. Because towns were spread out among mountain valleys and local city lords were either unwilling or unable to organize a unified resistance, the Assyrians could make effective use of speed and surprise to pick off individual strongholds. As the army progressed, the carnage continued, and the next town to succumb to the onslaught was Kindau, another apparently well-fortified citadel that the Assyrians took by storm after the infantry set fire to the gates. Though the reliefs give the impression of Assyrian invincibility, these repeated assaults could not have been easy on troops attacking without the benefit of siege machinery. Nevertheless, Sargon pressed on, since only one major obstacle remained. Having set out to pacify the wider area of Kishesim, Bit-Sagbat, and Harhar, Sargon arrived at Harhar prepared to do whatever was necessary to capture the city, particularly since its citizens had allegedly overthrown their Assyrian-backed rulers and asked Daltâ, the king of Ellipi and also an Assyrian client, to take over instead.[94] Here was yet another instance of a client exceeding his authority by acting without patron approval. To what degree Daltâ felt himself subject to the Assyrian king we cannot know, but it seems unlikely that he would have felt compelled to ask permission to conduct his personal political affairs. Be that as it may, Sargon determined that Harhar would suffer for its crimes.

The siege and capture of Harhar are illustrated in gruesome detail on the Room II reliefs, which depict a very large city with an outer rampart, an inner wall with multiple towers and two gates, as well as a fortified citadel and several monumental buildings (figure 9). What is perhaps most striking about the scene, however, is the row of fourteen naked men impaled on stakes in full view of the city as a graphic demonstration of the wages of resistance.[95] From the surrounding hills, Assyrian archers provide cover for the Gurrean spearmen and Assyrian levies, who, having breached the outer rampart, ascend the inner wall on ladders. In the background, the city's frenzied inhabitants keen miserably and fail to put out the fire that is spreading through the citadel—all in all, an uncompromising and unapologetic illustration of the calculated frightfulness of Assyrian tactics. It is also the only such incident to appear on the surviving reliefs or to get mentioned in Sargon's inscriptions.

Several factors likely influenced the Assyrian treatment of Harhar. First, Sargon had to punish miscreant subjects. Second, cultural difference played a part. As the Assyrians marched farther away from their familiar theater of operations and thus met enemies unacquainted with customary Near Eastern military and political practices, the Assyrian army applied overwhelming force to accentuate its power.[96] Time and logistics no doubt also figured prominently in tactical decisions. Weather and terrain restricted campaign season in the Zagros Mountains. The farther the army advanced and the longer it campaigned, the more it risked getting caught in the mountains at the onset of winter. Since the Assyrians had already marched some six hundred miles through difficult mountain territory and still faced the return journey, they resorted to any tactic that would produce results in a timely fashion. Moreover, the casualties incurred during the march and in storming so many mountain fortresses without the protection afforded by siege machinery must have taken a terrible toll on the troops, who were only too ready to take out their frustrations on the enemy.[97] Above all, the Assyrian king and his commanders were practical. If terror would achieve their goals efficiently, they would not hesitate to use it. According to the grim calculus of war, therefore, the ghastly execution of a few might well result in the survival of many.

After Harhar fell, Sargon's treatment of the city was, by contrast, deliberately magnanimous. Although he changed the city's name to Kar-Sharrukin (trading post of Sargon) in fulfillment of his broader commercial plans, his inscriptions stress that he restored its gods to their temples, which he rebuilt.[98] It is no accident that the only overtly religious activity mentioned in the account of this campaign took place at the site of the worst violence. On the one hand, public piety toward indigenous gods was meant to placate the surviving local population, who would now be governed by an Assyrian official as subjects of an Assyrian king. On the other hand, religious observance also helped the army to mitigate the taint of extreme violence and so continue to identify with and function within the corporate military entity. In other words, rituals helped the king and his officers restore discipline after the bloody fighting. In order to consolidate their hold on the Khorasan Road, the Assyrians carried out additional operations in the area, expanding the territory of Kar-Sharrukin by adding "six great districts" to it.[99] Although they could not expect to attain long-term pacification of this remote region instantaneously, the Assyrians could buy temporary security for their new province by depriving the lands beyond it of the means to wage war (e.g., food, wealth, and weapons). During this last portion of the campaign, the Assyrians plundered western Media, including the edge of the Hamadan plain. A fragmentary stele found at Najafehabad in Iran includes a detailed itinerary of the (still unidentified) locales that the Assyrians targeted. Of particular note in the otherwise standard list of plundered towns and people is Sargon's claim to tribute from "far-off districts which the kings who went before [me had not seen]."[100] As Tiglath-pileser did not go beyond Tikrakka and Kishesim, which he only mentioned once in his inscriptions, this claim seems legitimate. Thus, by forcing "twenty-eight city lords of mighty Media" to submit and pay tribute, Sargon not only achieved his objective of seizing control of the western trade, but he also fulfilled the ideological mandate to exceed the deeds of his predecessors.[101]

From Sargon's point of view, the campaign was another resounding success, yet it had been a particularly grueling experience compared to those of the previous two years that had involved little, if any, fighting. One indication of how hard Sargon had pushed his troops was his relieved admission upon arriving at the Hamadan plain that he "fed my troops to repletion on their harvest."[102] Implicit in this phrase is the notion that only a king as exceptional as Sargon could overcome the harsh realities of campaigning in the Zagros, where the terrain and weather were merciless. We have no way of determining the number of Assyrian casualties (let alone those of the enemy combatants and civilians), but given the large number of fortified strongholds captured in 716, the rigors of mountain travel, and the physical demands of campaigning, it seems safe to assume that the Assyrians lost a considerable number of men. A high casualty rate would explain the nearly constant deportations that, aside from being a useful way to pacify conquered areas, were necessary to replenish the male population eligible for conscription.

If the royal inscriptions are to be believed, then during the campaigns of 720–716, Sargon and his army covered more than six thousand miles, much of it over extremely inhospitable terrain well beyond the reach of ready supplies.[103] Three of these expeditions—to Tabal, against Carchemish, and to the Brook of Egypt—did not involve much fighting and therefore did not require the maximum strength of the army. By contrast, Sargon seems to have mustered the full force of Assyrian military capability for the Zagros campaigns. The plunder of rich cities such as Carchemish and the opening up of trade emporia helped to defray the cost of sustained military activity. Nonetheless, campaigns increasingly took the army well beyond the borders of the empire and its affiliates into territory that it had little hope of holding permanently—a fact that gave local leaders (city lords and buffer kings) more agency than one might otherwise think possible. Although Sargon's accomplishments were undeniable—he had established a tolerable détente with Babylonia and Elam, subdued Syria-Palestine, made peace with Egypt, put a wedge between Phrygia and Urartu by managing the Tabalian kingdoms, taken control of the Khorasan Road, and founded a new city—his troubles were far from over, and the specter of Urartu still loomed large.

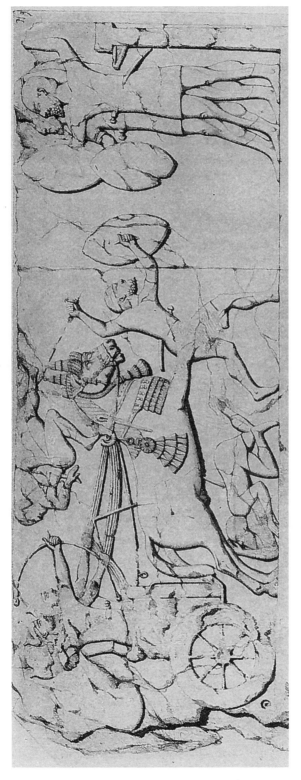

Figure 1. Relief from Room V of Sargon's palace at Dur-Sharrukin showing Assyrians fighting opponents from Syria-Palestine. Albenda, *Palace of Sargon II*, pl. 97.

Figure 2. Relief from Room V of Sargon's palace at Dur-Sharrukin showing the Assyrians besieging a Syro-Palestinian town with siege machinery in 720. Albenda, *Palace of Sargon II*, pl. 96.

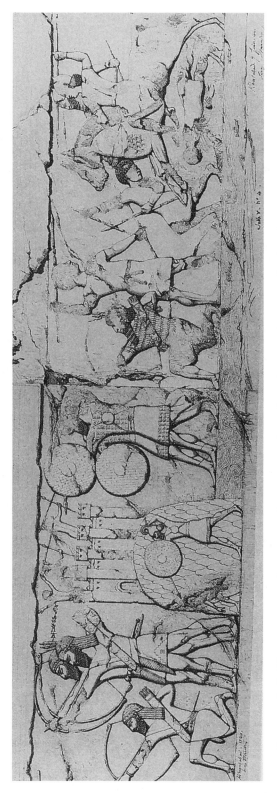

Figure 3. Relief from Room V of Sargon's palace at Dur-Sharrukin showing the siege of Gibbethon in 720. Albenda, *Palace of Sargon II*, pl. 95

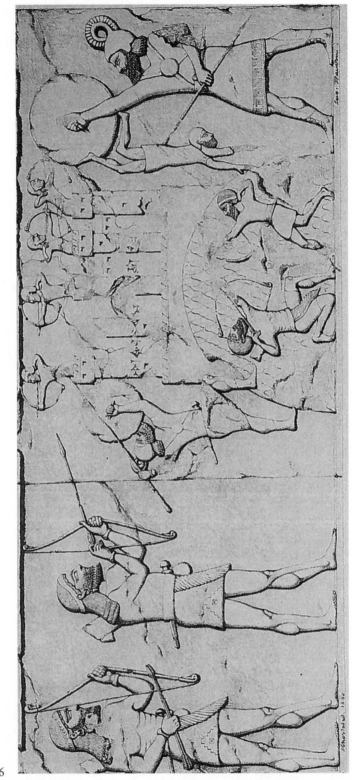

Figure 4. Relief from Room V of Sargon's palace at Dur-Sharrukin showing the siege of Ekron in 720. Albenda, *Palace of Sargon II*, pl. 98.

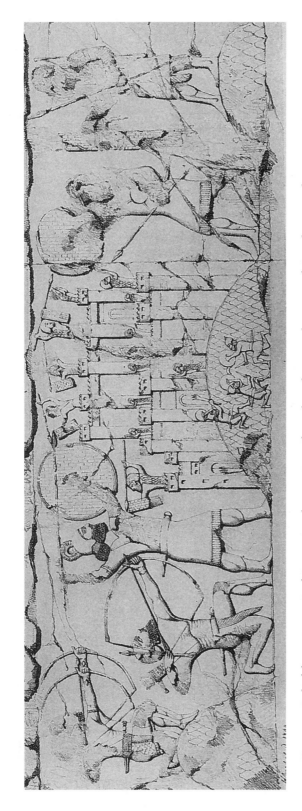

Figure 5. Relief from Room II of Sargon's palace at Dur-Sharrukin showing the siege of Ganghutu in the Zagros Mountains. Albenda, *Palace of Sargon II*, pl. 128.

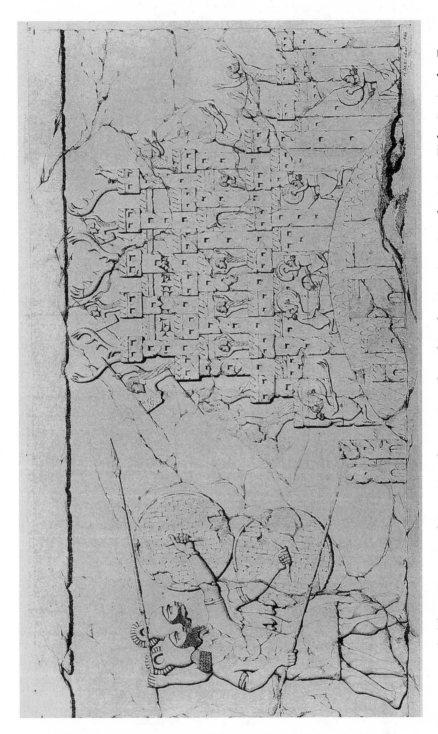

Figure 6. Relief from Room II of Sargon's palace at Dur-Sharrukin showing Assyrians besieging Kishesim in the Zagros Mountains. Albenda, *Palace of Sargon II*, pl. 126.

Figure 7. Relief from Room II of Sargon's palace at Dur-Sharrukin showing Assyrians besieging Bit-Bagaia in the Zagros Mountains. Albenda, *Palace of Sargon II*, pl. 123.

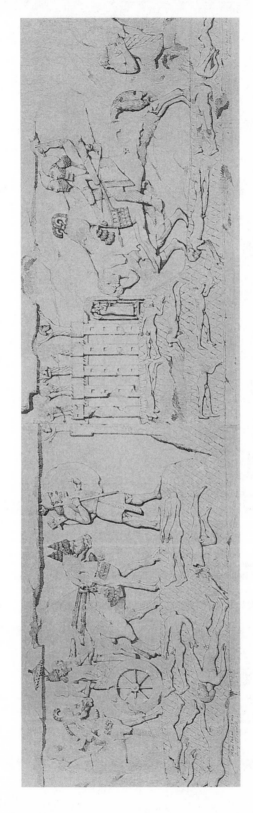

Figure 8. Relief from Room II of Sargon's palace at Dur-Sharrukin showing Assyrians besieging Tikrakka in the Zagros Mountains. Albenda, *Palace of Sargon II*, pl. 120.

Figure 9. Relief from Room II of Sargon's palace at Dur-Sharrukin showing Assyrians besieging Harhar in the Zagros Mountains. Albenda, *Palace of Sargon II*, pl. 112.

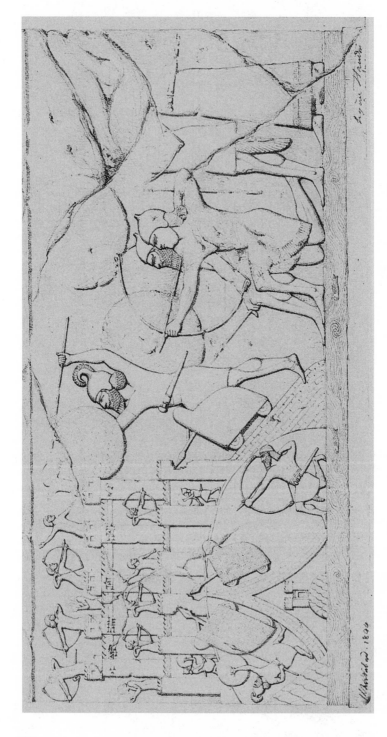

Figure 10. Relief from Room II of Sargon's palace at Dur-Sharrukin showing the siege of Kisheslu in the Zagros Mountains. Albenda, *Palace of Sargon II*, pl. 138.

Figure 11. Relief from Room II of Sargon's palace at Dur-Sharrukin showing the siege of Pazashi in the Zagros Mountains. Albenda, *Palace of Sargon II*, pl. 136.

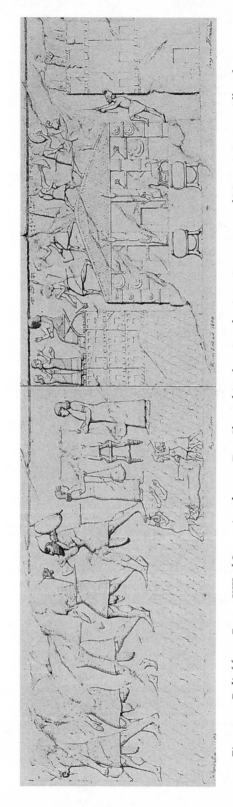

Figure 12. Relief from Room XIII of Sargon's palace at Dur-Sharrukin showing the Assyrian capture of Muṣaṣir in 714. Albenda, *Palace of Sargon II*, pl. 133.

Figure 13. Relief from Room II of Sargon's palace at Dur-Sharrukin showing the king in battle in the Zagros Mountains. Albenda, *Palace of Sargon II*, pl. 121.

CHAPTER 4

TRIUMPH OVER URARTU, 715–714 B.C.

The Cold War Heats Up: Mannea, 715

Despite the setbacks of 716, Rusa continued his attempts to secure a foothold in Mannea. According to Sargon's Annals, the Urartian king "spoke full of lies and deceit to Ullusunu and took away twenty-two of his fortresses. With slander and insults against Ullusunu he persuaded Dajukku, a governor of Mannea, (to support him) and received his son as hostage."[1] Another text attributes Rusa's territorial gain to Ullusunu, who allegedly gave the fortresses as gifts to his new overlord.[2] In any case, Rusa's occupation of Mannean frontier territory and his efforts to win over more of Ullusunu's subordinates represented an escalation of hostilities that pushed the fragile détente with Assyria to the limit. Honor-bound to respond, Sargon had to proceed carefully, lest he start a war before he had fully secured his flanks.

Under these circumstances, Sargon decided to concentrate on the Mannean rebels. In 715, the Assyrians attacked Dajukku, captured and deported him to Assyria with his family, and returned the fortresses to Ullusunu's care, thus restoring the status quo in Mannea with apparent ease.[3] As for the political payoff, Sargon saw to it that Rusa's continued harassment of the Manneans backfired. Far from encouraging additional defections, Urartian interference simply gave Sargon another opportunity to play the good patron by coming to Ullusunu's aid. The decision to deport rather than execute Dajukku filled both practical and symbolic objectives. As a hostage, Dajukku might secure his people's submission to Mannean (and, by association, Assyrian) rule, while the fact that Rusa did not come to Dajukku's aid highlighted Sargon's mercy all the more. That these events prompted Ianzu, the ruler of nearby buffer state Hubushkia, to reaffirm his loyalty and pay tribute to Assyria attests to the effectiveness of Sargon's gesture.[4] Gratifying as this outcome was to the Assyrians, it was not sufficient to satisfy royal honor, which demanded that Sargon push back hard against Rusa.

Seizing the initiative, Sargon attacked Urartian-held territory for the first time, capturing "nine forts, the inhabitants of five regions of Rusa . . . their cattle and their flocks."[5] Despite the provocation, Rusa remained inactive while the Assyrians raided Andia, where they destroyed eight more forts and collected some 4,200 inhabitants with their cattle for deportation to Assyria.[6] The city, Pazashi, "a fortress city of the land of Mannea which is in front of the pass leading to the land of Zikirtu," became the Assyrians' next target.[7] The siege of this double-walled mountain stronghold involved the construction of a siege ramp and a coordinated assault at multiple points (see figure 11). Gurrean spearmen and Assyrian archers manned siege towers equipped with battering rams in an attack on the main gate, while a group of levies attempted to set fire to a postern, and others fought their way to the walls. From the top of a siege tower, an official read out surrender terms to the beleaguered inhabitants in an effort to provoke their capitulation.[8] Meanwhile, Itu'ean archers and Assyrian heavy infantry provided cover from the surrounding hills as the city succumbed to the onslaught. The capture of Pazashi afforded Sargon access to Zikirtu, located to the southeast of Lake Urmia and bordering Wishdish and Urartu to the north. Control of the mountain pass leading to Zikirtu gave Sargon the means to punish those Mannean provinces loyal to Urartu as well as threaten Rusa's eastern flank.

Although Mitatti of Zikirtu was a long-standing Urartian ally, Rusa made no effort to help him. The Assyrians had now summarily reversed Rusa's gains in Mannea, but the Urartian king was by no means on the defensive. He still held sway over Waisi, Zikirtu, Andia, and Wishdish, from which he could continue to mount attacks against Mannea. Beset by difficulties elsewhere, Sargon could not capitalize on Rusa's misfortunes. An uprising in Harhar (Kar-Sharrukin) and Phrygian incursions into Quwê threatened stability on the Assyrian flanks. That Rusa was involved in both the revolt in Harhar and the Phrygian action seems likely. Temporarily brought to a stalemate against Urartu, Sargon quickly moved to eliminate the new threats.

In the vicinity of Harhar, the Assyrian army destroyed numerous towns and collected the heads of some four thousand rebel warriors that were then presented, along with a roughly equal number of the living and their cattle, to Sargon at his camp. Once again the area received particularly harsh treatment. The soldiers took heads in order to provide tangible evidence of their accomplishments to Sargon and because Assyrian hegemony over the area, being in its early stages, required extreme measures.[9] Harhar now marked Assyria's eastern frontier, beyond which the dangerous and unpredictable Medes lived. Therefore, it behooved the Assyrians to make the consequences of resistance obvious. At this point, the king sent his general, Taklak-ana-Bel, the Assyrian eponym (year name) for 715 and the governor of Naṣibina, to subdue Kisheslu and the surrounding area.[10] In honor of this campaign, sculptured reliefs at Dur-Sharrukin not only depicted the successful siege of Kisheslu, but also the fortified camp of Taklak-ana-Bel himself, identified by epigraph.[11] For any Assyrian other than the king to be immortalized by name in a monumental inscription was a rare honor. Judging from the siege scene, Taklak-ana-Bel earned the distinction. A double-walled fortress town guarded by a towered outpost, Kisheslu was perched on a high hill overlooking a river, and its capture required the full array of Assyrian siege expertise (see figure 10). As at Pazashi, Gurrean spearmen and Assyrian levies mounted a coordinated attack at several locations, using siege towers equipped with battering rams to breach the walls while Itu'ean auxiliaries and Assyrian regulars supported the assault.

Taklak-ana-Bel successfully concluded his mission with the conquest of Kisheslu and neighboring Anzaria, and the reconquest of Kindau and Bit-Bagaia, which had fallen to Assyria the previous year. Though Sargon authorized the conquering army to apply necessary force, he was well aware that lasting pacification of the Median polities required the establishment of a consistent, just government. Over the course of his reign, letters from successive governors of Harhar (Kar-Sharrukin) attest to Sargon's long-term, benevolent policy in the area.[12] The Assyrians varied their approach to governance to meet the exigencies of each situation. While they routinely took hostages, monitored their subjects' movements, and demanded loyalty, tribute, and information, in return they promised protection and treated subject rulers with due respect. Moreover, since Sargon's primary interest in the region was commercial, he concentrated on transforming area settlements into fortified entrepôts.

Sargon designated the newly pacified cities, Kisheslu, Anzaria, Kindau, and Bit-Bagaia, trading centers and renamed them Kar-Nabu, Kar-Sin, Kar-Adad and Kar-Ishtar after four of the most important gods in the Assyrian pantheon (not coincidentally, those whose standards led the main divisions of the army). In effect, the new names tacitly acknowledged the army's efforts to take the towns. Although the depots were meant to attract trade, their function was as much military as commercial; therefore, Sargon also improved their fortifications. Here, as in the west, he superimposed Assyrian administration on already existing systems. The Assyrian takeover of this part of the Khorasan Road had significant ramifications for the economies of other Near Eastern states. The Assyrians could now regulate the flow of goods from the east into Babylonia and, to a lesser extent, Elam, while continuing to divert resources away from Urartu for their own fiscal benefit. Economic triumphs notwithstanding, Sargon had not yet succeeded in cornering Urartu or alleviating Phrygian pressure on his western flank, so while Taklak-ana-Bel wrapped up the Zagros campaign, Sargon turned his attention to Quwê.[13]

Thwarting Midas: Western Operations, 715

At the midpoint of Sargon's reign, a local king, Urikki, ruled Quwê under the stewardship of an Assyrian governor, Ashur-sharru-uṣur.[14] Hegemony over Quwê gave the Assyrians access to the area's natural resources as well as oversight of the main roads between central Anatolia and Syria, thus allowing them to monitor commercial, military, and civilian movement through these areas. Although the Assyrian take-over of Quwê and the Levant had the added benefit of cutting off both the Urartians and Phrygians from key Mediterranean seaports (e.g., Tyre and Arwad), on the downside these gains galvanized the enemy into action. In an attempt to undermine the Assyrian presence in Quwê and adjacent regions, Midas stepped up anti-Assyrian espionage and started picking off frontier forts.[15] The Assyrians' appropriation of the eastern Mediterranean trade stymied their enemies' economic ambitions and destabilized the Iamnaia ("Ionians," the Assyrian ethnonym for Greek islanders, not those Greeks settled on the coast of Anatolia). At this point, the Greeks had begun to emerge from the Dark Age, the period of cultural desolation after the collapse of the Mycenaean kingdoms at the end of the Bronze Age (ca. 1150). A renewed Greek presence in the Aegean thus posed a threat to trade. A letter from an Assyrian official in Tyre to Tiglath-pileser III that reports Ionian raids on coastal towns in the area corroborates the assertion made in Sargon's Annals that the Ionians had been killing the men of Tyre "since the distant past."[16] The latest raids came at a pivotal time and could not be ignored. Though the island-dwellers did not dare to attack Assyrian territory directly, they felt free to raid Assyria's Phoenician ally, Tyre, and also harass Quwê.[17] Furthermore, circumstantial evidence suggests that the Ionians were in league with Midas.[18] Certainly it would have suited their interests to work together against the Assyrians. Sargon was not obligated to respond to minor enemy raids against clients, who were expected to deal with local disturbances by themselves. But the potential spread of anti-Assyrian activity required swift countermeasures. Sargon responded to this dangerous situation by launching a rare naval campaign into the Mediterranean against the Greek islanders.

As a land-locked power, the Assyrians were not equipped for naval warfare and consequently had to rely on Phoenician nautical expertise and ships. During this period, Phoenician warships were primarily triakonter biremes (two banks of thirty oars on ships about forty-five feet long) equipped with a single sail, a raised fighting deck, and a ram that gave each ship the ability to pierce the hull of an enemy vessel.[19] Assyrian depictions of Phoenician vessels also include troop transports that were basically constructed as unarmored warships.[20] The object of naval warfare was to ram and disable or sink an enemy vessel, while marines on the fight deck blanketed the target ship with arrows. Occasionally, boarding led to hand-to-hand combat. These principles aside, exactly how the Assyrian-Phoenician allies conducted the campaign is difficult to determine. In his cylinder inscription, Sargon calls himself the "battle-experienced (one), who caught the Ionians in the midst of the sea like a fisherman does fish and (thus) made Quwê and Tyre tranquil."[21] In the Annals, which are quite fragmentary at this point, he reports broadly: "In order to pac[ify the Ionians, whose homeland] is located [in] the mi[dst of the s]ea, who, from long [ago] had killed the inha[bitants of Ty]re and Quwê, and [blockaded?] the roa[d?] (disrupted trade?) . . . I went out to the sea against them and killed them, [sma]ll and large, with my weapon."[22] Given the Assyrians'

inexperience with sea battle and the fact that Sargon mentions killing Ionians of all ages, it is likely that most, if not all, of the fighting
took place on land when the Assyrians raided Greek island settlements. In any case, the objective was not to conquer the Aegean
islands but to deter their inhabitants from further interference and
to prepare for the campaign into Quwê by preventing the Greeks
from aiding the Phrygians.[23]

Having thus achieved Sargon's preliminary goals, the Assyrians
landed in Quwê where they immediately recaptured the lost border forts. They then pursued the retreating Phrygians through the
Taurus Mountains and onto the Konya plain where they "inflicted
a defeat on Mita (Midas), King of Muski (Phrygia), in his wide district."[24] For Sargon, this resolution was ideal: he discouraged further
Phrygian-Ionian cooperation, solidified Assyrian control of Quwê,
demonstrated to the kings of Tyre and Quwê the benefits of Assyrian
hegemony, and, above all, gave the Phrygians a taste of Assyrian vengeance. Soon after, or so the Annals claim, the Egyptian pharaoh,
the queen of the Arabs, and the ruler of Saba (tribal territory on the
middle Euphrates) felt it expedient to send gifts of "gold, ore from
the mountains, precious jewels, ivory, seeds of ebony, all kinds of
perfumes, horses and camels."[25] Though in the field the Assyrians
appeared unstoppable, Sargon could not quite manage to eradicate the
opposition; while he suppressed it in one area, it inevitably popped
up somewhere else, and his Mannean problem continued unresolved.

As Sargon campaigned in the west, Rusa reacted to Ullusunu's
defection by mounting anti-Assyrian operations on two fronts:
in the Urmia basin and along Assyria's northern border. Back in
Nineveh, the crown prince, Sennacherib, monitored the developing
situation in his father's absence and in August (probably 715) he
sent a detailed intelligence report informing Sargon of Rusa's latest
activities.[26] Sennacherib's dispatch not only offers a vivid portrayal
of Assyrian intelligence operations but also underscores the disjunc-
tion between the immediacy of such reports, whose authors did not
know what was going to happen next, and the retrospective view
presented in royal inscriptions written after the fact. In the first part
of the brief, Sennacherib quotes a message from Arije, the king of
Kumme, a small client state on Assyria's northern frontier:

A messenger [of Arije] has come [reporting]: "[The Ukkean has
written to] the Urartian king that the king of Assyria's [governors]

are building [. . .], and the Urartian king has [establi]shed the order
for his governors: 'get your troops, go and seize the governors of the
king of Assyria alive from the Kummeans, and bring them to me.'
At this point I have not found out [all the] information; as soon
as I hear, I will send an express messenger to the crown prince so
that they should send troops to me quickly." This was the report
of Arije.[27]

According to Arije, the king of Ukku had discovered information
about Assyrian activities in Kumme and sent the information to
Rusa, who then called for the Ukkeans to intervene on his behalf.
Notably, Rusa's objective was to capture, not kill, the Assyrian governors. Presumably he hoped thereby to acquire information and
gain bargaining power in order to drive the Assyrians out of the
area. The taking of prisoners and hostages reduced the probability that war would break out. Arije, who had informers of his own
in Ukku, discovered the plans, informed his patrons, and thereby
foiled Rusa's plot.

In the meantime, Assyrian agents operating in Urartu reported
Rusa's military endeavors to Ashur-reṣua, who passed the information on to Sennacherib with additional observations. Sennacherib
duly informed the king:

> On the 11th of Elul (August) I (Sennacherib) got a tablet from Ashur-
> reṣua (reporting): "The Urartian did not get anything where the
> Zikirteans brought him, but had to turn back empty-handed; he
> went with his troops to Waisi, entered and left his troops in Waisi.
> He went with a few of his troops and entered into the Manneans'
> domain. At this point I have not heard about the incursion, but I
> will write you as soon as I have heard more. The governor oppo-
> site me was (also) in Waisi; I heard that he went out behind him
> (the king), but nobody has seen his departure from Waisi. They are
> making the roads before me better and treading down ramps; as
> soon as I have heard what it means, whether he is coming with his
> troops or whether he is harmless, I will write quickly to the crown
> prince." This was the report of Ashur-reṣua.

The Assyrian delegate knew that improvements to roads and cause-
ways could signal an upcoming attack and was careful to report the
possibility to his superiors. At the end of his report Sennacherib
appended a diplomatic note: "A messenger of the Mannean (Ullusunu)
has come before me bringing to me a horse as the audience gift and

speaking the salutations of the Mannean (king). I clothed him and put a silver bracelet on his arm. . . . I am sending this letter to the king, my lord, on the 11th of Elul."[28] Regular communication (sending news and greetings) and gift exchange were an essential part of the patron-client relationship, and failure to comply properly could mean ruin for the client. In this case, Ullusunu was rewarded for fulfilling his obligations. Sennacherib's letter reveals additional aspects of the interplay between the rival powers and their clients, who spied on one another constantly and rapidly passed information up and down the chain of command. The Kummeans, clients of Assyria, had spies in Ukku. The Ukkeans, nominally independent but leaning toward Urartu, had spies in Kumme. The Assyrians had spies in Urartu, Kumme, and Ukku, and doubtless the Urartians fielded a similar coterie of informants. Whatever their supposed affiliations, the petty rulers trying to survive under pressure from the larger powers clearly maintained diplomatic relations with Assyria and Urartu, both of whom continued to rely on clients for information and to take action as their proxies.

Under these complex circumstances, the formation of good strategy depended on the reliability of the information collected and the speed with which it could be disseminated. In this the Assyrians appear to have had the upper hand. Both Arije and Ashur-reṣua emphasized the preliminary nature of their information and that they would write again as soon as they knew more. That Sennacherib sent his report the very day he received Ashur-reṣua's letter is characteristic of Assyria's efficient intelligence practices. Considering what Sennacherib had discovered about Rusa's intentions, it is no wonder that the crown prince treated Ullusunu's ambassador with special care or that Ullusunu sent gifts to Sargon. Without Assyrian backing, the Mannean king had little hope of retaining power.

Tension Mounts: Operations in Mannea, 714

The situation at the end of 715 suggests that Sargon conceived of his next campaign not as the coup de grace against a serious rival that his inscriptions later celebrated, but simply as the next stage of a struggle he expected to continue for the foreseeable future. Rusa remained unrepentant. Nor was there any indication that he had modified his ambition to take over Mannea. The eighth campaign duly began with fairly limited objectives: the Assyrians would go east, collect tribute, and carry out punitive action against Andia and Zikirtu in order to place these districts firmly in Mannean hands again.[29]

In late June or early July (the month of Du'uzu) Sargon mustered troops in Calah, took them across the Upper and Lower Zab Rivers, then "in full flood," and marched to Zamua where he made a thorough inspection of his army.[30] Logistical considerations may have prompted the late start, as the army had to calculate its movement into enemy territory (thus beyond the reach of forward supply depots or client supplies) to correspond to harvest times and the availability of lowland animal pasturage.[31] Additionally, severe winters sometimes closed the mountain passes until early summer. In any case, the army's journey following the Lower Zab drainage system through the mountains to Mannea proved extraordinarily difficult, as Sargon's lyrical account of the campaign, the Letter to Ashur, attests: "I passed between Nikippa and Upa, high mountains covered with impenetrable trees, whose interiors were labyrinthine and whose passes were frightful; a shade is cast over their region as if it were a cedar grove and the one who goes on their paths cannot see the shining sun. I crossed the River Puia, (in) the ravine between them as many as twenty-six times and my army in its might did not fear the flood water."[32] Unfit for horses and chariots and too difficult for foot soldiers, passage over another mountain required the vanguard to hack a way forward with pickaxes.[33] Though heroicized, the description nonetheless reveals a bitter truth: without proper roads, mountain travel and river crossings entailed real risk and an enormous amount of strenuous hard work. Right from the start, the army's advance was slow and exhausting.

Aside from the arduous journey, the first part of the campaign was routine, involving diplomacy and the collection of tribute rather than combat. Much to the surprise and pleasure of Sargon, Ullusunu and his entire court met the Assyrians as they advanced out of the mountains. By now Ullusunu had enough confidence in Sargon to dispense with the customary hostage exchange before he (Ullusunu) arrived at the Assyrian camp with his tribute of horses, cattle, and sheep—vital supplies without which the ensuing campaign would be impossible.[34] That normal relations required the insurance of hostage-taking indicates how little trust existed between kings, even those with a history of cooperation. After meeting Ullusunu,

Sargon moved south to Allabria and collected the annual dues from Bel-apla-iddina for the same purpose. Word of the Assyrian army's presence spread quickly, and soon the city rulers conquered during Sargon's previous campaigns gathered in Parsua to pay the Assyrians off. Thus far the campaign had been as much an armed diplomatic mission as a military operation.

At this point, however, the Assyrians backtracked and met the Manneans in Sirdakka, where Ullusunu tried to convince Sargon to help him against Urartu. After feeding the Assyrian army and paying additional tribute, Ullusunu dutifully asked Sargon to approve the formal investment of the Mannean crown prince. Finally Ullusunu and his magnates, "crawling before me (Sargon) on all fours like dogs," begged the Assyrian king for military aid. Playing the benevolent overlord, Sargon "took pity on them and paid attention to their entreaties."[35] As part of the formalities, he threw a banquet for Ullusunu and "exalted his throne above that of Iranzi his father who begot him." In causing "those people to sit down at a joyous table with the people of Assyria," Sargon aimed to demonstrate Ullusunu's obligation to him, awe the Mannean elite, and forge tighter bonds of loyalty.[36] In the Near East, as in many cultures, the formal banquet played an important role in the diplomatic process. The lavish feast, seating order, conversation, and entertainment both expressed and reinforced power relationships. By hosting Ullusunu in his own land, Sargon not only established the Mannean king's subordinate position publicly but simultaneously marked him as a royal favorite.

On the surface, the way Sargon treated Ullusunu seems almost perversely manipulative—after all, the stated purpose of the campaign was to help the Manneans. But several factors were at play here, not the least of which was the need for Sargon to gain prestige among the tribal city lords of the eastern Zagros. By simultaneously humbling and supporting Ullusunu, a well-established client, Sargon effectively drew attention to his own authority. However much it might suit his purposes to help the Manneans, the Assyrian king could not appear to be at the beck and call of a subject ruler. The spectacle of obeisance followed by feasting (not to mention the memory of previous Assyrian campaigns) struck exactly the right note outside Mannea. Soon after, according to the Letter to Ashur, chieftains from Gizilbundi, a remote district in the mountains, heard of the Assyrian campaign and Sargon's "terrifying radiance" and promptly delivered their tribute to him at Sirdakka "so that their fortresses would not be destroyed."[37] Successive campaigns in the central Zagros combined with carefully managed displays of benevolent Assyrian power had paid off. Now it only took commanding behavior and the threat of violence to cow people into submission—at least for as long as they perceived the Assyrians as an imminent threat.

The spectacle of power politics notwithstanding, it also appears that Sargon delayed military action for a more compelling reason; he was carefully monitoring the developing situation in Urartu. Several documents from the palace archives at Nineveh and Calah report that the Urartians suffered a catastrophic defeat while campaigning against the Cimmerians around this time.[38] While the reports are not explicitly dated, their prosopographical content and context argue for a 714 date. For example, we can date one letter in the group on the grounds that it refers to the situation in Tabal, where Sargon's daughter, Ahat-abisha, resided with her spouse, Ambaris, the Tabalian king.[39] Since Sargon removed Ambaris from the throne and deported him with his family to Assyria in 713, the letter must have been written prior to that date. Even this seemingly firm date is open to interpretation, and scholars have proposed several possible scenarios, including dating the group to 709.[40] Although the scenario developed throughout this chapter cannot be considered definitive, it represents the role of Assyria's intelligence gathering very clearly.

A nomadic people living in northern Anatolia and Transcaucasia, the Cimmerians appear in Assyrian records for the first time in reports of the crisis.[41] Apparently Rusa led a spring campaign against the Cimmerians in order to secure his troublesome northeastern border before resuming action against Mannea with allies Andia and Zikirtu.[42] The plan went awry, however, and the Urartian army suffered a serious setback in battle. News of the disaster reached Sennacherib in Assyria in several waves from various informants, including the rulers of Ukku and Muṣaṣir, both, as we have seen, with ties to Urartu. In an early dispatch, for example, Sennacherib reported: "[Shulmu]-Bel, the deputy of the palace herald, came before me (and said): "Urzana has written to me: 'When the Urartian king went against the Cimmerians, his troops were killed. The governor of Waisi has been killed. At this point, we have not found out (much) information, but as soon as we have found out, we will send you whatever intelligence (we get).'"[43] Since the Assyrian palace herald's province was located on the frontier closest to Muṣaṣir, he got news of the Urartian defeat first. A fragmentary letter (author unknown) claims that the Urartian king barely escaped with his life and that his departure was so sudden that "the rear part of the camp did not see their [k]ing and did [not] know that he had sa[ved himself]."[44] In the chaotic aftermath of battle, the surviving soldiers, thinking that Rusa was dead, apparently enthroned his son, Melartua, who may have been executed shortly afterward when the mistake was discovered.[45]

Back in Assyria, Sennacherib continued to receive testimony and quickly forward news to Sargon. In another letter, the crown prince wrote:

> The Ukkean (king) has written to me (that) "when the king of Urartu went to Cimmeria, his troops, as many as there were, got killed. 11 of his (Rusa's) governors with their troops have been wiped out; his field marshal (and) 2 governors [. . .]." This was the report of the Ukkean.
>
> Ashur-reṣua has written to me: "the report which I wrote earlier about the Urartians—there was a massacre and many were killed. Now the country is calm and his magnates have gone, each to his land. Kaqqadanu, his (Rusa's) field marshal, has been captured. The king of Urartu is in Wauzan." This is the report of Ashur-reṣua.

The first reports paint a dramatic picture of the crisis and suggest that losses were indeed critical. However, less dire news came from another official, as Sennacherib's letter goes on to state:

> Nabu-le'i, the governor of Birate, has written to me: "I have written to the guards of the forts along the border concerning the report about the Urartian king and they (say): 'When he went against the Cimmerians, his troops, as many as there were, got killed. Three of his magnates along with their troops have been killed; he himself ran away and entered his country, but as of now his army has not arrived.'" This is the report of Nabu-le'i.
>
> The (ruler) of Muṣaṣir (Urzana) and his brother and son have gone to greet the Urartian king, and the messenger of the Hubushkian (ruler) has also gone to greet him. All the guards of the forts along the border have sent me reports like this.[46]

Assuming that Sennacherib recorded the reports in the order he received them, then the earliest ones make greater claims of

Urartian deaths, while the later one reduces the number of mag-nates lost to three and notes that the situation in Urartu seems stable. Another point that suggests that the loss was not quite as devastating as the early reports avow is that neither Urzana nor the king of Hubushkia felt it politic to snub Rusa. Even so, their different responses were carefully fashioned political statements. By making a personal appearance accompanied by close male rel-atives, Urzana affirmed his ties to Rusa, whereas Ianzu signaled his tepid support by staying home and sending a mere messenger. Information of this type was crucial to Assyrian decision-making on both the strategic and tactical levels, and later this incident helped Sargon justify a raid on Muṣaṣir.

Among the final accounts of the Cimmerian victory, Sennacherib sent his father news from an Itu'ean spy operating in Ishtahup: "The Itua'ean [. . .] who [. . .] from the city of Ishtahup has now been brought to me from [. . .]ratta. I asked him [about the Urarti]ans and he told me: "When they went against the Cimmerians, the Urartian [and his magnates were defeated], and they are very afraid of the king, my lord. They quake and are silent like women and nobody [threatens?] the forts of the king, my lord. The news is very good."[47] With several of their top officials dead or captured and the army in some disarray, the Urartians were right to fear the Assyrians. Recent excavations at a site near the head of the Gelishin pass suggest that Rusa attempted to forestall a potential Assyrian attack by hastily building a new fort there.[48] Yet instead of attacking Urartu imme-diately, Sargon opted to accede to Ullusunu's entreaties and move against Andia and Zikirtu, those subdistricts of Mannea that had turned traitor and sided with Rusa. Sargon's decision was strategi-cally sound. To invade Urartu proper without first making sure of allies and dealing with Rusa's known confederates (e.g., Andia and Zikirtu) would leave the Assyrians vulnerable to attack from the rear. Better to secure Mannea by striking Ullusunu's enemies and see whether Rusa could offer them any support.

To this end, Sargon and his army rapid-marched thirty "dou-ble-hours" (about 185 miles) over very rugged ground to Pazashi, where they improved the defenses and reprovisioned the fortress preparatory to invading Zikirtu.[49] Sargon continued to gather intel-ligence about Rusa's whereabouts before committing to a plan of action.[50] In this regard, a dispatch from Bel-apla-iddina, the ruler of Allabria, contained particularly vital information:

As to the news of the Urartian, a messenger of the Andian and a messenger of the Zikirtean have gone to Waisi and they said to him, "The king of Assyria is before us." The day he saw the messengers he set out to Zikirtu, that one together with his troops. The Hubushkian also went with him, for five stages (then) he returned and ordered his magnates: "Collect your troops; I shall deploy (my troops) against the Assyrian king." This is from [in]formers; the (news of) deploying is from informers.[51]

The letter offers another glimpse into the intricate political machinations of client rulers. The Andian and Zikirtean allies had scouts keeping track of the Assyrian whereabouts. The Assyrian-backed ruler of Allabria had informers in Waisi, a Urartian possession, while the supposedly pro-Assyrian ruler of Hubushkia appeared to have reneged on his ties to Assyria to support Rusa in the upcoming fight. Knowing how important this news was for assessing enemy strength prior to battle and fully aware of its political ramifications, Bel-apla-iddina carefully distinguished between verified and unverified information. The addition of Hubushkian troops to the combined forces of Andia, Zikirtu, and Urartu—if, indeed, the Hubushkians actually followed through—would help mitigate the losses recently suffered in the war against the Cimmerians and possibly even give the numerical advantage to the Urartian coalition.[52] Although Assyria required clients to send contingents of soldiers on Assyrian military operations, royal inscriptions did not acknowledge clients' contributions of military personnel. Hence, the Letter to Ashur makes no mention of allied troops on the Assyrian side. If Ullusunu and Bel-apla-iddina did contribute units to the army, as is likely, we have no way of knowing troop numbers or how they functioned.

Whatever the character of the Assyrian army, it was big enough to alarm Mitatti of Zikirtu, who did not chance an encounter but retreated, deserting his capital city, which "seemed of no value to him," and taking his people to safety in "a remote mountain amidst hardships, lest their location be detected."[53] Mitatti then posted a rearguard and joined Rusa with what troops he could muster. Whether Mitatti retreated in abject terror, as Sargon would have us believe, or sacrificed his own lands in order to draw the Assyrians to a battlefield of Rusa's choosing, as seems more likely, the Assyrians surged forward, slaughtering the Zikirtean rearguard and laying waste to the entire region "like a deluge."[54] The Assyrian army then moved along the shore of Lake Urmia into Wishdish, a district that Rusa had previously appropriated from Ullusunu. This seizure and the earlier incident, when Rusa violated his treaty with Assyria by attempting to impose hegemony over Muṣaṣir, allowed Sargon to hold the Urartian king solely responsible for the current state of war. From the Assyrian point of view, Rusa, "who did not cherish the command of Ashur and Marduk, who did not revere (his) oath to the lord of lords, (who was) a mountain man, murder spawn, (and) imbecile, whose lips babbled insolent speech and improprieties, who did not cherish the august command of the god (of justice) Shamash," had gone too far by attacking the Manneans, and Sargon had no choice but to respond in kind.[55] Indeed, the Letter to Ashur includes an equally long passage extolling Sargon's virtues in contrast to Rusa's bad qualities. Despite the claim made in the previous year that Sargon raided nine districts of Urartu, in the Letter to Ashur he admitted that he "had never transgressed the boundaries of Rusa the Urartian that demark his extensive country" or "shed the blood of his warriors."[56] The Assyrian king took great care to stress the fact that, although he was the invader, he was not at fault, for he had not started the war. In truth, both kings responded to circumstances: Rusa anticipated an Assyrian attack and sought to defend himself, while Sargon aimed to take advantage of his enemy's apparent weakness. By contrast, the Letter to Ashur describes the battle preparations in characteristically heroic terms, as a contest between two valiant kings to decide which was the better man.[57] Whoever was ultimately responsible, the cold war was well and truly over, and the two kings had come to fight.

War Breaks out in Ernest: The Battle of Mount Waush, 714

Readying for battle, which now appeared inevitable, Rusa set up camp in a ravine of Mount Waush (Mount Sahend, east of Lake Urmia) and then allegedly sent a messenger formally challenging Sargon to fight him there.[58] Although the formal challenge was probably added to the Letter to Ashur in order to stress the heroic nature of the contest, this does not make it less likely that Rusa had already deployed his troops for battle. Ancient armies habitually arrayed for battle in full view of each other. Given the circumstances, it is difficult to determine which side had the tactical advantage. After the Cimmerian debacle, the Urartian army cannot have been in top form but probably

consisted of what was left of the royal corps and contingents cob-
bled together from allies (e.g., Mitatti) and local mountain chiefs.
If Sargon's intelligence reports were correct, in the Cimmerian war
Rusa had lost at least three of his highest-ranking officers, including
his field marshal. It is easy to imagine that Urartian morale was at
low ebb, although Rusa may have had confidence in his battle plan.
After all, he had the home ground advantage. He had chosen the location and knew the terrain, whereas the Assyrians were now operating in unfamiliar territory well beyond ready supplies.

Assyrian morale also seems to have suffered, for the Letter to
Ashur emphasizes (most unusually) that the "bleary-eyed" king's
men, "who had traveled a distant road," were "weary and sluggish"
because they had "passed over countless remote mountains, whose
ascent and descent were very difficult so that their faces became
dazed."[59] Since the army had already traveled something like five
hundred miles, the last portion of which involved plenty of marching and destruction, if not too much actual fighting, it stands to reason that the troops were thoroughly fatigued. It is also possible that
in stressing the condition of his soldiers Sargon was attempting to
justify what he did next, which was to attack before his battle line
was fully arrayed. In so doing, he ignored customary practice. Under
normal circumstances he would have set up camp and organized his
battle line in full view of the enemy.[60] Sargon's decision to attack
was neither desperate nor rash, as has sometimes been assumed, but
the result of a keen tactical reckoning that understood the folly of
giving exhausted, demoralized men time to see what they were facing or the enemy the opportunity to assess their condition.[61] The
order of march also played a part in Sargon's decision.

Marching in column into a mountain pass, the army must have
been spread over several miles. Subsequent events compel us to
believe that in his approach to the battlefield Sargon maintained the
marching order described early on in the campaign. That is, he and
his entourage took the lead, followed by chariots, additional cavalry, combat troops, and support troops—all units of the standing
army—with *kallāpu* troops, pack animals, and the "surging flood of
Assyrian soldiers" (infantry levies and possibly allies) taking up the
rear.[62] Because his most reliable, elite units were in front and since
his main advantage was surprise, Sargon chose to attack straight-
away, leaving the main force to follow in his wake. The Letter to
Ashur describes the battle as follows:

I did not ease their (the soldiers') weariness, I did not give water to wet their thirst, I did not establish a base or build a walled camp. I did not send out my warriors or rally my troops, I did not turn my right and left wings to my side, (and) I disregarded my rear. I did not fear (Rusa's) massed army, I had contempt for his cavalry, I did not glance at the vast numbers of his armored chariot warriors. With only my single chariot and the horsemen who ride at my side, who never leave me in hostile or friendly territory, the cavalry troop of Sin-ah-uṣur, I fell upon him like a furious arrow; I caused his defeat and turned back his attack. I inflicted a huge massacre on him, spreading out the bodies of his warriors like malt and filling up the expanse of the mountain with them. I caused their blood to flow like a river in ravines and gullies, I dyed red the battlefield, countryside, and open country. I beheaded his fighters, the security of his army, and slaughtered at his feet the bowmen and lancers like fat sheep. In the midst of the battlefield, I broke the weapons of his foremost councilors, the ones who stand with him, and captured them with their steeds. I seized 260 members of his royal line, his eunuchs, governors, and cavalrymen; I broke their battle line.[63]

Though the account does not describe the Urartian battle array in any detail, it seems that Sargon and his brother, Sin-ah-uṣur, who led the cavalry guard, charged straight at Rusa's position through the Urartian center that was primarily composed of what remained of the Urartian royal guard.[64] The attack succeeded in driving Rusa from the field to seek refuge in his camp.[65] As the Urartian soldiers in the center panicked and attempted to flee, they ran straight into their own wings, which were thus prevented from trapping Sargon's cavalry in a pincer. Once the Urartian king had fled and more of the Assyrian troops came forward, the enemy army collapsed completely. Mitatti of Zikirtu was killed, many Urartians surrendered, and, with no one left to lead them, the rank and file either fled or died in the attempt. Though the sanguinary battle description emphasizes the merciless Assyrian onslaught, the fact that the Assyrians accepted the surrender of more than two hundred Urartian elites indicates that normal practice was not confined to killing but admitted more flexibility.

During the rout, Sargon and his company surrounded the Urartian camp, and when Rusa attempted to escape, the Assyrians shot his chariot horses, forcing him to mount a mare and make his desperate getaway shamefully "right in front of his troops."[66] After chasing the remnants of the Urartian army for "six stages of march" all the way to the next great mountain, Sargon called off the pursuit as the weather was turning bad and his own men and horses were spent.[67] Though it had been a terrible risk, Sargon's boldness had paid off, and he had proven himself decisively to be superior to Rusa, his primary rival. Triumph on the battlefield had more than military significance, however. It signaled divine approval and the Assyrian king's legitimacy. As the gods' chosen representative, Sargon celebrated his achievement with appropriate piety: "I entered into my camp with joy and exultation, with players on lyres and flutes. To Nergal, Adad, Ishtar, lords of battle, to the gods who dwell in heaven and the netherworld, and to the gods who dwell in Assyria, I offered splendid sacred sacrifices. I stood before them in prayer and supplication and praised their divinity."[68] Post-battle rituals were probably as long and involved as those that prepared the king and his army for war, and we are reminded that the Assyrians—and indeed everyone in the ancient Near East—believed that rituals offered men a means to communicate with the gods and thereby gain a measure of control over their short lives.[69] Of course, ceremonies also communicated political messages. Not long after (and possibly associated with) these celebrations, Sargon had Bagdatti of Wishdish flayed on Mount Waush as poetic justice for the murder of the Mannean king, Aza, in the same spot two years earlier.[70] The wages of victory were many, and Sargon was prepared to take full advantage of all of them.

Sweet Victory: Devastating Urartian Territory, 714

With the Urartian army and its allies dispersed and Rusa probably preparing to defend his capital, Tushpa, there was nothing to stop the Assyrians from entering Urartu. Therefore, Sargon abandoned his original plan to attack Andia and Zikirtu and headed west into Urartu. The objective was not conquest (nor had it ever been) but to put an end to Urartian interference in Mannean affairs once and for all.[71] Because Andia and Zikirtu needed Urartian military backing to retain their independence from Mannea (and by association Assyria), Sargon could now solve his Mannean problem more effectively by neutralizing Urartu than by restricting operations to Andia or Zikirtu. Mitatti's death in battle obviated that need in any case. By destroying settlements and wrecking as much agricultural land as possible, Sargon intended to prevent Rusa from undertaking military

operations against him for the foreseeable future. Devastation warfare was extremely effective, but it postponed rather than precluded
future military action. As we have seen, when executed efficiently,
it could buy a decade or more of peace. In terms of public display,
nothing could be better than a march unopposed through Urartian
territory to provide unmistakable proof of Sargon's superiority and
Assyrian dominance.

The exact route that the Assyrians took through Urartu has been
the subject of prolonged debate. Although it is possible that Sargon
led the army north, making a loop around Lake Urmia, logistical
constraints occasioned by the sparse settlement on the lake's eastern
side make it more likely that the Assyrians confined themselves to
Urartian territory to the southwestern and western side of the lake.[72]
Whatever road the army took, the invasion entailed substantial risk.
Campaign season was far advanced—it must have been September
by this time, and snow would make the mountains impassable by
November at the latest. Moreover, the invasion would penetrate
deeply into enemy territory, where the Assyrians could not be certain of the availability of food and fodder. In this situation Sargon
had little choice about the route he could take. If he wanted both to
inflict damage and feed his troops, he would have to navigate through
the high mountains and difficult terrain that separated his targets,
the isolated fertile valleys to the west and southwest of Lake Urmia
where the Urartians maintained large granaries and wine stores.[73]
Not an easy journey, especially for an already weary army, but well
worth the trouble, if only for the yield in political capital.

As the Assyrians moved into Urartu, area residents fled, aban-
doning their fortresses and villages to the Assyrians, who plundered
and destroyed everything in their path. In the Letter to Ashur, Sargon
boasts: "I set their stately roof timbers on fire; I burned their crops
and their fodder. I opened the grain stores and fed my troops with
untold amounts of grain. I let loose my army's cattle on his meadows like a swarm of locusts, (and) they rooted up the pasturage,
his security, and ravaged his fields."[74] This pattern was repeated in
Bari, which Sargon identified as a key royal grain store and where
the Assyrians captured the reserve mounts in the royal stable.
Adding insult to injury, at Uhlu, the site of Rusa's luxurious summer palace, Sargon let his troops feed on the stored grain and "drink
sweet wine like water from a river, from water skins and leather
buckets."[75] Wherever they went, soldiers cut down fruit trees,

wrecked buildings, trampled fields, ruined irrigation works, and stole anything of value for the king. Eventually Sargon had either amassed so much booty or found so little worth keeping that he let his men hold on to whatever they looted.[76] The lengthy section in the Letter to Ashur devoted to the invasion of Urartu achieves a lyrical rhythm in which appreciative descriptions of the magnificent Urartian countryside and cities are invariably followed by equally poetic accounts of Assyrian destruction, the better to emphasize the magnitude of Sargon's achievement.

According to Urartian ideology, kings made their power manifest by building everything from forts and palaces to granaries and aqueducts. In other words, public construction "forwarded a claim to political legitimacy based on the power of the king to subdue the 'wilderness' and call forth an ordered built environment."[77] The Assyrians had a similar understanding of the meaning of the built environment, and given Sargon's penchant for figurative politics it is likely that he (and elites on both sides) understood his destruction of Urartian property to be a direct attack on Rusa. Indeed, the Letter to Ashur may deliberately mirror the language of one of Rusa's inscriptions concerning irrigation.[78] Practically speaking, the devastation inflicted on the Urartian fields, pastures, towns, and food supplies was probably as damaging to Urartian military capability and imperial prestige as defeat on the battlefield, where at least they had attempted to defend themselves. Recent interpretations of these events discount the material impact of Sargon's invasion and suggest that he acquired little of value and did no lasting damage, since most Urartians simply fled with their belongings when mountaintop beacons signaled the enemy's approach.[79] Whatever its economic consequences for Urartu, the attack dealt a serious blow to Rusa, whose indifference to an enemy army marching unopposed through his territory shamed him irrevocably. Only when the Assyrians finally arrived at Waisi, the main starting point for Urartian campaigns into Mannea, did Sargon meet any organized resistance. But Rusa had built up the fortifications of the city to no avail, and the Assyrians took the lower town from the rear, slaughtering the defenders. In the march through Urartu, according to the Letter to Ashur, the Assyrians sacked some 430 farmsteads, villages, towns, and cities in seven provinces.[80]

At this point, the Assyrians left Urartu and entered Hubushkian territory. Suddenly sure of his loyalty to Assyria, Ianzu did not hesitate to approach Sargon, do homage, and pay tribute. We are reminded of two earlier incidents: the first when Ianzu did not visit the Urartian king in person but sent a messenger instead, thus indicating his closer association with Sargon, and the other the apparently incorrect report that Ianzu had decided to fight on the Urartian side. It was probably Ianzu's attention to protocol that saved him now. By contrast, Urzana of Muṣaṣir, who earlier made a point of his subservience to Rusa, failed to send even a messenger to Sargon, who complained:

> On my return journey, Urzana of Muṣaṣir, doer of wrong and crimes, breaker of the oath of the gods, who did not submit to my lordship, the dangerous mountain man who sinned against the loyalty oath of Ashur, Shamash, Nabu, and Marduk and revolted against me, he interrupted the advance of my return journey and expedition by (withholding) his ample gifts; he did not kiss my feet. He withheld tribute, gifts and presents and not once did he send his messenger in order to ask about my health.[81]

In disdaining to treat Sargon with the same level of respect he accorded Rusa, Urzana provided the Assyrian king with a convenient pretext for punitive action. However, so late in the season, Sargon dared not risk stranding the army on the enemy's side of the mountains without adequate food or shelter, so he decided on a radical solution. He sent his exhausted main force home to Assyria, and with only a thousand volunteers, "my impetuous cavalry, archers, shield-men and lancers, my fierce warriors, well-versed in combat," he undertook to punish Urzana.[82]

Political Theater: The Sack of Muṣaṣir, 714

The move made sense not only logistically but tactically as well. While the army's main body held the enemy's attention, Sargon and his men had a good chance of traveling unobserved toward Muṣaṣir and so achieve surprise. Although the potential benefits of the operation were many, Sargon's scheme probably seemed daring to the point of recklessness given the season, and it took more than one divine portent to convince the army to accept it. A lunar eclipse on October 24 (thus providing an absolute date for the campaign), plus the favorable reading of a liver omen and some clever theological rationalizing apparently decided the issue, and Sargon proceeded with the raid.[83] Characteristically, he had more compelling reasons for the attack than punishing Urzana. Like Carchemish, Muṣaṣir was a rich city, and its capture would provide a welcome influx of goods to support Assyria's temples, augment the royal treasury, and fund the construction of Dur-Sharrukin. Above all, the sack of Muṣaṣir would disgrace Rusa by striking at the very heart of Urartian kingship, for some part of the royal coronation traditionally took place at the city's temple of Haldi.[84] Since Haldi was the preeminent god in the Urartian pantheon and the one who accompanied the king on campaign (thus the Urartian equivalent of Ashur), the capture of his cult statue and plundering of his temple would simultaneously humiliate the Urartians and verify Assyrian supremacy. Sargon could not hope for a better opportunity to boost his reputation at the expense of his enemy's, and by choosing to attack with only a small force he drew further attention to the unbridgeable gulf between his own heroism and Rusa's cowardice.

The plan succeeded flawlessly. Since the raiding party could go where a large army could not, Sargon and his men bushwhacked a way through extremely difficult terrain where

> mighty cascades have cut their way, the din of their falls roaring like thunder a double league off, and every kind of useful tree, shrub, and vine grows in a tangle like a canebrake, intimidating to anyone who thinks of entering them, which no king whatsoever had traversed nor any prince who preceded me had seen the pathways thereof. I cut through their dense growth and broke up their narrow ridges with bronze axes. I made good going for my army among them with a narrow passage, a strait pathway, which the foot soldiers could get through only sideways. I laid my riding chariot on shoulders and proceeded on horseback at the head of my troops. I gave orders to my staff officers, as well as to their forces, that he (Urzana) must not escape.[85]

By scaling the walls and sneaking into the city, the Assyrians took Urzana completely by surprise (see figure 12). Once inside, they simply took over, announced the fate of the inhabitants, who were to be deported, and looted the place. In order to shame Urzana, Sargon made him sit by the city gate while his entire household (wife, sons, daughters, and courtiers), together with 6,110 citizens and animals, marched past him into Assyrian custody.[86] Consciously repeating, and thereby undoing, Rusa's earlier occupation of Muṣaṣir as described in his bilingual monuments, Sargon took up temporary residence in the palace and proceeded to plunder its contents and that of the temple of Haldi.[87] As for Urzana, with his family held hostage there was no reason to remove him from his throne, and he retained his precarious position, albeit under the watchful eye of Gabbu-ana-Ashur, Sargon's palace herald, whose province was near-est to Muṣaṣir.

The amount and quality of plunder from Muṣaṣir were stagger-ing. In the Letter to Ashur the detailed treasure list takes up more than fifty lines and enumerates a wide range of valuable objects, including precious metals and jewels from Urzana's treasury, vast quantities of silver and gold votive objects from the temple of Haldi, ceremonial clothes, and weapons, as well as the contents of the royal armory: 25,212 bronze shields, 1,514 bronze lances, and 305,412 bronze daggers.[88] Quantities emphasized the magnitude of the windfall, while other objects received special attention for their novelty or political interest. For example, censers and cups from Tabal, where Sargon's son-in-law, Ambaris, ruled as a client, pro-vided material evidence of traitorous contact between that state and Urartu (by way of Muṣaṣir).[89] The fact that the Tabalian arti-facts were the only ones in the list identified by point of origin indi-cates that they had special significance to the Assyrians, and indeed Sargon led a punitive campaign against Tabal the very next year. Another significant monument, a statue of Rusa in his chariot, bore the inscription "with my two horses and one charioteer, my hand won the kingdom of Urartu," thus implying that Rusa, like Sargon, had attained the throne in an unorthodox way.[90] The apparent simi-larities between the two kings transformed the war from a mundane conflict to a contest between heroes and, by extension, their gods, all of which imbued Sargon's triumph with cosmic significance.

Enormous as the material gains from Muṣaṣir were, the great-est satisfaction came from the knowledge that Sargon had bested his foe in the most humiliating way possible. The Letter to Ashur vividly imagines Rusa's response to the news of Muṣaṣir's capture: "Rusa heard and fell to the ground. He ripped his garments and bared his limbs. His headgear was thrown to the ground, (and) he tore out his hair and beat his breast with his fists. He threw him-self on his stomach. His heart stood still, his insides burned, in his mouth were painful lamentations."[91] If the march through Urartu had undone Rusa's achievements, the sack of Muṣaṣir resulted in his symbolic de-coronation as he actually threw away his crown.[92] In a world where so much depended on appearances, performance, and gesture, figurative descriptions like these were the very currency of power. Nowhere is the importance of political gesture more evident than in the Letter to Ashur that celebrated in high literary style, immediately after the events it described, not only Sargon's military exploits but the panache with which he had achieved them. There is no doubt that the text owes a great deal to its brilliant author, Nabu-shallimsunu, Sargon's chief scribe.[93] It stands to reason, however, that its core events, including the handling of Ullusunu, the bold attack at Waush, the execution of Bagdatti, the calculated demolition of Urartu's great monuments, and Urzana's disgrace—however artfully embellished in the telling—were not simply invented after the fact. On the contrary, Sargon did these things with an eye to their political payoff. The savvy elites and erudite scholars at his court would certainly have responded to the text's sophisticated political messages. This was a king who understood that pageantry, display, and protocol were as essential to power as violence deliberately applied.

He also appreciated the need to engage the continuing support of his own people—magnates, priests, and common people, including soldiers and deportees. Hence, on another level the text addressed these groups. Although royal inscriptions rarely acknowledged the hardship of campaigning, a growing reliance on conscripted deportees to mitigate chronic manpower shortages in the army underscored the high cost of warfare.[94] Morale required attention. In retrospect, the dramatic events of the eighth campaign were tailor-made for royal self-aggrandizement, but for the men on the ground living through the experience the campaign must have been extremely grueling—all the more reason to acknowledge their sacrifice with appropriate rituals and celebrations. It is in this context that we should consider the Letter to Ashur. When read or recited "to Ashur, father of the gods . . . to the gods of destinies and the goddesses who dwell in Ehursaggalkurkurra (Ashur's temple), their great temple . . . to the city and its people, to the palace and those who dwell in it," the authorities not only recognized the army's hard work and accomplishments by stressing the rigors of campaigning and the magnificence of the enemy's land, but, more importantly, explained what it all meant in political and religious terms.[95] The text even admits campaign casualties, if in a formulaic way: "One charioteer, two horsemen, and three *kallāpu*-troops were killed."[96] The Assyrians had traveled far, suffered much, risked everything, and triumphed. Once again their king had proved himself a bold but flexible military leader and the legitimate representative of Ashur. Just as the king of Urartu could not match Sargon, the god of Urartu could not rival Ashur, and the Assyrians had the statue of Haldi to prove it.

Despite the unpropitious start to his reign, by the end of 714 Sargon had achieved a string of outstanding successes. Not only had he bested his arch-rival, Rusa, but it also appeared that he had tamed the Tabalian principalities, the Zagros polities, and the fractious Syro-Palestinian states. Moreover, his commercial endeavors helped to allay the cost of repeated campaigning and the ongoing construction of Dur-Sharrukin. It would not do to get complacent, however. Phrygia continued to plot, if not actually fight, against Assyria. Urartu was down but not out of the fray, and the small buffer states could never be relied on to remain loyal. Most of all, the continuing independence of Babylonia rankled. Under these circumstances, not even Sargon could afford to bask in his Urartian triumph for long.

CHAPTER 5

COMPLETING THE EMPIRE OF ASHUR, 713–708 B.C.

Assyria's triumph over Urartu in 714 did not mark the end of hostilities between the two states, though it was the last time they fought over Mannea during Sargon's reign. Within a year or so of the Assyrian invasion, fear of attack and the sack of Muṣaṣir drove Rusa to suicide (or so Sargon claimed), after which Argishti, Rusa's son, ascended the Urartian throne.[1] Rather than continue the war with Assyria, the new king reverted to cold war operations—diplomatic intrigue, show of force, and minor acts of aggression—in order to demonstrate that Urartu still had a strong military and that its new king was made of sterner stuff than his father. At this critical juncture—the uncertain period of adjustment any new king faced plus the aftermath of the previous year's disasters—Argishti needed to increase his prestige, ideally at the expense of the Assyrians, while prudently avoiding open war. The restoration of Urartian privileges at Muṣaṣir and the temple of Haldi would be ideal in this respect. Regaining access to this important cult center was the most direct way for the new king to prove his legitimacy and declare his intentions to the Assyrians.

In the meantime, Sargon made use of the unstable situation in Urartu to bolster his relationship with Urzana. Although he had taken Urzana's family hostage, Sargon treated Muṣaṣir with studied benevolence and returned the refurbished statue of Haldi in 713, possibly after making improvements to the god's temple as a sign of patronage.[2] A common feature of Assyrian imperialism was "godnap," the removal of the statues of foreign gods to Assyria. The act signified that the deities in question had abandoned their people in favor of the Assyrians. Inevitably such seizures also implied that the Assyrian god, Ashur, was stronger than the foreign gods.[3] Sometimes, as in the case of Haldi, the king chose, for political reasons, to return the statue(s) and restore the temple(s). Such prestige-building tactics demonstrated the supremacy of Assyria's own

gods and king without directly involving the military. Most telling in this respect is the fact that Sargon did not garrison Muṣaṣir
but simply commanded Urzana to report to the nearest Assyrian
governor (Gabbu-ana-Ashur, the palace herald), pay his annual
tribute, and fulfill the standard client requirements, including
regular visits to Assyria. The royal correspondence reveals that
Urzana was not a particularly enthusiastic subject. Though he did
visit Assyria at least once, on other occasions he excused himself
because "snow has blocked the roads" or sent his brother to report
to Gabbu-ana-Ashur in his place.[4] Painfully aware of his precarious position, Urzana could neither ignore the Assyrians, who held
his family, nor appear too eager to serve Sargon, lest this behavior
attract Urartian retribution.

In any case, it did not take long for Argishti to challenge the
Assyrian hold on Muṣaṣir. In direct contravention of Sargon's orders
to Urzana—delivered via the palace herald—that "no one may take
part in the ritual without the king's order," Argishti reinitiated the
Urartian elites' participation in the cult of Haldi. When Gabbu-ana-
Ashur inquired about the situation, Urzana answered with a resigned
shrug: "When the king of Assyria came here, could I stop him? He
did what he does. And this one (Argishti), how could I stop him?"[5]
A mere pawn in the struggle between the stronger powers, Urzana
had no choice but to comply with their demands and endure their
periodic visits, whether these entailed solemn religious observation
or armed robbery. Argishti's maneuver to assert his authority—the
gathering of governors and troops at Muṣaṣir—has often been taken
to mean that he reconquered the city, deposed Urzana, and deported
his people.[6] But the evidence, such as it is, suggests that Argishti's
response was nonviolent and that, once again, Urzana retained his
throne. At any rate, whatever deportations Argishti carried out (if
any) would simply have replicated Sargon's earlier actions. For his
part, Sargon did not require direct control of Muṣaṣir and had apparently never intended to annex it, since he had not invested the city.
As long as Urzana provided intelligence about the Urartians and
kept up the appearance of polite submission by sending greetings and
exchanging gifts, it was in Sargon's best interest to let the Urartian
king move freely in and out of the city. Now that the Assyrians had
proved their supremacy over Urartu, Sargon needed to stabilize relations between the two states, so that he could turn his attention to
the fulfillment of his long-term plans to reconquer Babylonia.

As a means to this end, Sargon received a Urartian embassy to negotiate the return of prisoners. An undated order, which almost certainly belongs to the period between 714 and 710, describes this visit:

> The word of the king to Nabu-duru-uṣur: Now I am sending the royal bodyguard, Mannu-ki-Ashur, to those Urartian envoys. He will bring them to Arzuhina in front of these prisoners who are eating bread in your presence. You, the day you see this tablet, summon these captives; let them be alert and stand ready, and the day that Mannu-ki-Ashur, the bodyguard, writes to you that "The envoys have arrived in Arzuhina, get the prisoners moving," gather the prisoners, go to Arzuhina, and entrust them [. . .] to the [city-over]seer of Arzuhina. [I have ordered] Ashur-balti-nishe: "Go [. . .] in the presence [of . . .] and assi[st] them." Truly, the [Urartia]n women who [are] in your presence with [these] prisoners in Arrapha should not [go] with the prisoners.
>
> But now the women whom [he is seek]ing, taking out and bringing to the city of [. . .] let them live with these women in Arrapha, and let them be given bread to eat and water to drink until I come. The palace chariots which are bringing these women are to give the people bread and the teams fodder.[7]

The return of prisoners or hostages may have played a part in wider treaty negotiations, which probably also stipulated that the Urartians cease interference in Mannean affairs. The fact that the Manneans were able to raid Urartian territory with minimal fear of reprisal and that the ruler of Zikirtu started supplying horses to Assyria supports this assertion.[8] Even if Argishti and Sargon came to some agreement, which is by no means certain, it did not settle the conflict completely, and tensions remained high. What Sargon did achieve was the breathing room to prepare for his invasion of Babylonia, albeit not before he resolved a few minor problems elsewhere first.

Maintaining Control: Punitive Campaigns in Tabal and Media, 713

The 714 campaign, though undeniably successful, led to one unwelcome discovery that required attention: Sargon's son-in-law, Ambaris, the ruler of Bit-Purutash, had been plotting with Midas, Rusa, and the other Tabalian kings to expel the Assyrians from Anatolia.[9] News of the treason may have come during the Urartian campaign of 714, when Sennacherib began sending intelligence information about the Cimmerians' victory over Urartu to Sargon in the field. One report was so important that the crown prince did not summarize its contents, as was customary, but commented that "they have brought me from Tabal a letter from Nabu-le'i, the major-domo of Ahat-abisha. I am sending it to the king, my lord."[10] We do not know what information the forwarded letter contained, but apparently it alerted the Assyrians. Consequently, when they captured Muṣaṣir, the telltale presence of Tabalian luxury items where they should not have been—dedicated at the temple of Haldi—confirmed their suspicions.[11] It stands to reason that the objects from Tabal that ended up in Muṣaṣir had originally been given as gifts or tribute to a Urartian king, who then re-gifted them to the temple, although other explanations are possible: the Tabalian cups and censers could have dated to the earlier period of Urartian hegemony over Tabal in the ninth century or even arrived at Muṣaṣir legitimately through trade. Be that at it may, Sargon chose to see the objects as damning evidence of a privileged client's disloyalty.

Ambaris's betrayal stung. The Annals contain a long passage enumerating the favors that Sargon and his predecessors had bestowed on Ambaris's family. Not only had they lifted his father, Hulli ("the son of nobody"), from obscurity to the throne of Bit-Purutash, but Sargon had even married his own daughter to Ambaris, awarding a generous dowry that included additional territory as well. The ungrateful king had responded by colluding with Sargon's main enemies and fomenting rebellion among his fellow rulers, including Kurti of Atunna. After mustering the army, Sargon marched unopposed to Tabal, which he laid waste "to its furthest border." That is, he made a show of force by looting and wrecking, while supplying his troops in the process. Once again, the Assyrians met little, if any, resistance. Kurti, who had allegedly been plotting with Midas, immediately avowed loyalty to Assyria, and no one—not Midas, Argishti, or any Tabalian rulers—made an effort to aid Ambaris. The Assyrians annexed Bit-Purutash, deported Ambaris, his entire family (presumably including Sargon's daughter), and officials to Assyria, and then put a eunuch governor in charge.[12]

The annexation of Bit-Purutash was not an ideal outcome for the Assyrians, who preferred hegemonic relationships to direct rule in areas where distance and mountainous terrain hindered control. Moreover, the area's isolation from other Assyrian provinces, the nearest of which was Quwê, also argued against annexation as it would take a great deal of money, time, and people to invest the territory properly. The archaeological evidence from this area of Anatolia, meager though it is, suggests that Sargon never completed the Assyrian occupation. No unequivocally Assyrian buildings or military installations have so far been identified, and though the Annals claim that Sargon repopulated Bit-Purutash with deportees, no evidence of exogenous communities has come to light so far.[13] For the time being, Sargon managed to reestablish Assyrian control of Tabal and to remind his clients that he would not tolerate disloyalty.

While Sargon was punishing Ambaris, he sent his magnates east to deal with a rebellion in Karalla and to consolidate the Assyrian possession of the Khorasan Road from Ellipi into western Media.[14] The people of Karalla had expelled their Assyrian governor and enthroned Amitashi, the brother of Ashur-le'i, whom the Assyrians had deported to Assyria as a hostage in 716. Compared to Sargon's relatively mild treatment of Bit-Purutash, punishment of Karalla was particularly harsh. The magnates laid waste to the countryside, but Amitashi fled to take refuge with Adâ of Shurda, a neighboring territory. Unwilling to risk Assyrian reprisals, Adâ promptly murdered Amitashi, captured his retinue, and presented the rebel's head and two living sons to the Assyrians. The Assyrians rewarded Adâ by accepting him as a client, subordinate to the governor of Zamua. Back in Assyria, Sargon had Ashur-le'i flayed.[15] No guests of the crown, hostages such as Ashur-le'i acted as insurance against the treasonous behavior of clients and allies. Anyone who dared to ignore that fact was likely to reap the cruelest of punishments. More important, Sargon's impending plans to take back Babylonia made Karalla a special case. He could not proceed against Babylonia unless he had a firm grip on the Zagros polities. Any whiff of rebellion on the Assyrians' rear flank would invite Elamite intervention and thus jeopardize Assyrian operations.

After reestablishing their hold on Karalla, the magnates moved to suppress internecine strife in the client state, Ellipi, which occupied the strategically important area on the northeastern flank of Babylonia, not far beyond Assyrian-held Der. Maintaining influence over Ellipi was essential to Sargon's plans for the reconquest of the south. Thus, keeping its pro-Assyrian ruler, Daltâ, secure became a priority. The arrival of the Assyrian army there sent the rebels scurrying for the hills until the magnates, acting on Sargon's behalf, "let them come down from the mountains and counted them as booty," thereby rendering "the heart of Daltâ glad and let(ting) the inhabitants of Ellipi in its entire extent live in peace."[16] Afterward, the magnates moved deeper into the Zagros to "remote tracts of land in the area of the Arabs of the sunrise and those lands of the powerful Medes, who had thrown off the yoke of Assyria and roamed the mountains and desert like thieves." Meeting little resistance, the Assyrians "burned all their cities and turned all their land into nameless piles of rubble."[17] Despite the bellicose rhetoric, this remote operation probably entailed little more than plundering and destroying impoverished hamlets, isolated farmsteads, and the occasional mountain fortress. During the rest of the campaign, the magnates collected the annual tribute—mostly animal stock—from the rulers of Mannea, Ellipi, Allabria, and the myriad city lords of Media. In truth, by this time, the Assyrian conquest of the Zagros was so thorough that, with the exception of their necessary intervention in a civil war in Ellipi in 707, the Assyrians did not have to launch another major campaign to the east during Sargon's reign.[18]

By the end of 713, Sargon seemed to have a solid grip on the empire's territories: Argishti maneuvered to stabilize his borders; Midas was reduced, as usual, to diplomatic intrigue, and clients in Palestine appeared docile. The Assyrian magnates were busy with administrative duties. For the first time since his troubled accession, Sargon could afford to suspend major military operations for a year while he concentrated on domestic matters, the construction of Dur-Sharrukin, and, most important, his plans for the reconquest of Babylonia. Despite progress, the more territory Assyria brought under its sway, the more complex holding it became. A mixed blessing, opportunities for territorial or commercial expansion always led to further complications and potential delays in the achievement of long-term goals. Thus, the interlude between 713 and the kickoff of the Babylonian campaign in 710 entailed nearly as much military action and political maneuvering—though not the same level of intensity—as the previous campaign years.

Domestic Activities: Sargon in Assyria, 712–711

Nothing certain is known about Sargon's activities during the time he remained in Assyria. However, a number of letters from the royal archives involve the day-to-day problems Sargon, his magnates, and governors regularly encountered. Although it is impossible to assign specific dates to these documents (other than generally identifying them as falling after 714), they form a relatively clear picture of the state of the empire during the second half of Sargon's reign.

The constant campaigning of the previous years had had a mixed impact on the Assyrian heartland. We can only guess at the number of casualties the Assyrian army suffered, but, given the conditions under which it operated, it stands to reason that lengthy annual campaigns—often through terrible terrain—took a high human toll. While war depleted the male population, the regular influx of foreign deportees altered Assyria's demographic profile. As a result, the ethnic diversity of the army increased accordingly. Administrative documents show that up to one-fifth of the men serving in Sargon's army had West Semitic (as opposed to Assyrian) names, and letters attest to soldiers serving from all over the empire.[19] In order to hold on to his conquests, Sargon needed to attend to administrative matters and to project a coherent image of a unified and invulnerable Assyrian core, one with a loyal army that could strike fast and hard anywhere. Central to achieving his goals was the construction of Dur-Sharrukin, a clear projection of Assyrian power that took on special meaning after Sargon's defeat of Urartu. His magnificent new city would outshine even the most outstanding feats of Urartian engineering. By this reasoning, since the Assyrians could destroy and create with equal ease, they were greater by far than the Urartians or anyone else. The reality, of course, proved to be somewhat different.

A few years into the project, most of the work at Dur-Sharrukin still remained to be done. In order to make progress quickly, Sargon mustered all the human and material resources at his disposal, and, under the skilled guidance of Tab-shar-Ashur, the royal treasurer, managed to organize the largely deportee work force of laborers, skilled craftsmen, and artisans, while also providing them with construction materials, food, and shelter. All told, this endeavor resembled the largest military campaign in scale, though it lasted far longer and entailed greater logistical complexity. It took just over ten years to build the city's basic infrastructure, and at least twenty-six governors participated in the project.[20] Building materials, such as wood, stone, and even straw for the mud brick, had to be imported from all over the empire. The coordinated effort this required complicated things for the provincial governors, who had to adhere to the king's strict policies while attempting to govern their provinces, fill royal quotas, and pursue their own interests. Since Sargon could ill afford to support idle workers as they waited for materials, prompt delivery of resources was essential. Bottlenecks and delays did occur, however. One frustrated official, trying to fulfill his construction obligations at Dur-Sharrukin, wrote to the palace reporting that there was no straw for the bricks and asking "by what means will they make bricks for their work assignment in the morning?"[21] Sometimes local people simply refused to cooperate, as when the palace herald complained, "Stone slabs and bull colossi are placed before me, but the people of the country, none agree to g[o forth] to my wor[k], saying: 'Are we [your] men?' They do not lis[ten to me] . . . these (people), whatever (I say)—it is or it isn't— they do not listen to me at all."[22] Continuous delays forced Sargon to take draconian measures. At one point, he wrote to the governor of Calah insisting that "700 bales of straw and 700 bundles of reeds, each bundle more than a donkey can carry, must be at hand in Dur-Sharrukin by the 1st of Kislev (November). Should one day pass by, you will die."[23] A similar letter fragment suggests that Sargon sent the same threat to other officials.[24]

Other imperial policies caused problems for provincial administrators. For example, tight restrictions on trade—regulations on where it could occur, what commodities could be exchanged, and who might participate—arrogated control and profits to Assyria. Nevertheless, those provincial governors trying to enforce royal standards sometimes met with passive resistance, overt hostility, or outright rebellion. A letter from the governor (or vice-governor) of Hamath reveals some of the negative consequences of the king's policies. Answering Sargon's accusation, quoted in the letter ("You have made Huzaza into a merchant's town. People have been giving iron to the Arabs for silver"), the author, Bel-liqbi, responded, "Who are they, the merchants who have been selling in there? Three people, old 'Atean men, [are . . .] there; they keep grapes, 20 or [30 homers], as many as we bring in, and sell them to the Arabs. I sell iron to the deportees, [only] copper to the Arabs." The beleaguered official continued by claiming that "a toll collector has been installed at Ṣupat's city gate and now they have installed the other one in Huzazu; the Arabs are leaving and not going inside (anymore); they have become afraid."[25] Presumably, the Arabs did not want to get caught with illicit merchandise or pay tax on what they bought. In any case, Sargon's regulations put Bel-liqbi in a difficult position, especially vis-à-vis the Arabs, who played a crucial role in maintaining trade relations with Egypt and providing access to the spice road through Arabia.

The vagaries of trade relations aside, the Assyrians had a complicated relationship with the Arabs during this period. On the one hand, the nomads' ability to survive the harsh desert environment made them ideal trading partners for the Assyrians, who were not habituated to the rigors of desert travel. On the other hand, the Arabs' tribal organization and unpredictable movements made them difficult to monitor, let alone control.[26] Though Sargon's inscriptions claim that Samsi, queen of the Arabs, paid him tribute, letters confirm that he made concessions to nomads, allowing them to wander unchecked through much of Assyrian territory in return for their cooperation.[27] This liberal policy was not entirely successful, and a number of reports dating to the middle years of Sargon's reign attest to Assyria's increasingly problematic relationship with intractable Arab nomads.[28]

The tribes were not the only challenge to provincial authority, however. Some subject polities suffered so that Sargon could fulfill his long-range objectives. When reporting on tax collection and provincial organization, for example, the governor of Hamath points out that he is short-staffed and that "it is constantly hostile, but I do not neglect the guard." Moreover, when, as a result of the deals they made in 716, the Assyrians established their own trade center at the Brook of Egypt, the new arrangement inevitably diverted business and profit from some of the Philistine kingdoms, whose economies depended on the coastal trade with Egypt. Though cities such as Gaza continued to profit under Assyrian rule, others were not so lucky.

More Punitive Measures: Ashdod, Gurgum, and Kammanu, 711

Philistine Ashdod was one of the less fortunate ones. By 712, Azuri, its king, could no longer tolerate Assyrian hegemony and stopped paying tribute. That he thought he had a reasonable chance of breaking free from Assyria seems unlikely unless, as the Bible suggests, rumor of Sargon's death prompted him to take action. One of Isaiah's prophecies, usually dated to around 715, seems to refer to the death of the Assyrian king: "Rejoice not, O Philistia, all of you, that the rod which smote you is broken." Since Sargon's death occurred in 705, we may conclude that Isaiah, and the Philistines of whom he spoke, acted in response to a false rumor.[29] Rumor-inspired rebellion was certainly not unheard of in the ancient world. When Alexander the Great campaigned in the Danube region not long after his accession, the false report of his death fueled insurrection among the Greek city-states.[30] It is possible that something similar occurred when Sargon disappeared for long periods on campaign in the Zagros Mountains. In any case, Isaiah was right to warn, "Wail, O gate; cry, O city; melt in fear, O Philistia, all of you! For smoke comes out of the north, and there is no straggler in his ranks."[31] This evocative warning notwithstanding, given past experience it did not require a great prophet to predict swift Assyrian retribution.

Since keeping power within the ruling family could help maintain a semblance of legitimacy and avoid future problems, Sargon removed Azuri "on account of his crime" and appointed Ahimeti, his brother, to rule in his place. The people of Ashdod did not accept the change and soon overthrew Ahimeti in favor of a commoner, Iamani (the "Ionian"), whose name suggests an association with the sea trade.[32] Anticipating Assyrian retaliation and knowing that he could not survive without help, Iamani sought support from neighboring rulers in Philistia, Judah, Edom, Moab, and Egypt. Determined to retaliate but busy elsewhere, Sargon entrusted command to his field marshal, who marched unopposed to Philistia. Ashdod's massive fortifications and complex four-entry gate could not stop the determined besiegers, who sacked the city, its port, Ashdod-Yam, and Gath.[33] Afterward, true to form, they deported the inhabitants and made the area an Assyrian province. The remains of three thousand bodies, discovered in a mass grave during excavations at Ashdod, could represent victims of the Assyrian attack.[34] Ultimately, however, no one came to Iamani's aid. After all, the Egyptians had little to gain by disrupting their lucrative commercial arrangement with the Assyrians, and the kingdoms of Israel and Judah clearly understood the improbability of success. Not only did Iamani receive no help, but after he found refuge in Egypt for a few years the Kushite pharaoh, Shabitku, chose to extradite him in 707 or 706 in order to cultivate good relations with Assyria.[35] The Philistine rebellion of 711 marked the final attempt of any Syro-Palestinian state to break free of Assyria during Sargon's reign.

In the same year, the Assyrian army marched to suppress another internecine struggle, this time in Gurgum, a client polity north of Sam'al in southern Anatolia. There the ruler's son, Mutallu, had murdered his father, Tarhulara, and seized power. According to the very fragmentary Nineveh Annals, the murder was a crime of passion, as Mutallu "flew into a rage" prior to the killing.[36] Whatever family squabble inspired this act, it would not do to let the crime go unpunished, and Sargon took advantage of the sordid episode to annex the area. The Assyrians captured Mutallu and "burned his hands" as appropriate punishment for the heinous double crimes of patricide and regicide. Though Sargon made Gurgum an Assyrian province, he left the general populace alone, preferring to pillage the royal palace and deport the local elites, including Mutallu, to Assyria.[37] Once again he used elite hostages to ensure the proper behavior of those left behind.

After tidying up the disorder in Gurgum, the Assyrian army moved north into Kammanu to punish another malcontent, Tarhunazi, whom Sargon had placed in charge a few years earlier, after deposing the prior ruler for some unstated offense. When Sargon discovered that Tarhunazi had "written calumny about Assyria" to Midas, he intervened again. In his Annals, Sargon proclaimed that "in the anger of my heart, I conquered Kammanu to its furthest extent; I shattered his royal city, Melid, like a clay pot."[38] Sargon made Kammanu an Assyrian province but gave Melid, which was adjacent to Urartu, to the king of Kummuh, Mutallu (not the patricide of the same name from Gurgum), in order to maintain a buffer zone along the Urartian border. Over the next few years, the Assyrians strengthened Kammanu by building ten forts there and garrisoning them with tribal auxiliaries moved in from the south.[39] Despite the justification given in the Annals, it is possible that increasing tensions along the Urartian-Assyrian border prompted the annexation of Kammanu. If that was the case, the campaign only exacerbated the already volatile situation in the northern provinces.

Struggles on the Periphery after 712

The governors of these provinces struggled to maintain security while filling the king's resource quotas. Construction at Dur-Sharrukin required a huge amount of wood. By way of comparison, archaeologists have calculated that the construction of the seventh-century Urartian fortress Ayanis, with a footprint of about 650,000 square feet, required forty thousand trees to build.[40] Most of the wood and stone for the construction of Dur-Sharrukin, whose walls enclosed more than one square mile (or about 27,878,400 square feet), came from the forested highlands on the upper reaches of the Tigris and Euphrates Rivers. When the Assyrians exhausted the wood supply in their own territory (or in order to conserve it), they sought fresh forests in independent Shubria and sometimes even in Urartian territory. In order to protect work details, governors of frontier provinces built forts and brought in deportees to boost agricultural production. A fully equipped fort, manned by 100 to 150 soldiers, included administrative buildings, defenses, and a good water supply.[41] Forts protected work details, local inhabitants, and travelers in the immediate vicinity, but they did not form an effective perimeter defense of imperial territory, nor were they meant to withstand the concerted attack of a large army.

Internal economic imperatives—particularly the search for resources for Dur-Sharrukin and for military use—gradually pushed the Assyrians into neighboring territory that the Urartians controlled. This encroachment, in turn, caused strained diplomatic relations, increased espionage, a steady military buildup and, finally, violent skirmishes. A number of letters from the governors and vice-governors of the provinces of Amedi and Tushan relate such incidents. Writing from Tushan, an official named Ashipa (probably the governor) reported the buildup of Urartian troops in the adjacent provinces and assured Sargon that "we are standing guard opposite them. All the people are in fortified dwellings; they, the oxen and sheep are on this side [o]f the river. We are standing guard."[42] Similarly, Nashur-Bel, the governor of Amedi, wrote to Sargon about how a clash over logging had nearly led to open war:

> Concerning the news of the Urartians, the scouts I sent to look around have told me this: "The governor opposite us is standing guard with the deputy governor in the city Harda; opposite the

Vizier, conscripts are distributed town by town in battle array up
to Tushpa. Argishti's messenger has come by saying, 'Concerning
the work I ordered you to do, don't do the work! Feed your horses
until I send a messenger to you.'"

I sent the Itu'eans with the village inspector for the logs that
were withheld in Eziat, and he brought them over in a fight. The
deputy of their village inspector and nine of his soldiers were hit
with a bow (arrows); two of them died. They wounded three of
their soldiers. This was their report.[43]

These letters, which cannot be precisely dated and are included here
as an example of continuing hostilities between Assyria and Urartu
during this period, indicate that Assyrian activity provoked Argishti
to deploy his army along the Tushpa–Elazig road on the Murat River
east of Melid and north of Amedi and Tushan.[44] Nashur-Bel managed
to extract his men and logs from Eziat but not without bloodshed.

In another, probably associated letter, Nashur-Bel followed up
an earlier request for instructions with the news:

My messenger, [wh]om I sent [to] the (Urartian) governor opposite
me has returned; he spoke to him as the king, my lord, wrote me,
saying: "We are at peace, so why do you seize our forts?"

He said, "What should I do? If I have trespassed on your border
or against your forts, hold me accountable." His troops are collected with him; he is standing guard in Harda. This was the news
about them.[45]

Although Sargon instructed Nashur-Bel to resolve the issue through
diplomacy, the Urartian governor's insolent reply effectively prevented further negotiation. In spite of continuing tensions, hostilities apparently went no further than the squad-level skirmish
reported in the first letter. The Urartians stood down and the tenuous peace held. The Assyrians did not respond to such situations
directly but opted instead to make a show of force by campaigning
in neighboring areas, such as Kammanu.

With the annexation of Gurgum and Kammanu, Sargon gained
complete control over all of the north–south passes of the Taurus
Mountains leading into Syria, and thus he secured his territory
against potential Phrygian and Urartian attacks during the Assyrians'
upcoming invasion of Babylonia. Moreover, though the takeover
of Carchemish in 717 had brought the northern metal trade under

Assyrian control, these latest advances gave them direct access to the area's rich iron deposits and forests.[46] In this context, the strategic importance of the 711 campaign becomes clear, for without a secure hold on the empire, a strong defense against his northern enemies, and a reliable wood and metal supply, Sargon could not proceed with the long-awaited campaign against Merodach-Baladan.

The Conquest of Babylonia, 710–709

For the ten years following the battle of Der in 720, Babylonian independence served as a constant reminder of the inauspicious start to Sargon's reign. The empire would not be complete until Assyria reclaimed the south, but the subjugation of Babylonia was not a straightforward matter of military conquest. Alone among Assyria's enemies, the Babylonians shared with their northern rivals a millennia-old cultural affinity: they spoke the same language (different dialects of Akkadian) and practiced associated religious and intellectual traditions. Acutely aware of their shared history, the Assyrians had a profound respect for the ancient institutions of urban Babylonia, whose cult centers had been in existence since "before the flood."[47] Reverence aside, mastery over Babylonia also meant that Assyria could exploit both the Persian Gulf trade and the overland trade into Arabia. Thus, in order to complete Assyria's control over Mesopotamian commerce, Sargon had to conquer Babylonia.

Despite their shared culture, the two states had developed quite differently during the first millennium. In the late eighth century, Babylonia was not a cohesive, centralized state in the same sense as Assyria but a hybrid collection of diverse ethnic and social groups that the Babylonian king struggled to unite (map 2). The Akkadian-speaking population lived in the area's large, ancient cities, while seminomadic Chaldean and Aramaean tribes occupied the steppe, marshes, and Zagros foothills.[48] The most powerful Chaldean tribes, Bit-Iakin, Bit-Amukani, and Bit-Dakkuri, occupied the lower Tigris and Euphrates and the delta (at that time much farther north than it is today). Aramaean tribes such as the Puqudu, Itu'u, Ru'u, and Gambulu inhabited the central Euphrates area and the lands to the east of the Tigris. Over time, some tribal people gradually settled in cities, especially those in the far south, such as Ur, Uruk, and Eridu.[49] Political tensions among the cities and between the urban population and the tribes hindered centralization, while shifting tribal alliances and endemic feuding provided additional barriers to unity. Geography and the environment posed extra challenges.

When he invaded the south, Sargon had to contend with several types of terrain: flat, irrigated farmlands and uncultivated desert; the Zagros piedmont, and the vast marshy area that bordered the Persian Gulf, called the "Sealand." The Tigris and Euphrates Rivers and tributaries such as the Diyala, Uqnu, and Tubliash Rivers also presented considerable obstacles, while recent shifts in the Euphrates course had changed settlement and agricultural patterns.[50] Sargon's Annals describe the affected area between Assyria and Babylonia as follows:

> It was desert, into the midst of which the access had been cut off from distant days. Its course was laborious. Tracks had not been established. The inaccessible paths—thorn, thistles and thickets flourished over them. Dogs and jackals lurk in their midst, cavorting like lambs. In that desert country, Aramaeans and Sutians—tent-dwellers, fugitives, bandits, a plundering bunch—pitched their dwellings and made desolate its course. Dikes and furrows did not exist upon the meadows of the habitations in their midst, which for many days past had gone to ruin. It was woven with spider webs.[51]

Although the river's shift forced the abandonment of some settlements, more serious challenges awaited the Assyrians than the desolate landscape of northwestern Babylonia. To the east, the Tigris was prone to violent flooding in spring, and its tributaries often became impassable.[52] Moreover, while the Assyrian army had plenty of experience crossing mountain torrents and dealing with rugged terrain, the Sealand—home to Merodach-Baladan's tribe, Bit-Iakin, and the location of the tribal capital, Dur-Iakin—presented a new type of challenge. The area's marshes, with their miles of reeds, occasional islands, and maze of uncharted, shallow waterways, invited ambush from the criminals, fugitives, and tribal peoples who took refuge there. Thus, in order to retake Babylonia, Sargon had to overcome physical obstacles, win over the cities, subdue the various Chaldean and Aramaean tribes, and prevent the Elamites from getting involved—all without recourse to the kind of violence that would spur resistance and undermine his claim to Babylonian legitimacy.

Although the reconquest of Babylonia would be difficult and time-consuming, several key factors favored Assyria. Proximity and

favorable terrain allowed the Assyrians to campaign there throughout the year. More important, political and military conditions
were ripe for intervention. Over the course of ten years free from
external threat, Merodach-Baladan had fulfilled the main ideological requisites of Babylonian kingship: he had maintained irrigation
systems and canals, developed trade, and funded building projects
in major cities such as Babylon, Kutha, Borsippa, Uruk, and Ur.[53]
Yet, for all that, he had not managed to forge the urban and tribal
populations into anything approaching lasting unity. In short, he
could not count on personal loyalty or a cohesive Babylonian identity to prevail over local self-interest.[54] Moreover, in 717 a new
Elamite king, Shutruk-nahunte, had succeeded Humban-nikash on
the Elamite throne, thus requiring the Babylonian king to renegoti-
ate an alliance in order to receive help from that quarter.[55] Worst of
all, Merodach-Baladan could not field the type of well-trained army
needed to oppose Sargon's seasoned veterans. The Babylonians' military shortcomings should be understood not as a strategic failure
but as an indication that Merodach-Baladan had limited authority
over his diverse subjects, who formed numerous factions with conflicting interests.[56] Even so, he had proven a wily opponent in the
past by taking a defensive stance, avoiding battle, and relying on the
Elamites to do the fighting for him. It would not do for the Assyrians
to underestimate him.

   For Sargon too the circumstances in 710 were vastly different
from those of 720. At that time he had been a new king in a precarious political position fighting on the defensive. Now he ruled a vast
empire and led the most successful army in the Near East. Sargon's
strategy required the deployment of both a large conventional
force and smaller, mobile units that could move rapidly through
Babylonia as necessary. The invasion plan compensated for the
fact that the army could not use its customary devastation tactics
indiscriminately in Babylonia, and it fully anticipated Merodach-
Baladan's response, including the possibility of Elamite intervention. Instead of pushing straight south to Babylon and getting mired
in a war of attrition, during which he might have to besiege each
major city in succession, Sargon opted for a more cautious, economical approach. He would mount a conventional operation on
Babylonia's eastern frontier, in order to prevent the Elamites from
coming to Merodach-Baladan's aid, and then reduce the military
capabilities of the allied Chaldean and Aramaean tribes and isolate

Bit-Iakin.[57] Sargon realized that circumstances favored unconventional warfare. While his main force focused on Babylonia's eastern flank, Sargon's agents, including some native Babylonians, Chaldeans, and Aramaeans, would foment insurrection among targeted tribes, while encouraging or coercing high officials in the cities to switch sides.

Not everyone had supported Merodach-Baladan's seizure of power in 722, and in the aftermath some of his opponents fled to Assyria. A sizeable number of Chaldeans, for example, moved to Assyria, where by 715 they formed an auxiliary unit in the standing army.[58] Thus, the Assyrians could turn refugees and exiles into agents provocateurs in order to win over local populations by peaceful means and stimulate rebellion against Merodach-Baladan. Once they had converted Merodach-Baladan's supporters to their cause, the Assyrians could prevail with minimal force of arms. In other words, Sargon's brilliant strategy exploited intelligence assets, military capability, and Babylonian disunity. By contrast, Merodach-Baladan appears to have been as unprepared for the Assyrian invasion as he was unsure how to respond to it, so when the Assyrians implemented their plans, Merodach-Baladan defaulted to his old strategy of avoiding battle and letting his Elamite allies do the fighting. Apparently he believed that what had worked once might work again. Although Merodach-Baladan neither anticipated Sargon's clandestine operations nor effectively counteracted them, he also failed to respond effectively to the Assyrian army's invasion on his eastern flank.

A large number of tablets from Sargon's letter corpus pertain to the Babylonian campaign. Based on these reports, Assyriologist Andreas Fuchs has recently reconstructed the chronology of the campaign, and I adopt his arrangement here.[59] At the start, Sargon attempted to win the support of the Aramaean tribes living south of Der. The governor of Arrapha reported about his diplomatic efforts among the Ru'ueans, who lived between the Tigris and Uqnu Rivers:

> Nabu-zeru-ibni, the Ru'[uean] eunuch whom the king, my lord, retur[ned] from Damascus from the presence of Bel-duri and sent to Abdudu to Be[l. . . .] perchance the Ru'u[ean] and his people would co[me] to him—Merodach-Bal[adan] heard of his having come (and) he had all of his brothers brought and said to them: "Now that his brother has come, you will run o[ff] to him!" They said to him,

"Why would we run off? Our brother who has come is on the other side. He came, but he will leave."[60]

Having tracked down a member of the tribe living as a deportee in Damascus, the Assyrians returned him to his homeland to convince tribal leaders to back Sargon. In this case, Merodach-Baladan's operatives were able to foil Sargon's plans, and the Ru'ueans remained loyal to the Chaldean king throughout the war. Despite the initial setback, other Assyrian efforts at subversion proved more fruitful, and the several Aramaean tribes in the Diyala River region subsequently joined Sargon.[61]

In the meantime, the Assyrian army marched south from Der to take control of the tribal lands of Rashi, Iadburu, Puqudu, Gambulu, and parts of Bit-Iakin on the Elamite-Babylonian frontier.[62] Initially, Merodach-Baladan attempted to forestall the Assyrians by ordering the Gambulu tribe plus six hundred cavalry and four thousand infantry to garrison the city Dur-Abihara (also known as Dur-Athara), where he had the fortifications hastily improved.[63] Despite the preparations, the Assyrians took the city in a single day, after which they deported the inhabitants together with their possessions. On this front the Assyrian army employed its routine devastation tactics to great effect as it swept through the area burning, looting, and taking prisoners. The Assyrians' irresistible speed so impressed the other Gambulu in the vicinity that eight of their leaders brought tokens of submission to Sargon, who then formed the area into a new province.[64] The Elamites remained inactive throughout these operations. Unable or unwilling to engage the main Assyrian army, Merodach-Baladan looked for an opportunity to strike at their secondary force in northern Babylonia while he waited to see whether the Assyrian invasion in the east would goad the Elamites into action.

In an effort to counteract the Assyrians, Merodach-Baladan's cavalry made raids in the area around Assyrian-held Dur-Kurigalzu and Dur-Sharruku (not to be confused with Dur-Sharrukin), fortress towns on opposite sides of the Tigris River about twenty miles apart.[65] Dur-Kurigalzu protected the Patti-illil canal that connected the Euphrates and Tigris at a point where the rivers' courses brought them into proximity. Both forts provided the Assyrians with excellent bases from which to conduct the Babylonian portion of the campaign. After Merodach-Baladan received intelligence to the effect that Dur-Sharruku was vulnerable to attack due to a water shortage, he set forth from Kutha to besiege the northern town.[66] Tracking enemy movements, Assyrian agents reported Merodach-Baladan's progress northward to Sargon, who remained in the east with the main forces.[67] One agent, Shamash-abu-uṣur, noted, "The son of Zeri (Merodach-Baladan) is crossing (the Tigris) at Bab-bitqi. The Itu'u, the Rubu'u, and the [Li]ta'u [have c]rossed in front of them [at] the town Apallâ."[68] It is not clear whether the Aramaean tribes mentioned in the letter were part of Merodach-Baladan's advance force or were shadowing the Babylonian army on behalf of Sargon.[69] A shadow force could keep track of the enemy and also harass them as they crossed the river, disrupt their supply lines, and slow their attack.

As these events unfolded, Bel-iqisha, a highly placed informant in Babylon, which was still in Merodach-Baladan's hands, argued forcefully for Sargon to send an army to meet the Chaldean troops as they crossed the Tigris at Bab-bitqi:

> The king did not listen to any of the previous words that we sent to the king, my lord. Now, after the delegates of Bit-Dakkuri all together had written to Merodach-Baladan, and the *šandabakku* official (the governor of Nippur) together with Nabu-le'i the governor, and the troops of Bit-Iakin marched with them to (Bab)-Bitqi and the prefect turned the horsemen of Bit-Dakkuri, the Aramaeans, and the men of Bit-Dakkuri against him (Merodach-Baladan), the delegates have been silent as they have gotten scared. The others, having heard, have turned back. And now the leading men, who do not secure the land and whose words the king has heard, after going out, are now incessantly sending deceitful messages and strengthening their cities. The king should not wait for the result. May the troops come to Bab-Bitqi.

The fearful author added one final plea: "I have written to the king because it is critical! The king should not delay, for we are now divided, and your servants and the land of Akkad (Babylonia) threaten to slip from your hand."[70] The letter vividly portrays the dilemma of those trying to navigate a safe way through the hostilities, and we are reminded that this was not a war driven by nationalism or ideology but by elite self-interest in the quest for survival and power. Lack of confidence in Merodach-Baladan's ability to defeat the Assyrians compelled tribal and city leaders, whatever their personal preferences, to side with Sargon. But until they felt secure, they not only plotted with both sides, but also prepared to withstand attacks from both. Although the pro-Assyrian prefect succeeded in turning Bit-Dakkuri and other local tribes against Merodach-Baladan, the timing left the new allies in an awkward position. There were not sufficient Assyrian forces in the vicinity to provide security against Merodach-Baladan. To make matters appear worse, Merodach-Baladan had ordered the fortifications of Larak (located somewhere east of the Tigris in Puqudu territory) repaired in order to impede Sargon's progress in that theater of operations.[71] Not privy to Sargon's strategy or cognizant of Assyrian success elsewhere, Bel-iqisha saw only the potential for disaster.

In actuality, however, everything was going according to plan. Il-iada', the Assyrian official in charge in Dur-Sharruku, calmly prepared to meet Merodach-Baladan's advancing army.[72] He answered Sargon's directive to "be alert and make your guard strong for these two months until I come" with the reassurance that "the soldiers and horses are drawn up together to stand guard in the area of the king, my lord. [I] am constantly moving about in the presence of my guard." In the same text, Il-iada' noted that "there is a lot of water in the Diyala River (and) the waters go to Dur-Sharruku . . . [The rep]ort concerning Merodach-Baladan: [he has tur]ned back and he is in his country."[73] Merodach-Baladin's abortive attempt on Dur-Sharruku had probably been undertaken in order to galvanize support in the area, while he waited to see whether Sargon would inadvertently do him the favor of provoking the Elamites into war. When this did not happen and it became clear that Dur-Sharruku had sufficient water to withstand a siege, he gave up and retreated to Babylon to await further developments. As the letter of Il-iada' revealed, Sargon expected that he would only need another two months to secure the border with Elam. During the interval, Il-iada' continued operations with the help of some Assyrian magnates, who brought vital supplies and reinforcements, including "10 homers of salt, 16 [. . .] of cardamom, 30 jugs of oil, 18 jugs of naphtha, 30 bows, 20,000 arrows, 10,000 wagon-wheel parts" as well as Itu'eans and Gurreans "of the palace." Next "they went to the mouth of the Patti-illil canal and are working inside the f[o]rt there. 10 of my Gurreans and 20 of my Itu'eans went with them."[74] From their base at Dur-Sharruku, the Assyrians were slowly fortifying northern Babylonia and stocking provisions preparatory to the next phase of conquest.

As the Assyrians continued to woo Babylonian supporters, and Merodach-Baladan did nothing to intervene, his power base eroded further. Increasingly, leaders contacted the Assyrians in hopes of brokering a deal favorable to themselves. One official advised the king to "speak kindly" to a potential new supporter in order to "encourage him so he will come and establish the kind words to the people of his country and his brothers."[75] As it became obvious to local leaders that Merodach-baladan could not prevail, defections to the Assyrian side increased. Soon the rulers of Sippar, one of the most important cities in northern Babylonia, invited the Assyrians into the city.[76] Pushing the initiative further, Sargon outmaneuvered Merodach-Baladan yet again by placing troops in Dur-Ladini, a ruined fort within a few miles of Babylon.[77] The move not only isolated the Chaldean leader but also offered protection for the tribe, Bit-Dakkuri, whose support was crucial to Sargon's strategy.

The presence of the Assyrians gave the people of Bit-Dakkuri more confidence. Although the initial Assyrian takeover of Borsippa, the main city in the region, apparently caused some civil disorder, subsequent reports portrayed the residents as enthusiastically pro-Assyrian, particularly after their leaders returned from exile in Assyria.[78] One of those repatriated was a woman named Barsipitu, who wrote to Sargon:

> Under the protection of the gods of [the king, our lord], we entered Bit-[Dakkuri] in good health. Ana-Na[bu-taklak] (the Assyrian delegate) and the entire population of Bit-Dakkuri rejoiced in our presence, and they constantly bless the king our lord, saying "now we know that the [king] our lord has reestablished Bit-Dakkuri and will give it the advantage, as he has sent us the son of our lord! And we shall be living under the protection of the king, our lord, forever."[79]

Barsipitu was probably the daughter of Balassu, the former chief of Bit-Dakkuri, who supported Tiglath-pileser III during the Mukin-Zeri rebellion.[80] As Assyrian emissaries to Bit-Dakkuri, Barsipitu and her brother, who is mentioned in the letter, returned to their homeland in order to secure it for Sargon and their own family. Balassu appears to have remained in Assyrian territory as a hostage. This tactic created opportunities not only for those who had a grievance against Merodach-Baladan but also for anyone with ambitions for personal gain. In one instance, a Chaldean, perhaps even a member of Bit-Iakin, offered to support the Assyrians in exchange for "all my people, as many as I subdue."[81] The situation encouraged people to put personal benefit before collective interest at the expense of central and tribal authority. Rising factionalism and instability caused problems for both Merodach-baladan and Sargon. Even so, the situation in Babylonia was shaping up nicely for the Assyrians, who now had a military presence in friendly territory close to Babylon and informers within the city. Meanwhile, the main army continued to secure the eastern flank.

As the Assyrians campaigned in the east across the Tubliash River in the area of Iadburu, they inevitably came into contact with Elamites, who had invested two towns there sometime earlier. The Assyrians quickly captured these along with their Elamite garrisons and, according to the Annals, 12,062 of the local population, whom they deported. This victory inspired a number of local tribal headmen to submit to Sargon, who gained control of Iadburu as a result. Once again the Elamites failed to respond.[82] Having achieved his objectives in the southeast, Sargon swung back to the north through Rashi, Elamite-held territory in the Zagros foothills bordering Ellipi, an Assyrian client. As the Assyrians invaded, the people of Rashi retreated to the fortified mountain stronghold, Bit-Imbi, accompanied by the Elamite king, Shutruk-nahunte, who still made no move to challenge the Assyrians, despite overt provocation. Correctly interpreting Shutruk-nahunte's passivity as clear evidence that he did not intend to interfere, Sargon withdrew most of the army from the east and embarked on the next phase of his campaign in Babylonia.

While the Assyrian army marched to join their advance troops in Dur-Ladini, Merodach-Baladan left Babylon, joined his army in Kish, and then made his way via Nippur across the Tigris toward Iadburu. Here he hoped to meet the Elamites and procure their help with a gift of "his royal accoutrements; his bed, his chair, his footstool, his royal ewer, (and) his necklace."[83] The fact that Merodach-Baladan could travel unopposed in Iadburu so soon after Sargon campaigned there indicates that the Assyrians had not fully garrisoned the area but had simply passed through in order to make allies and warn off the Elamites. This turn of events also suggests that many (if not most) of the people living in Babylonia did not feel loyal to either side and simply supported whoever was close enough to threaten. Though informants kept track of the Chaldean's whereabouts, Sargon made no attempt to engage Merodach-Baladan's retreating forces. He didn't need to. Merodach-Baladan had gotten himself into a critical situation, and since the Elamites had done all the fighting against Assyria in 720, the request for a repeat performance did not impress. Merodach-Baladan duly made his appeal to Shutruk-nahunte, who accepted his gifts but denied aid. This time around, the odds strongly favored Assyria and there was no incentive to help Merodach-Baladan. The Elamites could afford to await a better opportunity. Rebuffed but undaunted, Merodach-Baladan retreated to the Sealand where he prepared to make a stand at his base, Dur-Iakin.

While his enemy sought help and then refuge, "certain Babylonians, members of the nobility, (and) friends of the king," began agitating to support Sargon. In order to explain their defection, they claimed that the god Marduk had "ordered the son of Iakin (Merodach-Baladan) out of Babylon" in favor of Sargon.[84] Shortly after, key priests of Babylon and Borsippa invited Sargon to enter Babylon and the great temple, Esagil, and grasp the hands of Marduk in the New Year ceremony (akītu) that all legitimate Babylonian kings performed and that was the focus of the Babylonian cultic calendar.[85] The investiture involved a great deal of ritual pomp, including beginning reconstruction of the ruined canal linking Borsippa and Babylon so that Nabu, the main god of Borsippa, could travel in style to Babylon for the annual festivities.[86] The whole expensive enterprise eventually forced Sargon to make huge donations to "all the cult cities of Sumer and Akkad."[87] Nevertheless, that spring the akītu festival provided an important "moment of maximal political symbolism" that inspired others, including the citizens of Nippur, to follow Babylon's example and submit willingly to Sargon.[88]

Despite Babylon's importance, Sargon did not make the city his base of operations. Instead he left it in the hands of a governor, Sharru-emuranni, and chose to stay with the army in Kish.[89] This arrangement had both political and military significance. Sargon's decision to remain with the army was not only safer, but also reassured his men that he was still very much an Assyrian king, whose actions would benefit their homeland. Moreover, in Kish, Sargon could avoid the worst of the local politics and leave Sharru-emuranni to filter the incessant complaints, appeals, demands, and denunciations that came in from Babylonians wishing to profit from the new regime.[90] The Assyrians had by now won at least nominal control over northern Babylonia. However, Sargon could not move south after Merodach-Baladan until he was satisfied that the country would not erupt into violence behind him. So far, his campaign strategy had worked splendidly, and he had made great progress without fighting a costly pitched battle, alienating the Babylonian people, or (probably) sustaining large numbers of casualties. Major military endeavors had been confined to standard devastation operations on the Elamite-Babylonian border, and, as far as we can tell from the sources, Babylonia proper had incurred no significant damage at all. Notwithstanding the many setbacks he had suffered, Merodach-Baladan was by no means ready to quit but continued to seek support among the Aramaean and Chaldean tribes near Bit-Iakin, some of whom, like the Puqudu, had recently submitted to Assyria. If Merodach-Baladan could raise a large enough army, he might yet induce Shutruk-nahunte to offer military aid. According to Sargon's Annals, Merodach-baladan evacuated the towns Bit-Zabidaia, Iqbi-Bel, and Hursaggalli and forced the inhabitants of Ur, Kissik, and Nemed-Laguda to move into Dur-Iakin, where they worked frantically to improve the defenses in anticipation of a siege.[91]

A couple of missives from leaders in the Tubliash River area probably date to this part of the war and reveal Assyria's tenuous hold on the region.[92] In one letter to a high-ranking Assyrian official, the "tribal leaders of Tubliash" declared that "the army should quickly get there! There is talk that people are rising up in great numbers. Persuade the magnates and come in five days' time! You must not lose the land! Come quickly! Come!"[93] Another reported in greater detail:

> Fort Shama'unu is abandoned. There is nobody there except 200 verminous soldiers, and there are no rations there except for the provisions that they carry with them. They have cut off the water between us and the land of Rashu. Nobody from Rashu has c[ome] to you. However, I have spoken with the leaders of [GN], of Dummuqu, and of [GN]. All of them are servant[s of the king, my lord]. They have sent their messages to the king, my lord, with my [messen]ger. It cannot be put off to the future! May the troops reach us quickly, that I can turn the whole country and give it back to the king, my lord . . .
>
> [Abi-i]aqar, the Pu[qu]dean, does not want the well-being of the land in the king's presence; he seeks revenge. The deadline that he set he has (now) changed. Obliging poverty and robbery, he (wants) to take booty for himself. He does not want the clasping of hands . . .
>
> Now the whole country has raised its hand toward the king. May the army come and take its hand! I swear by Bel and Zarpanitu,

Nabu and Marduk, the wise one, that the words which we have sent to the king our lord in this letter are true, out of our heart.[94]

The letters describe widespread unrest in the area and illustrate the fluctuations typical of wartime power struggles. The fort, Shama'unu, which had fallen to Sargon only a few months earlier, could not mount an effective defense, and someone (the identity is unclear) had sabotaged the water supply coming from Rashu. A renegade Puqudean was fomenting insurgency, and only a few tribal leaders struggled to support Assyria. Though the appeals do not explicitly associate Merodach-Baladan with the trouble they report, it stands to reason that he would welcome, or actively encourage, any behavior that diverted attention from him or increased the number of his followers. In any case, the situation in the south demanded Sargon's immediate attention.

The Siege of Dur-Iakin, 709–708 (707)

In Ajaru (April–May) 709, Sargon and his army marched to besiege Dur-Iakin. Sargon met little resistance on his way there, and some places, such as the Iakinite city, Iqbi-Bel, capitulated willingly.[95] Presumably, other southern cities, now largely depopulated, followed suit. In Dur-Iakin, Merodach-baladan prepared for a siege by taking "a measuring rope from its great wall 200 cubits (about 330 feet); he caused a moat to be dug one and a half nindan (about 30 feet) deep and reached ground water. He cut a channel from the Euphrates and flooded its meadows; the flood plain of the city, the battle zone, he filled with water and broke the bridges."[96] The specifications, which claim that Merodach-Baladan's workers moved some three million cubic meters of earth, were included to emphasize the Assyrian achievement in breaching the defenses, rather than to record a mathematical reality.[97] By flooding the fields around the city, Merodach-Baladan hindered, but probably did not wholly prevent, the Assyrians from deploying their chariots or cavalry.[98] Sargon's inscriptions describe the ensuing engagement evocatively:

That one (Merodach-Baladan), together with his auxiliary troops and battle troops, set his lordly tent and prepared his camp in the midst of the canals like pelicans. I sent my warriors over his ditches like eagles and they accomplished his defeat. With the blood of his soldiers they dyed the water of his canals red like red wool. The Suteans, his reinforcements, who turned to his side and came to his aid, together with the Marsane, I slaughtered like sheep and I rained down the poison of death on those remaining people. That one (Merodach-Baladan) left his royal tent, golden throne, golden couch, golden scepter, silver chariot, golden sun-shade and the ornament on his neck inside his camp and fled alone. Like a cat, sneaking along its wall, he entered the city.[99]

According to the Annals, Merodach-Baladan deployed his troops "among the rivers" in front of the main city gate, while the Assyrians responded with standard tactics; they ignored the water and simply built an earthen ramp over the obstacles. When the two forces engaged in battle, the Chaldeans held off the Assyrians until Merodach-Baladan was wounded in the hand by an arrow and retreated into the city (variously, like a cat or a mongoose) to withstand a siege.[100] The Chaldean withdrawal was so well executed that, despite killing large numbers of enemy troops, the Assyrians were not able to force the gate. To draw attention from this fact, Sargon's inscriptions emphasize the Assyrians' rich take in plunder, specifically Merodach-Baladan's royal furniture and accoutrements. In political parlance, the capture of Merodach-Baladan's personal belongings dealt a symbolic blow to his prestige similar to the one Sargon had delivered against Rusa. Still, the cornered Chaldean leader refused to submit.

That Merodach-Baladan believed Dur-Iakin might withstand the Assyrians was not as foolhardy as it might seem. After all, attackers could only sustain a siege for as long as they could supply themselves and maintain fighting effectiveness. Lengthy sieges were always a race against starvation for both sides. Although the Assyrians could transport food down the Euphrates from northern Babylonia as necessary, the flooded area around Dur-Iakin probably made it difficult to procure sufficient quantities of potable water. Furthermore, the stagnant floodwaters not only hindered siege operations but made encampments unhealthy and difficult to construct. The spread of disease and the possibility of sustaining high casualties during an attack also posed significant risks. The opponents had arrived at another stalemate.

Sargon's royal inscriptions are understandably cryptic about what happened next, but it appears that after some months, during which the Assyrians rounded up everyone in the vicinity, cut down Dur-Iakin's date orchards, and kept the Chaldeans bottled up inside, Merodach-Baladan negotiated a surrender. The Annals mockingly avow that "because he (Merodach-Baladan) was afraid, he laid down scepter and throne, and kissed my messenger. When I told him to surrender the large walls and their ramparts and he agreed to my command, I took pity on him."[101] In exchange for the city and the contents of Merodach-Baladan's treasury, Sargon let his enemy go. Even if we accept the outcome related in Sargon's version, the sequence of events is not clear. The Assyrian Eponym Chronicle mentions that the booty of Dur-Iakin was removed and the city destroyed in 707, well over a year after the siege began.[102] Sargon himself remained in Babylonia until the situation was resolved and the country secure. The final result, while not ideal, did permit the Assyrians to complete their takeover of Babylonia.

The compromise that allowed Merodach-Baladan to live in exile in Elam attests to the extreme difficulty of conquering Babylonia. That Sargon had managed the feat without fighting numerous, costly pitched battles or besieging any of the ancient, highly revered cities not only testifies to the effectiveness of his careful preparations but belies the common view that violence and terror were the primary means of Assyrian conquest. Deliberate economy of force in Babylonia allowed Sargon to achieve his objectives there while maintaining a hold on the rest of the empire. Knowing that his army was a limited resource that required careful husbandry, Sargon spent nearly as much effort keeping up the appearance of military invincibility as he did maintaining actual military effectiveness. Given these circumstances, the logical thing for him to do was to stay in Babylonia until the conquest was completed in 707.

ENDGAME, 709–705 B.C.

Ruling Babylonia, 709–707

For the next couple of years (709–707), Sargon consolidated his rule over Babylonia by deporting large portions of the tribal population, rewarding those who had supported him, and encouraging the compliance of the urban dwellers. His pacification program involved the same type of patronage activities that he had used to mollify the Assyrians after he ascended the throne—and indeed that Merodach-Baladan had used to legitimize his own rule.[1] That is, Sargon sought to establish himself as a just, legitimate Babylonian king through highly visible public acts of munificence, including participating in religious rituals, freeing the old regime's political prisoners, settling disputes, and funding public works projects and temples.[2]

After he mounted the throne in Babylon in 709, Sargon sent an official, Bel-iddina (not to be confused with the ruler of Allabria, Bel-apla-iddina), to inspect cult centers around the country, presumably in order to inventory their contents, assess their requirements, and identify those that were politically significant.[3] Subsequently Sargon restored the special privileges (exemption from taxes and corvée duty) to the populations of some of the oldest and most important cult cities, Babylon, Nippur, and Sippar, just as he done for Harran and Ashur at the beginning of his reign.[4] Divine statues that Merodach-Baladan had taken to Dur-Iakin from the cities Ur, Uruk, Nemed-Laguda, Larsa, Eridu, and Kissik were restored to their temples, and funding was renewed as well.[5] It was no accident that many of the temples that Sargon patronized were in cities (Ur, Uruk, Eridu, and Larsa) located in the territory of Bit-Iakin. He was eager to pacify the region without undue military involvement.

In addition to awarding civic privileges and restoring normal temple operations, the Assyrian king made lavish donations to specific sanctuaries, including Esagil, the temple of Marduk in Babylon, to which he gave

154 talents, 26 minas, 10 shekels of red gold, 1,604 talents, 20 minas of polished silver, bronze and iron without number, obsidian, lapis lazuli, agate, precious stones in quantity, purple and crimson cloth, multicolored textiles and linen, boxwood, cedar and cypress, every spice, products of the Amanus mountains, whose scent is sweet, from my first year to my third year I gave as gifts to Bel, Sarpanitum, Nabu, Tashmetum, and the gods who dwell in the cult centers of Sumer and Akkad.[6]

Significantly, in this section of the Display Inscription, Sargon measured his reign not from his accession in Assyria but from the moment he "took the hands of Marduk" in Babylon. According to this reckoning, the "third year" of his rule was 707, not 719. Instead of claiming the title "king of Babylon," he chose the more politic, "viceroy (*šakkanakku*) of Babylon; king of Sumer and Akkad." Implicit in these distinctions was the message that Sargon did not rule as a foreign invader but as the one whom the gods had chosen to be the architect of a new order, and that it was the god, Marduk, who ruled as king of Babylon.[7] The written explanation of such prestige-building acts was pro forma and therefore essential to their reception.

Sargon's texts from this period display a familiar mix of tact—in adopting the title "viceroy of Babylon," for example—and triumphant self-glorification. By appropriating Merodach-Baladan's accomplishments in much the same way that he had undone Rusa's, Sargon emphasized his own superiority and divine mandate. For example, Merodach-Baladan had commemorated his improvements to the Eanna temple in Uruk with an inscription that included the following justification of his accession:

[At that] time, the great lord, the god Marduk, had become angry with the land of Akkad, and the evil enemy, the Subarians (the Assyrians), exercised dominion over Akkad for [. . . until] the days were fulfilled, the time had arrived, (and) the great god Marduk made peace with the land of Akkad, with which he had gotten angry. He looked (favorably) upon Marduk-apla-iddina (Merodach-Baladan), king of Babylon, a prince who venerates him, to whom he (Marduk) extended his hand, true heir, eldest son of Eriba-Marduk, king of Babylon, the one who made firm the foundation of the land. The king of the gods, the god Asarri, duly raised him up [to] the shepherdship of the land of Sumer and Akkad (and) [sa]id from his own mouth: "This is indeed the shepherd, the one who will gather the scattered (people)."[8]

Explaining away Tiglath-pileser's Babylonian rule as the result of Marduk's wrath, Merodach-Baladan then claimed that his own accession fulfilled the gods' will. When the Assyrians found Merodach-Baladan's inscription (presumably as they renovated the temple), Sargon sent it to Calah for his scribes to use as a model for his own Eanna text. The text that the Assyrians scribes produced actually plagiarized parts of Merodach-Baladan's, though it prudently omitted overt reference to recent events or Assyrian gods such as Ashur.[9]

Like his former rival, Sargon offered a divine explanation for his assumption of the Babylonian throne. When writing for an Assyrian audience in the Annals, he presented himself as the liberator of Babylonia, divinely appointed to reestablish the natural order of things. Sargon justified himself using the same religious rationale that Merodach-Baladan had presented:

> For twelve years, against the will of the gods, he (Merodach-Baladan) ruled and administered Babylon, the city of Enlil, lord of the gods. Then Marduk, the great lord, saw the evil enterprises of the land of Chaldea, which he hated, and the (order) was on his lips that his royal scepter, throne, and kingship be taken away. Me, Sargon, the reverent king, he chose from among all kings and exalted me. In order to turn back the feet of the hostile and evil Chaldeans from the land of Sumer and Akkad, he made my weapons mighty.[10]

Divine selection was a common trope in the royal inscriptions of both Assyria and Babylonia—as was its inverse, divine abandonment.[11] Following centuries-old practice, royal scribes manipulated the narrative to make it compatible with Babylonian and Assyrian ideologies and to align mundane events with their understanding of the cosmic hierarchy. This type of rationalization was fundamental to the exercise of kingship in Assyria and Babylonia, and most kings, especially those who achieved power in an irregular fashion, sought to legitimate themselves by such means. Indeed, throughout the Near East, kings justified themselves through retrospective reasoning and by citing divine abandonment whenever they failed.[12]

In addition to maintaining Babylonian temples and rebuilding Babylon's city walls, Sargon went to unprecedented lengths to win over the urban population by restoring order and prosperity to the cities at the expense of the Aramaean and Chaldean tribes.[13] After the fall of Dur-Iakin, Sargon deported large portions of the tribal population, while he re-civilized areas in the northwest that had been abandoned to wild animals and bandits. He put a stop to Arab raids against Sippar.[14] He also freed political prisoners held in Dur-Iakin, returning them to their homes in Sippar, Nippur, Babylon, and Borsippa and restoring the lands that Sutean tribesmen had allegedly taken from them.[15] How well these political acts succeeded in winning over the Babylonians is difficult to determine, since we know little about the next years of Assyrian rule there. But in view of the deliberate restraint Sargon exercised in taking over the region, it is likely that he continued to rely on diplomacy and persuasion backed by solid intelligence and the threat of force. There is no evidence of armed resistance or punitive action in Babylonia for the remainder of Sargon's reign, though some tribes, such as Bit-Amukani, proved uncooperative. One officer wrote to the king exhorting him to "send a tablet to Sharru-emuranni: let him gather the whole of Bit-Amukani and say this to them: 'why do you not listen to [N] asib-il about the [ki]ng's work?' [H]e told me that the men [do not] listen to him."[16] Lingering difficulties notwithstanding, Babylonia was firmly in Assyrian hands again; careful planning had paid off and the ideological prerequisites had been met.

Although Sargon attended diligently to the symbolic aspects of Babylonian rule, this did not replace practical military planning. Over the next few years, Sargon fortified the route through the Elamite-Babylonian border and improved the region's infrastructure in order to neutralize the threat from Shutruk-nahunte and Merodach-Baladan. Deportees from Kummuh (taken during a campaign in 707) settled undeveloped land on the border, while Sargon chose an official, Nabu-damiq-ilani, to "build a fort in the city Sagbat on the border of Elam in order to repel the Elamite enemy."[17] Babylonia was divided into two new Assyrian provinces: Babylon, including other important cities, and Gambulu, which encompassed the tribal areas. Word of what had transpired in Babylonia spread, and according to the Annals, "Uperi, the ruler of Dilmun (Bahrain), like a fish whose lair is located 30 double-hours (away) in the midst of the Sunrise Sea (Persian Gulf), heard of my great might and sent audience gifts."[18] As anticipated, the conquest of Babylonia brought the Persian Gulf trade via Dilmun as well as the overland Arab trade under Assyrian sway. In effect, Sargon established an Assyrian monopoly on Near Eastern trade, the only exception being the most northerly, roundabout, and difficult route through eastern Iran, northern Urartu, and along the south coast of the Black Sea. Naturally, Assyria's enemies could not sit idly by while their economies suffered.

Midas of Phrygia Seeks Peace, 709–708

Both allies and enemies continued their political machinations while Sargon handled the situation in Babylonia, and several important developments occurred around the empire during this period. As with other material we have encountered, different dating schemes are possible here. Hence, in what follows, the chronological arrangement of the letters remains provisional.

In 709–708 an unexpected peace overture from Midas transformed the relationship between Assyria and Phrygia. When a Phrygian delegation presented itself to Ashur-sharru-uṣur, the governor of Quwê, he immediately sought instructions from Sargon, who responded to each query point by point:

> The word of the king to Ashur-sharru-uṣur: I am well, Assyria is well; you may be glad.
>
> Concerning what you wrote me: "A messenger [of] Midas, the Phrygian, has come before me, bringing me 14 men from Quwê, whom Urikki caused to be sent to Urartu as envoys." This is extremely good! My gods Ashur, Shamash, Bel and Nabu have now acted, and [wi]thout a battle [or any]thing, the Phrygian has given us his word and made peace!
>
> Concerning what you wrote: "I will not send my messenger to the Phrygian without the king, my lord's (order)—Now, today, I am writing to you that you should not keep your messenger from the Phrygian's presence. Write kind words to him and constantly listen to whatever news is about him, until I have free time!
>
> Concerning what you wrote: "Should I send his servants to him just as he sent me the servants of the king, my lord?"—send them to him soon so his heart will relent towards us. Whether 100 of his men or 10, write to him like this: "I wrote to the king, my lord, about the men of Quwê whom you sent to me, and he became extremely joyful; and in return he wrote to me thus: 'Do not hold back even one of the Phrygians in your presence, but send them to Midas [immediately].' "Thus at the king, my lord's, command I am sending you th[ese] men."

So far in his response to the governor, Sargon had expressed pleasure at Midas's unexpected overture and urged Ashur-sharru-uṣur to send an envoy to the Phrygian king and to proceed with a prisoner exchange regardless of the number of men involved. What Sargon did not clarify was the status of the Phrygians in Quwê—whether they were prisoners of war, fugitives, or hostages. As for how the governor should deal with the Tabalian rulers involved in these complex negotiations, Sargon ordered the following:

> Concerning what you wrote: "Urpala'a's messenger came with the Phrygian messenger to greet me—let him come, and let the gods Ashur, Shamash, Bel and Nabu command that all these kings wipe your sandals with their beards!"
>
> [section omitted]
>
> Concerning what you wrote: "Urpala'a [. . .] from the king, my lord, because the Atunneans and the Istuandeans came and stole the cities of Bit-Purutash away from him"—now that the Phrygian has made peace with us and [. . .] what can all the kings of Tabal do anymore? You will pressure them from this side and the Phrygian from that side so that (soon) you will immobilize them. On account of my gods Ashur, Shamash, Bel and Nabu, you are now treading this land under your feet. Mill about as you wish, do whatever work you have, "cut the long and lengthen the short" until I come and give you [. . .] work![19]

Eager to take advantage of the situation, Sargon ordered Ashur-sharru-uuṣur to do whatever necessary to secure results. The archived tablet was incomplete, which could mean either that the original was never sent due to changing circumstances or the copyist accidentally filed an unfinished copy. In either case, the letter implies that Midas was willing to enter into a détente with Assyria at the expense of Urartu, the Tabalian kingdoms, and Urikki's plans to gain Quwê's independence from Assyria. As a mark of good faith, the Phrygians turned over to Assyria the men whom Urikki treasonably sent on a diplomatic mission to Urartu. How the Phrygians intercepted that delegation is not explained, nor is the presence in the same embassy of a messenger from Urpala'a, the ruler of Tuhana and an Assyrian client. Presumably the Tabalian rulers maintained diplomatic relations with numerous outside powers, despite Assyrian claims to sovereignty over them. When Midas decided to make peace, Urpala'a realized that he had better contact Sargon, who did not appear surprised or bothered by his client's participation in the embassy. On the contrary, the king realized that the Tabalian rulers had been effectively neutralized. The fact that Sargon actually told Ashur-sharru-uṣur how to word his message to Midas is indicative of the care with which the Assyrian king approached foreign relations. In particularly delicate diplomatic matters, he did not allow his governors much initiative.

The reason for Midas's volte-face with respect to Assyria has been much debated. Sargon's Annals claim that after "the governor of Quwê plundered three times in Midas's territory, easy terrain with chariots and over hard terrain on foot," Midas decided to make peace.[20] Although earlier Assyrian raids could have influenced the Phrygian king, it is likely that other factors played a role as well.[21] We know, for example, that, at roughly the same time that Midas made peace with Assyria (709–708), Shilta, the king of Tyre, called upon his Assyrian allies to help him maintain control over part of Cyprus. In response, Sargon sent a "eunuch who is brave in battle" (probably the turtān) to deal with the problem. In short order, "seven kings of the land Iadnana (Cyprus)" not only submitted once again to their Tyrian overlord but sent an embassy laden with audience gifts to Sargon in Babylonia. Within a year, Sargon had erected a stele on Cyprus as visible proof that his reach surpassed that of his forefathers.[22] Midas is not mentioned in connection with these events. However, since the Assyrian-Tyrian alliance had interfered with Phrygian commercial interests in the Mediterranean for years, it stands to reason that events concerning Cyprus had had an impact on Phrygia. In any case, for Sargon, peace with Phrygia was worth celebrating: Phrygian and Urartian imperial ambitions in the Anti-Taurus had been thwarted, and without those states to turn to for support, the fractious Tabalian kingdoms had no choice but to submit.

Assyria, Urartu, and the Northern Buffer States, 709–707

On the downside, the new accord with Phrygia fed the cold war enmity between Assyria and Urartu and led to an escalation of threats and armed incidents that kept Assyria's northern frontier provinces on perpetual alert. As a result, the focus of competing interests shifted to northern buffer states such as Shubria. Located in the mountains between the Assyrian provinces, Amedi and Tushan, and the Urartian territories on the Murat River, Shubria managed to retain its independence due to its rugged terrain, its status as a religious sanctuary, and its presumed role as a neutral buffer between the two powers.[23] Shubrian kings became adept at playing the greater powers against each other, sometimes acquiescing to and sometimes defying their incessant demands. Hu-teshub, the Shubrian ruler during Sargon's reign, proved to be both wily and aggravatingly independent. Although he occasionally sent intelligence reports about the Urartians to the Assyrians, as any dutiful client would, he was no Assyrian puppet.[24] Nor would he submit meekly to Urartu. At one point, Hu-teshub so provoked Argishti that the Urartian king demanded the return of the jewelry he and his father had given to the Shubrian in gift exchange.[25] Throughout this period, Hu-teshub remained (to no one's surprise) unapologetically self-serving.

Several incidents involving Shubria reported in the Assyrian correspondence reveal that logging and the hunt for deserters were particularly sensitive issues, ones that heightened the possibility of open war, though the Assyrians, at least, took pains to avoid that outcome. Deserters from the Assyrian army, criminals fleeing prosecution, and unwilling deportees frequently sought refuge in Shubria or Urartu, where they could barter information for asylum.[26] The Urartians experienced the same situation in reverse. Hence, the kings of both countries were eager to recapture fugitives even as they welcomed refugees from the enemy. Despite external pressure, Hu-teshub often granted sanctuary and refused to surrender refugees.

A letter to Sargon from Sha-Ashur-dubbu, the governor of Tushan, reported how the attempted recovery of deserters nearly caused an international incident:

> I sent two of my eunuchs and six soldiers with a seal[ed tablet] in hand for the fugitives in Penza; they went with two cohort commanders and had the men brought down. They ate bread inside; the brother of the Shubrian (Hu-teshub) ate bread with them there. They left together and were going home, when the Shubrians set upon them from an ambush and captured my two eunuchs and the six soldiers. My two cohort commanders escaped.
>
> I wrote him (Hu-teshub), saying: "Release the troops!" He said, "I will ask around. [I]f they are in my country, I shall give them back."

I [se]t out on their trail in person, but they had caused the soldiers to go up to his fort. May the king, my lord, send word that the officers of the royal Taziru and Itu'u (troops) stationed here should come and stand guard with me until those logs are brought out. The king, my lord, knows that my men are doing [wor]k [in] Dur-Sharrukin and only cavalrymen stand with me.[27]

In this case, the governor sent a handful of men to accompany his representatives because he assumed the mission involved a standard extradition from a friendly kingdom. However, the Shubrians had plans of their own. After handing over the prisoners and dining with the Assyrians, they ambushed the group on its way home. Only two officers escaped capture. When Sha-Ashur-dubbu protested, Hu-teshub pretended to know nothing about what had transpired and blithely promised to investigate. Circumstances supported Hu-teshub's obvious equivocation, since he had neither been present at the banquet nor met the Assyrian delegation. Too shorthanded for retaliatory action, Sha-Ashur-dubbu asked Sargon for permission to muster the Itu'eans and Taziru auxiliaries who lived in the area "at the ready." In order to avoid escalation, Sargon instructed him to "se[ize] his (Hu-teshub's) men in eq[ual number] to your men, [until] he releases [them]."[28] Since Sha-Ashur-dubbu could not field a large force and the Assyrians did not want hostilities to escalate into war, Sargon tried to force a prisoner exchange instead. In this case, the outcome is not known, though Hu-teshub continued his conniving undaunted.

At about the same time, Sha-Ashur-dubbu discovered that Hu-teshub had prevented Urartian fugitives from reaching Assyria, settling them in Shubria instead. When confronted, Hu-teshub replied that he had acted because he was "god-fearing." The subsequent extradition of a runaway Urartian mule driver to Urartu revealed Hu-teshub's hypocrisy and prompted the Assyrian governor to write accusingly, "Why are you not fearful of the gods, *abati*, foal of the Urart[ian]!?" Caught in an embarrassing lie, Hu-teshub wrote appeasingly to Sha-Ashur-dubbu, promising to return his men (presumably Assyrian fugitives or those captured earlier).[29] Although Shubria claimed the status of religious sanctuary during this period, and its king was, in theory, morally bound to protect those seeking shelter, Hu-teshub brazenly exploited the situation for his own benefit. Self-interest, however rationalized, trumped everything, even the demands of religion.

Despite the ongoing diplomatic chicanery, the Assyrians still risked logging operations in Urartian territory, as Sha-Ashur-dubbu reported to Sargon:

> Concerning what [I wrote] to the king, my lord: "They have [. . .] 500 logs [in the territory] of the Urartian"—[now] my "third man," who [. . .], has cut them and piled them up a[long the river]. As so[on as] he has completed [the work], he will set [out] and muster the troops. I can spare 100 men to enter (Urartian territory) and throw the beams in the river; the rest I will ba[se] in the[ir] garrisons and outposts. Perhaps there will be some kind of rebellion; I am strengthening the guard—I am afraid of a rebellion.[30]

Though no follow-up report has survived, Sha-Ashur-dubbu's letter is indicative of Assyrian activities on the frontier. The understandably anxious Assyrian governor was in a difficult position. In order to fulfill his quota of logs for the Assyrian heartland, he had been forced to send men into Urartian territory, risking them and the détente between the two states. Perennially short-handed, he could only spare one hundred men to launch the logs downstream, while he deployed the rest of his troops closer to home in anticipation of a Urartian attack or a (Urartian/Shubrian-incited) rebellion among the local populace. Although good intelligence helped him stay ahead of the opposition, his manpower shortage made him vulnerable. The Urartians were poised to incite disgruntled Assyrian subjects here as elsewhere.

The Assyrian client state, Kumme, offers a case in point. Here Ashur-resua coordinated Assyrian intelligence operations and kept an eye on the local ruler. In spite of this Assyrian presence (and because of it), the people became angry over deportations, tribute demands, and corvée duties and plotted to kill both their ruler and the Assyrian delegate.[31] Seizing the opportunity to undermine the Assyrians, the Urartian king tried to win over the disaffected parties. A fragmentary Assyrian intelligence report quotes a message from Argishti to the Kummeans in which he initially complained: "[Ever s]ince [I ha]ve occupied the throne, there has not really been a greeting you have sent to me; (everybody) comes to me [on acco]unt of Ashur and your gods." Here Argishti is making a pointed reference to the protocol that required the rulers of buffer states to maintain diplomatic relations with opposition kings. Since the Kummeans' failure to do this gave Argishti a pretext to attack, which he did not intend to do, he simply assured the Kummeans that "I have heard that you became afr[aid]. Why did you get scar[ed]? Even Rusa did not speak about destroying [your country. Nor have I] spoken about it." The Kummeans' answer, reported in the same letter, was non-committal: "Since we are the servants [of Assyria], a cavalry officer is ahead [of us]. The houses of Kumme are left to us . . . we do not have the ability to put our feet anywhere."[32] Despite the Kummeans' obvious discontent with Assyria, Argishti's effort to provoke trouble did not work because effective intelligence allowed Ashur-reṣua to identify the four agents provocateurs who were "inciting the country" and to recommend: "let them eat [foo]d and drink water; when the ti[me is right] let them be removed."[33] As usual, Sargon kept abreast of events, but because he and the army were preoccupied in Babylonia, he simply sent a "sealed order" to be read aloud to Kummean officials. They responded submissively: "The king, our lord, is the lord of everything—what can we say?"[34] After this exchange, Kumme drops out of the Assyrian correspondence. So far, it has not been possible to ascertain the outcome of the crisis or the city-state's status during the next several decades.

Incomplete evidence notwithstanding, these reports about international relations in the north reveal a great deal about the Assyrian intelligence corps and military operations. Provincial troops were spread thin; frontier governors could not muster forces large enough to fend off a determined invasion. Instead they relied on fortified choke points and small contingents of soldiers to raid, lay ambushes, and carry out espionage. These same troops (possibly supplemented by conscripted locals) also made up work details to cut wood and acquire other resources. In other words, on the imperial periphery, where soldiers were dispersed among forts, the military played an auxiliary but vital role as laborers and as a tool in the service of imperial politics. Without excellent communication and intelligence, the Assyrians could neither acquire the resources they needed nor defend their territory. Ultimately, however, what really maintained border security was the enemy's belief that invasion would attract the full force of the Assyrian army.

Clearly, Sargon did not want to campaign in the north. Still, it was important that the Assyrians appear strong there in order to impress his new friend Midas, his enemy Argishti, and the unpredictable northern buffer kings. Consequently, in 707, Sargon sent his "eunuchs along with their vast troops and the main troops of my royal army" against Muttallu of Kummuh, on the standard pre-text that Muttallu had withheld tribute from Assyria.[35] According to the Annals, rather than face the Assyrians, Muttallu abandoned his entire family and fled to the mountains "never to be seen again." The subsequent punitive campaign followed the usual pattern: the Assyrian magnates seized Melid, the capital city, plundered it, and presented the royal family and massive amounts of booty to Sargon, who had by then left Babylon and returned to Assyria. Since the annexation of Kummuh put Assyrian troops in close proximity to Urartu, Sargon appointed a new military official, the "field marshal of the left" (turtān šumeli), to govern the area. For defensive pur-poses, he also provided the new appointee with an unprecedented number of troops: 150 chariots, 1,500 cavalry, 20,000 bowmen, and 10,000 shield-bearers and lancers.[36] The Assyrians settled the new province with people deported from Bit-Iakin, which had by now been thoroughly subdued. The purpose of this campaign was to strengthen Assyria's hold on the north and dissuade the Urartians from further interference in Assyrian interests there.

Civil War in Ellipi, 708–707

While Sargon was still in the throes of the Babylonian campaign and as events on the northern periphery simmered, a new problem emerged. His long-time client, Daltâ, the ruler of Ellipi, died, leav-ing two nephews and at least one son to struggle for the throne. Initially the contest involved the two nephews, Nibê and Ashpa-bara. Similar in organization to the other Zagros polities, Ellipi was ruled by a king or chief, to whom the city lords in the area owed allegiance through blood ties, social obligation, and political neces-sity. A buffer between Elam and the Assyrian provinces along the Khorasan Road and on the Diyala River, Ellipi was of great strategic importance. What complicates matters here is that Daltâ died late in 708, just around the time Sargon appointed Mannu-ki-Ninua to succeed Nabu-belu-ka"in as governor of Kar-Sharrukin (Harhar and the surrounding area).[37] A priority for the new governor was to reaf-firm client ties with all the city lords in his territory by traveling among them to oversee new oath-taking ceremonies. Until Mannu-ki-Ninua established his authority as the king's representative to the local headmen, Assyria's hold over the mid-Zagros was in jeopardy.

Given the developing situation in Ellipi and Assyria's military involvement in Babylonia and the northern provinces, it was imperative that Mannu-ki-Ninua manage the changeover without having to undertake military operations. Several letters from the royal archives attest to Assyrian diplomatic efforts in the province of Kar-Sharrukin. Just after Daltâ's death, for example, Sargon instructed Mannu-ki-Ninua to "speak kindly" to the city lords under him and treat them justly.[38] In another text, Mannu-ki-Ninua reported on his relations with various city lords:

> [Concerning the Zabg]agaeans about whom the king, my lord, wrote to me: "Ask about and watch when they come in and go out, and write to me!" They have now returned from the house of Daltâ (king of Ellipi) . . . And when I went and established a treaty with the Kulumaneans, and made peace with them, they too (the Zabgagaeans) [mad]e peace with them. They approached me about Zabgaga, saying: "Return our ci[ty lord] and [ins]tall him ove[r us]" I [. . . a]s the king, my lord, [had wr]itten to me: [. . .] *broken section* [. . .] I told them [. . .]
>
> For the sake of peace, they should not stop the[ir] messengers [. . . I dres]sed them in robes, put silver bracelets [on their wrists and] sa[id to them]: "[Just] as [you] previo[usly stoo]d by Nabu-belu-ka"[in, found out wha]tever news there was, and [tol]d it to him, [stan]d [like] this with me and send me whatever news [of th]e Medes you hear. I shall watch over you just as Nabu-belu-ka"in watched over you and I shall say a good word about you before the king, my lord."
>
> And they spoke to me thus: "The king ordered us to stand with the governor of [Kar-Sharrukin], so we shall now stand [with you] . . ."
>
> They also said: "As for you, come with your [. . .] and estab[lish] the treaty with us at the head of the city, Satarnu. We have made peace." [Now] then I am speaking kind words [to] them until the king, my lord writes whatever (he wants me to do).[39]

Here a local clan begged for the return of their leader, whom the Assyrians held hostage. Mannu-ki-Ninua responded in a soothing manner and pacified the area through diplomacy. By bestowing robes and jewelry as symbols of Assyrian respect and patronage, the governor followed standard diplomatic procedure. In return, the city lords were also obliged to provide labor for work details, men for military duty, and relevant news.

The Assyrians also encouraged the acquiescence of local elites by undertaking major construction at Kar-Sharrukin, which facilitated trade, created work, and rendered the city suitably impressive.[40] The benign policy evinced in reports from this province stands in stark contrast to the earlier Assyrian conquest in 716. By invading with "shock and awe" tactics, the Assyrians eventually acquired the leverage to govern by peaceful means, which they understood would earn better long-term results than force alone. At this juncture, in particular, it was desirable that Sargon maintain his grip on the central Zagros without having to campaign there. In fact, Mannu-ki-Ninua's reports regularly reassure that "all the garrisons of the king, my lord, are well, and all the city lords around me have inquired about the health of the Palace," thus fulfilling the prerequisites of clientship.[41] As a result of sound policy, late in Sargon's reign, Assyrian campaigns in western Media amounted to armed (show-of-force) tribute collection without recourse to actual fighting.

However, even though Mannu-ki-Ninua acquitted his duties successfully, it became clear that conflict in Ellipi would require an active response. In seeking the throne, Nibê procured Elamite support, which consequently drove Ashpa-bara to the Assyrian side. Thus, a small polity's internal power struggle became a proxy war between Assyria and Elam in the same way that the earlier succession struggle in Mannea had pitted the Urartians and Assyrians against one another. Opting out of the endeavor, Sargon sent seven of his magnates—governors from the Assyrian heartland and the eastern provinces—to support Ashpa-bara.[42] The king was evidently anxious about entrusting the campaign to others for he commanded them: "Do not neglect your guard; [you] must be intensely [on your guard]! . . . Let the speciali[sts] tell [the oracles] to you; Ashur and my gods [will go before you]!"[43] The Assyrian army mustered in a well-defended position in the province of Namri, south of Zamua and just north of Ellipi. A letter from one of the magnates (or the king) included the rationale for choosing this location:

[. . .] "come wi[th your troops and camp in the pass] of Ura[mmu]."
    [I am writing to you] now this word, the [location], is extremely good. You [know] that this pass [leading to] the city Urammu is [ver]y difficult [. . .]; there is no possible way at all that the Elamite [army] will be able to come at you. Don't be concerned; at the city of Urammu where you are to set up camp there is steppe

that is [very] good for camping; it is also [very] good for making
forays, there is [a lot of] grass there, and it is a [bounteo]us resting
place [. . .].[44]

The site met military requirements perfectly. It was spacious, within
easy reach of the area of operations, well-defended, and offered ample
pasturage for horses and pack animals—just what one would expect
from seasoned military leaders.

Inevitably, the civil war became complicated when the Ellipian
city lords, who saw in the situation an opportunity to improve
their own positions, became involved. Hoping to gain the advantage, they took risks willingly and switched sides whenever politic.
The Assyrians, who had plenty of experience with fickle local elites,
made efforts to secure the support of the most powerful among them.
Of particular interest was Kibabashe, ruler of Bit-Barrû, whose territory lay near Kar-Sharrukin.[45] According to one dispatch, "Ashur-
resh-ishi the royal bodyguard [has met with the chiefs] of Bit-Barrû;
they ate bread together, and he [. . .] [lifted] a cup in the presence
of Ki[babashe]."[46] The shared meal was a standard part of the diplomatic process, though it did not always achieve the desired goal,
as the earlier incident in Shubria attests.[47] In this case, Kibabashe
or some other city lord quickly became a turncoat, prompting the
king to order: "If this traitor [. . .] comes to you in person or sends
his messenger [to you, he m]ay not enter; speak to him outside the
camp."[48] The miscreant (whatever his identity) could not be allowed
inside the Assyrian camp lest he divulge the army's strength and the
disposition of the troops.

Aside from one or two brief comments, the surviving correspondence includes no further details about the magnates' movements or
their conduct of the campaign, although several intelligence briefs
indicate that the Assyrians were especially concerned about keeping track of the king of Elam.[49] Writing to Sargon from Der, one
official reported Shutruk-nahunte's movements: "He entered Bit-
Bunakka on the 11th of Tammuz, went out on the 13th, and went
up to the mountain. [My] messenger [has written to me] thus: "A
town called Burati, (one of) his forts outside the 'house of Daltâ'
(Ellipi), has become hostile to him. He is going inside, and will
either make peace with it or bring them down in battle. From there
he will go to Ellipi on account of the s[on of Dalt]â."[50] Shortly afterward, another official wrote to his superior, the governor of Der,

with news that Shutruk-nahunte was mobilizing "the spearhead of his chariotry" in Bit-Bunakka (in the mountains about seventy-five miles east of Der).[51] Fearing that the Elamites might attack Der, the Assyrian administration prepared to defend itself. The correspondence does not preserve what happened next, although the Annals claim that the magnates put to flight the Ellipians and 4,500 Elamite bowmen. After the enemy forces took refuge in the Ellipian city of Maribishtu, a fortress located "on top of a massive mountain that rises to the realm of the clouds," the Assyrians starved them out in a brief siege ("shut them up like a bird in a cage") and took the survivors to Sargon.[52] Ashpa-bara ascended the throne, and Lutû, the son of Daltâ, took a subordinate position.[53] The Assyrians garrisoned Maribishtu, improved its defenses, and attached some Ellipian border territory to Assyrian provinces such as Sangibutu. Despite these arrangements, strife in Ellipi had not been resolved, and by the spring of 706 more city lords had become restive, and Ashpa-bara was fighting with Lutû.

The ensuing struggles, which mirrored the petty squabbles and byzantine politics seen among other buffer states, were by now exceedingly familiar to the Assyrians, who handled the situation with characteristic aplomb. Knowing full well that Assyrian spies were reporting their every move, the scheming local rulers prevaricated as a matter of course. Marduk-sharru-uṣur, the Assyrian governor of Sangibutu, reported:

> [Ashpa-ba]ra [has t]old Kibabashe and Dasukku: "The king gave Ellipi to me and I enjoy it. He gave Sangibutu to Marduk-sharru-uṣur. Your towns have been taken away. If you (want to) make battle, do. Otherwise, leave. I am not involved in it." He spoke thus before the people of the country. Now Kibabashe and Dasukku are constantly moving around opposite [me] with a hundred cavalrymen. The king, [my] lord, [knows] that their [cavalrymen] are (only) twenty: [x of them] are Lutû's and the rest [of the cavalrymen are] Ashpa-bara's. They do not openly show [that] they are run[ning around] with them.[54]

Although Ashpa-bara publically proclaimed his neutrality, both he and the supposedly pro-Assyrian Lutû privately lent their own cavalry to the offending city lords. Kibabashe and Dasukku did not pose a serious threat, but their actions signaled the Ellipian elites' anger over the way the war had been resolved initially, while also exposing

Ashpa-bara's and Lutû's duplicity. The Assyrians apparently chose to ignore these events, although the accurate information they gained helped them gauge the likelihood of future disruptions.

In fact, the incident presaged a rupture between the erstwhile allies, Ashpa-bara and Lutû. Soon after, Mannu-ki-Ninua reported, "As to the news of Lutû, he and Ashpa-bara are engaged in battle against each other in Hadalpa and killing each other's men."[55] In order to gain control of the deteriorating situation, Sargon had Lutû's son kidnapped and then ordered Mannu-ki-Ninua to "go meet Sharru-emuranni. He will entrust you the son of Lutû. No human being must see him until you have brought him into Kar-Sharrukin."[56] The clandestine operation went off exactly as planned. The transfer took place in a remote mountain pass, and the son became the pawn by which Mannu-ki-Ninua brought the recalcitrant father to heel.[57] In this case, diplomacy and nonviolent coercion achieved success, and while nothing is known about the fate of Lutû and his son, Ashpa-bara remained a client until he attempted (unsuccessfully) to establish independence from Assyria early in the reign of Sargon's successor, Sennacherib.[58]

Celebrations in Dur-Sharrukin, 706

The final war recorded in Sargon's inscriptions, the magnates' campaign to Ellipi, took place in 707, the same year that the king returned to Assyria from Babylonia, a plague swept through Assyria (a decidedly inauspicious event), and "the gods of Dur-Sharrukin entered their temples."[59] The temple investiture occurred on the twenty-second day of Tishri (September–October), just a couple of weeks after Marduk-sharru-usur reported on the nefarious activities of Kibabashe and Dasukku.[60] About six months later, on the sixth day of Iyyar (April) 706, Sargon inaugurated the investiture of his capital by hosting a huge gathering of rulers and elites from all over the empire. The occasion commemorated one of Sargon's greatest achievements, and he did not stint on the celebrations. The Annals describe the festivities:

> I invited Ashur, the father of the gods, the great lord, (and all) the great gods who dwell in Assyria inside (my palace). I presented them with . . . gifts without number, and offered pure sacrifices, given out of (my) heart's desire, before them. Sitting down in my

palace together with rulers from the four quarters (of the world),
with the governors of my land, with the princes, the eunuchs, and
the elders of Assyria, I celebrated a feast and accepted from the rulers of east and west valuable masterpieces made from gold, silver,
(and) all kinds of precious things befitting those palaces.[61]

Assyria had not recorded a group of such dignitaries gathered in
one place since Ashurnaṣirpal II celebrated the expansion of Calah
back in the ninth century, and grand though that had been, it did
not match Sargon's accomplishment. Calah was ancient when
Ashurnaṣirpal revived it, whereas Sargon built an entire, magnificent city replete with palaces, fortifications, and temples where
earlier there had been only farmland and a village so poor as to be
hardly worth mentioning. Unlike previous kings, Sargon claimed to
be the intellectual source of the project. His own ideas and planning
brought it to fruition, never mind the contributions of the magnates,
governors, and thousands of workers.[62]

The city was truly impressive. Supported by towered bastions
at fifty-foot intervals, fortification walls measured over forty-six
feet thick and sixty-five feet high and enclosed an area of about
1.2 square miles (three square kilometers), making Dur-Sharrukin
"one of the largest cities in antiquity," even larger than "such
ancient metropoles as Athens, Jerusalem and Susa."[63] The citadel,
which boasted the royal palace, four smaller mansions, temples,
and a 165-foot-high ziggurat, was built on a high platform that jut-
ted out beyond the city wall so as to astonish approaching travelers with its splendor. The palace alone covered almost twenty-five
acres. Massive *lamassu* and *šēdu* (winged bulls and hybrid bull-ge-
nie figures), the largest weighing about thirty tons and reaching a
height of nineteen feet, guarded the doorways to the great courts
and reception rooms.[64] Sculptured reliefs depicting military campaigns, hunts, and tribute delivery covered the walls in the main
reception rooms and hallways. The door colossi, stone thresholds,
and the fronts and backs of wall slabs, had summary or annalis-
tic accounts of the king's deeds inscribed on them.[65] Other rooms
sported colorful painted decoration or glazed tiles, and the most
prominent of the huge wooden doors bore metal bands with narrative scenes etched and hammered in repoussé. The decoration
depicted every corner of the empire and transformed the palace
(with the throne room at its heart) into a microcosm of the whole.[66]

Imperial ideology informed not only the citadel but the entire site and its verdant hinterland.

Sargon was especially proud of his exotic *bit ḫilāni*, a building with a portico fashioned on a Hittite model, which he describes lovingly: "Eight pairs of lion colossi, each weighing 4,610 talents of shining bronze, which had been cast with Ninagal's skill and were full of brilliance; four tall cedar columns, whose thickness was twelve cubits each, the products of Mount Amanus, I sat upon the lion bases and I set wooden beams as the crown of its doorways."[67] To carry the message of his mastery over the Hittite lands (Syria and central Anatolia) further, Sargon planted a large royal pleasure park with trees from the Amanus Mountains and filled it with birds and animals that he and his magnates could hunt for sport. A canal augmented the area's natural watercourses, and together these secured sufficient irrigation for orchards, fields, and the royal park. Deportees, who built Dur-Sharrukin, settled the lower city, which archaeologists have yet to explore thoroughly. The richest home-owners occupied the area closest to the citadel, while the majority lived in densely packed, small mud-brick houses that lined the narrow streets of the lower town. Excavation has not been sufficient to delineate the city's craft and merchant districts, assuming that they were established there as in other Assyrian cities. Even the new inhabitants fulfilled an ideological purpose, as Sargon claimed to have brought together people from around his empire, made them speak one language (Assyrian), and taught them "to fear god and king."[68] Since the Assyrian king represented civilized order, people thought it natural that he should have a civilizing influence on new subjects.

In planning his capital, Sargon did not neglect his army. Straddling the city's southwest wall on another raised platform lay the review palace (*ekāl māšarti*), where the army maintained its equipment and mustered for campaign, and where the king stored tribute, booty, and military paraphernalia. Though the basic layout was typically palatial, the review palace's utilitarian purpose obviated the need for the type of elaborate decoration found in Sargon's palace. Yet, even here, apotropaic colossi guarded the main doors, and a few of the most important rooms sported colorful glazed brick tiles.[69] In fact, if the review palace ever fulfilled its purpose, it probably did so only once, for the muster of Sargon's last campaign to Tabal in 705.

Death and Defeat: The Final Campaign, 705

During the summer following celebrations at Dur-Sharrukin, the magnates campaigned in Karalla. A terse entry in the Eponym Chronicle—"the magnates to Karalla"—is the only record of the operation, which probably amounted to a routine tribute collection and "trooping of the colors," in any case.[70] Sargon stayed at home. By 705 he must have been approaching sixty, and he had not campaigned with the army since the reconquest of Babylonia. In two inscriptions found at Dur-Sharrukin, Sargon declared that "the gods who dwell in heaven and earth, and also in this city, were pleased with my command and therefore granted me for all times the privilege of building this city and growing old in it."[71] Having achieved all of his objectives, the king seemed ready to rule in peace from his magnificent capital. Yet despite the contented tenor of his inscriptions, Sargon left Dur-Sharrukin a few months later to lead the army to distant Tabal one more time.

Did the mundane routine of governance bore Sargon? Did he miss the excitement of campaigning? Did his magnates begin to grumble about the aging king's inaction? Was the crown prince becoming restless? Or was the campaign business as usual? We will probably never know what motivated the king to take the field again or what transpired on campaign. Only terse chronicle entries and a political-literary text, The Sin of Sargon, written years after the fact, testify to events. The Eponym Chronicle reports that "in the eponymy of Nashur-Bel (705) the king [marched] against Gurdi the Kulummaean; the king was killed; the camp of the king of Assyria was pl[undered]; on the 12th of Ab (late July), Sennacherib [became] king."[72] The Babylonian Chronicle records bluntly that "Sargon went to Tabal,"[73] whereas the poorly preserved Sin of Sargon informs us of "the death of Sargon, [. . .] who was killed in [enemy country] and who was not interred in his house."[74] These tantalizing fragments yield more questions than answers, and a full reconstruction of events awaits new evidence. Nevertheless, some observations are possible.

The exact location of Kulummu is not known, though circumstantial evidence puts it somewhere between Bit-Purutash and Til-garimmu.[75] Gurdi (alternatively Qurdi or Kurti) was evidently one of various Tabalian rulers. This name has an Anatolian-Luwian origin and appears in several texts and monuments from the area.[76] A letter from Tab-shar-Ashur, the royal treasurer and governor of a northern border province, indicates that a ruler named Gurdi (in all likelihood the Kulummaean) was an Assyrian client, having formally entered into a treaty with the Assyrians at some point earlier in Sargon's reign.[77] Presumably, international political circumstances in the north or Gurdi's treaty-breaking (or both) prompted Sargon to take the field against him. Expecting the usual result, the Assyrians launched a typical punitive campaign. That is, the army marched into Gurdi's territory to cow him into submission. Given the relative ease of previous disciplinary actions in Tabal (and against Carchemish, Muṣaṣir, Kummuh, and Karalla, among others), the Assyrians no doubt expected Gurdi to submit quickly, without offering much resistance. When Kulummaean forces attacked, possibly in an ambush or through treachery, the Assyrians were taken by surprise, and disaster followed. One can easily imagine a seemingly repentant Gurdi or his representative entering the Assyrian camp to plead for mercy, but spearheading an attack instead. The wonder is that no one had tried it earlier.

However it happened, a petty ruler from the mountains managed to kill the great Assyrian king and enough of his troops so that the king's body was not recovered and did not receive a proper burial.[78] How many magnates suffered the same fate is not known, although it is probable that at least one important official, such as Ashur-sharru-uṣur, the governor of Quwê, perished alongside his king.[79] The manner of Sargon's death sent shock waves through the empire. Though many cultures have considered death in battle the apogee of male achievement, far preferable to any other kind of death, the opposite view prevailed in ancient Mesopotamia, at least with respect to kings. A king's death in combat signaled divine anger and abandonment, and since he acted as the people's advocate before the gods, his defeat spelled disaster for them as well. Worse still was the loss of the king's body. Under normal circumstances, Assyrian kings were interred in Ashur, where their descendants and priests could offer sustenance (food and water or wine offerings) to provide the deceased with a modicum of comfort in an otherwise dark and desolate underworld.[80] The desecrated or abandoned corpse doomed the king's spirit to eternal wandering and implied devastating consequences for Assyria itself.

Beliefs about the burial of the dead were age-old and nearly universal among Near Eastern cultures. Every soldier faced the very real possibility that should he perish in battle his corpse would remain unburied, food for carrion, his restless spirit doomed to wander. Near Eastern sources make no mention of the practice of a post-battle truce for the recovery and burial of the dead that is so prevalent in classical Greek sources. Even if such a thing had been possible in the Near East, royal reluctance to admit casualties no doubt prevented its inclusion in the official record.[81] Still, literary sources imply that burial normally followed battle. For example, the twelfth tablet of the Standard Babylonian Epic of Gilgamesh includes a dialogue between the hero, Gilgamesh, and the ghost of his friend, Enkidu, in which the two vividly portray how the treatment of the dead would determine the quality of their afterlife. After Gilgamesh asks, "Did you see the one who was killed in battle?" Enkidu responds, "I saw. His father and mother hold his head and his wife weeps over him." This represents the best-case scenario in which the family of the deceased can treat the body properly. The next question Gilgamesh asks his friend, "Did you see the one whose corpse was thrown into the steppe?," elicits the lugubrious reply, "I saw. His ghost does not find rest in the Underworld."[82]

The importance of proper burial was so ingrained among Near Eastern cultures that curse formulae, which formed an integral part of treaties and legal documents, threatened oath-breakers that their corpses would fall victim to scavengers. One such treaty invokes, "Below in the netherworld, may they make your ghost thirst for water. . . . May the earth not receive your corpses but may your burial place be in the belly of a dog or a pig."[83] Likewise, the roughly contemporary Greek epic, The Iliad, places similar emphasis on the necessity of funerary rites. Not only do heroes on both sides risk their lives to retrieve the bodies of fallen comrades, but toward the end of the poem, even Priam, the king of Troy, imagines with horror that after his death, "the dogs that I fed at my table, My own watchdogs will drag me outside and eat my flesh raw."[84] In his desire for revenge, Achilles initially intends the same fate for Hector's corpse.[85] The shocking fact that the body of the great king Sargon II suffered such a fate shook the Assyrian Empire to its very foundation.

While the regime shift after the death of any king frequently occasioned rebellion among subject lands, the appalling nature of Sargon's death dealt an especially severe blow to Assyrian prestige. Subject rulers and enemies alike understood it as explicit evidence of divine rejection. The biblical prophet Isaiah picked up the theme and admonished:

> But you (Sargon) are brought down to Sheol, to the depths of the Pit. Those who see you will stare at you: "Is this the man who made the earth tremble, who shook kingdoms, who made the world like a desert and overthrew its cities, who would not let his prisoners go home?" All the kings of the nations lie in glory, each in his own tomb; but you are cast out, away from your grave, like loathsome carrion, clothed with the dead, those pierced by the sword, who go down to the stones of the Pit, like a corpse trampled underfoot.[86]

Assyria's enemies quickly parlayed the situation into a bid for freedom and saw the opportunity to recover lost lands. After all, the gods—especially those of mighty Assyria—had essentially invited them to act. The disaster in Tabal affected more than royal prestige. The defeat of the feared, seemingly invincible Assyrian army at the hands of uncivilized mountain rabble exposed the army's vulnerabilities and gave impetus to nascent rebellions everywhere. Within months, Merodach-Baladan came out of exile to retake Babylonia, and this time he got plenty of support from fellow countrymen. The first three campaigns of Sargon's successor, Sennacherib, suppressed revolts throughout the empire and prevented him from seeking revenge against Gurdi for another ten years.[87]

Although Sennacherib apparently ascended the throne without internal opposition, his father's ignoble end posed a serious problem. What had Sargon done to earn the gods' wrath? What could Sennacherib do to lay his father's ghost to rest? Until the new king found answers to these questions and propitiated the gods in an appropriate manner, all of Assyria was at risk. Assyrian priests scrambled to address the horrible problem of the unburied king. Recently, Assyriologist Eckart Frahm has suggested that the celebration of the annual resurrection of the god Dumuzi, in the month Du'uzu (June–July) offered a possible solution. In the Dumuzi myth, the young god came back to life every year for three days before returning to the underworld. During that period, people could rid themselves of bad luck or sin and send it back to the underworld with the god. Frahm noticed that in 705 the festival fell shortly after Sargon's death, on the twenty-sixth to the twenty-ninth of the month, the twenty-seventh being the day of Dumuzi's release.[88] He also observed that on that very day, Nabu-zuqup-kenu, an exorcist living in Ashur, copied out the twelfth tablet of the Epic of Gilgamesh that includes the relevant passage quoted above. It seems clear that Assyrian scholars sought to appease the ghost of Sargon or even effect symbolic interment indirectly by means of Dumuzi or Enkidu.[89]

The unnatural end to such a brilliant and successful reign continued to haunt successive Assyrian kings. None risked a similar fate by leading troops into battle, although they did accompany the army on campaign. Hoping to placate their capricious gods, late Assyrian kings increasingly came to rely on prognostication and the performance of apotropaic and cleansing rituals. Sargon's death may have contributed to the intensified interest in ritual. With hindsight, the unfavorable omens heralding his demise were unmistakable: the plague that swept through Assyria in 707 when the gods entered the new city and the earthquake that shook Dur-Sharrukin just a few months later.[90] Since in retrospect these omens could be associated both with Sargon's death and with his city, the Assyrians naturally concluded that in building it the king had been guilty of hubris. Now it seemed that Sargon had bragged too much about his plans and his ability to see them to fruition. Wishing to disassociate himself from his father, Sennacherib abandoned Dur-Sharrukin as a royal seat and omitted his patrimony from the titular portion of his inscriptions. Though people continued to live at Dur-Sharrukin, the administration quit the citadel, and no king lived in the palace or worshipped at the temples again.

Decades later, Sargon's death was still so notorious that his grandson Esarhaddon used it to promote his new religious and political policies, especially with regard to Babylonia. In the long tradition of justifying current political decisions in terms of past events, Esarhaddon's scribes produced a text called The Sin of Sargon.[91] In this work, Esarhaddon's father, Sennacherib, having returned from the dead to instruct his son, described how diviners tried to discover what his own father, Sargon, had done to deserve death and dishonor in a foreign land. Eventually divination revealed to Sennacherib that the gods had punished Sargon not for self-glorification (for having built the new city of Dur-Sharrukin), but for having disrespected the gods of Babylonia.[92] For his part, Esarhaddon exploited this reading of Sargon's fate to justify his reconstruction of Babylon, which Sennacherib had destroyed in 689. Although this text illustrates an ideological system in which "the realm of the divine and the realm in which the king acts are, for all intents and purposes, indistinguishable," The Sin of Sargon sheds little light on what actually happened.[93] It speaks more to Esarhaddon's immediate needs as king than to the actual events that tarnished his grandfather's otherwise exemplary rule. Reduced to a symbolic object lesson by his own descendants, Sargon's unpropitious death prevented him from being remembered as one of Assyria's (and antiquity's) greatest kings. In life, Sargon fulfilled his own heroic vision by transforming his country into a massive empire. Through the fortunes and misfortunes of war, he forfeited the chance to be viewed as a worthy successor of his namesake, Sargon of Akkad. What happened to Sargon, an incredibly successful king, highlights the fragile nature of life and power in the ancient world, where a single moment of bad luck could overturn a lifetime's work.

CONCLUSION

A ny final assessment of the career of Sargon II must first acknowledge that he did not build an empire from nothing. By the time he became king, the patterns of military and political discourse among the various Near Eastern polities were very well established. Though Sargon was not heir to the throne, he did grow up as a member of the royal family amid the court intrigue, political maneuvering, and diplomatic deceit typical of those jockeying for power in an unforgiving environment. After he became king, he consciously took advantage of all that his predecessors had accomplished and that his contemporaries taught him. Above all, Sargon owed a debt to the kings who had created the military and administrative organization necessary to conquer and maintain a vast territorial empire. Without their achievements, Sargon would not have had sufficient human and material resources to fulfill his objectives as quickly as he did.

As a result of Tiglath-pileser's territorial gains and Shalmaneser's more modest endeavors, by the time Sargon won the throne, Assyria already had efficient lines of communication and administrative experience throughout Syria-Palestine and Babylonia, areas of great strategic importance. In addition, Sargon's predecessors had established a tenuous hegemony over a number of important kingdoms in the Taurus and Zagros Mountains. Both political logic and royal ideology dictated that Sargon follow through on his father's plans. To have done less would have reflected poorly on him personally and delayed the progress of Assyrian domination, whose purpose was to bring order to the Near East.[1] Sargon was no mere imitator, however. What distinguished him from his talented forbearers was a crystalline vision of empire, political aptitude, an economy-of-force-driven military policy, superior intelligence-gathering capability, an instinct for opportunity, and the ability to react quickly and decisively to setbacks. An outstanding military leader, Sargon also knew how to delegate authority while maintaining the loyalty of both his magnates and his troops.

Over the course of Sargon's reign, the Assyrian army saw action every year but one (712), sometimes more than once in a year, and often in widely separated areas far from the Assyrian homeland. On a single campaign, soldiers regularly marched more than a thousand miles, much of it over staggeringly difficult terrain. A conservative estimate of the number of total miles that the army traveled would be in the range of ten thousand to fourteen thousand miles. While it is highly unlikely that any single person participated in every campaign—Sargon himself did not—the great distances covered speak to Assyria's superior operational capability. How could the army maintain such a pace? In fact, as table 7.1 reveals, Sargon marshaled his forces with due care and diligence. Early on, shorter, less strenuous campaigns alternated with lengthier, more challenging ones. Their intensity fluctuated as well. Assuming that our sources record all major events, then large-scale, set-piece battles occurred only in years 720 (at Der, Qarqar, and perhaps Raphia), 714 (at Waush), and 709 (outside Dur-Iakin). The rarity of major battles contrasts sharply with the regularity of relatively low-intensity engagements—raids, cavalry skirmishes, and ambushes—that the inscriptions and letters report.

Significantly more numerous than major battles, sieges also varied in intensity. Sargon's inscriptions claim that he conquered well over a hundred enemy habitations, while the Letter to Ashur, a text that describes a single campaign, boasts that the Assyrians sacked over four hundred Urartian "cities." A closer look reveals that the Assyrian inscriptions tended to conflate a range of settlement types, from barely protected hamlets to fortresses and heavily fortified cities. It is safe to assume that the majority of conquered places listed in the inscriptions offered little, if any, resistance. What makes this noteworthy is that the Assyrians bothered to discover and record their names at all. Presumably they did so in order to authenticate conquest so as to ease future administration of the area and to fulfill ideological imperatives. Likewise, the sculptured reliefs offer insight into how the Assyrians dealt with physical obstacles. Of the seventeen city conquests depicted on Sargon's sculptured reliefs, at least ten represent frontal assaults unsupported by siege engines, while only four show the use of towers and battering rams. Two reliefs indicate that cities capitulated without a fight, two others are too poorly preserved for accurate interpretation, and one relief depicts the burning city in the aftermath of an assault.[2] This pictorial information, though unverifiable as to accuracy and by no means complete, strongly suggests that difficult terrain, coupled with logistical shortages and seasonal constraints, often inhibited the use of military technology. That is, when the army campaigned in the Zagros or Taurus Mountains, far from the Assyrian heartland, it could not always produce the material to build siege machinery or take the time to starve out the besieged inhabitants. That Sargon understood the high cost of long marches followed by frontal assaults on defended positions goes without saying and partially explains the deliberate, economical rhythm of his campaigns.

In retrospect, Sargon's campaigns separate easily into three distinct phases, each focusing on the achievement of particular objectives. As shown in table 7.1, from 720 to 716a, Sargon sought to establish himself as king and gain mastery over the west. From 716b to 714, he focused on the north and east, and from 710–707 his attention shifted to the south and southeast. During the interval 713–711, Sargon consolidated his hold on the empire preparatory to the invasion of Babylonia. This is not to suggest that he held strictly to a predetermined timetable or that he never campaigned outside his target area. While pursuing his own interests, the king had to remain flexible, seize opportunities, and react to enemy activity. Hence, ad hoc operations punctuated the steady flow of strategic campaigns. For example, the Quwê and Aegean campaign of 715, which took place outside the target theater of operations, responded to Phrygian machinations. Military activity after 709 involved punitive action and opportunity (Kummuh in 707), imperial security (Ellipi in 707), or routine tribute collection (Karalla in 706).

During the first phase (720–716a), the king led campaigns in every major theater of operations. Particularly hard-hitting was the crucial campaign to the west against Ilu-bi'di's coalition in 720. All other military operations during this phase, including the battle of Der in 720, were more limited in scope. After securing his throne, the king exerted his authority on the Empire's frontiers, in this case Mannea (719) and Tabal (718). The annexation of Carchemish in 717 and the expedition to the Brook of Egypt the following year were low-intensity efforts that brought Assyria domination over Syro-Palestinian overland trade routes. For the maritime trade, however, Sargon continued to rely on the Phoenicians and Philistines. The king's first years focused on securing the throne and bolstering Assyria's economy, while the string of victories augmented military capability through deportations and conscription of defeated enemies. Resource depletion in the Assyrian heartland caused by Tiglath-pileser's relentless campaigning and the years of turmoil at

TABLE 7.1. The Campaigns 720–705

Year	Campaign location	Combat (battle/devastation/siege)	Deportation/plunder	Extreme or political violence	Campaign leader
720a	Der	Battle			Sargon
720b	Syria-Palestine	Two battles, lots of devastation, several sieges	Deportation, plunder, and additions to the army	Ilu-bi'di flayed; Hanunu blinded	Magnate/Sargon
719	Mannea	Devastation	Deportation and plunder		Sargon
718	Tabal	Show of force? Little or no violence?	Deportation, plunder, and additions to the army		Sargon
717	Carchemish	Little or no violence?	Deportation, plunder, and additions to the army		Sargon
716a	The Brook of Egypt	Commercial/no violence	Diplomatic		Sargon or a magnate?
716b	Mannea, Karalla, Allabria, and into Media	Lots of devastation, sieges, and fighting	Deportation (Ashur-le'i and Itti deported) and plunder	"Slaughtered their multitudes"; beheading of corpses; impalements	Sargon
715a	Mannea	Devastation and sieges	Deportation and plunder	4,000 heads to king in camp	Taklak-ana-Bel (and Sargon?)
715b	Aegean Sea and Quwê	Amphibious warfare and devastation	Plunder	"I killed them small and large with my weapons"	Sargon or a magnate

Year	Region				Commander
714	Mannea/Urartu	Tribute collection, devastation, battle	Plunder of 400+ towns; taking of Urartian prisoners; deportation	Bagdatti of Wishdish flayed (poetic justice)	Sargon
713a	Tabal	Devastation	Annexation, deportation, and plunder		Sargon
713b	Karalla	Devastation	Deportation	Ashur-le'i flayed	Magnates
711a	Ashdod	Devastation and siege	Deportation		Turtan
711b	Gurgum	No military violence?	Deportation of Mutallu but not the populace	Mutallu's hands burned	Turtan
711c	Kammanu	Devastation	Annexation, deportation		Turtan
711d	Northern border provinces	Skirmishes			Local governors
710	Babylonia	Devastation in the east	Deportation, plunder, additions to army		Sargon
709–707	Dur-Iakin	Battle and siege	Deportation and plunder; diplomacy		Magnates, Sargon?
708–707	Ellipi	Show of force, skirmish, siege, and hostage taking	Deportation		Magnates
706	Karalla	Tribute collection			Magnates
705	Tabal	Punitive			Sargon

the end of Shalmaneser V's reign necessitated this buildup phase. Essential materials and manpower having been procured, Sargon could then turn to much more difficult tasks.

By contrast to the early years, the campaigns of 716b–714 proved significantly more challenging, with four successive incursions into the Zagros Mountains and two trips nearly as arduous (albeit not as bloody) into Anatolia. The fulfillment of Sargon's long-range commercial plans, as well as the acquisition of resources such as horses, necessitated the conquest of the central and northern Zagros, while the political situation with respect to Urartu, Elam, and Babylonia made subjection of the area an urgent priority. For this strategic phase, Sargon relied on the full complement of Assyrian military power: the standing army, levied troops, and deportee battalions. According to the royal inscriptions, the campaigns to the east were much more violent than those carried out elsewhere. During the 716 campaign to Mannea, Karalla, and Media, the Assyrians became more aggressive as they pushed into the wild mountains of western Media, where they carried out beheadings and impalements in order to make the maximum impact quickly and with the least cost to themselves. In the next year, in the same area, troops under the leadership of Taklak-ana-Bel took some four thousand enemy heads. It is a commonplace of war that violence becomes worse as conditions deteriorate. The harsh environment of the Zagros undoubtedly took a toll on troops, who had to assault fortified mountain aeries without the benefit of protective siege machinery, while operating under the constraints of time, logistics, weather, and distance. For the most part, however, the violent suppression of the Zagros polities resulted from coldly rational command decisions. Simply put, Sargon needed to control the area quickly and decisively, and he applied necessary force to the task.

The penetration of the Zagros inevitably brought the Assyrians into conflict with the Urartians, a formidable power in their own right. After a tense period of cold war, the two powers clashed briefly in 714, when Sargon won a decisive victory at the Battle of Mount Waush, which he followed with a triumphant and highly symbolic march through Urartian territory. At no time was his intention to conquer Urartu. Rather, the objective was to curtail further Urartian expansion west and south, to secure the eastern trade, and to prove to the world his own superiority to the Urartian king, Rusa. These goals he accomplished with characteristic efficiency and the required panache. Prestige acts such as those described in the Letter to Ashur were as essential to the retention of power as brute force. Above all, the eighth campaign victory bought Sargon the breathing space necessary to consolidate his holdings, concentrate on domestic matters, and prepare for the reconquest of Babylonia, which in many ways became the crowning achievement of his reign.

The Babylonian campaign of 710–707 demonstrated more than any other just how subtle and well-executed Assyrian military operations could be. Although the conquest of Syria-Palestine and the Anatolian and Zagros polities required a measure of political dexterity and perseverance, the subjugation of Babylonia presented a special case in which the delicate political situation exacerbated all the problems normally associated with campaigning. In order to facilitate a peaceful takeover, Sargon eschewed the normal devastation tactics in favor subversion and estrangement. The strategy required careful coordination, as the army waged conventional war on the eastern front, while agents subverted the enemy's power among the Babylonian cities and rurally placed tribes. That the plan achieved the desired results, if not Merodach-Baladan's capture, indicates that Assyrian intelligence and military capability had attained a high level of sophistication. The relative ease of the Assyrian victory cannot be attributed wholly to enemy weakness. Most of the credit belongs to Sargon and his officials, who spent years deliberately undermining Babylonian unity and creating the impression of Assyrian invincibility. In this case, careful preparation and political maneuvering paid off.

Throughout his reign, whether his campaigns fulfilled strategic plans, seized opportunity, or reacted to setbacks, Sargon met the exigencies of each situation with a carefully calculated level of intensity. Political choreography and the threat of force sometimes achieved the objective without recourse to widespread violence, as at Shinuhtu (719), Carchemish (717), and Muṣaṣir (714). More often, the army used devastation (property damage and looting) to accomplish its objectives, which, as the nearly constant deportations and hostage taking indicate, rarely entailed exterminating the enemy. According to Sargon's inscriptions, the king carried out thirty-eight separate deportations that moved more than two hundred thousand men, women, and children to different parts of the empire.[3] Deportations allowed Sargon to balance violence with reconstruction, economic development, and cordial diplomatic exchange,

while the use of force won him both the leeway for future leni-
ency and the prestige to govern effectively without overextending
his military. But if it seems that Sargon realized a kind of enlight-
ened absolutism, it was the product of shrewd calculation rather
than the deliberate implementation of abstract philosophical principles. His vision for Assyria—unassailable domination throughout the Near East—accorded well with the prevailing ideology of
kingship, but he utilized particular political and military method-
ologies because they worked. When it came to decision-making he
was intuitive rather than doctrinaire. However, Sargon's penchant
for Realpolitik inevitably had a negative impact on some people,
including his own officials.

The demands of rapid expansion, building, and economic development pushed the imperial administrators to the limit. The whole
organizational edifice appears fragile in retrospect. A drought,
plague, or rebellion could cause significant deprivation, and provincial officials often struggled to maintain order and fulfill the king's
demands. Through careful management, military success, political acuity, and a measure of luck, Sargon kept it all running until
he met his death on the battlefield in 705. After years of relentless effort, Sargon's ill-omened demise tarnished his memory and
sparked widespread rebellions that inevitably led to more violence.
Sennacherib, Sargon's son and successor, pursued his father's economic interests but chose to consolidate, rather than expand the
empire, by retrenching on the periphery and ceding territory when
necessary. Babylonia proved to be an intractable problem, for which
Sennacherib and his successors could find no lasting solution. The
pattern of rebellion, resistance, competition, and conflict that
marked Sargon's reign had begun much earlier and would continue
to plague the Assyrian Empire until its final collapse.

Historians often attribute the empire's periodic instability to
the violent and oppressive methods with which its kings dominated
conquered peoples. But instability and brutality were not confined
to the Assyrians, nor was violence their preferred means of action.
Limited resources and a harsh environment made life "nasty, brut-
ish, and short" for everyone, Assyrians included. Reflex opportunism
fueled volatility and created a repeating pattern of conflict among all
Near Eastern polities. The story told in these pages reveals a complex world, in which all political actors—not Sargon alone—connived, bargained, postured, and fought to attain the advantage over

enemies and win a measure of security for themselves. International relations involved a wide array of activities, including espionage, diplomatic marriage, treaty-alliance, hostage taking, gift exchange, public pageantry, murder, and war. Still, political power depended on a strong military and the wealth to pay for it. The ability to apply overwhelming force when and where he chose gave Sargon the advantage over competitors.

The Assyrians ran a sophisticated imperial organization in a rational way that befitted the practices and expectations prevalent throughout the Near East at the time. Indeed, all of the political intrigues and military operations described in this book could find parallels at any given time in history. Thus, it is time to revise the standard view of the Assyrians as being somehow more cruel and rapacious than their contemporaries. They were not. Ultimately we must attribute the dominant position that Assyria achieved under Sargon to the serendipitous confluence of many factors, among them his predecessors' achievements, a thriving economy, competitors' weakness, an astonishingly effective military, and good fortune. At the center of these stands Sargon, a brilliant king and general, whom the passage of time has rendered enigmatic and unknowable—a man whose deeds matched his vision but whose personal legacy fell victim to the Assyrians' deep-seated fear of divine retribution.

APPENDIX A

DRAMATIS PERSONAE AND GEOGRAPHICAL LIST

Dramatis Personae (all dates are B.C.)

Abaliuqunu: Urartian governor, possibly of Muṣaṣir, sometime after 714

Adâ: ruler of Shurda, a principality in the vicinity of Karalla; made Assyrian client in 713

Adad-nirari III: king of Assyria, 811–783; father of Tiglath-pileser III

Ahat-abisha: daughter of Sargon; wife of Ambaris, king of Bit-Purutash

Ahimeti: ruler of Ashdod appointed by Sargon in 712 to replace his brother, Azuri

Ambaris: ruler of Bit-Purutash (Tabal); son of Hulli; son-in-law of Sargon II, removed from office in 713

Amitashi: usurper; brother of Ashur-le'i, ruler of Karalla; killed in 713

Argishti II: king of Urartu, ca. 713–685; son of Rusa I

Arije: ruler of Kumme; Assyrian client

Ashipa: Assyrian official (probably governor) in Tushan before ca. 710

Ashpa-bara: son of Daltâ, king of Ellipi; brother of Lutû, cousin of Nibê

Ashur-dur-paniya: Assyrian magnate, possibly the governor of Til-Barsip or the treasurer (*masennu*) after Tab-shar-Ashur, ca. 706

Ashur-le'i: ruler of Karalla; Assyrian client removed from office in 716, executed 713

Ashur-nirari V: king of Assyria, 755–745; son of Adad-nirari III; brother of Tiglath-pileser III

Ashur-reṣua: Assyrian spymaster and delegate in Kumme

Ashur-sharru-uṣur: Assyrian governor of Quwê

Aza: king of Mannea, ca. 718–716; murdered in 716; son of Iranzi; brother of Ullusunu

Azuri: ruler of Ashdod; brother of Ahimeti; Assyrian client removed from office in 712

Bagdatti: ruler of Wishdish; Urartian client; killed in 714

Balassu: pro-Assyrian ruler of Bit-Dakkuri and Borsippa; uncle of Mukin-zeri of Bit-Amukani

Barsipitu: probably the daughter of Balassu, Assyrian emissary to Bit-Dakkuri in 710

Bel-apla-iddina: Assyrian-appointed ruler of Allabria in 716

Bel-duri: Assyrian governor of Damascus

Bel-iddina: Assyrian official in Babylonia after 710

Bel-liqbi: Assyrian governor or vice-governor of Hamath

Bel-sharru-uşur: ruler of Kishesim; deported to Assyria in 716

Dajukku: Mannean governor; deported to Assyria in 715 after defecting to the Urartian side

Daltâ: king of Ellipi; Assyrian client; died 707

Dasukku: Ellipian city ruler

Gabbu-ana-Ashur: Assyrian chief cupbearer and provincial governor

Gurdi: Kulummaean ruler; possible Assyrian client; responsible for the death of Sargon

Hanunu: ruler of Gaza; Assyrian client; removed from office in 720

Hulli: ruler of Bit-Purutash; father of Ambaris; Assyrian client

Humban-nikash: king of Elam, ca. 743–717

Hu-teshub: king of Shubria

Iamani: ruler of Ashdod; usurper; removed from office in 711

Ianzu: ruler of Hubushkia, Assyrian client

Il-iada': Assyrian official; governor of Der; coordinator of Assyrian operations in northern Babylonia, 710–709

Ilu-bi'di (Yau-bi'di): king of Hamath in Syria; leader of a rebellion against Sargon in 720; executed in 720

Iranzi: king of Mannea; died ca. 717, Assyrian client; father of Aza and Ullusunu

Isaiah: Hebrew prophet

Issar-duri: Assyrian official; governor of Arrapha

Itti: ruler of Allabria; removed from office in 716

Kaqqadanu: Urartian magnate and field marshal; captured by Cimmerians ca. 714

Kaqqadanu: Urartian governor, possibly to be equated with the Kaqqadanu described above

Kiakki: ruler of Shinuhtu; Assyrian client, deported 718

Kibabashe: Ellipian city ruler

Kurti: ruler of Atunna; Assyrian client

Lutû: son of Daltâ, king of Ellipi, cousin of Nibê

Mannu-ki-Ninua: Assyrian governor of Kar-Sharrukin after 708

Marduk-sharru-uṣur: Assyrian governor of Sangibutu after ca. 708

Merodach-Baladan ruler of the Chaldean tribe, Bit-Iakin; king of Babylonia, 721–709

Midas (Mita): king of Phrygia, ca. 738–700

Mitatti: ruler of Zikirtu, a Mannean subdistrict; Urartian client; killed at Waush in 714

Mukin-zeri: leader of Bit-Amukani; king of Babylon, 731–729; nephew of Balassu of Bit-Dakkuri

Mutallu: prince in Gurgum; murdered his father, Tarhulara, the king, and took the throne; deported to Assyria in 711

Mutallu: king of Kummuh, not to be confused with the prince of Gurgum of the same name; Assyrian client; deported in 707

Nabu-belu-ka"in: Assyrian governor of Kar-Sharrukin before 708

Nabu-le'i: Assyrian governor of Birate

Nabu-le'i: Assyrian official in Tabal; majordomo of Sargon's daughter Ahat-abisha

Nabu-shallimsunu: Sargon's chief scribe and probable author of the Letter to Ashur

Nashur-Bel: Assyrian governor of Amedi

Nibê: nephew of Daltâ; king of Ellipi; cousin of Ashba-bara and Lutû

Osorkon IV (Shilkani): ruler of Lower Egypt, ca. 730–715

Padi: installed as king of Ekron in 720

Pisiri: ruler of Carchemish; Assyrian client; removed from office in 717

Qurdi: see Gurdi

Rē'ē: Egyptian general under Osorkon IV; defeated at Raphia in 720

Rusa, son of Erimena: king of Urartu (dates uncertain)

Rusa, son of Sarduri: king of Urartu, ca. 730–713

Samsi: queen of the Arabs

Sargon: king of Assyria, 721–705; son of Tiglath-pileser III; brother of Shalmaneser V and Sin-ah-uṣur; father of Sennacherib and Ahat-abisha

Sennacherib: son of Sargon II; crown prince and then king of Assyria, 704–681

Sha-Ashur-dubbu: Governor of Assyrian province Tushan after ca. 710

Shabakḫo: Kushite ruler of Egypt, ca. 721–707 or 706

Shalmaneser V: king of Assyria, 726–722; son of Tiglath-pileser III; half-brother of Sargon II

Sharru-emuranni: governor of Zamua; eponym for 712; governor of Babylon after 710

Shulmu-Bel: deputy of the Assyrian palace herald

Shutruk-nahunte: king of Elam, 717–699

Sin-ah-uṣur: full brother of Sargon II; *sukkalmah* (grand vizier) and leader of the elite royal cavalry guard

Tab-shar-Ashur: Assyrian magnate; governor; royal treasurer

Taklak-ana-Bel: Assyrian governor of Naṣibina and eponym for 715

Tarhulara: king of Gurgum; Assyrian client; murdered by his son, Mutallu

Tarhunazi: king of Kammanu; Assyrian client; removed from office in 711

Tiglath-pileser III: king of Assyria, 745–727; father of Shalmaneser V, Sargon II, and Sin-ah-uṣur

Uassurme: ruler of Bit-Purutash; Assyrian client; removed from office by Tiglath-pileser III in 729

Ululaya: birth name of Shalmaneser V

Ullusunu: king of Mannea; son of Iranzi; brother of Aza; Assyrian client

Uranzu: ruler of Hubushkia; Assyrian/Urartian client

Urikki: ruler of Quwê; Assyrian client

Urpala'a: ruler of Tuhana; Assyrian client

Urzana: ruler of Muṣaṣir; Assyrian/Urartian client

Unlocated Place Names

Abitikna	Burati	Kindau
Amaet	Durdukku	Shama'unu
Anzaria	Eziat	Shuandahal
Apallâ	Gizilbundi	Shurda
Bab-biqti	Hadalpa	Satarnu
Ba'il-gazara	Harda	Sukkia
Bala	Hursaggalli	Tikrakka
Bari	Iqbi-bel	Urammu
Bit-Imbi	Ishtahup	Zibia
Bit-Zabidaia	Kar-siparri	

APPENDIX B

SOLVING THE PUZZLE OF ASSYRIAN-URARTIAN CHRONOLOGY

Certain aspects of Near Eastern chronology for the period of Sargon's reign remain a matter of significant debate because evidence that is undated, fragmentary, and scattered over time and across cultures precludes certainty. Scholars often reach widely different conclusions depending on how they arrange texts, assign dates, and understand the historical context. Few would dispute the basic chronology of Sargon's reign. Rather, the debate arises from efforts to fit his correspondence into the chronological framework that the royal inscriptions and Eponym Chronicle establish. Letters reporting a Cimmerian victory over Urartu present a particularly thorny case. Sometime during Sargon's reign, the king of Urartu led his army against the Cimmerians only to suffer a significant defeat, the loss of several of his governors, and the capture of his field marshal. Since the only sources describing this incident are several undated Assyrian letters that do not name the Urartian king involved (SAA I 30, 31, 32; SAA V 90, 92, 173), a debate over the exact date of the battle and the identity of the king has ensued. Related problems are the sequence of Assyrian and Urartian interference in Urzana of Muṣaṣir's affairs and the order of Urartian kings. In the following, which is by no means exhaustive, I review recent theories and argue in favor of the chronology put forth in this book.

The Cimmerian Victory over Urartu

One of the most persistent problems of Neo-Assyrian chronology, the date of the Cimmerian victory over Urartu, has yet to find a clear solution, and without unequivocal new evidence scholars are unlikely to reach a consensus. There are two main competing theories: the traditional one, which I espouse (with some tweaking), asserting that the Cimmerian-Urartian battle took place *before* Sargon's confrontation with Rusa in 714, and a second theory, supported by Fuchs (among others), claiming that the battle occurred about five years later, during Sargon's occupation of Babylon.[1] Mayer prefers an even later date of 705 or the early years of Sennacherib.[2] These scholars argue against a pre-714 date based on the following key assertions.

1. The Urartians could not have fought the Assyrians at Mount Waush soon after suffering a terrible battlefield loss against the Cimmerians.
2. If the defeat had occurred around 714, Sargon would have mentioned it or the Cimmerians in his inscriptions, which he did not.
3. Since Urzana reported the defeat to the Assyrians, he must have done so *after* Sargon "conquered" Muṣaṣir in 714 because that was when Urzana became an Assyrian client.
4. Had the Cimmerian battle occurred when Sargon was on campaign in 714, reports would have been sent directly to him in the field. By contrast, it would have made sense to filter reports through Assyria to Babylonia when the king was in residence there in 710–708.
5. Sargon would not have dared to annex Kummuh in 707 unless the Urartians had just suffered a severe battlefield defeat.
6. Since most of the datable letters from Nineveh belonged to the period 710–708, all of them probably did.

In the rest of this section, I address each of these points.

Let us begin by reviewing the information contained in the letters. News of the battle reached Sennacherib, who summarized the information in three letters (SAA I 30–32), which he forwarded to Sargon. At least two additional, independent reports (SAA V 90 and 173) also addressed the topic. Some people include other letters in this group as well, but I consider only those texts that clearly refer to the same events.

- SAA I 30: Urzana has reported the Cimmerian defeat and that the governor of Waisi has been killed.
- SAA I 31: The king of Ukku has claimed the loss of eleven Urartian governors and the capture of the field marshal and two other governors. Ashur-reṣua has written that the field marshal (Kaqqadanu) has been captured, but the country is

now quiet, and the governor of Birate has relayed that only
three magnates have been killed and the field marshal captured. Urzana, his son, his brother, and the king of Hubushkia
have gone to meet the Urartian king.

- SAA I 32: A spy has reported that the defeated Urartians now
  fear the Assyrians.
- SAA V 90: (Sender not preserved) claimed nine governors
  killed.
- SAA V 173 (Sender not preserved) reported a severe defeat.

One of Sennacherib's letters, SAA I 31, includes two pieces of evidence that appear to prove that the Cimmerian debacle occurred
before Sargon battled Rusa in 714. First, we are told that Urzana has
gone with his son and brother to meet the Urartian king. Since Sargon
deported Urzana's "wife, sons, daughters and family" to Assyria
after he looted Muṣaṣir in 714, the letter, in which Urzana's son is
said to accompany him, must date before the deportation.[3] Second,
Sennacherib notes that he is forwarding a message to Sargon from
"Nabu-le'i, the majordomo of Ahat-abisha" in Tabal. As Sargon married his daughter to the Tabalian king, Ambaris, in 716, but deported
him and "his whole family and household" to Assyria in 713, it has
long been assumed that Ahat-abisha must be Sargon's daughter and
that the letter, and thus the Cimmerian incident, predates 713. Not
everyone accepts this evidence as conclusive. In the case of Urzana's
son, for example, Roaf ignores the implications and simply assumes
that "not all of his family remained hostages in Assyria."[4] Be that as
it may, there is no evidence that Sargon ever reinstated a ruler that
he had deported, although he occasionally restored someone that a
predecessor had removed from office (e.g., Hulli), or let prisoners of
war go, as in the case of captive Phrygians that he set free.[5] Quite the
contrary, Sargon kept deported elites as hostages and did not hesitate to punish them if their people rebelled.

Similar rationalizing has been applied to the case of Ahat-abisha.
In order to circumvent the evidence, scholars have proposed several inventive solutions: the woman in the letter "could have been
someone else"; Sargon might have left Ahat-abisha in charge when
he removed Ambaris; he could have reinstated Ambaris at a later
point, or Nabu-le'i could have been managing Ahat-abisha's interests in Tabal.[6] None of these speculative solutions works. While
it is technically true that absolute proof of the woman's identity

has yet to surface, no logical alternative exists. Ahat-abisha had an Assyrian name, was personally known to Sargon, and lived in Tabal where she had sufficient rank and controlled a large enough household to employ a majordomo. Who but the royal daughter and wife of the local potentate could she be? Not a governor's wife, for Sargon's inscriptions clearly state that he replaced Ambaris with a (presumably unmarried) eunuch. Nor would we expect the wife of a lower-ranked official to be so well known to the king that mention of her name could gain her (or her majordomo) his attention. Likewise, it is not even remotely likely that Sargon made his daughter ruler of Tabal after Ambaris's deportation. Not only would that solution contradict Sargon's own inscriptions, but it has no precedent. There is no evidence that any Assyrian king ever appointed a woman as governor anywhere, let alone a remote polity that had been annexed only recently. The suggestion that Nabu-le'i remained behind in Tabal to look after Ahat-abisha's interests is more feasible, although known royal female-owned estates are all located in the Assyrian heartland or just outside.[7] As to the proposal that Sargon could have reinstated Ambaris at some later date, this too has neither evidence nor precedent to support it. As mentioned above, Sargon did not (according to the available evidence) reinstate a subject after first ordering him to be deported to Assyria. Most rulers that Sargon deported (e.g., Pisiri and Tarhunazi) simply vanish from the historical record. Thus, the only way to avoid dating the letter to the period before 713 is by rejecting outright what Sargon himself claimed or by rationalizing unprecedented alternatives. The evidence, such as it is, does not support these proposals. It now remains for us to examine the other points raised in support of a late date for the Cimmerian victory.

The letters that report the Cimmerian battle only agree on two events—namely that the Urartians had been defeated decisively and that their field marshal, Kaqqadanu, had been captured.[8] Since someone named Kaqqadanu was also mentioned in a few other undated letters (SAA V 86, 87 and 89), it stands to reason that they might shed light on the issue. The late-date view assumes that since these other reports involve Urartian troop movements in the area around Waisi, they must refer to the Urartian "reconquest" of Muşaşir after 714, in which case the Cimmerian battle, in which Kaqqadanu was captured, must have occurred later as well. There is no firm basis for this reasoning, since SAA V 86, 87, and 89 could have been written at any time during Sargon's reign and do not necessarily concern a conquest of Muṣaṣir at all. In fact, two of the aforementioned missives (SAA V 87 and 89) likely do not refer to the field marshal. Ashur-reṣua, almost certainly the author of all three texts, names Kaqqadanu the field marshal in SAA V 86, but in the others, SAA V 87 and 89, he references Kaqqadanu the governor. Apparently Ashur-reṣua needed to distinguish between two different officials. It is also possible that Kaqqadanu was promoted from governor to field marshal at some point. In any case, the field marshal's (possible) appearance in other letters does not help us arrive at a date for his capture by the Cimmerians.

As for the assumption that the Urartians could not have fought a second battle soon after such a defeat, let us consider what we know about Rusa's invasion: he took his army and entered Cimmerian territory, was soundly beaten, and then retreated; Rusa went to Tushpa, while some of his soldiers escaped to Guriana or to their own home cities. The Cimmerians do not appear to have pursued their fleeing enemies for long.[9] We do not know what type or how many troops invaded Cimmeria, whether the Urartians did so to punish or conquer (two very different types of operation), whether they fought a pitched battle or a running cavalry engagement (the latter seems likely given that the Cimmerians were horse archers), or how many casualties they suffered. One letter noted that while Rusa escaped the battle, the army had not yet returned to Tushpa, thus suggesting that some units had retreated in order. Considering the paucity of information, we should be cautious about making assumptions about Urartu's subsequent military capability.

What we can do is evaluate the practical realities of Rusa's post-battle situation. The Assyrian reports indicate that the Urartians lost a few key officials—somewhere between three and eleven—and suffered significant casualties against the Cimmerians. During this period, kings and nobles not only went on campaign but fought in battle. Although we cannot determine how many died as a result, regular campaigning must have taken a toll. Near Eastern battle casualty records have not survived (if they ever existed), but we have only to look at classical parallels to learn how frequently top officials got killed in battle. For example, during the Second Punic War, between December 218 and July 216—about a year and a half—the Romans lost three major battles (Trebia, Trasimene, and Cannae) and, in effect, three armies. At Cannae alone, one consul, two quaestors, twenty-nine out of forty-eight military tribunes, and eighty senators died, yet Rome still continued the war because its system of government anticipated battlefield casualties among the ruling class and dealt with the problem.[10] Differences in time and circumstances notwithstanding, the Urartian and Assyrian imperial systems, which depended similarly on the military participation of governors and other high officials, also included a hierarchical fail-safe to manage the inevitable attrition. Someone—be it son, brother, deputy governor, or other official—would have been poised to move up in status to fill a vacancy, if only on a temporary basis. Not all officials went on campaign; some remained behind to administer the provinces. More important, when great kings campaigned they rarely, if ever, fielded the entire strength of the country. Rather, they mustered forces selectively and prudently left troops in reserve for security.[11] There is no reason to believe that the army that lost to the Cimmerians represented the whole of Urartian military strength. Admittedly, a major battlefield defeat would have caused some turmoil, but any state completely immobilized by a single loss could not expect to survive for long. By way of analogy, we note that Sargon himself fought the Elamite army to a draw (at best) in 720, but during the same year campaigned on a second front, where his army fought and won two additional battles. Those campaigns occurred during or immediately after a period of intense instability in Assyria, yet Sargon was able to field two armies in one year.

Whatever the exact nature of the Cimmerian battle, military necessity (in this case, fear of an Assyrian invasion) required the Urartians to cobble together another army. For the defeated Urartians, the question became not whether they could field a second army but what it would look like. According to the Assyrian sources, the army that fought Sargon at Mount Waush was composed of Urartian shock troops (infantry), 260 royal cavalrymen (from the king's own clan), allied Andian, Zikirtean, and Wishdishian forces, and those of other dependencies as well.[12] Konakçı and Baştürk suggest that Rusa's 260 riders represented members of "a class of elite warriors chosen from among the tribesmen or clansmen of the monarch himself"—something comparable to Sargon's thousand-strong mounted bodyguard. If this assertion is true, losses suffered against the Cimmerians may have contributed to the unit's subsequent surrender at Waush.[13] That the Urartians could have regrouped and fought again shortly after losing to the Cimmerians is well within the realm of possibility, especially if the bulk of their infantry had not engaged the Cimmerians.

A second point that Fuchs and Roaf raise is that that none of Sargon's inscriptions, not even the Letter to Ashur, mention the Cimmerians. They contend that if the battle had occurred at around the same time as the 714 campaign, Sargon's inscriptions would have alluded to it.[14] By this rationale, the omission indicates that the battle did not take place at that time. Not only is this an argument *ex silentio*, but it also contravenes the fundamental purpose of the royal inscriptions, which was to promote the Assyrian king to the exclusion of all else. Had Sargon mentioned the Cimmerian victory in the context of his own triumph over Urartu, he would have cheapened his achievement by intimating that he had bested an already weakened foe. The Letter to Ashur did no such thing. Following convention, Sargon related the details of the Assyrians' battle against Rusa but gave no credit to his Mannean allies or anyone else. Instead he stressed, in mythopoeic terms, his and his army's heroism as well as the inevitability of their victory over a formidable foe. The omission of the Cimmerians is entirely compatible with the ideological requirements of Assyrian royal inscriptions and therefore does not preclude the possibility that the Cimmerian-Urartian battle predated Sargon's eighth campaign.

Another example of circular reasoning involves Urzana. Observing correctly that since Urzana reported the Cimmerian battle to Sennacherib, he did so as an Assyrian client, the late-date proponents then assert incorrectly that this proves that the battle occurred after Sargon captured Muṣaṣir in 714, the point at which they assume incorrectly that Urzana became a client.[15] In the Letter to Ashur, written in 714, Sargon gave Urzana's failure to ask after his health or send greeting presents as the reason for despoiling Muṣaṣir and deporting Urzana's family.[16] Clearly the Assyrian king already regarded Urzana as a client in 714. Moreover, two of the letters (SAA I 30 and 31) that report the Cimmerian victory prove that Urzana was also a Urartian client at the time. The first one contains Urzana's account of the Urartian defeat, and the second one, already discussed, relays the news that Urzana and his brother accompanied the Hubushkian ruler to meet the Urartian king in the battle's aftermath. That Urzana felt the need to communicate this news to the Assyrians as well as visit the defeated Urartian king plainly indicates that he dealt with both sides at the same time. Thus, Urzana's client status does not necessarily indicate a late date for the letters.

Another point cited in favor of a later dating involves Assyrian communication channels. By this reckoning, had the Cimmerian victory taken place in 714, the officials reporting it (Urzana of Muṣaṣir, the governor of Birate, the vice-governor of the palace herald's province, the Assyrian delegate in Kumme, and at least one spy) would have sent their letters straight to the king on campaign, rather than to Sennacherib in Assyria.[17] Fuchs argues that it makes more sense if the letters were forwarded to Sargon years later while he remained in Babylon, wrapping up his campaign there. One cannot help noting that if it were so easy to send letters straight to Sargon in the Zagros, it would have been even easier to send them directly to him when he was in Babylon. All the messengers had to do was travel straight downstream to reach the king himself. By contrast, when Sargon campaigned in the Zagros, finding him would have posed a serious problem to anyone not constantly apprised of his changing whereabouts. In other words, when Sargon went on campaign in 714, the central administration under the crown prince's direction had a much better chance of keeping in touch with the king than the provincial officials would have had. In this case, it would have been much faster, easier, and safer for officials located in the provinces and client states to the north of Assyria to send their reports to Nineveh or Calah, where the crown prince could compile incoming intelligence for forwarding. The same goes for Urzana of Muṣaṣir, despite his location relatively near the theater of operations. Direct contact with Sargon would have entailed sending a messenger east through Urartian territory southwest of Lake Urmia and into Mannea, thus inviting discovery and Urartian retribution. The indirect routing of reports of the Cimmerian victory to Sargon fits the circumstances of 714 far better than those of 709, although either date is possible. Nor does the speed at which the information could travel preclude a 714 date.

Lastly, it has been argued that since most of the other letters found at Nineveh date to the period after 711, the Cimmerian letters also found there must as well.[18] Mayer also alleges that since one of Sennacherib's twelve known letters to Sargon certainly dates after 709 (SAA 1 33), all of them did.[19] On the contrary, several letters from Nineveh demonstrably date earlier than 711—for example, SAA V 162, 164, 250, and SAA I 7, 9, 10, and 179.[20] Furthermore,

one of the Cimmerian dispatches (SAA I 32) and one letter mentioning Urzana (SAA V 144) were excavated at Calah, where most of the
letters from early in Sargon's reign were found. Without more information about the original organization and disposition of the letter
corpus—where, how, and by whom letters were stored—it seems
unlikely that the findspot can reveal much about their dates. Nor
should we consider contemporary all the letters from a single person
on the basis of one dated exemplar. After all, an official's involvement in the Babylonian campaign of 710 does not mean that he was
not in office four years earlier.

Having now considered the main factors involved in the dating argument, there remains the important matter of how the
Cimmerian victory over Urartu best fits into the wider geopolitical setting of Sargon's reign. Positing a late date, Fuchs argues that
Sargon annexed Kummuh in 707 soon after learning about Urartu's
disastrous loss in Cimmeria. Sargon's move, he reasons, would have
been extremely rash at any other time, since it removed the buffer area that had previously separated the two enemy states.[21] I do
not see the shared border as a prominent factor. Although it is convenient for modern historians to discuss the relationship between
Assyria, Urartu, and small, regional polities in terms of buffer or
client states and clearly demarcated borders, we cannot suppose
that the ancients understood the situation exactly this way. After
all, the ancient understanding of geographical space did not accord
with our modern bird's-eye view of the world.[22] Nor did they share
the modern nation-state's obsession with guarding the integrity of
a notional borderline. On the contrary, the fact that Assyrian officials writing from provinces and client states frequently refer to
"the (Urartian) governor opposite me" suggests that the Assyrians
conceptualized a shared border with Urartu all across the north, not
just in Kummuh.[23]

As to the rashness of Kummuh's annexation, let us consider
the context. By 707 Sargon had accomplished all of his main objectives. The Assyrians held sway from the Sinai Desert to the Persian
Gulf. Rulers in Cyprus had recently sent gifts, while Midas of
Phrygia's peace overtures had neutralized the fractious Tabalian
polities. Concord prevailed in the central Zagros provinces. There
was nothing to stop Sargon from acting when the opportunity to
annex Kummuh arose—that is, when the situation in Babylonia sta-
bilized. Anticipating the possibility of a Urartian pushback against

Kummuh, he appointed a second field marshal, the "*turtān* of the left" (*turtān šumeli*) to secure the area (and indeed police the whole western Empire) with a large army of over twenty thousand bowmen, 150 chariots, fifteen hundred cavalrymen, and one thousand heavy infantry.[24] Had the Urartians just suffered the kind of disastrous battlefield defeat that Fuchs imagines, such precautions would not have been necessary. If, however, the Urartians had enjoyed seven years of relative peace with Assyria in which to recover their military capability, then Sargon's defensive measures seem natural and in character. Thus, the annexation of Kummuh signified the logical completion of a series of events set in motion at the beginning of Sargon's reign. The move was neither rash nor dependent upon a sudden Urartian failure.

By contrast, Sargon's abrupt, mid-campaign change of plan in 714 makes little sense unless some important event like the Cimmerian victory over Urartu inspired it. For the five years leading up to Sargon's confrontation with Rusa at Mount Waush, the two kings had avoided battle prudently. Though they both attempted to control Mannea and regularly campaigned there, they did not meet in battle during that time. Open warfare posed too great a risk, because the armies appeared evenly matched and both kings needed to deal with pressing matters elsewhere. Syria-Palestine, Anatolia, and the middle Zagros occupied Sargon's attention, while Rusa targeted the area around Lake Sevan and plotted with Assyria's enemies to gain some advantage over Sargon. After five years of cold war, what would make these kings suddenly risk open warfare? The most likely explanation is that in early 714 Rusa went back to the Lake Sevan area and attacked the Cimmerians, who routed the Urartian army and caused Rusa to retreat back to Tushpa. The round trip probably would have been in the range of five hundred to six hundred miles and taken a month or two to accomplish, though without a clearly identified itinerary we cannot be certain. In terms of distance and elapsed time, the operation would have been roughly comparable to Sargon's 720 Der campaign. Just as the Assyrians mounted two campaigns to widely different areas in that year, Rusa initiated a second campaign in 714. To be sure, circumstances were not the same for Rusa as they had been for Sargon. I make the analogy simply to demonstrate that it was possible to undertake two arduous campaigns in one year. Just as Sargon had fought for survival in 720, Rusa did what he thought necessary in

714. Knowing that Sargon was in Mannea and believing that the Assyrians would invade Urartu as soon as they discovered what had happened in Cimmeria, Rusa took steps to defend himself. He mustered troops from the survivors (including his clansmen), men still in Urartu, and clients. Together they joined his allies near Mount Waush in Wishdish to await further developments. Sargon, who began the annual campaign as a routine tax-gathering and punitive expedition, paused to weigh his options in Mannea while reports of the Urartian debacle caught up with him. News could travel quite fast via messengers working in relays. Once he understood the significance of the opportunity that Rusa's recent defeat presented him, Sargon adjusted his plans, moved to Panzish, and thence northward into Wishdish, where he defeated Rusa decisively. Rusa fled, and the Urartians were routed just as they had been when fighting the Cimmerians. The Assyrians then marched in triumph through Urartian territory, looting every settlement in their path. Eventually Sargon sent his main force home, while he and handpicked volunteers veered aside to punish Urzana of Muṣaṣir for neglecting his client duties. The Urartian crisis had created an opportunity for the Assyrians. Recognizing this, each king had to react quickly and decisively; hence the staccato timing of subsequent events.

The overall context makes this scenario preferable to that of Fuchs and Mayer. Given the deliberate, restrained tenor of the Assyrian-Urartian conflict before 714, the sudden eruption of all-out war would be difficult to fathom without the Cimmerian catalyst, particularly in view of the relative ease of the Assyrian victory at Waush, followed by their march unopposed through Urartu. Moreover, the excited, urgent tone of letters, one of which triumphantly claims, "they (the Urartians) are very much afraid of the king, my lord. The situation is very good" (SAA I 32), does not fit the situation in 710–709. At that time, the Assyrian army, which was occupied with the pursuit and defeat of Merodach-Baladan, did not pose an immediate threat to Urartu. By contrast, in 714 the stunning fact of Rusa's defeat was indeed breaking news, since the Assyrian army was already in position on the Urartian frontier. The whole episode makes sense if Rusa, assuming that Sargon would attack after hearing of his foe's vulnerability, arrived at Waush to defend himself. When the Assyrians duly acted, the weakened Urartians broke and ran. Having lost their second major battle within a few months, they had no hope of stopping the Assyrians' invasion. Humiliated and defeated, Rusa killed himself or was forcibly removed from the throne.

Assyrian and Urartian Relations with Urzana of Muşaşir

Central to the reconstruction of the chronology of the period is an interpretation of the political relationships between Urzana, the ruler of the small buffer state Muşaşir, and the kings of Assyria and Urartu. Historians often assume that possession of Muşaşir shifted violently between the Assyrians and the Urartians, so that when one held the city, the other lost all contact with it.[25] For example, Roaf equates the Urartian troop movement in the vicinity of Muşaşir, referred to in several undated Assyrian letters (e.g., SAA I 29 and SAA V 1, 86, 87, 88, 147), with "the invasion of Muşaşir described in Rusa's steles."[26] In fact, neither set of texts alludes to an invasion (at least not in the standard sense), and nothing indicates that they describe the same events. Rusa's bilingual steles from Movana, Merghe Kavan, and Topzawa state that he battled Urzana in Assyrian territory and then went to Muşaşir, which he (Rusa) occupied for a couple of weeks before leaving again. A siege appears to have been unnecessary. Although the inscriptions say that Rusa reinstated Urzana, they do not indicate that he annexed the city formally (left troops or officials in charge), though he obviously considered Urzana a client.[27] Sargon's eighth campaign account echoes Rusa's inscriptions, similarly celebrating a short stay in Muşaşir after seizing it, and bragging pointedly about looting the very temple to which Rusa had donated earlier. One might argue that the reverse is true and Rusa's inscriptions echo Sargon's actions, but given that Rusa died within a few months of Sargon's visit, this seems extremely unlikely. Although Sargon's Letter to Ashur claims that he "incorporated the people of the district of Muşaşir as people of the land of Assyria and imposed on them duties and labor service as if they were Assyrians," he does not say that he left troops in the city.[28] Moreover, no source concerning Muşaşir suggests that either the Assyrians or the Urartians inflicted much (if any) damage on it or garrisoned it on a permanent basis.[29]

As to the violent conquest of Muşaşir, the closest any text comes to suggesting combat is a passage describing how Sargon's troops terrified the inhabitants into submission: "Against that city

I let my troops' battle cry roar like thunder and the inhabitants
[. . .], the old men and women of its people went up on the roofs of
their houses to weep bitterly [. . .] they groveled on all fours to save
their lives."[30] In other words, the citizens surrendered without a
fight. The surviving relief drawing depicting the takeover of Muṣaṣir
suggests that the Assyrians scaled the walls surreptitiously and
simply seized control.[31] Similarly, the Assyrian letters that report
Urartian forces on the march to Muṣaṣir do not allude to combat of
any kind.[32] In those cases the Urartians seem to have been gathering to perform the pre-campaign rituals set to take place in the city,
which was an important cult center near Waisi, the general muster
point for campaigns into Mannea. Certainly, troop movements to a
city did not necessarily indicate an attack upon it.[33] On the contrary,
maneuvers in friendly territory usually occurred in preparation for
a campaign elsewhere, as SAA I 29 attests. The relatively urgent
tone of the reports on Muṣaṣir stems from the need to discover the
Urartians' campaign destination (for obvious reasons), rather than
from concern over losing possession of the city, which the Assyrians
did not hold in any case. At present there is no way to date these letters (SAA I 29 and SAA V 1, 86, 87, 88, 147) or to make them fit with
Rusa's inscriptions. If they do concern a pre-campaign muster, then
proximity makes Mannea the likeliest Urartian target. Hence, a date
before 714 seems probable.

During most of Sargon's reign, neither the Urartian king nor
Sargon held Muṣaṣir in a physical sense, albeit both claimed sovereignty over it, demanded tribute and troops, and expected fealty
from its ruler. How these kings treated Urzana depended on what
political message each wanted to send the other and Urzana. What
happened there over the course of Sargon's reign was all part of the
political game, and all three kings understood that implicitly. A
pawn in the wider contest between the two great powers, Urzana
simply did what he had to do in order to survive. As previously mentioned, in his Letter to Ashur, Sargon justified plundering Muṣaṣir
on the grounds that Urzana had neglected to ask after his health, thus
implying that Sargon already considered Urzana a client in 714. In a
letter probably written after 714, Urzana himself freely admitted that
he had made no attempt to prevent the Urartians from performing
rituals in the temple, despite Sargon's prohibition against this.[34] As
mentioned earlier, one of the letters concerning the Cimmerian loss
contains a report from Urzana (SAA I 30), while another (SAA I 31)

relates that he has gone to meet the Urartian king. This evidence indicates that Urzana, like other petty kings, maintained contact with both great powers simultaneously and succumbed to their will when necessary. Throughout this period, both Assyria and Urartu claimed sovereignty over Muṣaṣir, which was of vital strategic interest to both of them. The level of influence that each king exerted over Urzana fluctuated. Neither Sargon nor Rusa ever achieved exclusive control of the city, except for the very brief interludes (a period of a few weeks) when they actually occupied it.

Considering these factors together, the likeliest sequence of events begins with Rusa taking over Urartu sometime around 730, while Tiglath-pileser or Shalmaneser V reigned in Assyria. During the period between Rusa's accession and Sargon's, the former avoided conflict with Assyria and campaigned in the northeast. Sargon's contested accession gave Rusa the opportunity to reassert Urartian hegemony over Mannea and buffer states like Muṣaṣir, and thus to reclaim for Urartu the prestige lost during Tiglath-pileser's reign. Erected after more than a decade of successful rule, Rusa's bilingual steles celebrated his victory over Urzana and brief occupation of Muṣaṣir. These actions may also have broken an existing treaty with Assyria and sparked a power struggle with Sargon that lasted until Rusa's death in 714 or 713. At first the two tested each other through proxy wars and prestige acts until finally, in 714, the conflict escalated into open war. Throughout this period, the rulers of buffer states, such as Ukku, Muṣaṣir, and Hubushkia, colluded, connived, calculated, and bought and sold information, all the while fawning upon or resisting the great kings as expedience dictated. The prestige game continued until something critical happened to change the stakes: that something was the Cimmerian defeat of Urartu in 714. There is some question, however, about the identity of the Urartian king who opposed Sargon.

The Sequence of Urartian Kings

Since no Urartian king list has been recovered so far, our understanding of the order in which their kings ruled depends largely on the concordance between Urartian and Assyrian royal inscriptions. The latter affirm that between 719 and 714 Sargon fought against a king called Rusa. The lack of identifying patronymic in the Assyrian texts has led to disagreement about whether Sargon struggled with Rusa, son of Sarduri, hereafter "Rusa (S)," or Rusa, son of Erimena, hereafter "Rusa (E)." Since the reign of Sarduri II, the presumed father of Rusa (S), overlapped with that of Tiglath-pileser III, it has generally been assumed that Sargon faced Rusa (S), who would have become king sometime around 730. Placing Rusa (E) in the sequence of Urartian kings has proved more difficult. In a recent, exhaustive review of the possible scenarios, Michael Roaf has proposed a new one—namely that from 719–714 Sargon fought Rusa (E) and not Rusa (S). By his reckoning, Rusa (E) usurped the throne sometime before 722 and then spent the first several years of his reign on building projects, only turning his attention to military endeavors after Sargon asserted himself in the east. After hostilities broke out in 719, the conflict escalated until 714, when Sargon defeated Rusa (E), who was deposed or killed himself shortly thereafter. According to Roaf, Rusa (S) then took his rightful place as king.[35]

The idea that Sargon's opponent was a usurper originates from the Letter to Ashur that describes a statue of Rusa (lineage unstated) among the plunder taken from Muṣaṣir in 714. The statue's inscription states that Rusa won the throne with just his chariot and a team of horses.[36] In other words, the Rusa represented by the statue did not inherit the throne by birthright but rather won it by force. Based on this interpretation, Roaf argues that, as the son of a legitimate king, Rusa (S) would not have had to fight for the throne; hence, the statue must depict Rusa (E). In my view, this argument carries little weight for several reasons. For one, it is well known that even king's sons sometimes had to fight to succeed their fathers. Sargon himself and his grandson, Esarhaddon, are two prime examples. Furthermore, Roaf's hypothesis also creates an unlikely scenario, one in which a usurper, Rusa (E), won the throne but allowed the rightful heir and the member of a different dynasty, Rusa (S), to survive, a constant, public reminder of the new king's illegitimacy. As Altan Çilingiroğlu notes, "No new dynasty has ever shown this tolerance to the members of the old dynasty, which had been taken down by force."[37] Even if it is possible that Rusa (S) somehow eluded his usurping namesake (and for a lengthy period), a more likely circumstance would simply be that Rusa (S) won the throne over other claimants.

Additional factors militate against Roaf's proposed chronology. Since Assyrian sources demonstrate that Argishti II ruled Urartu by 709 at the latest, Roaf's arrangement would compress the reign of Rusa (S) into a scant three or four years (713–709) that would leave little time for him to accomplish the deeds enumerated in his inscriptions.[38] For example, one text, the Tsovinar rock inscription, records the conquest by Rusa (S) of twenty-three kingdoms in the area of Lake Sevan, including the land of Guriana, the very location to which the defeated Urartian army retreated after they lost to the Cimmerians (a point to which I will return).[39] Similarly, the Movana stele inscription, which celebrates Rusa (S)'s punishment of Urzana, contains the summative statement: "In my years I enlarged the country of Biainili (Urartu), I oppressed the enemy country. The gods gave me days of joy, a multitude of good days of joy they establ[ished]."[40] The claims made in these texts reflect the accomplishments of a long-term and mature king, not someone who had been on the throne four years at most. By contrast, Rusa (E)'s surviving narrative inscription, the Gövelek/Keşiş Göl stele, emphasizes his building projects and temple dedications, the latter including the unique gift of "a sheep and a fat sheep to the god, Ashur."[41] Such a dedication would have been particularly incongruous during Sargon's lifetime, given the animosity that existed between the two countries. On the contrary, Rusa (E)'s mention of Ashur makes sense only if it took place sometime *after* another Rusa—Rusa (ca. 680–640), son of Argishti II—deported Assyrians to Urartu and settled them at Ayanis.[42] That Rusa (E) was Sargon's opponent, therefore, appears highly unlikely. That said, other factors require consideration.

Sargon's inscriptions dating to 714 claim that Rusa killed himself shortly thereafter, but those of 713 protest that Ambaris of Tabal wrote to Rusa asking for help against Assyria. Roaf sees this as a contradiction that proves that there must have been two Rusas ruling in succession, and so Rusa (S) must have followed Rusa (E) on the throne. The traditional view, he argues, leaves no time for the collusion between Rusa and Ambaris to have taken place before Rusa's suicide. Assuming that the crime and its punishment happened almost simultaneously, Roaf does not consider that Assyrian kings did not—indeed could not—always react immediately to intelligence received, particularly if they were already campaigning in another theater of operations. Inscriptions mention clients' infractions as a way to justify the resulting (and later) punitive campaign, but there is simply no reason to suppose a strict temporal connection between the two. Even assuming that Sargon did act immediately after learning about Ambaris's disloyalty, the collusion still could have happened at any time before 713. In other words, discovery of the crime and the crime itself need not have been contemporaneous. The fact that the Letter to Ashur singles out the Tabalian objects among the booty from Muṣaṣir implies that the Assyrians already knew about Ambaris's disloyalty in 714. Therefore, there is no need to find a second Rusa to act as Ambaris's coconspirator.

Finally, Roaf also introduces iconographic evidence in support of the supposition that Rusa (E) ruled before Rusa (S). Urartian kings, like many Near Eastern monarchs, marked royal belongings such as shields with incised lion figures to symbolize ownership. As many scholars have noted, the lions of Urartian kings exhibit subtle differences. According to Roaf, these differences represent a clear iconographic development that reveals the proper chronological order of the kings, as Rusa (E)'s lions fit nicely between those of Sarduri II and Rusa (S).[43] Since this subjective argument is based on the unverifiable assumption that Urartian lion-representation progressed in this linear fashion, it must be rejected. We cannot determine when the lions were produced without also knowing where and how—whether by the same workshop, in the same city, under like orders to create something new but not wholly different.[44] In the interest of space, I have not attempted to consider every point that Roaf raises. Even so, given the objections I have raised here, I must reject Roaf's hypothesis and maintain the view that Sargon's opponent was Rusa, son of Sarduri, who ruled from about 730 until late 714 or early 713. Throughout the book, when I refer to Rusa, I mean Rusa, son of Sarduri.

This excursus has not been exhaustive. I have discussed only the salient points of contention, for a detailed treatment of every competing theory or potential shred of evidence would require a book in its own right. The present body of evidence leaves us in the odd position of being able to arrange it in almost any number of ways, depending on what pieces we include and how we interpret them. It is important to stress that other chronological solutions—particularly those of Fuchs, Mayer, and Roaf—are technically possible, although, for the reasons just addressed, I maintain that the evidence-based chronology proposed in this work—in effect, the traditional one—is far preferable.

Notes

Citing Ancient Texts

When citing an ancient text, it is the custom to note the publication volume and text number without intervening punctuation (SAA I 25), so that the reader does not mistake the text number for a page number. Detailed citations follow the sequence: text, column number, and line number with periods between them. The citation "RINAP 3 49.iii.14" refers to the third volume in the Royal Inscriptions of the Neo-Assyrian Period, text 49, column 3, line 14. However, publications of cuneiform texts vary widely in terms of format, so citation style may vary accordingly. In the endnotes, text citations are designed so that readers going to the original source can find the reference easily. When citing a modern source, the convention is to separate the title from the page with a comma: Radner, "Between a Rock and a Hard Place," 215. When citing the editor's comments in a volume of texts, I give author, volume abbreviation, and page number after a comma: Parpola, SAA I, xi. If, however, only one of the editors wrote the commentary in a text edition, the citation reads as follows: [name] in [volume abbreviation], page number (e.g., Fuchs in SAA XV, iii).

Abbreviations for Cuneiform Texts

ABC	Grayson, A. K. *Assyrian and Babylonian Chronicles*. Winona Lake, Ind.: Eisenbrauns, 2000.
AJ 711	Fuchs, Andreas. *Die Annalen des Jahres 711 v. CHR*. State Archives of Assyria Studies 8. Helsinki: Neo-Assyrian Text Corpus Project, 1998.
CAD	*The Assyrian Dictionary of the University of Chicago*. Edited by Martha T. Roth. 26 volumes. Chicago: University of Chicago Press, 1956–2011.
CT 22	H. W. King and R. Campbell Thompson. *Cuneiform Texts from Babylonian Tablets in the British Museum*. London: Trustees of the British Museum, 1906.
CTN II	J. N. Postgate. *The Governor's Palace Archive*. Cuneiform Texts from Nimrud II. London: British School of Archaeology in Iraq, 1973.
CTN III	Dalley, Stephanie, and J. N. Postgate. *The Tablets from Fort Shalmaneser*. Cuneiform Texts from Nimrud III. London: British School of Archaeology in Iraq, 1983.
CTN V	H. W. F. Saggs. *The Nimrud Letters, 1952*. Cuneiform Texts from Nimrud V. London: British School of Archaeology in Iraq, 2001.

CTU   Mirjo Salvini. *Corpus dei testi urartei: Le iscrizioni su pietra e roccia*, vols. 1–3. Documenta Asiana 8. Rome: Ist. di Studi sulle Civilta dell'Egeo e del Vicino Oriente, 2008.

ISK   Fuchs, Andreas. *Die Inschriften Sargons II. aus Khorsabad*. Göttingen: Cuvillier, 1994.

Najafehabad   Levine, Louis D. *Two Neo-Assyrian Stelae from Iran*. Royal Ontario Museum of Art and Archaeology Occasional Paper 23. Toronto: Royal Ontario Museum, 1972.

RIMB   Frame, Grant. *Rulers of Babylonia: From the Second Dynasty of Isin to the End of the Assyrian Domination (1157–612 B.C.)*. Royal Inscriptions of Mesopotamia: Babylonian Periods, vol. 2. Toronto: University of Toronto Press, 1995.

RINAP 1   Tadmor, H., and S. Yamada. *The Royal Inscriptions of Tiglath-Pileser III (744–727 B.C.) and Shalmaneser V (726–722 B.C.), Kings of Assyria*. Royal Inscriptions of the Neo-Assyrian Period 1. Winona Lake, Ind.: Eisenbrauns, 2011.

RINAP 3   Grayson, A. Kirk and Jamie Novotny. *The Royal Inscriptions of Sennacherib, King of Assyria (704–681 B.C.)*. The Royal Inscriptions of the Neo-Assyrian Period 3, parts 1 and 2. Winona Lake, Ind.: Eisenbrauns, 2012, 2014.

RINAP 4   Leichty, Erle. *The Royal Inscriptions of Esarhaddon, King of Assyria (680–669 B.C.)*. The Royal Inscriptions of the Neo-Assyrian Period 4. Winona Lake, Ind.: Eisenbrauns, 2011.

SAA   State Archives of Assyria I–XIX. Helsinki: Neo-Assyrian Text Corpus Project, 1987–2012.

TCL III   Thureau-Dangin, F. *Une relation de la huitième campagne de Sargon*. Textes cunéiformes du Louvre 3. Paris: 1912.

Introduction

1. This is not to say, however, that the Assyrians necessarily controlled all the land within their territory. For further discussion, see Liverani, "The Growth of the Assyrian Empire," 90–92; Parker, "Geographies of Power," 126–28; Parker, "Hegemony, Power, and the Use of Force," 283–87.

2. Radner, "Traders in the Neo-Assyrian Period," 102; Kozuh, "A Hand Anything but Hidden," 77–86. Dalley, "Foreign Chariotry and Cavalry," 47, notes that "when the word 'trader' (*tamkaru*) is specified during the neo-Assyrian period, it is almost always qualified with ANŠE. KUR.RA ('horses')."

3. However, Sargon did not practice economic imperialism in the modern sense. For more on the economic strategy of Neo-Assyrian kings, see Kozuh, "A Hand Anything but Hidden," 77–86.

4. Bahrani, *The Graven Image*, 134.
5. Adam T. Smith, "Urartian Spectacle," 125.
6. State Archives of Assyria Online, Oracc ("Open Richly Annotated Cuneiform Corpus"), University of Pennsylvania, http://oracc.museum.upenn.edu/saao; The Royal Inscriptions of the Neo-Assyrian Period, Oracc, University of Pennsylvania, http://oracc.museum.upenn.edu/rinap/.
7. See, for example, BM 11882, a relief from the palace of Tiglath-pileser III now in the British Museum.
8. SAA XVII 2.
9. Liverani, "The King and His Audience," 374–75.
10. Ponchia, "Mountain Routes in Assyrian Royal Inscriptions, Part II," 244.
11. Liverani, "The Ideology of the Assyrian Empire," 306–307.
12. Lanfranchi, "Consensus to Empire," 82. Lanfranchi notes that Sargon's inscriptions "are apt to distort past events in the perspective of the celebration of the successful conclusion of a long-term progamme." See also Tadmor, "History and Ideology of the Assyrian Royal Inscriptions"; Tadmor, "Propaganda, Literature, Historiography"; Liverani, "Memorandum on the Approach to Historiographic Texts"; Van de Mieroop, *Cuneiform Texts and the Writing of History*, 55.
13. Fagan, "I Fell upon Him Like a Furious Arrow," 87.
14. For a brief but illuminating study of the language of conquest in Sargon's Annals, see Tappy, "The Final Years of Israelite Samaria," 261–66.
15. Assman, *Cultural Memory and Early Civilization*. See also Jonkers, *The Topography of Remembrance*.
16. Niven and Berger, *Writing the History of Memory*, 11.
17. Renger, "Neuassyrische Königinschriften," 109–28.
18. Gadd, "Inscribed Prisms of Sargon II."
19. Fuchs, *AJ 711*, 81–96.
20. *ISK* Stier 1–106.
21. *ISK* S1–4 (Türschwellen/thresholds). For an overview of the type and placement of Sargon's inscriptions, see Russell, *The Writing on the Wall*, 106–10.
22. *ISK* Ann. (Annals) and Prunk. (Display).
23. Fuchs, *AJ 711*, 85–88.
24. Hawkins, "The New Sargon Stele from Hama," 160, lines 5–8; Lambert, "Portion of Inscribed Stela of Sargon II," 83.
25. Frame, "The Tell 'Acharneh Stela," 56, fig. 7.
26. TCL III; Mayer, "Sargons Feldzug gegen Urartu." For an excellent English translation, see Foster, *Before the Muses*, 790–813. In this volume, chapter 4 discusses the eighth campaign in detail.
27. Saggs, "Historical Texts and Fragments of Sargon II."
28. Parpola in SAA I, xi, xvi, estimates that Sargon's total correspondence (letters sent and received) amounted to as many as 15,300 letters a year. See also Radner, "An Imperial Communication Network," 81–83.

29. *The Prosopography of the Neo-Assyrian Empire*, vols. 1–3. Helsinki: Neo-Assyrian Text Corpus Project, 1998–2001. Published as six separate parts.

30. See, for example, SAA V 113, in which Gabbu-ana-Ashur, the palace herald, wrote that "my messengers have been going back and forth to Nabu-le'i (governor of Birati), Ashur-belu-da''an (possibly governor of Halziatbar), and Ashur-reṣua (the Assyrian delegate in Kumme)."

31. Liverani, *Prestige and Interest*.

32. SAA I; SAA V; SAA XV; SAA XIX.

33. For the Bukan stele, see Eph'al, "The Bukan Aramaic Inscription"; Lemaire, "Une inscription araméene"; Sokoloff, "The Old Aramaic Inscription from Bukan"; Fales, "Evidence for West-East Contacts." For Rabat Tepe, see Kargar and Binandeh, "A Preliminary Report of Excavations at Rabat Tepe."

34. See, for example, Hawkins, *Corpus of Hieroglyphic Luwian Inscriptions*.

35. Albenda, *Ornamental Wall Painting*.

36. Russell, *The Writing on the Wall*, 99.

37. On the ideology of Dur-Sharrukin, see Battini, "Un example de propagande néo-assyrienne," 219; Novák, "From Ashur to Nineveh," 181. On building the city, see Parpola, "The Construction of Dur-Šarrukin," 66–67.

38. Botta and Flandin, *Monuments de Ninive*; Loud, *Khorsabad Part I* and *Khorsabad Part II*; Albenda, *Palace of Sargon, King of Assyria*.

39. There is some debate about whether each room depicts a single campaign. See Franklin, "The Room V Reliefs," 265; Reade, "Narrative Composition in Assyrian Sculpture;" Reade, "Sargon's Campaigns of 720, 716 and 715 B.C."

40. A relief fragment in the Oriental Institute may once have been part of a series depicting the Babylonian campaign. The slab was found among debris in Room VIII, the throne room. Loud, *Khorsabad Part I*, 60.

41. Bahrani, *Rituals of War*; Ataç, *The Mythology of Kingship in Neo-Assyrian Art*; Winter, *On Art in the Ancient Near East*, vol. 1.

42. Liverani, "The King and His Audience," 380–82.

43. Collon, "Examples of Ethnic Diversity on Assyrian Reliefs"; Reade, "Sargon's Campaigns of 720, 716 and 715 B.C."

44. Reade, "Narrative Composition in Assyrian Sculpture"; Nadali, "Assyrians to War." See also Winter, *On Art in the Ancient Near East*, vol. 1, 3–108.

45. Most scholars, while acknowledging that ideology influenced royal inscriptions and reliefs, agree that artists and scribes also attempted to be as accurate as possible. See, for example, Gunter, "Representations of Urartian and Western Iranian Fortress Architecture," 103–104. See also Tadmor, "Propaganda, Literature, Historiography"; Liverani, "Memorandum on the Approach to Historiographic Texts."

46. Jacoby, "The Representation and Identification of Cities on Assyrian Reliefs."

47. Blakely and Hardin, "Southwestern Judah in the Late Eighth Century B.C.E.," 40–41.
48. See especially Adam T. Smith, "Archaeologies of Sovereignty"; Harmanşah, "Beyond Aššur"; Harmanşah, *Of Rocks and Water.*
49. Parker, "Hegemony, Power, and the Use of Force," 291.

Chapter 1

1. Liverani, *Prestige and Interest,* 150–59.
2. Foster, *Before the Muses,* 880–913.
3. Ehrenreich, *Blood Rites,* 134. See also Melville, "Ideology, Politics, and the Assyrian Understanding of Defeat."
4. *ISK* Klein. Inschr. 3.2.6.
5. Postgate, "Assyria: The Home Provinces"; Postgate, "The Economic Structure of the Assyrian Empire."
6. Pečírcova, "Administrative Organization of the Neo-Assyrian Empire"; Pečírcova, "Administrative Methods of Assyrian Imperialism"; Postgate, "The Economic Structure of the Assyrian Empire," 211; Postgate, "The Invisible Hierarchy"; Ponchia, "Administrators and Administrated in Neo-Assyrian Times."
7. Na'aman, "Ekron under the Assyrian and Egyptian Empires," 87; Wilkinson et al., "Landscape and Settlement," 41; Melville, "Kings of Tabal."
8. Radner, "Provinz"; Postgate, "Assyria: The Home Provinces."
9. Mattila, *The King's Magnates*; Parpola, "The Neo-Assyrian Ruling Class"; Parpola, "The Assyrian Cabinet"; Radner, "Royal Decision-Making."
10. Mattila, *The King's Magnates,* 138.
11. Pečírcova, "The Administrative Methods of Assyrian Imperialism," 168–75.
12. SAA XIX 89; CTN II 196.
13. Mattila, *The King's Magnates,* 141. The practice of spreading estates began earlier, probably under Adad-nirari III. See also Postgate, "Assyria: The Home Provinces," 2–5. For more on Sargon's administrative reforms, see May,"*m*Ali-talīmu or What Can Be Learned from the Destruction of Figurative Complexes?"
14. SAA I 34. See also Mattila, *The King's Magnates,* 145; Whiting in SAA XII, xxi–xxxvi; Postgate, "The Ownership and Exploitation of Land in Assyria," 147; Bedford, "The Economy of the Near East," 78.
15. For the *ilku* system, see Postgate, *Taxation and Conscription,* especially 221–23; Postgate, "The Economic Structure of the Assyrian Empire," 210.
16. Postgate, "The Assyrian Army at Zamua," 95. For the problem of identifying eunuchs in the army, see Dalley and Postgate, CTN III, 28.
17. On foreign soldiers in the Assyrian army, see Dalley, "Foreign Chariotry and Cavalry"; Y. Kaplan, "Recruitment of Foreign Soldiers."
18. Postgate, "Itu'." See also Fales, "The Assyrian Words for '(Foot) Soldier,'" 82.
19. General studies of the Neo-Assyrian military organization and warfare include Manitius, "Das stehende Heer der Assyrerkönig"; Saggs,

"Assyrian Warfare in the Sargonid Period"; Malbran-Labat, *l'Armée et l'Organisation Militaire de l'Assyrie*; Mayer, *Politik und Kriegskunst der Assyrer*; Fales, *Guerre et paix en Assyrie*.

20. Reade, "The Neo-Assyrian Court and Army"; Dezső, "The Reconstruction of the Assyrian Army—reliefs."

21. For the most recent and thorough attempt to sort out all the available evidence for the structure of Sargon's army and for the Neo-Assyrian army in general, see Dezső, "Reconstruction of the Assyrian Army of Sargon II"; Dezső, *The Assyrian Army I*, vol. 1; Dezső, *The Assyrian Army I*, vol. 2.

22. Dezső, *The Assyrian Army I*, vol. 1; Dezső, *The Assyrian Army I*, vol. 2. See also Fales, "The Assyrian Words for '(Foot) Soldier'"; Scurlock, "Review of Fales *Guerre et paix en Assyrie*," 313. As Scurlock points out, the tribal contingents in the Assyrian army did not enjoy the same status as, say, Roman auxiliaries. Nor did they function in the same way. Nevertheless, since the Assyrians clearly distinguished these groups from other soldiers, the term "auxiliary," used broadly, seems to apply.

23. After Postgate, "The Invisible Hierarchy," 344.

24. Dalley and Postgate, CTN III, 28. Parpola in SAA I, xiv. Parpola asserts that *ša qurbūti* were comprised "largely if not exclusively" of eunuchs, but the evidence—especially the pictorial evidence—does not support such a categorical conclusion.

25. See, for example, Albenda, *Palace of Sargon, King of Assyria*, plates 94, 95, 97, 99.

26. Mattila, *The King's Magnates*, 153; Dezső, "Reconstruction of the Assyrian Army of Sargon II," 127 and Fig. 7; Dalley and Postgate, CTN III, 37–38.

27. Dalley and Postgate, CTN III, 33, 39. See also Dezső, *The Assyrian Army I*, vol. 2, 74.

28. TCL III 320–21.

29. Postgate, *Taxation and Conscription*, 225. See also Dezső, "Reconstruction of the Assyrian Army of Sargon II," 116. For a different view, see Dalley and Postgate, CTN III, 31. For the full range of texts in which these officials appear, see CAD Q, 315–16.

30. See, for example, SAA I 240, in which an unnamed official writes to Sargon: "Now, the king, my lord, should send a royal bodyguard to them (with the order)."

31. Postgate, "The Assyrian Army at Zamua," 95–96.

32. Littauer and Crouwell, *Wheeled Vehicles and Ridden Animals*. Although Sargon's reliefs never depict more than two superimposed horses, the plumes and reins shown sometimes indicate the presence of three. See, for example, Albenda, *Palace of Sargon, King of Assyria*, plates 103, 116 and 121. We can get a good idea of general wheel design from three small (less than ten inches in diameter) eight-spoked iron wheels with bronze bearings and hubs found in the Nabu temple at Dur-Sharrukin, where they probably belonged to some type of cult furniture or cart. Loud, *Khorsabad Part II*, 62 and plate 24.

33. Dezső, "Reconstruction of the Assyrian Army of Sargon II," 123.
34. There is some evidence that under Sargon chariots sometimes had four-man teams. Albenda, *Palace of Sargon, King of Assyria*, plate 116; Littauer and Crowell, *Wheeled Vehicles and Ridden Animals*, 104.
35. Dezső, "Reconstruction of the Assyrian Army of Sargon II," 115–16.
36. Mattila, *The King's Magnates*, 151.
37. Dalley, "Foreign Chariotry and Cavalry, 39." For officers of the Samarian unit, see CTN III 99 §E.
38. Littauer and Crouwell, *Wheeled Vehicles and Ridden Animals*, 141.
39. Dezső, "Reconstruction of the Assyrian Army of Sargon II," 120.
40. *ISK* Prunk. 35–36; Ann. 5.
41. See, for example, Botta and Flandin, *Monuments de Ninive*, plate 66; Noble, "Assyrian Chariotry and Cavalry," 65.
42. Littauer and Crouwel, *Wheeled Vehicles and Ridden Animals*, 142.
43. Noble, "Assyrian Chariotry and Cavalry," 65. On Sargon's reliefs all the horses have heavily tasseled bridles and reins, and it is possible that these tassels prevented the reins from slipping over the horse's head. It should be noted that although cavalry all carry bow and quiver cases strapped to their backs, they are never shown actually discharging a weapon on the gallop, and it may be that they still preferred to shoot from a stationary position.
44. Archer, "Chariotry to Cavalry," 71. Archer has recently made the interesting proposal that cavalry were an Assyrian innovation, having developed in the ninth century in "an attempt to develop a rough terrain chariot." He goes on to argue that "the early cavalry depicted on the Balawat gates (of Shalmaneser III) operated exactly as the chariot teams of the late second millennium did and as contemporary first millennium chariots continued to do . . . all that is missing is the chariot itself."
45. On the horse trade, see Dalley, "Foreign Chariotry and Cavalry, 45–48"; Heidhorn, "The Horses of Kush." On the prestige role of horses, see Cantrell, "Some Trust in Horses."
46. Postgate, *Taxation and Conscription*, 144; Dalley and Postgate, CTN III, 36–37.
47. Postgate, *Taxation and Conscription*, 210; Dezső, *The Assyrian Army I*, vol. 2, 43.
48. Dezső, "Reconstruction of the Assyrian Army of Sargon II," 95–96; Dalley and Postgate, CTN III, 28–31.
49. SAA V 119.
50. Dalley and Postgate, CTN III, 33–34; Dezső, "Reconstruction of the Assyrian Army of Sargon II," 94–95.
51. Postgate, *Taxation and Conscription*, 210.
52. SAA V 202.
53. SAA I 22.

54. SAA I 181.
55. SAA I 241.
56. Fales, "The Assyrian Words for '(Foot) Soldier,'" 82–84.
57. On scale armor, see Barron, "Late Assyrian Arms and Armor," 173. On Assyrian helmets, see Dezső and Curtis, "Assyrian Iron Helmets from Nimrud."
58. The evidence for slingers on Sargon's reliefs is problematic. Dezső finds only one possible example, but I have been unable to confirm his identification. Dezső, "Reconstruction of the Neo-Assyrian Army," 109.
59. Dezső, Assyrian Army I, vol. 1, 36–8.
60. See Botta and Flandin, Monuments de Ninive, vol. 2, plates 67, 96.
61. Postgate, "Itu'," 222; Dezső, "Reconstruction of the Assyrian Army of Sargon II," 98.
62. For further argumentation and references, see Postgate, "The Assyrian Army at Zamua," 103; Dezső, Assyrian Army I, vol. 1, 38–51.
63. In letters both groups are frequently mentioned performing various duties: SAA I 93, 97, 176 (internal security); SAA I 32 (intelligence gathering); SAA XV 136, 166, 238 (fort garrison duty).
64. SAA I 97.
65. SAA V 215. See also Postgate, "The Assyrian Army at Zamua."
66. SAA I 241; SAA V 21, 220.
67. Scurlock, "kallāpu," 730.
68. SAA V 46 (accompanying a messenger), 215 (mustering for campaign); SAA XV 68, 69 (accompanying messengers). See also Scurlock, "kallāpu," 731.
69. Barron, "Late Assyrian Arms and Armor," 38. On Assyrian ironworking during Sargon's reign, see Pleiner, "Three Assyrian Iron Artifacts from Khorsabad."
70. Barron, "Late Assyrian Arms and Armor," 39.
71. Ibid., 173.
72. See Balfour, "On a Remarkable Ancient Bow," for a possible example of a seventh-century Assyrian bow made of wood, sinew, and bone and covered in birch bark. This specimen was recovered in the nineteenth century from an Egyptian tomb that purportedly dated to the appropriate time period. The author, writing in 1897, claimed that he would donate the bow to Oxford, but I have not been able to verify that he did so. A relief dating to the reign of Sargon's great grandson, Ashurbanipal (669–627 B.C.), shows soldiers stringing a recurve bow. See Barnett, Assyrian Sculpture, plate 98.
73. Barron, "Late Assyrian Arms and Armor," 49.
74. Albenda, Palace of Sargon, King of Assyria, plates 136, 138. See also Barnett, Assyrian Sculpture, plate 56 (Tiglath-pileser III siege); panels from Sennacherib's South-West Palace (British Museum Room 28, nos. 7–9).
75. Cantrell, The Horsemen of Israel, 122.
76. Postgate, Taxation and Conscription, 222–24. See also SAA XV 105.

77. Review palaces have been discovered at Calah, Nineveh, and Dur-Sharrukin. For the Nineveh review palace, see Turner, "Tell Nebi Yūnus." For the *ekal māšarti* at Calah, see Oates and Oates, *Nimrud*, 144–54. For Dur-Sharrukin, see Loud, *Khorsabad Part II*, 75–77. Sargon's army typically mustered at Calah but is also known to have gathered at Arbela and in provinces such as Zamua.

78. RINAP 4 1.v.40–46.

79. Cantrell, *The Horsemen of Israel*, 126n56.

80. SAA XI 28; CTN V NL 2643. See also Postgate, "Assyrian Uniforms"; Fales, "Preparing for War in Assyria."

81. SAA V 152.

82. SAA I 241.

83. SAA XV 369.

84. SAA I 149.

85. SAA V 200; SAA V 79. On the "mule stable man" being the overseer of deportees, see Gallagher, "Assyrian Deportation Propaganda," 64–65. For the translation of "mule-stable man" as corvée officer, see Parker, *The Mechanics of Empire*, 146–47.

86. SAA I 155 and 154, respectively.

87. Fales, "Grain Reserves, Daily Rations"; Fales, "Preparing for War in Assyria." The letters on which Fales bases these studies are SAA V 250 and SAA I 257. See also De Odorico's comments in *Numbers and Quantifications*, 108–11; Marriott and Radner, "Sustaining the Assyrian Army," 132–33 (discussing the size of the army for Sargon's eighth campaign).

88. Fales in SAA XI, xxvii. For the actual texts, see CTN III 99–109; SAA XI 123, 125.

89. SAA XV 142. Unfortunately, this letter is quite fragmentary and the sender's name is not preserved.

90. Fales, "Central Syria in the Letters to Sargon II," 137–38. For an overview of the project and all it involved, see Parpola, "The Construction of Dur-Šarrukin."

91. SAA V 119. Straw was an essential component of mud brick, which was (and still is) the main building material in the Near East.

92. Engels, *Alexander the Great and the Logistics of the Macedonian Army*, 1.

93. Liverani, "The Growth of the Assyrian Empire"; Postgate, "Assyria: The Home Provinces"; Parker, "Geographies of Power."

94. Engels, *Alexander the Great and the Logistics of the Macedonian Army*, 18; Jonathan Roth, *The Logistics of the Roman Army*, 7–12; Spalinger, *War in Ancient Egypt*, 35, 40–42.

95. See, for example, SAA I 14; SAA XV 217, 234, 250. For the provincial system of supply, see Pečírcova, "Administrative Methods." Engels, *Alexander the Great and the Logistics of the Macedonian Army*, 19, figures that an army at the time of Alexander could carry enough food for only about ten days. Depending on the size of his army, the situation would have been similar for Sargon.

96. Fales, "Grain Reserves, Daily Rations." For a different view, see Marriott and Radner, "Sustaining the Assyrian Army," 134–37. While it is true that a large number of noncombatants traveled with the army to support the king and elites, it is highly unlikely that food service personnel catered to the whole army. Indeed, Ashurbanipal's reliefs depict soldiers butchering and cooking their own meat (Room 28, SW palace of Sennacherib at Nineveh, now in the British Museum).

97. TCL III 53.

98. TCL III 166. For similar incidents, see TCL III 186, 197, 219.

99. SAA V 215.

100. See, for example, Albenda, *Palace of Sargon, King of Assyria*, plate 137.

101. SAA II 6, quoted in Scurlock and Andersen, *Diagnoses in Assyrian and Babylonian Medicine*, 62.

102. SAA I 97.

103. SAA V 200.

104. SAA XV 83; SAA V 146, 200 (snow); SAA XV 60, 83 (snow); SAA V 249 (storm); SAA XV 61 (rivers in flood). For further examples, see Van Buylaere, "I Feared the Snow and Turned Back." For travel in general, see Favaro, *Voyages et Voyageures à l'Époque Néo-Assyrienne*.

105. TCL III 18–24.

106. Howarth, *People of the Wind*.

107. Henshaw, "The Assyrian Army," 2. On the various *akītu* festivals, see Pongratz-Leisten, "The Interplay of Military Strategy and Cultic Practice."

108. Dalley and Postgate, CTN III, 40; Dezső and Curtis, "Assyrian Iron Helmets," 110.

109. For the depiction of a standard, see Albenda, *Palace of Sargon, King of Assyria*, plates 113, 114.

110. TCL III 25–27.

111. Dubovský, "Neo-Assyrian Warfare," 67.

112. Nadali, "Assyrian Open Field Battles," 118. Nadali goes so far as to assert that the Assyrians avoided battle whenever possible, "confining the direct confrontation to occasional brief field operations," but this statement is an oversimplification. With rare exceptions, battle cannot occur unless both sides agree to fight. No competent commander seeks battle unless he thinks he has a reasonable chance of victory. Since the Assyrians were almost always the aggressors, it is probably fair to assume that they were at least as prepared to fight their enemies in battle as vice versa. And, in fact, the large numbers of sieges that the Assyrian army undertook indicate the enemy's unwillingness to meet the Assyrians in battle rather than an Assyrian preference for siege work, which generally has a much higher casualty rate.

113. Noble, "Assyrian Chariotry and Cavalry," 66–67; Archer, "Chariotry to Cavalry," 77–78.

114. Scurlock, "Neo-Assyrian Battle Tactics"; de Backer, "Some Basic Tactics of Neo-Assyrian Warfare"; Nadali, "Assyrians to War"; Nadali,

"Assyrian Open Field Battles." Scurlock compares Assyrian tactics to those identified by the Roman author Vegetius (fifth century A.D.).

115. Oates and Oates, *Nimrud*, 31.

116. Melville and Melville, "Observations on the Diffusion of Military Technology," 155.

117. SAA XV 131.

118. SAA XV 199.

119. See, for example, Albenda, *Palace of Sargon, King of Assyria*, plates 95, 98 (spearmen alone, archers alone), 105 (archers protected by spearmen with a tower shield and a smaller shield). For more on siege tactics, see Eph'al, *The City Besieged*; De Backer, *L'art du siège néo-assyrien*.

120. See, for example, Postgate, *Early Mesopotamia*, 230. The author mistakenly asserts, based on some Old Babylonian mathematical problem texts, that scribes used math to calculate the time needed to build a ramp of a given height. On the contrary, the nonpractical math problems calculate the distance to the wall or the height of the partially built ramp, neither of which would have been remotely useful to an attacking army. Melville and Melville, "Observations on the Diffusion of Military Technology," 153–54.

121. Wright, "Warfare and Wanton Destruction," 443. For a different view, see Cole, "Destruction of Orchards," 34–36; Tadmor, *The Inscriptions of Tiglath-Pileser III*, 79; Oded, "Cutting down Orchards."

122. See, for example, Albenda, *Palace of Sargon, King of Assyria*, plate 137.

123. For alternative views, see Cogan, *Imperialism and Religion*; Holloway, *Aššur Is King!*

124. Mentioned in CT 22 1, a letter from Ashurbanipal (Sargon's great-grandson) to a scribe that included a "shopping list" of tablets for the king's library. See also Frame and George, "The Royal Libraries of Nineveh," 280–81.

125. Menzel, *Assyrische Tempel*, nos. 39–41 (T 82–89); Deller, "Neuassyrische Rituale für den Einsatz der Götterstreitwagen." See also Fales and Lanfranchi, "The Impact of Oracular Material"; May, "Triumph as an Aspect"; Jean, "Magie et Histoire: les rituels en temps de guerre."

126. May, "Triumph as an Aspect," 462–63.

127. See, for example, SAA V 84 ("The Urartian is making his sacrifices. All the governors are with him") and 165 ("as to the Urartian, he set out [. . . .] and was making sacrifices in the city of A[. . .]").

128. For the *akītu*, see Pongratz-Leisten, "The Interplay of Military Strategy and Cultic Practice." For the ritual aspect of the letter to the gods, see Oppenheim, "The City of Assur in 714," 144–47.

129. Friday, *Samurai, Warfare and the State*, 32.

Chapter 2

1. Millard, *The Eponyms of the Assyrian Empire*, 58–59. For the years 762–759, the Eponym Chronicle records revolts in "the citadel" (presumably Calah), Arrapha, and Guzana respectively. It also notes an outbreak of plague in 759 as well as the telling fact that internal instability allowed Ashur-nirari V (753–746) to campaign only twice during his reign (749 and 748).

2. The evidence for Tiglath-pileser's patrimony is conflicting and scarce, but indicates that his father was Adad-nirari III. See Frahm, "Observations on the Name and Age of Sargon II"; Frahm, "Family Matters," 176. For different interpretations of the rebellion, see Garelli, "The Achievement of Tiglath-pileser III," 46–51; Zawadzki, "The Revolt of 746 B.C.," 53–54. Zawadzki reasons that Tiglath-pileser initiated the revolt on the grounds that the governor of Calah remained in office after Tiglath-pileser ascended the throne. However, the governor need not have been involved in the rebellion and could even have helped Tiglath-pileser suppress it.

3. On the different family members, see Melville, "Neo-Assyrian Royal Women"; Dalley, "Yaba, Atalya, and the Foreign Policy of Late Assyrian Kings"; Radner, "Shalmaneser V. in den *Nimrud Letters*"; Baker, "Shalmaneser V"; Baker and Mattila, "Sīn-ahu-uṣur," 1128; Niederreiter, "L'insigne de pouvoir et le sceau du grand vizir Sîn-ah-uṣur"; May,"ᵐAli-talīmu or What Can Be Learned from the Destruction of Figurative Complexes?," 199–202.

4. If the fragmentary inscription on which the name appears has been interpreted correctly, Ra'īmâ was the mother of Sennacherib. Frahm, "Family Matters," 179–80. Sennacherib's name, "Sin-ahhē-erība," means "the god Sin has replaced the brothers."

5. For references to Sennacherib's siblings, see Frahm, *Einleitung in die Sanherib-Inschriften*, 1. For Atalia, see Al-Rawi, "Inscriptions from the Tombs of the Queens of Assyria"; Dalley, "The Identity of the Princesses in Tomb II."

6. RINAP 1 35.iii.1–29; Hawkins and Postgate, "Tribute from Tabal."

7. RINAP 1 41.21b; 49.3.'

8. For a full treatment of the war, see Luukko SAA XIX, xxvii–xxxiii.

9. SAA XIX 87.

10. RINAP 1 40.15b; 47.11b; 51.9b; *ABC* I.i.23. See also Brinkman, *Prelude to Empire*, 42–44.

11. On the probability that Shalmaneser took control of Sam'al and Quwê, see Radner, "Shalmaneser V in den *Nimrud Letters*," 95; Baker, "Shalmaneser V," 586–87. For the siege and capture of Samaria and further bibliography, see especially Younger, "The Fall of Samaria"; Na'aman, "The Historical Background to the Conquest of Samaria"; Becking, *The Fall of Samaria*; Park, "A New Historical Reconstruction of the Fall of Samaria."

12. For different treatments of Sargon's accession, see Vera Chamaza, "Sargon II's Ascent to the Throne," 27–30; Frahm, *Einleitung in der Sanherib Inschriften*, 1–2; Mayer, "Der Weg auf den Thron Assurs," 546–47.

13. *CAD* Š, pt. 3, 16–18.
14. *ABC* I.i.23. For an explicit record of regicide in the Babylonian Chronicle, see *ABC* I.iii.7–8. See also Younger, "The Fall of Samaria," 468.
15. Woods, "Mutilation of Image and Text," 42.
16. Fuchs, "Šarru-kēnu, Šarru-kīn, Šarru-ukīn," 1239, 1247.
17. Ibid., 1239.
18. Vera Chamaza, "Sargon II's Ascent to the Throne," 23–25.
19. Radner, "Assyrian and Non-Assyrian Kinship," 26.
20. Note, for example, that not one of the four kings following Shalmaneser V—Sargon, Sennacherib, Esarhaddon, and Ashurbanipal— was the eldest son. For more on this problem, see Melville, "Neo-Assyrian Royal Women," 55.
21. See also Mayer, "Der Weg auf den Thron Assurs," 548–54.
22. On the possibility that Shalmaneser had a son, Ashur-da''in-aplu, see Baker, "Salmānu-ašarēd," 1077.
23. Na'aman, "Sargon II's Second *Palû*," 168–69. Na'aman argues that since the Tell 'Acharneh inscription describes events of the campaign in the third person instead of the first person, it is clear that Sargon was not present. However, the Room V reliefs depict him in his chariot at Ekron (Albenda, *Palace of Sargon, King of Assyria*, plates 98–99), indicating that he was present for at least some of the campaign.
24. *ABC* I.i.32. In his Annals, Sargon accuses Merodach-Baladan of buying Elamite aid, for which see *ISK* Ann. 309. See also Brinkman, "Merodach-Baladan II"; Brinkman, "Elamite Military Aid to Merodach-Baladan."
25. The sequence of events is not entirely clear. In the Ashur Charter, mention of Ilu-bi'di's rebellion comes after that of Merodach-Baladan, but this probably reflects a scribal convenience rather than when the rebellions began. In any case, he dealt with both in the year 720. For a different view, see Younger, "Recent Study on Sargon II," 292.
26. Tadmor, "Philistia under Assyrian Rule," 87–90; Parpola, "Assyria's Expansion in the 8th and 7th Centuries," 100–101; Aubet, *The Phoenicians and the West*, 92–93.
27. SAA XIX 133.
28. Brinkman, "Merodach-Baladan II," 14.
29. Scurlock "Marduk and His Enemies"; Fales, "Moving around Babylon."
30. For the geopolitical situation in Babylonia, see Frame, *Babylonia 689–627 B.C.*; Cole, *Nippur in Neo-Assyrian Times*; Brinkman, *Prelude to Empire*. On intercity rivalries in Babylonia during this period, see Scurlock, "Marduk and His Enemies."
31. Liverani, *The Ancient Near East*, 541.
32. Frahm, "Ashurbanipal at Der," 52–53.
33. Radner, "An Assyrian View on the Medes," 51–52. On the strategic location of Der, see Frahm, "Ashurbanipal at Der," 51; during Sargon's reign in particular, see Postgate and Mattila, "Il-Yada' and Sargon's Southeast Frontier."

34. *ABC* I.i.36–37; Brinkman, "Elamite Military Aid to Merodach-Baladan," 162n11.
35. *ISK* Ann. 18–20; Prunk. 23; Zyl. 17.
36. *ABC* I.i.33–35.
37. RIMB B.6.21.1. 6–18.
38. Melville, "Win, Lose, or Draw?," 529–30.
39. A later (ca. 672) query about whether Sargon's breach of treaty with the Babylonians caused his death implies the existence of such an agreement. See Tadmor, Landsberger, and Parpola, "The Sin of Sargon," 48–49.
40. Grayson, "Problematical Battles in Mesopotamian History"; Younger, "Recent Study on Sargon II, King of Assyria," 292.
41. Waters, *A Survey of Neo-Elamite History*, 15. See also Ponchia, "Mountain Routes in Assyrian Royal Inscriptions, Part II," 236.
42. Kuhrt, *The Ancient Near East*, vol. 2, 498.
43. Novák, "Arameans and Luwians," 252–55.
44. 2 Kings 15–16; 2 Chronicles 28; Isaiah 7.
45. RINAP 1 42.8′–9′; 48.14′–15′; 49. 113–115.
46. Eph'al, "'The Samarians(s)' in Assyrian Sources," v 36; Lipiński, *On the Skirts of Canaan*, 70–82, 184–89, 221; Dubovský, "Tiglath-pileser III's Campaigns in 734–732 B.C."
47. Yamada, "*Karus* on the Frontiers of the Neo-Assyrian Empire," 67–69; Aubet, *The Phoenicians and the West*, 92–94.
48. Oded, "Observations on Methods of Assyrian Rule," 181–83. On the Assyrian communication system, see Radner, "An Imperial Communication Network," 71–74.
49. Frahm, "A Sculpted Slab with an Inscription of Sargon II," 49n9. Frahm notes that the "exact details of how the Assyrians controlled Hamath under Tiglath-pileser III and Shalmaneser V are still somewhat unclear."
50. Ibid., 46.
51. *ISK* Prunk. 33.
52. Younger, "The Fall of Samaria in Light of Recent Research," 472.
53. Engels, *Alexander the Great and the Logistics of the Macedonian Army*, 57–59.
54. For examples, see Na'aman, "Forced Participation in Alliances"; Dubovský, "Tiglath-pileser III's Campaigns in 734–732 B.C."
55. Yamada, *The Construction of the Assyrian Empire*, 155–63.
56. For the stele, see Lauinger and Batiuk, "A Stele of Sargon II at Tell Tayinat."
57. For example, Albenda, *Palace of Sargon, King of Assyria*, plate 96.
58. Frame, "Tell 'Acharneh," 52, ii.'9–'12 (translation and restorations quoted here are Frame's).
59. *ISK* Prunk. 34–35.
60. *ISK* Zyl. 25; Frame, "Tell 'Acharneh," 52, ii.'12; Albenda, *Palace of Sargon, King of Assyria*, plate 78.
61. *ISK* Prunk, 35; Frame, "Tell 'Acharneh," 49–51.
62. Fortin, ed., "Tell 'Acharneh 1998–2004"; Lipiński, *On the Skirts of Canaan*, 221.

63. Frame, "Tell 'Acharneh," 52, iii 6'–'10.
64. These cities are identified by epigraphs written on the badly broken (now lost) reliefs 14–17 in Room V. Albenda, *Palace of Sargon, King of Assyria,* plate 92 (barely visible). On the evidence for the possible location of Ba'il-gazara in Phoenicia, see Reade, "Sargon's Campaigns of 720, 716 and 715 B.C.," 100; Franklin, "Room V Reliefs at Dur-Sharrukin," 271; Na'aman, "Sargon II's Second *Palû*," 167. Russell's suggestion that Ba'il-gazara "is related to" biblical Gezer, located near Ekron, is not compatible with the campaign itinerary. See Russell, *The Writing on the Wall,* 121n54; Unger, "Ba'il-gazara," 392. Sinnu is probably to be equated with Siannu (Tel Siyanu) on the coast about thirty miles north of Arwad.
65. SAA I 93, 230.
66. Younger, "The Fall of Samaria," 472–73.
67. Gadd, "Inscribed Prisms of Sargon II," 180, column 4, lines 25–34. A slightly different version of events is included in the Display Inscriptions, for which see *ISK* Prunk. 23–24.
68. Dalley, "Foreign Chariotry and Cavalry," 32. Note, however, that Eph'al, "'The Samarians' in Assyrian Sources," suggests that some of the "Samarians" named in muster lists for this unit do not bear Hebrew names and may, therefore, actually represent people moved into the region later by the Assyrians.
69. Millard, *The Eponyms of the Assyrian Empire,* 59; RINAP 1 20.8'–17.' According to his Annals, rather than assaulting the city, Tiglath-pileser blockaded Damascus for forty-five days, during which his army cut down all the area's fruit trees and rampaged through the surrounding countryside. When he returned the next year, he captured the city (or it surrendered to him).
70. Sargon does not include the conquest of these cities in his inscriptions, and it has sometimes been suggested that they were actually captured during a later campaign. I concur with Reade, Na'aman, and Russell in associating all the reliefs in Room V with the campaign of 720. Reade, "Sargon's Campaigns of 720, 716 and 715 B.C.," 99–102; Na'aman, "Ekron under the Assyrian and Egyptian Empires," 82–83; Russell, *The Writing on the Wall,* 114. For a different view, see Franklin, "The Room V Reliefs," 265. The identification of Gabbatunu with biblical Gibbethon is likely but not completely certain.
71. Albenda, *Palace of Sargon, King of Assyria,* plate 95. The battle outside the city shows Kushites (Nubians)—identified by their clean-shaven faces and tightly curled hair—fighting with a spear in each hand. For Hanunu's association with the Egyptians, see *ISK* Ann. 56; Prunk. 25, 26; Zyl.19. Lipiński, *On the Skirts of Canaan,* 136, points out that the depiction of the Egyptians as Kushites (Nubians) is an anachronism. The Kushite Dynasty was not yet in power in Egypt. The reliefs, which were carved after this change occurred, reflected the situation in Egypt at carving time, rather than that of 720.
72. The cities are depicted on slabs 5 and 2 of Room V. According to Younger, "Assyrian Involvement in the Southern Levant," 239n15, Ekron covered only about four hectares or ten acres at that time.

Note, however, that Ussishkin, "The Fortifications of Philistine Ekron," 61–63, and Na'aman, "Ekron under the Assyrian and Egyptian Empires," argue that the city was large and prosperous at the time.

73. Na'aman, "Ekron under the Assyrian and Egyptian Empires," 83.
74. *ISK* Ann. 53–57; Prunk. 25–26.
75. *CAD* R, 304.
76. *A/711* VII.b. 25–28.
77. Dubovský, "King's Direct Control."
78. *ISK* Sicht. 16–17. For a different interpretation of these events, see Younger, "Assyrian Involvement in the Southern Levant," 237–40.
79. Fales, "Central Syria in the Letters of Sargon II."
80. Room VIII, the throne room of Sargon's palace, depicts the flaying of Ilu-bi'di and the blinding of a captive. Both scenes have identifying epigraphs, although the one associated with the blinding is illegible, so we cannot be certain that Hanunu is the victim. However, there is no other obvious candidate. Albenda, *Palace of Sargon, King of Assyria*, plate 75.
81. First noted in the Ashur Charter and then celebrated in most of his royal inscriptions, the restoration of privileges is also mentioned in a letter, SAA I 99. For the Ashur Charter, see Saggs, "Historical Texts and Fragments of Sargon II," 17, lines 36a–38b; Vera Chamaza, "Sargon's Ascent to the Throne," 25; See also Fales in SAA XI, xxxii–xxxiii, where he suggests that the Harran Census (SAA XI 200–219) was undertaken to help identify those who became exempt.
82. Saggs, "Historical Texts and Fragments of Sargon II," 16–17, lines 40–41.
83. Lambert, "Portion of Inscribed Stela of Sargon II," 125; Hawkins, "The New Sargon Stele from Hama," 151–64; Malbran-Labat, "Le text de l'inscription." Exactly when the deportations occurred is impossible to say. Since kings commonly edited content to reflect current circumstances and all of these inscriptions were written years after 720, it is possible that the deportation occurred any time after the 720 campaign.
84. Van de Mieroop, "The Literature and Political Discourse," 333. See also Galter, "Sargon der Zweite."
85. *ISK* Zyl. 34–35.

Chapter 3

1. Kurht, *The Ancient Near East*, 562–67; Bryce, *The World of the Neo-Hittite Kingdoms*, 39–43; Kealhofer, ed., *The Archaeology of Midas and the Phrygians*.
2. Herodotus, *Histories* 1.14; Arrian, *Campaigns of Alexander* 2.3; Justin *Epitome* 11.7. See also Roller, "Legend of Midas"; Berndt-Ersöz, "The Chronology and Historical Context of Midas."
3. Zimansky, "Urartian Geography," 12. See also Zimansky, "Urartian Material Culture as State Assemblage"; Adam T. Smith, "The Making of an Urartian Landscape," 70; Bernbeck, "Politische Struktur"; Tarhan, "The Structure of the Urartian State."
4. Kroll, Gruber, Hellwag, Roaf, and Zimansky, introduction to

Biainili-Urartu, 21–24; Dan, "The Archaeological and Geographical Landscape of Urartu," 333. See also Körüğlu and Konyar, eds., *Urartu—Transformation in the East.*

5. Çilingiroğlu, "Mass Deportation in the Urartian Kingdom"; Konakçı and Baştürk, "Military and Militia in the Urartian State," 193–94.

6. There is some disagreement about whether Sargon fought Rusa, son of Erimena, or Rusa, son of Sarduri, although, in my view, the evidence favors the latter. For a full discussion, see Appendix B.

7. SAA V 88 ("3,000 soldiers, their officers, and the commanders of the *kallāpu* troops of Setini, the (Urartian) governor opposite me, have set out towards Muṣaṣir").

8. Konakçı and Baştürk, "Military and Militia in the Urartian State," 182; Dan, "The Archaeological and Geographical Landscape of Urartu," 333; Biber, "Urartu Silahlari/Urartian Weapons."

9. Bryce, *The World of the Neo-Hittite Kingdoms*, 60–62. Bryce points out that by the late eighth century, many Luwians probably spoke Aramaic and by that time Luwian may have become a "chancery" language.

10. Parker, *Mechanics of Empire*, 89–97; Mayer, "Die Stadt Kumme," 353–355; Radner, "Between a Rock and a Hard Place," 254–60.

11. For example, see SAA I 30 (Urzana reports to the deputy of the palace herald) or SAA I 31 (the kings of Muṣaṣir and Hubushkia in contact with Rusa).

12. See Melville, "Ideology, Politics, and the Assyrian Understanding of Defeat."

13. Mauss, *The Gift*, 3.

14. See, for example, SAA V 85 ("Send your spies to the environs of Tushpa and find out a detailed report!"). For the Neo-Assyrian intelligence system, see Follet, "Deuxième Bureau"; Dubovský, *Hezekiah and the Assyrian Spies*; Desző, "Neo-Assyrian Military Intelligence."

15. Ashur-reṣua is the author of letters SAA V 84–103 and SAA XV 288, and is mentioned in several others (e.g., SAA V 106 and 107).

16. SAA V 12 (captured Urartian spies).

17. Only a few sites in the Urmia basin have been excavated, and none of them can be certainly identified with the locations given in Assyrian texts. However, the positions of Izirtu and surrounding polities relative to each other make some site identifications likely. Here, I follow Parpola and Porter, *The Helsinki Atlas*, although I must stress the provisional nature of site identifications in the Zagros. See also Mollazadeh, "The Pottery from the Mannean Site of Qallaichi"; Zimansky, "Urartian Geography"; Kroll, "The Southern Urmia Basin"; Hassanzadeh and Mollasalehi, "New Evidence for Mannean Art."

18. Postgate, "Mannäer," 341–42; Zadok, "The Ethno-Linguistic Character of Northwestern Iran"; Fales, "Evidence for West-East Contacts," 141. The language of the Manneans remains unknown as the only excavated written evidence from the area is a stele found at

Bukan inscribed in Aramaic, which was definitely not the indigenous language. Eph'al, "The Bukan Aramaic Inscription"; Lemaire, "Une inscription araméene"; Sokoloff, "The Old Aramaic Inscription from Bukan." For evidence of horse-breeding, see SAA V 169 (the Zikirtian king sells horses to Assyria), 171 (Andian and Mannean emissaries bring horses as tribute), 224 (buying horses in the east), and SAA XV 53, 59.

19. SAA V 217.

20. Levine, "East-West Trade," 178.

21. The mountains directly north of Assyria did not have any passes suitable for an army to traverse. The army could only get to Urartu by going east and then north or by a circuitous western approach. Parker, *Mechanics of Empire*, 37–40, 94–95.

22. TCL III 148; Fuchs, *AJ711*, 57n26.

23. On the prossible location of Muṣaṣir, see Danti, "The Rowanaduz Archaeological Program," 28–29; Marf, "The Temple and the City of Muṣaṣir/Ardini," 13.

24. Three of Rusa's inscriptions mention these events: the Topzawa stele and two variants, the stele from Merge Kavan, and the Movana inscription, for which, see Salvini, "La bilingue urarteo-assiri di Rusa I," 79–96; André-Salvini and Salvini, "The Bilingual Stele of Rusa I from Movana." Dating of the events they describe is much contested. For discussion, see Appendix B.

25. The deliberate destruction of boundary monuments as an act of war has a long history in Mesopotamia. See, for example, Woods, "Mutilation of Image and Text in Early Sumerian Sources," 315.

26. *ISK* Ann. 58–70.

27. Levine, "Geographical Studies I," 3.

28. This route is based on maps 4–5 in Parpola and Porter, *The Helsinki Atlas*. See also Lanfranchi, "Assyrian Geography and Neo-Assyrian Letters," 132; Ponchia, "Mountain Routes in Assyrian Royal Inscriptions, Part II," 237–45. The distance given here has been calculated using Google Earth.

29. Levine, *Two Neo-Assyrian Stelae from Iran*, 31. See also Marriott and Radner, "Sustaining the Assyrian Army," 129.

30. *ISK* Ann. 64–67.

31. For a recent history of the area, see Aro, *Tabal*. For Neo-Assyrian involvement in particular, see Melville, "Kings of Tabal"; Hawkins, "Kings of Tabal in the Later 8th Century"; Hawkins, "The Neo-Hittite States"; Bryce, *The World of the Neo-Hittite Kingdoms*, 141–62.

32. König, *Handbuch der chaldischen Inschriften*, 64, Text 25, III.11; Melville, "Kings of Tabal," 92.

33. In Assyrian texts, "Tabal" is used as a general region-wide name as well as the designation for a kingdom within that area. In order to avoid confusion, I have adopted the nomenclature used by Sargon, whose texts refer to Tabal proper as Bit-Purutash.

34. Although Shinuhtu does not appear in the extant tribute lists from Tiglath-pileser's reign, it is likely that it became a client of Assyria at this time. See SAA XI 30; RINAP 1 15.1; 27.2b; 32.1; 35.iii.1; 47.r6b.

35. RINAP 1 47.r115; 49.r28.
36. Gadd, "Inscribed Prisms of Sargon II," 180; *ISK* Ann. 68.
37. *ISK* Ann. 69–71; Prunk. 28; Zyl. 22. The Display Inscription (Prunk.) adds that Sargon took thirty of Kiakki's chariots and crews into his army.
38. Najafehabad, 18–19.
39. Although some ivory might have come from elephants in Syria at this time, most was imported from Africa into Anatolia through the Levant or Cyprus. Since ebony also appears on the list, a source in Africa is most likely. Moorey, *Ancient Mesopotamian Materials and Indsutry*, 116–18; Collon, "Ivory," 220–21.
40. A route from Calah to Shinuhtu via Naṣibina, Guzana, Kullania, Sam'al, Tarsus, and the Cilician Gates is about 660 miles as calculated on Google Earth.
41. *ISK* Ann. 71.
42. *ISK* Ann. 195–96. Bryce, *The World of the Neo-Hittite Kingdoms*, 144.
43. *ISK* Ann. 196–97; Prunk. 28–30.
44. For a different view, see Bryce, *The World of the Neo-Hittite Kingdoms*, 144–45.
45. Melville, "Kings of Tabal," 99–100.
46. RINAP 1 14.10b. See also Fuchs, "Pisiri(s)," 997.
47. Fales, "Rivers in Neo-Assyrian Geography," 208.
48. *ISK* Ann. 72–73.
49. *ISK* Ann. 72b–c.
50. On the concept of just war in Assyria, see Oded, *War, Peace, and Empire*, 4–5; Oded, "The Command of God"; Bahrani, *Rituals of War*, 11–12; Crouch, *War and Ethics*.
51. Millard, *The Eponyms of the Assyrian Empire*, 60.
52. The literature on Assyrian kingship is abundant. See most recently Radner, "Assyrian and Non-Assyrian Kingship"; Parpola, "Neo-Assyrian Concepts of Kingship"; Parker, "The Construction and Performance of Kingship"; Frahm, "Rising Suns and Falling Stars."
53. Saggs, "Historical Texts and Fragments of Sargon II," 16–17, lines 36a–40.
54. *ISK* Zyl. 39.
55. Radner, "The Assur-Nineveh-Arbela Triangle," 325. See also Russell, *The Writing on the Wall*, 234–39.
56. Barbanes, "Planning an Empire," 16.
57. *ISK* Zyl. 34–36, 43.
58. Harmanṣah, "Beyond Aššur," 68.
59. The royal correspondence shows that twenty six Assyrian governors contributed to the construction of Dur-Sharrukin. Parpola, "The Construction of Dur-Sharrukin," 51.
60. Van de Mieroop, "The Literature and Political Discourse," 335–38.
61. Van de Mieroop, *The Ancient Mesopotamian City*, 59–60.
62. *ISK* Zyl. 50–52.
63. *ISK* Zyl. 65.

64. Parpola, "The Construction of Dur-Sharrukin," 69n1. See also van de Mieroop, "The Literature and Political Discourse," 335–39; Battini, "Des rapports géométriques en architecture."

65. For an explanation of the gematria, see Frahm, "Observations on the Name and Age of Sargon II," 48. For additional references to *Enūma eliš* in Sargon's cylinder inscriptions, see Frahm, "Counter-Texts, Commentaries, and Adaptations," 24n21.

66. Stronach, "Notes on the Fall of Nineveh," 307–34; Novák, "From Assur to Nineveh," 181.

67. Russell, *The Writing on the Wall*, 237–38.

68. Radner, "The Assur-Nineveh-Arbela Triangle," 326.

69. Oded, *Mass Deportation and Deportees*. For the financing of Dur-Sharrukin and the fiscal consequences of Sargon's conquests, see Albenda, *Palace of Sargon, King of Assyria*, 34–36; Parpola, "The Construction of Dur-Šarrukin"; Radner, "Money in the Neo-Assyrian Empire," 129. "Money" refers to metals measured according to an official weight standard and used as a source of exchange. Coinage had not been invented yet.

70. Najafehabad, 22; SAA I 34.

71. SAA I 159.

72. Nahal Muṣri has long been equated with Wadi el-Arish, but note that there are other possibilities. Na'aman, "The Brook of Egypt," 74–80; Lipiński, *On the Skirts of Canaan*, 134–41; Na'aman, "The Boundary System and Political Status of Gaza," 63.

73. Gadd, "Inscribed Prisms of Sargon II," 179–80, column 11, lines 46–49.

74. Kahn, "The Inscription of Sargon II at Tang-i Var." Kahn argues that Osorkon was ruler of Bubastis in the Nile Delta under Shabakho, the Kushite Pharaoh, but this point is still controversial. According to a fragment of the 711 Annals from Ashur (*AJ 711* III.e: Ass 8–11), Osorkon's (that is, Shilkani's) gift is chronologically associated with events of 716.

75. Zamazalová, "Before the Assyrian Conquest in 671 B.C.E.," 317.

76. Yamada, "*Karus* on the Frontiers of the Neo-Assyrian Empire."

77. Dalley, "Foreign Chariotry and Cavalry," 43; Heidhorn, "The Horses of Kush."

78. SAA I 110 and Postgate, *Taxation and Conscription in the Assyrian Empire*, 388–89, ND 2672 (a tablet from Nimrud/Calah). Since the letter (SAA I 110) mentions Egypt, and since we know that Marduk-remanni was out of office by 712, we can securely date the report between 715 and 713. Na'aman, "The Boundary System and Political Status of Gaza," 58.

79. *ISK* Ann. 78–83.

80. SAA V 217. The letter is undated but almost certainly describes events just after the death of Iranzi. The city lords mentioned are probably the rulers of local fortresses loyal to Assyria. Dubovský, *Hezekiah and the Assyrian Spies*, 71.

81. SAA V 218.
82. *AJ 711* II.d: Ass. 12; *ISK* Ann. 84, Prunk. 55.
83. *ISK* Ann. 86–87.
84. Najafehabad, 31–32; *AJ 711* Ann. II.d (Ass. 11–13). Although Annals (Ann. 90) assert that Sargon had Assur-le'i flayed, the execution did not occur until 713 when Assur-le'i was executed for his brother's rebellion.
85. *AJ 711* Ann. II.d (Ass. 11–13).
86. Albenda, *Palace of Sargon, King of Assyria*, plates 109–30. The reliefs in Room II were arranged in two registers divided by the summary inscription. Most of the bottom register depicts the campaign starting on slab 34 with the march and continuing through the siege of Harhar and its aftermath. Epigraphs identify the cities Bit-Bagaia, Kindau, Kishesim, Ganghutu, Tikrakka, and Harhar. The top register is devoted to the post-campaign banquet (slabs H1/21 through at least slab 7, moving counterclockwise). Two sieges have survived from the upper register, but the cities are not identified and it is not possible to determine how they fit into the sequence of events, so I do not consider them here.
87. Albenda, *Palace of Sargon, King of Assyria*, plate 128.
88. Radner, "An Assyrian View on the Medes," 53; Lanfranchi, "The Assyrian Expansion in the Zagros," 113; Levine, "East-West Trade," 181–82.
89. Radner, "An Assyrian View on the Medes," 53.
90. Najafehabad, 36–40.
91. Albenda, *Palace of Sargon, King of Assyria*, plates 125–26.
92. *ISK* Ann. 93–96; Prunk. 59–60; *AJ 711* Ann. iii.b 11–21; Najafehabad, 39–41.
93. Radner, "An Assyrian View on the Medes," 50, observes that "the rebellion of Harhar was certainly part of the events surrounding the brother war in Mannea caused by the ill feelings of many against the pro-Assyrian politics of such rulers as Iranzu of Mannea and Kibaba of Harhar."
94. *AJ 711* III.b: 26–27.
95. Najafehabad, 43: "I brought about their great defeat. Their warriors I impaled on stakes."
96. Lee, *Barbarians and Brothers*, 8.
97. Liverani, "The King and His Audience," 381, notes that extreme punishments such as impalement and flaying not only served to end resistance but also reflected the frustration of Assyrian soldiers.
98. *AJ 711* III.c: 1–12.
99. *AJ 711* III.c: 10–11.
100. Najafehabad, 48.
101. *ISK* Ann. 100. See Liverani, "The Ideology of the Assyrian Empire," 308–309, for a discussion of what he calls "royal priority, the Assyrian impulse to accomplish something for the first time."
102. Najafehabad, 53.

103. This does not seem excessive when compared to Alexander's rate of march, which sometimes reached over forty miles a day. Engels, *Alexander the Great and the Logistics of the Macedonian Army*, 153.

Chapter 4

1. *ISK* Ann. 101.
2. *ISK* Prunk. 38–39.
3. *ISK* Ann. 101–103.
4. *ISK* Ann. 104; SAA V 133 (the king of Hubushkia pays tribute). The exact location of Hubushkia is a matter of contention. See especially Salvini, "On the Location of Ḫubuškia"; Lanfranchi, "Assyrian Geography"; Medvedskaya, "The Localization of Hubuškia."
5. *ISK* Ann. 104–105.
6. *ISK* Ann. 106–107.
7. Walker, "The Epigraphs," 112. Pazashi (sometimes spelled Panzish) was probably in the vicinity of modern Takāb.
8. The Bible captures something similar in the famous speech of the Rab Shaqê to the people of Jerusalem from 2 Kings 18:19–25.
9. *ISK* Ann. 109–12. Many different cultures have used human trophies for similar reasons. For example, in the sixteenth century, Chinese and Japanese warriors took enemy heads or noses in order to earn battle rewards. See Swope, *A Dragon's Head and a Serpent's Tail*, 3. For other Near Eastern examples, see Dolce, "The Head of the Enemy."
10. Reade, "Sargon's Campaigns of 720, 716 and 715 B.C.," 99. Aside from several undated letters Taklak-ana-Bel wrote, nothing else is known about his career. SAA I 235–49 are attributed to him.
11. Albenda, *Palace of Sargon, King of Assyria*, plate 10.
12. SAA XV 90, 91. For further discussion, see chapter 6.
13. It is not clear how much of either campaign Sargon participated in personally, but given the great distances involved (about 1,200 miles round trip per campaign) it is doubtful that Sargon could have completed both in a single season.
14. Na'aman, "The Brook of Egypt," 71n7. Na'aman suggests that the Assyrians only annexed the coast of Quwê and left Urikki to rule the northern regions. This would explain the presence of both an Assyrian governor and a native ruler.
15. *ISK* Ann. 125–26.
16. *ISK* Ann. 117–19; SAA XIX 25. See also Saggs, *The Nimrud Letters*, 164–65, ND 2370; Parker, "The Earliest Known Reference to Ionians in Cuneiform."
17. Lanfranchi, "The Ideological and Political Impact," 13–22; Luraghi, "Traders, Pirates, Warriors," 31–33.
18. Lanfranchi, "The Ideological and Political Impact," 17–18; Bing, "A History of Cilicia during the Assyrian Period," 195.
19. Casson, *Ships and Seamanship in the Ancient World*, 49–60.
20. Troop transports differ markedly from cargo vessels of the type depicted on Façade N of Court III in Sargon's palace at Dur-Sharrukin. Albenda, *Palace of Sargon, King of Assyria*, plates 21–23; Albenda, "A

Mediterranean Seascape from Khorsabad"; Linder, "The Khorsabad Wall Relief."
21. *ISK* Zyl. 21.
22. *ISK* Ann. 117–19.
23. Lanfranchi, "The Ideological and Political Impact," 18.
24. *ISK* Ann. 125–26.
25. *ISK* Ann. 124.
26. Although Sennacherib names the month in which he sent the letter, he omits the year. Nevertheless, the content and context fit the circumstances of 715. The Assyrians' removal of Ashdod's king in 712 because he stopped paying tribute (*ISK* Ann. 241; Prunk. 90) indicates an earlier client-patron relationship between the two.
27. SAA I 29. The restoration of the king of Ukku at the beginning of the passage is nearly certain based on what we know from other letters. The nominally independent king appears to have had diplomatic relations with both Assyria and Urartu and to have been in frequent contact with the rulers of Kumme and Arzabia as well. Parker, *Mechanics of Empire*, 94–97; Dubovský, *Hezekiah and the Assyrian Spies*, 54–55.
28. SAA I 29. Since the visit of the Mannean ambassador shows that Ullusunu had already been brought back to the Assyrian side (thus post 716) and since the letter's August date means that campaign season was well underway, it is safe to assume that Sargon was no longer in Mannea when Rusa struck. Likewise, the efforts of Zikirtu and Urartu against Mannea indicate a date before 714. Dubovský, *Hezekiah and the Assyrian Spies*, 70n153.
29. TCL III 13–14: "For the third time (in a row) I arranged the march into the mountains. I guided the (chariot) yoke of Nergal and Adad, whose standards go before me, towards Zikirtu and Andia." For a translation that beautifully captures the literary dimensions of the text, see Foster, *Before the Muses*, 790–813. For a different interpretation of Sargon's strategy, see Fuchs, "Assyria at War," 392–93.
30. TCL III 12: "In the district of the land Sumbi I inspected my troops and I checked the number of their horses and chariots."
31. Marriott and Radner, "Sustaining the Assyrian Army," 128.
32. TCL III 15–16. Translation from Melville, "Sargon II," 337.
33. TCL III 22–24.
34. TCL III 30–36. On the practice of taking hostages, see Zawadzki, "Hostages in Neo-Assyrian Royal Inscriptions."
35. TCL III 58–59.
36. TCL III 62–63.
37. TCL III 64–72.
38. SAA I 30, 31, 32; SAA V 90, 92, 173, 174.
39. SAA I 31.
40. For a full discussion of the dating, see Appendix B.
41. References to the Cimmerians in ancient sources are scant and conflicting. Recent studies include Kristensen, *Who Were the Cimmerians?*; Lanfranchi, *I Cimmeri*; Ivantchik, *Les Cimmériens*; Ivantchik, "The Current State of the Cimmerian Problem"; Adalı, *The Scourge of God*;

Strobel, "Kimmeriersturm." Just where the confrontation between the Urartians and the Cimmerians took place is much contested. See, for example, Salvini, "The Eastern Provinces of Urartu," 588.

42. Strobel, "Kimmeriersturm," 805.

43. SAA I 30.

44. SAA V 90.

45. SAA V 90, 93. Whether the murder of the king referred to in SAA V 93 refers to Melartua or someone else is unclear.

46. SAA I 31.

47. SAA I 32. For the possible location of Ishtahup in Zikirtu, see Saggs, "The Nimrud Letters, 1952—part IV," 199, 211.

48. Jakubiak, "Some Remarks on Sargon II's Eighth Campaign."

49. According to the CAD, 208, as a distance measure a *bēru* is "more than 10 kilometers."

50. Oganesjan, "Assiro-urartskoe sraženie na gore Uauš," 112. Oganesjan considers the fortification of Pazashi as contingency planning in case the Assyrians lost the battle and, retreating, had to withstand a siege.

51. SAA V 164.

52. On the size of Sargon's army for this campaign, see Marriott and Radner, "Sustaining the Army," 132–33.

53. TCL III 84–85.

54. TCL III 90.

55. TCL III 92–93

56. TCL III 112–14.

57. TCL III 103–108.

58. For the identification of Mount Waush with Mount Sahend, see Thureau-Dangin, TCL III, vii. It is impossible to identify the battle site. The "invitation to fight" has a long history in Mesopotamian literature. For example, in the Middle Assyrian Tukulti-Ninurta Epic, the Assyrian king invites his Babylonian enemy, Kashtiliash (ca. 1232–1225), to stand and fight. Foster, *Before the Muses*, 311.

59. TCL III 127–28.

60. Implicit in Sargon's description of the ensuing battle is the assumption that under normal circumstances armies built a fortified camp, deployed scouts and guards, ate and rested, and arrayed for battle before engaging the enemy. Fagan, "I Fell upon Him Like a Furious Arrow," 90–91.

61. See, e.g., Blanchard-Smith, "A Tactical Reinterpretation of the Battle of Uaush," 229.

62. TCL III 25–26.

63. TCL III 129–39.

64. TCL III 132 refers to the horsemen as the *pirru* of Sin-ah-uṣur. The term "*pirru*" is a hapax legomenon (otherwise unattested), but must indicate a specialized unit. Grekyan's supposition that the unit was made up of infantry cannot be correct, since the text explicitly refers to horses (ANŠE.KUR.RA.MEŠ). Grekyan, "The Battle of Mt. Uauš Revisited," 85.

65. Scholars have proposed a number of different battle scenarios. Although our interpretations differ in detail, Scurlock, "Neo-Assyrian Battle Tactics," 498–503, and Blanchard-Smith, "A Tactical Reinterpretation of the Battle of Uaush," argue for an attack on the Urartian center, as do I. In contrast, Oganesjan, "Assiro-urartiskoe sraženie na gore Uauš," supposes that Sargon's companions attacked from the flank, and most recently Grekyan, "The Battle of Mt. Uauš Revisited," suggests that Sargon and his companions snuck around behind the Urartian camp and attacked from the rear. Grekyan's hypothesis is clever but unsupported in the text. Though the text is open to interpretation in some respects, there is no indication that Sargon did other than attack frontally with cavalry.

66. TCL III 140. Despite the formulaic description—the fleeing king had by Sargon's time become a trope in Assyrian inscriptions—there is no reason to doubt that Rusa retreated when the rout began.

67. TCL III 145.

68. TCL III 156–63. It is possible that the singling out of Nergal, Adad, and Ishtar as the "lords of combat" is a subtle nod to the performance of the three regiments that marched under their standards in the battle.

69. For a recent discussion of war rituals in Assyria, see May, "Triumph as an Aspect."

70. *ISK* Ann. 83; Prunk. 49.

71. Vera Chamaza, "Der VIII. Feldzug Sargon II, Teil II," 265.

72. Marriott and Radner, "Sustaining the Assyrian Army," 139. For a map of known Urartian settlements, see the introduction to Kroll et al., *Biainili-Urartu*, 23. For different proposals of Sargon's route, see Levine, "Sargon's 8th Campaign"; Zimansky, "Urartian Geography and Sargon's 8th Campaign"; Vera Chamaza, "Der VIII. Feldzug Sargon II," Parts I and II; Kroll, "Sargon II's 8th Campaign," 12–14; Maniori, *Le campagne babilonesi ed orientali di Sargon II d'Assiria*.

73. Grekyan, "When the Arrows Are Depleted," 99. According to Grekyan, the capacity of the largest granary was more than seven hundred tons, more than enough to feed an army as it passed through. See also Marriott and Radner, "Sustaining the Assyrian Army," 133–34.

74. TCL III 186.

75. TCL III 220.

76. TCL III 290.

77. Adam T. Smith, "Rendering the Political Aesthetic," 131.

78. Zaccagnini, "A Urartian Royal Inscription," 285.

79. Fuchs, "Assyria at War," 392.

80. TCL III 422.

81. TCL III 310. Translation by Melville, "Sargon II," 338–39.

82. TCL III 320.

83. TCL III 315–20. For the date of the eclipse and discussion of the extispicy, see Oppenheim, "The City of Assur in 714 B.C.," 137–38.

84. TCL III 336–43.

85. TCL III 325–32. Translation by Foster, *Before the Muses*, 807–808.

86. TCL III 348–49.
87. Salvini, "La bilingue urarteo-assiri di Rusa I," 79.
88. TCL III 352–406. For an analysis of the booty list, see Mayer, "Die Finanzierung einer Kampagne."
89. TCL III 358, 361.
90. TCL III 403–404. See also Fuchs, *AJ 711*, 108–11.
91. TCL III 411–18. Translation by Melville, "Sargon II," 339.
92. Kravitz, "A Last-Minute Revision to Sargon's Letter to the God," 88.
93. The colophon dates the text as the eponymy of Ishtar-duri, thus 714. Although the colophon identifies the scribe as Nabu-shallimsunu, we cannot be certain that he composed the text. For more on its authorship, see Levine, "Observations on 'Sargon's Letter to the Gods,'" 114–15; Van de Mieroop, "A Study in Contrast," 431. For more on the literary merits of the text, see Van de Mieroop, "A Study in Contrast"; Fales, "Narrative and Ideological Variations"; Hurowitz, "'Shutting Up' the Enemy."
94. Oded, *Mass Deportations and Deportees*, 48–54.
95. Though it does not explicitly say so, the text implies that Tab-shar-Ashur, Sargon's treasurer and "the best orator," read the Letter to Ashur at some sort of public ceremony. Whether every campaign was commemorated in a similar fashion is not known. Fragments of only two (or possibly three) other Neo-Assyrian "letters to a god" campaign reports have survived. Oppenheim, "The City of Assur," 145; Borger, "Gottesbrief."
96. TCL III 426.

Chapter 5

1. The earliest inscription mentioning the incident, *ISK* Zyl. 27, which was written in 713, claims only that Rusa killed himself out of fear. At least one later source, *ISK* Prunk.76, which dates to 707, gives the sack of Muṣaṣir as a reason for the suicide. It is also possible that Rusa was deposed. Undated letters, SAA V 93, 166, and 191, report rebellion in Urartu. Lanfranchi, "Some New Texts about a Revolt against the Urartian King"; Dubovský, *Hezekiah and the Assyrian Spies*, 135–36.
2. The Eponym Chronicle entry for 713 is fragmentary—"[. . .] entered his new house; [t]o Muṣaṣir"—but likely refers to Sargon's return of Haldi to a new or improved temple. See also SAA I 7, a fragmentary letter containing tantalizing but ambiguous references to the return of gods and to Muṣaṣir.
3. On godnap in the Near East, see Johnson, "Stealing the Enemy's Gods."
4. SAA V 146 (Urzana visits Assyria); 148 (Urzana's brother visits the palace herald). These letters are not explicitly dated but fit well with SAA V 147, whose reference to Sargon's previous visit to Muṣaṣir assures a post-714 date.
5. SAA V 147.

6. For further discussion, see Appendix B.
7. SAA I 10.
8. SAA V 84 and 131 report a Mannean attack on Urartian cities in the vicinity of Lake Urmia. SAA V 45, a fragmentary report to Sargon from the king of Shubria, might report a Urartian counterattack on Mannea. Even if this occurred after 714, it did not require Assyrian intervention. SAA V 169 (ruler of Zikirtu trades horses).
9. *ISK* Ann. 198–200; Prunk. 31.
10. SAA V 31.
11. TCL III 358.
12. *ISK* Ann. 201–204; Prunk. 31–32.
13. For the archaeology of the area, see Aro, "Art and Architecture," 288–91.
14. As was customary, the Annals relate the campaign briefly in the first person. However, the Eponym Chronicle entry for the year reads, "[The] magnates in Ellipa." Millard, *The Eponyms of the Assyrian Empire*, 60.
15. *ISK* Zyl. 33; Ann. 167–69.
16. *AJ 711*, VI.b 8–13.
17. *ISK* Ann. 184–90.
18. On the war in Ellipi, see Fuchs in SAA XV, xxix–xxxi, and chapter 6 in this book.
19. Fales, "West Semitic Names in the Assyrian Empire," 104.
20. Parpola, "The Construction of Dur-Šarrukin," 51.
21. SAA I 143. See also SAA I 144.
22. SAA V 118.
23. Translation by Parpola, SAA I 26.
24. SAA I 27.
25. SAA I 179. Fales, "Central Syria in the Letters of Sargon II," 136, dates the letter to the "central part of Sargon's reign."
26. Epha'al, *The Ancient Arabs*, 90–91. See also Fales, "Central Syria in the Letters of Sargon II"; Byrne, "Early Assyrian Contacts with Arabs."
27. See, for example, SAA I 82.
28. On the date of these letters, see Fales, "Central Syria in the Letters of Sargon II," 135–36.
29. According to the Bible (Isaiah 14.28), Isaiah gave the oracle the year of King Ahaz's death, which most scholars agree occurred in 716 or 715. It is often assumed that the passage refers to the death of Tiglath-pileser III, but since that occurred more than ten years earlier, this seems doubtful. See Gary V. Smith, *Isaiah 1–39*, 324.
30. Arrian 1.7.1–3.
31. Isaiah 14.28–31 (translation from *The New Oxford Annotated Bible*). Isaiah 18 and 20.1–4 also refer to the Ashdod campaign. See also Machinist, "Assyria and Its Image in First Isaiah," 721n5.
32. *AJ 711* VII.b 1–5. See also Lipinski, *On the Skirts of Canaan*, 76.
33. *AJ711* VII.b 15–17. Although Ashdod and its port, Ashdod-Yam, have both been excavated, archaeologists have not yet found evidence of a moat. See J. Kaplan, "The Stronghold of Yamani at Ashdod-Yam," 143–44.

34. Dothan, *Ashdod II–III*, 21. But see Finkelstein and Singer-Avitz, "Ashdod Revisited," 244–45.
35. *ISK* Prunk. 95–111; Ann. 241–53.
36. *AJ 711* VII. c:7. See also Frame, "A 'New' Cylinder Fragment of Sargon II," 67–68.
37. *ISK* Ann. 237–38; Prunk. 86; *AJ 711* VII.c.
38. *ISK* Ann 204–207; Gadd, "Inscribed Prisms of Sargon II," 183.
39. Gadd, "Inscribed Prisms of Sargon II," 183–84; *AJ 711* VII.e 1–8 and VIII.b 1–15.
40. Çilingiroğlu, "How Was an Urartian Fortress Built?," 214.
41. See, e.g., SAA V 15, in which Nashur-Bel (formerly read Liphur-Bel), the governor of Amedi ca. 713–705, describes such a fort. For Assyrian fort construction, see Parker, "Garrisoning the Empire."
42. SAA V 21. Though no text explicitly identifies him as such, a variety of evidence indicates that Ashipa was the governor of Tushan before Sha-Ashur-dubbu, who became governor sometime before 707, the same year he held the office of eponym. I agree with Dubovský who dates this letter after 714. Dubovský, *Hezekiah and the Assyrian Spies*, 35n84. For a different view, see Parker, *The Mechanics of Empire*, 222–24; Parker, "Ašipâ Again."
43. SAA V 3. For the probable location of Harda, see Dubovský, *Hezekiah and the Assyrian Spies*, 38n88.
44. Sevin, "The Oldest Highway"; Dubovský, *Hezekiah and the Assyrian Spies*, 38–39.
45. SAA V 2.
46. Maxwell-Hyslop, "Assyrian Sources of Iron," 150. Despite the presence of rich iron deposits in the area, Maxwell-Hyslop cautions that proof of Assyrian mining operations is still lacking.
47. Frame, "Babylon: Assyria's Problem and Assyria's Prize," 21–23.
48. Frame, *Babylonia 689–627 B.C.*, 33. For the tribal presence in Babylonia, see Fales, "Moving around Babylon."
49. Frame, *Babylonia 689–627 B.C.*, 32–51.
50. Cole, "Marsh Formation in the Borsippa Region," 88.
51. Gadd, "Inscribed Prisms of Sargon II," 192, column 7, lines 45–65.
52. See, for example, SAA XV 156 ("his men have not been able to go up to the mouth of the river because of the amount of water").
53. Brinkman, "Merodach-Baladan II," 15–17; Brinkman, *Prelude to Empire*, 48–50.
54. Brinkman, "Merodach-Baladan II," 17–18; Fuchs in SAA XV, xvi.
55. Waters, *A Survey of Elamite History*, 19–22.
56. *ABC* I.i.43–44 mentions a campaign in an unidentified tribal region, *Bit-* [. . .]-ri, but that seems to be the only evidence of military activity to survive. See also Brinkman, "Merodach-Baladan II," 18.
57. Potts, *The Archaeology of Elam*, 265.
58. Dalley and Postgate, CTN III, 35.
59. Fuchs in SAA XV, xiv–xxii.
60. SAA XV 1. See also Dubovský, *Hezekiah and the Assyrian Spies*, 169. See also Fuchs in SAA XV, xvii.

61. Dubovský, *Hezekiah and the Assyrian Spies*, 170–73.
62. For the political geography of the area, see Brinkman, "The Elamite-Babylonian Frontier."
63. *ISK* Ann. 266–69.
64. *ISK* Ann. 271–94.
65. SAA XV 164. The letter is fragmentary but seems to report hostile action from the vicinity of Dur-Kurigalzu. The Assyrians probably held the city at the time. See Postgate and Mattila, "Il-Yada' and Sargon's Southeast Frontier," 239.
66. SAA XV 189.
67. SAA XV 155, 156, 188, 189; SAA XVII 22.
68. SAA XV 186. Fuchs in SAA XV, xv–xvi, has argued convincingly that Merodach-Baladan is sometimes referred to by the nicknames "son of Zeri" and "son of Iakin," but this is not certain. For the location of Bab-bitqi in the vicinity of Opis, see SAA I 95; Cole, *Nippur in Neo-Assyrian Times*, 33n74.
69. Fuchs in SAA XV, xvii, assumes that the Aramaean tribes were part of Merodach-Baladan's advance guard, but in view of the Itu'eans' long association with Assyria, this seems unlikely. Note, for example, SAA XV 166, dated to the same period, in which Il-iada' mentions Itu'eans among his forces.
70. SAA XVII 22.
71. Ibid.
72. Il-iada' was the governor of Der under Shalmaneser V but seems to have been removed from that office and put in charge of Dur-Sharruku under Sargon. See Fuchs in SAA XV, xvi–xvii. For a different view, see Postgate and Mattila, "Il-yada' and Sargon's Southeast Frontier," 237–38.
73. SAA XV 156.
74. SAA XV 166.
75. SAA XV 159. Although the greeting formula is broken, the volume's editors ascribe it to Il-iada' on orthographic grounds.
76. SAA XV 158 and 159 (Sippar defects to the Assyrian side).
77. SAA XV 177, 178, 245 (on the Assyrian presence in Dur-Ladini in friendly Bit-Dakkuri territory). See also CTN III 108 for an Assyrian muster list associated with Dur-Ladini. The Assyrians probably took stock of their forces immediately after taking Dur-Ladini or a few weeks later, when Sargon's main divisions joined them there.
78. SAA XVII 75 refers to unrest in Borsippa. Dietrich, SAA XVII, xxv, dates the letter to 710 on the grounds that it refers to Nabu-le'i, who was the governor of Borsippa under Merodach-Baladan. The letter could also date to Esarhaddon's reign (680–669 B.C.).
79. SAA XVII 73. On the date of the letter, see Dietrich in SAA XVII, xviii; Vera Chamaza, *Die Omnipotenz Aššurs*, 26–43.
80. Dietrich, in SAA XVII, xxv. See also Villard, "Barsipitu," in SAA I 1, which likely dates to 709, his name may appear (the text is partially broken) in a list of deportees who have been given a choice between living in Quwê or Tabal.

81. SAA XV 216. See also Fuchs in SAA XV, xx.
82. *ISK* Ann. 295–301.
83. *ISK* Ann. 307–309. See also SAA XVII 10, in which an official reports that Merodach-Baladan has left Babylon and gone to Dur-Iakin.
84. SAA XVII 20.
85. *ISK* Ann. 313–14. See also SAA XV 161, a letter from Il-iada' that mentions previous communication between Etiru, the prelate of Esagil, the temple of Marduk in Babylon, and Sargon. For further discussion of the role of the Babylonian priesthood in events of 710–709, see Vera Chamaza, *Die Omnipotenz Aššurs*, 26–43. On the Babylonian New Year festival, see van de Mieroop, "Reading Babylon," 270–73.
86. *ISK* Ann. 316–17.
87. *ISK* Ann. 321–25 lists the donations Sargon made.
88. Holloway, *Aššur Is King!*, 236. For the situation in Nippur, see Cole, *Nippur in Late Assyrian Times*, 73. For additional defections to the Assyrian side, see SAA XV 184, 214, 218.
89. Millard, *The Eponyms of the Assyrian Empire*, 47. The entry for 710 reads "to Bit-Zeri; the king stayed in Kish." Apparently the Assyrians referred to "the conglomerate of tribes and cities" led by Merodach-Baladan as Bit-Zeri. Fuchs in SAA XV, xv.
90. See, for example, SAA XVII 39, 40, 48.
91. *ISK* Ann. 330–41. Other towns were involved as well, but their names are not preserved in the broken text.
92. The letters do not fit an earlier date, but it is possible that they belong to the period in 708 during which the Assyrians were involved in the succession war in Ellipi. Given the geographical source of the letters, a 709 date is most likely.
93. SAA XVII 150.
94. SAA XVII 152.
95. SAA XV 242.
96. *ISK* Prunk. 127–29.
97. For further remarks on the defenses, see Powell, "Merodach-Baladan at Dur-Jakin."
98. Since the Chaldeans fielded chariots, it follows that the Assyrians could also have done so. For a different view, see Scurlock, "Neo-Assyrian Battle Tactics," 504.
99. *ISK* Prunk. 129–32. Translation by Melville, "Sargon II," 341.
100. *ISK* Ann. 347.
101. *ISK* Ann. 359. See also van der Spek, "The Struggle of King Sargon II of Assyria." The exact timetable of these events is not clear.
102. Millard, *The Eponyms of the Assyrian Empire*, 60.

Chapter 6

1. Holloway, *Aššur Is King!*, 237.
2. *ISK* Ann. 316–20, 373–78; Gadd, "Inscribed Prisms of Sargon II," 186, 192.
3. SAA XVII 43, 44.

4. *ISK* Ann. 376–77; Prunk. 2–3, 5–8, 137; Zyl. 4. See also SAA XVII 145. On *kidinnu* and other exemptions, see Holloway, *Aššur Is King!*, 293–302.

5. *ISK* Ann. 376–78; Prunk. 136–37; Gadd, "Inscribed Prisms of Sargon II," 187, column 6, lines 75–79.

6. *ISK* Prunk. 141–43.

7. Vera Chamaza, *Die Omnipotenz Aššurs*, 62–63.

8. RIMB B.6.21.1, 8–15.

9. Gadd, "An Inscribed Prism of Marduk-apla-iddina II"; RIMB B.6.22.3.

10. *ISK* Ann. 258–63.

11. Cogan, *Imperialism and Religion*, 9–21; Holloway, *Aššur Is King!*, 54–55, 145–50.

12. Melville, " Ideology, Politics, and the Assyrian Understanding of Defeat."

13. RIMB B.6.22.1–2.

14. *ISK* Ann. 372–74; Prunk. 134–35; Gadd, "Inscribed Prisms of Sargon II," 187, column 6, lines 63–67. See also SAA I 84, a letter from Tab-shar-Ashur to the king that mentions Arabs plundering Sippar.

15. *ISK* Zyl. 4.

16. SAA V 63.

17. *ISK* Ann. 382; Prunk. 139.

18. *ISK* Ann. 383–84.

19. SAA I 1. The letter dates to the period after 710 because it mentions what the governor is to do with people from various Babylonian cities (section not included here). See also Postgate, "Assyrian Texts and Fragments," 21–34; Lanfranchi, "Sargon's Letter to Aššur-šarru-uṣur." Postgate establishes the 709 or 708 date. Lanfranchi argues for an earlier date of 715 on the grounds that the letter's claim that Midas sought peace "without a battle" does not fit with the Annals statement about three Assyrian raids. In fact, the wording is compatible. A typical Assyrian devastation campaign did not necessarily meet any organized resistance and certainly was not the same thing as a pitched battle.

20. *ISK* Ann. 386a–c.; Prunk. 149–51.

21. Fuchs, *ISK*, 463, suggests that the causative connection between the two events presented in the Annals and Display Inscription was probably a narrative convenience.

22. *ISK* Ann. 392–93. See also Na'aman, "Sargon II and the Rebellion of the Cypriote Kings"; Na'aman, "The Conquest of Yadnana"; Radner, "The Stele of Sargon II at Kition."

23. Dezső, "Šubria and the Assyrian Empire," 37; Radner, "Between a Rock and a Hard Place," 263–64.

24. SAA V 44, 45 (letters from Hu-teshub to Sargon reporting on Urartian activities). On Shubrian foreign policy, see Dezső, "Šubria and the Assyrian Empire"; Dubovský, *Hezekiah and the Assyrian Spies*, 43–44; Radner, "Between a Rock and a Hard Place," 260–64.

25. Reported in a letter (SAA V 31) from Sha-Ashur-dubbu, the governor of Tushan after Ashipa.

26. See, for example, SAA 53 (an Assyrian officer commits murder and flees with his men to Shubria); 54 (deserters in Shubria).
27. SAA V 32.
28. SAA V 33.
29. SAA V 35. "*Abati*" is a Shubrian (Hurrian) word meaning calf or heifer, and according to Radner its inclusion suggests that the Shubrian king communicated to the Assyrians in his native language, which was then translated. Radner, "Between a Rock and a Hard Place," 261.
30. SAA V 33.
31. SAA V 106, 107. See also Parker, *Mechanics of Empire*, 89–94; Dubovský, *Hezekiah and the Assyrian Spies*, 50–52; Mayer, "Die Stadt Kumme," 353–55.
32. SAA V 95.
33. SAA V 106.
34. SAA V 105.
35. *ISK* Ann. 403–404.
36. *ISK* Ann. 405–11. See also Radner, "Assyrians and Urartians," 740.
37. In this section, I generally follow Fuchs's chronological arrangement of the letters that concern the Ellipian civil war as outlined in his introduction to SAA XV, xxvi–xxx. The province of Kar-Sharrukin included all the renamed trading posts conquered in 716 except Kar-Nergal (Kishesim), which was a separate province.
38. SAA XV 91.
39. SAA XV 90.
40. SAA XV 84, 94. Construction began under Nabu-belu-ka"in.
41. SAA XV 101. See also SAA XV 98 and 100.
42. *ISK* Ann. 418.
43. SAA I 14.
44. SAA I 13. For the likely dating of the letter, see Fuchs in SAA XV, xxx, and note 86 on page liii.
45. On the location of Bit-Barrû, see Fuchs in SAA XV, xxxi and note 87 on page liii.
46. SAA I 14.
47. See, for example, SAA V 32, when an Assyrian embassy in Shubria dined with the brother of Hu-teshub only to be attacked on the way home.
48. SAA I 13. Fuchs in SAA XV, xxxi, suggests that Kibabashe was the unnamed traitor of the letter.
49. SAA XV 3, 95, and probably 35.
50. SAA XV 113. See also SAA XV 114, 115, which include follow-up reports of Shutruk-nahunte's whereabouts.
51. SAA XV 129. See also Dubovský, *Hezekiah and the Assyrian Spies*, 76–77.
52. *ISK* Ann. 420–21.
53. SAA I 16; SAA XV 69.
54. SAA XV 69.
55. SAA XV 101.

56. SAA XV 100.
57. SAA XV 100. For a somewhat different interpretation of this episode, see Dubovský, *Hezekiah and the Assyrian Spies*, 80–83.
58. Frahm, *Einleitung der Sanherib Inschriften*, 10. Lutû, son of Daltâ, is mentioned in one of the horse lists from Calah (ND 2451), indicating that at some point he paid tribute to the Assyrians. For ND 2451, see Postgate, *Taxation and Conscription in the Assyrian Empire*, 376–78.
59. *ABC* I.ii.4–5.
60. See Millard, *The Eponyms of the Assyrian Empire*, 48, 60 for the date of the ritual in Dur-Sharrukin and SAA XV 69 for Marduk-sharru-uṣur's report.
61. *ISK* Prunk. 167–74.
62. Van de Mieroop, "The Literature and Political Discourse," 336–37.
63. Parpola, "The Construction of Dur-Šarrukin," 49.
64. Loud, *Khorsabad Part I*, 44. According to Albenda, *Palace of Sargon, King of Assyria*, 49–50, archaeologists found about thirty-five colossi.
65. For an overview of the various text types, see Russell, *The Writing on the Wall*, 100–123.
66. Liverani, "The Ideology of the Assyrian Empire," 314.
67. *ISK* Prunk. 162–63.
68. *ISK* Zyl. 72–74.
69. For the *ēkal māšarti* at Dur-Sharrukin, palace F, see Loud, *Khorsabad Part II*, 75–78.
70. Millard, *The Eponyms of the Assyrian Empire*, 60.
71. *ISK* Zyl. 75, Bro., 55–57.
72. Millard, *The Eponyms of the Assyrian Empire*, 60.
73. *ABC* I.ii.6–7.
74. Tadmor, Landsberger, Parpola, "The Sin of Sargon," 10–11, 117–18.
75. For discussion of the various possibilities, see Frahm, "Nabû-zuqup-kēnu, das Gilgamesch-Epos und der Tod Sargons II," 75–76; Fuchs, *ISK*, 411–12, 461–64.
76. Aro-Veljus "Gurdî." Scholars previously read the name in the Eponym Chronicle as Eshpai instead of Gurdi and supposed that it was Cimmerian. Now that the name is correctly understood there is no basis for a Cimmerian connection. Fuchs in *ISK*, 464, and Frahm, "Nabû-zuqup-kēnu, Gilgamesh XII and the Rights of Du'uzu," 8n29, suggest that Gurdi be equated with Kurti of Atunna. However, since Atunna was located on the Anatolian plateau south of the Halys River and evidence from Sennacherib's reign puts Gurdi in Tilgarimmu, the identification is unlikely, and we are almost certainly dealing with more than one Kurti/Gurdi/Qurdi. See Aro, *Tabal*, 142–43.
77. SAA I 76 ("As to the treaty tablet of Gurdi about which the king, my lord, wrote to me, the adjutant of the palace superintendent came and picked it up on the 1st of Ab (July)." Since Tab-shar-Ashur was active during all of Sargon's reign, there is no way to date the letter.
78. SAA III 33.8–9.

79. Lemaire, "Aššur-šarru-uṣur," 5–6.
80. On royal deaths in Mesopotamian tradition, see Hallo, "The Death of Kings." On Mesopotamian funerary traditions, see Jonkers, *The Topography of Remembrance*, 187–211; Postgate, "The Tombs in the Light of Mesopotamian Funeral Traditions."
81. Melville, "Ideology, Politics, and the Assyrian Understanding of Defeat."
82. Gilgamesh XII148–53 as quoted in Frahm, "Nabû-zuqup-kenu, das Gilgamesch-Epos und der Tod Sargons II," 77–78. Frahm first recognized the association of this passage with Sargon's death.
83. SAA II 6 §56.
84. *The Iliad* 22.74–79, translated by Stanley Lombardo.
85. See, for example, *The Illiad* 22.86–87.
86. Isaiah 14.16–19 (New Revised Standard Version). Although the chapter identifies the king not as the ruler of Assyria but as the ruler of Babylon, scholars have long recognized that it must refer to Sargon, who was ruler of Babylon in 705. See, for example, Ginsberg, "Reflexes of Sargon in Isaiah after 715 B.C.E.," 49–53; Frahm, "Nabû-zuqup-kēnu, das Gilgamesch-Epos und der Tod Sargons II," 86.
87. RINAP 3 17.v.1–4. See also Frahm, *Einleitung der Sanherib Inschriften*, 88.
88. Frahm, "Nabû-zuqup-kenu, das Gilgamesch-Epos und der Tod Sargons II," 76–78; Frahm, "Nabû-zuqup-kēnu, Gilgamesh XII and the Rites of Du'uzu."
89. Frahm, "Nabû-zuqup-kēnu, Gilgamesh XII and the Rites of Du'uzu." See also George, *The Babylonian Gilgamesh Epic*, 54. George suggests that the twelfth tablet of the epic could have been performed at royal funerals. Frahm develops the idea further in his article.
90. For the earthquake, see SAA I 125. For the letter's date, see Parpola, "The Construction of Dur-Šarrukin," 76n121. For the plague, see *ABC* I.ii.'5.
91. SAA III 33; Tadmor, Landsberger, and Parpola, "The Sin of Sargon"; Weaver, "The 'Sin of Sargon.'"
92. Tadmor, Landsberger, and Parpola, "The Sin of Sargon," 45.
93. Weaver, "The 'Sin of Sargon,'" 62.

Conclusion

1. The notion of *pax Assyriaca* is still much debated, but see Fales's convincing argument in favor of the concept in "On *Pax Assyriaca* in the 8th and 7th Centuries." See also Scurlock's insightful comments in her "Review of Fales, *Guerre et paix en Assyrie*."
2. Albenda, *Palace of Sargon King of Assyria*: assault without siege engines (plates 94, 95, 98, 100, 101, 107, 112, 119, 126, 128); assault with siege ramps and battering rams (plates 96, 125, 136, 138), and capitulation without a siege (plates 120, 133).
3. Oded, *Mass Deportations and Deportees*, 70.

Appendix B

1. Fuchs, "Urartu in der Zeit," 155–57.
2. Mayer, "Die chronologische Einordnung der Kimmerier-Briefe," 173.
3. TCL III 348–49. By contrast to SAA I 31, SAA V 148 suggests that Urzana's brother remained with him in Muṣaṣir after the deportation of 714. The deportation description in the Letter to Ashur does not specify Urzana's brother(s) except by the general term "family," whereas it specifically mentions Urzana's sons among the deportees. Although the language is standard, the distinction seems significant as Urzana's sons do not get mentioned in other letters.
4. Roaf, "Could Rusa Son of Erimena Have Been King?," 207n77.
5. Since Tiglath-pileser III put Hulli on the throne of Bit-Purutash and Sargon also claims to have done that, the assumption is that either Tiglath-pileser or Shalmaneser V removed him from office.
6. Roaf, "Could Rusa Son of Erimena Have Been King?," 212n87. See also Lanfranchi, "Some New Texts about a Revolt against the Urartian King, Rusa I," 133–34; Postgate, "Assyrian Texts and Fragments," 31.
7. The only example of which I am aware of a female member of the royal family owning land outside the Assyrian heartland comes from the reign of Esarhaddon (680–669) when his mother, Naqi'a, owned an estate in Lahiru in southeastern Assyria (SAA VI 255).
8. Since only one sign (qa) of the name survives in SAA V 112, the reconstruction is extremely doubtful.
9. SAA V 144 and 145 refer to Cimmerian movements in Mannea and Urartu, but it is not clear whether they are associated with Rusa's campaign or date a few years later. The fact that in SAA I 31 Ashur-reṣua comments that "today his land is quiet and each of his magnates has gone to his own land" supports the latter view.
10. Livy, *History of Rome,* 22.49.
11. Konakçı and Baştürk. "Military and Militia in the Urartian State," 195.
12. TCL III 103–108.
13. Konakçı and Baştürk. "Military and Militia in the Urartian State," 181.
14. Roaf, "Could Rusa Son of Erimena Have Been King?," 211; Fuchs, "Urartu in der Zeit," 154.
15. Roaf, "Could Rusa Son of Erimena Have Been King?" Inexplicably, Roaf both acknowledges that Urzana played both sides and insists that Urzana can only have reported to the Assyrians after Sargon's capture of Muṣaṣir.
16. TCL III 310.
17. Fuchs, "Urartu in der Zeit," 155–56; Mayer, "Die chronologische Einordnung Kimmerier-Briefe," 170–76. Note that Mayer, "Sargons Feldzug gegen Urartu: militärische," 14, argues that Sennacherib would have been too young (around twenty) in 714 to have been left in charge in Assyria. Against this, I note the later examples of Alexander the Great,

left in charge in his father's absence at sixteen (Plutarch, "Alexander" 9), or the Persian prince, Cyrus the Younger, made satrap in Anatolia "when he was not yet seventeen" (Kagan, *The Peloponnesian War*, 437).

18. Fuchs, "Urartu in der Zeit," 156; Radner, "An Imperial Communication Network," 82. Radner remarks that "most of those letters from Nineveh that can be dated are from the later years of Sargon's reign, whereas the texts from Kalhu date to the first five years of his rule; there is a noticeable gap for the period of around 716–711 B.C." But, of course, that would depend upon how one dates the letters,

19. Mayer, "Die chronologische Einordnung Kimmerier-Briefe," 173. SAA I 33 can be dated after 710 because it mentions sending tribute from Kummuh to Sargon in Babylon. Other letters from Sennacherib are SAA I 29–40.

20. SAA V 162 must date before 713 because it mentions Rusa. For the dating rationale involving SAA I 110, see Na'aman, "The Boundary System and Political Status of Gaza," 58; for SAA I 179, see Fales, "Central Syria in the Letters of Sargon II," 136. For other letters, see Lanfranchi in SAA V, xvi–xvii, xxvii.

21. Fuchs, "Urartu in der Zeit," 156.

22. Mattern, *Rome and the Enemy*, 25.

23. See, for example, SAA I 29 ("The governor opposite me was in Waisi"); SAA V 2 ("I sent [to] the (Urartian governor opposite me"); SAA V 3 ("the (Urartian) governor opposite us"); SAA V 21 ("we are keeping watch opposite them (the Urartians)"). See also Parker, "Toward an Understanding of Borderland Processes."

24. *ISK* Prunk. 115–16.

25. See, e.g., Lanfranchi, "Some New Texts about a Revolt against the Urartian King, Rusa I," 134; Dubovský, "The Conquest and Reconquest of Muṣaṣir"; Roaf, "Could Rusa Son of Erimena Have Been King?," 207–11.

26. Roaf, "Did Rusa Commit Suicide?," 773.

27. CTU A 10-3. 10-4.

28. TCL III 410–11.

29. SAA V 84 refers to Abaliuqunu, the Urartian governor of Muṣaṣir, but it is not certain whether the title is a shortened form of the more common "governor opposite Muṣaṣir" or whether this means that the Urartians eventually annexed the city. See Parker, "Abaliuqunu," 1–2.

30. TCL III 343–44.

31. Albenda, *Palace of Sargon, King of Assyria*, plate 133.

32. SAA V 87, 88, 89. The editors of SAA V have reconstructed the very fragmentary text 89 to read "[*He has seized*] Urzana, [*the king*] of Muṣaṣi[r], ga[*thered*] his people, [*and taken them*] to Waisi," the assumption being that the Urartians have "reconquered" Muṣaṣir. Given the state of the text, whose only legible words are "Urzana," "Muṣaṣir," "his people," and "to Waisi," this interpretation stretches credulity.

33. See, for example, SAA I 29, in which Sennacherib reports that the Urartian king "went with his troops to Waisi, entered the city and left his forces there. Taking but a few troops with him, he set out and entered into the territory of the Manneans." In other words, troop movements to a city did not necessarily presage an attack on it.

34. SAA V 147. For further discussion, see chapter 6.

35. Roaf, "Could Rusa Son of Erimena Have Been King?"

36. TCL III 403–404.

37. Çilingiroğlu, "Rusa, Son of Argishti: Rusa II or Rusa III?," 24. To be sure, the Assyrian king, Esarhaddon, did not manage to imprison or kill his brothers when they fled abroad after fighting him for the throne. However, they represented family, not a separate dynasty, so by letting his brothers go (or failing to capture them), Esarhaddon distanced himself morally from them, the murderers who had killed their father (and king), Sennacherib, and thereby made himself look better.

38. See, for example, *ISK* Ann. 398–401.

39. CTU A 10–2.

40. CTU A 10–3. Translation from Roaf, "Could Rusa Son of Erimena Have Been King?," 193.

41. Salvini, "Una Stele di Rusa III Erimenahi," 122, line 12.

42. Salvini, "Una Stele di Rusa III Erimenahi," 138–39; Çilingiroğlu, "Rusa, Son of Argishti: Rusa II or Rusa III?," 26.

43. Roaf, "Could Rusa Son of Erimena Have Been King?," 196–98.

44. Following the subjective rationale, we note incidentally that Sargon's lions look more like those of Rusa (S) than those of Rusa (E). For Sargon's lions, see Niederreiter, "Le role des symbols figures."

Bibliography

Abusch, Tzvi, et al., eds. *Historiography in the Cuneiform World.*
Bethesda: CDL Press, 2001.

Adalı, Selim Ferruh. *The Scourge of God: The Umman-Manda and Its
Significance in the First Millennium* B.C. State Archives of Assyria
Studies 20. Helsinki: Neo-Assyrian Text Corpus Project, 2011.

Albenda, Pauline. "A Mediterranean Seascape from Khorsabad." *Assur* 3,
no. 3 (1983): 1–34.

———. *Ornamental Wall Painting in the Art of the Assyrian Empire.*
Cuneiform Monographs 28. Leiden: Brill, 2004.

———. *The Palace of Sargon, King of Assyria: Monumental Wall Reliefs
at Dur-Sharrukin, from Original Drawings Made at the Time of
Their Discovery in 1843–1844 by Botta and Flandin.* Paris: Éditions
Recherche sur la Civilisations, 1986.

Al-Rawi, Farouk N. H. "Inscriptions from the Tombs of the Queens of
Assyria." In Curtis et al., *New Light on Nimrud*, 119–38.

Álvarez-Mon, Javier, and Mark B. Garrison, eds. *Elam and Persia.* Winona
Lake, Ind.: Eisenbrauns, 2011.

Andreau, Jean, Pierre Briant, and Raymond Descat, eds. *Économie antique:
la guerre dans les economies antiques.* Saint-Bertrand-de-Comminges,
France: Musée archéologique départemental, 2000.

André-Salvini, Béatrice, and Mirjo Salvini. "The Bilingual Stele of Rusa
I from Movana (West-Azerbaijan, Iran)." *Studi Micenei ed Egeo-
Anatolici* 44 (2002): 5–66.

Archer, Robin. "Chariotry to Cavalry: Developments in the Early First
Millennium." In Fagan and Trundle, *New Perspectives on Ancient
Warfare*, 57–80.

Aro, Sanna. "Art and Architecture." In Melchert, *The Luwians*, 281–337.

———. *Tabal: Zur Geschichte und materiellen Kulture des Zentral-
Anatolischen Hochplateaus von 1200 bis 600 v. Chr.* Helsinki:
University of Helsinki, 1998.

Aro, Sanna, and Robert M. Whiting, eds. *The Heirs of Assyria: Proceedings
of the Opening Symposium of the Assyrian and Babylonian
Intellectual Heritage Project.* Helsinki: Neo-Assyrian Text Corpus
Project, 2000.

Aro-Veljus, Sanna. "Gurdî." In *The Prosopography of the Neo-Assyrian
Empire*, vol. 1, pt. 2, *B–G.*, edited by Karen Radner, 431–32. Helsinki:
Neo-Assyrian Text Corpus Project, 1999.

Assman, Jan. *Cultural Memory and Early Civilizations: Writing,
Remembrance, and Political Imagination.* Cambridge: Cambridge
University Press, 2011.

Ataç, Mehmet-Ali. *The Mythology of Kingship in Neo-Assyrian Art.* New York: Cambridge University Press, 2011.

Aubet, Maria Eugenia. *The Phoenicians and the West: Politics, Colonies, and Trade.* 2nd ed. Cambridge: Cambridge University Press, 2001.

Bahrani, Zainab. *The Graven Image: Representation in Babylonia and Assyria.* Philadelphia: University of Pennsylvania Press, 2003.

——. *Rituals of War: The Body and Violence in Mesopotamia.* New York: Zone Books, 2008.

Baker, H. D., and S. Yamada. "Salmānu-ašarēd." In *The Prosopography of the Neo-Assyrian Empire,* vol. 3, pt. 1, *P–S,* edited by Heather D. Baker, 1077. Helsinki: Neo-Assyrian Text Corpus Project, 2002.

——. "Shalmaneser V." *Reallexikon der Assyriologie und Vorderasiatischen Archäologie* 11 (2008): 585–87.

Baker, H. D., and R. Mattila. "Sîn-aḫu-uṣur." In *The Prosopography of the Neo-Assyrian Empire,* vol. 3, pt. 1, *P–S,* edited by Heather D. Baker, 1128. Helsinki: Neo-Assyrian Text Corpus Project, 2002.

Balfour, Henry. "On a Remarkable Ancient Bow and Arrows Believed to Be of Assyrian Origin." *Journal of the Anthropological Institute of Great Britain and Ireland* 26 (1897): 210–20.

Barbanes, Eleanor. "Planning an Empire: City and Settlement in the Neo-Assyrian Period." *Bulletin of the Canadian Society for Mesopotamian Studies* 38 (2003): 15–22.

Barnett, R. D. *Assyrian Sculpture.* Toronto: McClelland and Stewart, 1975.

Battini, L. "Des rapports géométriques en architecture: le cas de Dur-Šarrukin." *Revue d'Assyriologie et archéologie orientale* 94 (2000): 33–56.

——. "Un example de propagande néo-assyrienne: les défenses de Dur-Sharrukin." *Contributi e Materiali di Archeologia Orientale* 6 (1997): 217–31.

Barron, Amy. "Late Assyrian Arms and Armor: Art vs. Artifact." PhD diss., University of Toronto, 2010.

Becking, Bob. *The Fall of Samaria: An Historical and Archaeological Study.* Studies in the History of the Ancient Near East 2. Leiden: Brill, 1992.

Bedford, Peter R. "The Economy of the Near East in the First Millennium B.C." In Manning and Morris, *The Ancient Economy,* 58–83.

Berndt-Ersöz, Susanne. "The Chronology and Historical Context of Midas." *Historia: Zeitschrift für alte Geschichte* 57 (2008): 1–37.

Bernbeck, Reinard. "Politische Struktur und Ideologie in Urartu." *Archäologiche Mitteilungen aus Iran und Turen* 35/36 (2003–2004): 267–312.

Biber, Hanifi, "Urartu Silahlari/Urartian Weapons." In Köruğlu and Konyar, *Urartu,* 234–29.

Biggs, R. D., and J. A. Brinkman, eds. *From the Workshop of the Chicago Assyrian Dictionary: Studies Presented to A. Leo Oppenheim.* Chicago: University of Chicago, Oriental Institute, 1964.

Bing, John Daniel. "A History of Cilicia during the Assyrian Period." PhD diss., University of Indiana, 1968.

Blakely, Jeffrey A., and James W. Hardin. "Southwestern Judah in the Late Eighth Century B.C.E." *Bulletin of the American Schools of Oriental Research* 326 (2002): 11–64.

Blanchard-Smith, Jonathan. "A Tactical Reinterpretation of the Battle of Uaush: Assyria and Urartu at War 714 B.C." In Çilingiroğlu and French, *Anatolian Iron Ages 3*, 229–39.

Boardman, John, et al., eds. *The Cambridge Ancient History*, vols. 2–3. 2nd ed. Cambridge: Cambridge University Press, 1991.

Böck, Barbara, Eva Christiane Cancik-Kirschbaum, and Thomas Richter, eds. *Munuscula Mesopotamica: Festschrift für Johannes Renger*. Münster: Ugarit-Verlag, 1999.

Borger, Riekele. "Gottesbrief." *Reallexikon der Assyriologie und Vorderasiatischen Archäologie* 3 (1971): 575–76.

Botta, Paul Emile, and Eugène Flandin. *Monuments de Ninive*. Two volumes. Paris: Imprimerie nationale, 1849–50.

Brinkman, John A. "The Elamite-Babylonian Frontier in the Neo-Elamite Period, 750–625 B.C." In De Meyer, Gasche, and Vallat, *Fragmenta Historiae Elamicae*, 199–208.

———. "Elamite Military Aid to Merodach-Baladan." *Journal of Near Eastern Studies* 24 (1965): 161–66.

———. "Merodach-Baladan II." In Biggs and Brinkman, *From the Workshop of the Chicago Assyrian Dictionary*, 6–41.

———. *Prelude to Empire: Babylonian Society and Politics, 747–626 B.C.* Occasional Papers of the Babylonian Fund 7. Philadelphia: University Museum, 1984.

Bryce, Trevor. *The World of the Neo-Hittite Kingdoms: A Political and Military History*. Oxford: Oxford University Press, 2012.

Byrne, Ryan. "Early Assyrian Contacts with Arabs and the Impact on Levantine Vassal Tribute." *Bulletin of the American Schools of Oriental Research* 331 (2003): 11–25.

Cancik-Kirschbaum, Eva Christiane, Margarete van Ess, and Joachim Marzahn, eds. *Babylon: Wissenskultur in Orient und Okzident*. Berlin: de Gruyter, 2011.

Cantrell, Deborah O'Daniel. *The Horsemen of Israel: Horses and Chariotry in Monarchic Israel*. Winona Lake, Ind.: Eisenbrauns, 2011.

———. "'Some Trust in Horses': Horses as Symbols of Power in Rhetoric and Reality." In Kelle, Ames, and Wright, *Warfare, Ritual and Symbol in Biblical and Modern Contexts*, 131–48.

Casson, Lionel. *Ships and Seamanship in the Ancient World*. Baltimore: Johns Hopkins University Press, 1995.

Caubet, Annie, ed. *Khorsabad, le palais de Sargon II, roi d'Assyrie. Actes du colloque organisé au musée de Louvre par le Service culturel les 21 et 22 janvier 1994*. Paris: La documentation Français, 1995.

Chavalas, Mark, ed. *The Ancient Near East: Historical Sources in Translation*. Oxford: Blackwell, 2006.

Chavalas, Mark, and K. Lawson Younger, eds. *Mesopotamia and the Bible: Comparative Explorations*. Grand Rapids, Mich.: Baker Academic, 2002.

Çilingiroğlu, Altan A. "How Was an Urartian Fortress Built?" In Sagona, *A View from the Highlands*, 205–31.

———. "Mass Deportation in the Urartian Kingdom." *Anadolu Araştırmaları* 9 (1983): 319–23.

———. "Rusa, Son of Argishti: Rusa II or Rusa III?" *Ancient Near Eastern Studies* 45 (2008): 21–29.

Çilingiroğlu, A., and D. H. French, eds. *Anatolian Iron Ages 3: The Proceedings of the Third Anatolian Iron Ages Colloquium Held at Van, 6–12 August 1990*. Ankara: British Institute of Archaeology in Ankara, 1994.

Clark, Jessica, and Brian Turner, eds. *War Losses in the Ancient World*. Leiden: Brill, forthcoming.

Cogan, Mordecai. *Imperialism and Religion: Judah and Israel in the Eighth and Seventh Centuries B.C.E.* Society of Biblical Literature Monograph Series 19. Missoula, Mont.: Society of Biblical Literature and Scholars Press, 1974.

Cogan, Mordecai, and Israel Eph'al, eds. *Ah, Assyria . . . Studies in Assyrian History and Ancient Near Eastern Historiography Presented to Hayim Tadmor*. Scripta Hierosolymitana 33. Jerusalem: Magnes Press, 1991.

Cogan, Mordecai, and Daniel Kahn, eds. *Treasures on Camels' Humps: Historical and Literary Studies from the Ancient Near East Presented to Israel Eph'al*. Jerusalem: Magnes Press, 2008.

Cohen, Raymond, and Raymond Westbrook, eds. *Isaiah's Vision of Peace in Biblical and Modern International Relations: Swords into Plowshares*. Culture and Religion in International Relations. London: Palgrave, 2008.

Cole, Steven W. "The Destruction of Orchards in Assyrian Warfare." In Parpola and Whiting, *Assyria '95*, 29–40.

———. "Marsh Formation in the Borsippa Region and the Course of the Lower Euphrates." *Journal of Near Eastern Studies* 53 (1994): 81–109.

———. *Nippur in Neo-Assyrian Times: c. 755–612 B.C.* State Archives of Assyria Studies 4. Helsinki: Helsinki University Press, 1996.

Collon, Dominique. "Examples of Ethnic Diversity on Assyrian Reliefs." In Van Soldt, *Ethnicity in Mesopotamia*, 66–77.

———. "Ivory." *Iraq* 39 (1977): 219–22.

Collon, Dominique, and Andrew George, eds. *Nineveh: Papers of the 49th Rencontre Assyriologique Internationale*, 2 volumes. London: British School of Archaeology in Iraq, 2005. Also published as *Iraq* 66 (2004).

Crawford, Sidnie White, et al., eds. *"Up to the Gates of Ekron": Essays on the Archeology and History of the Eastern Mediterranean in Honor of Seymour Gitin*. Jerusalem: Israel Exploration Society, 2007.

Crouch, Carly L. *War and Ethics in the Ancient Near East: Military Violence in Light of Cosmology and History*. Beiheft zur Zeitschrift für die alttestamentliche Wissenschaft 407. Berlin: de Gruyter, 2009.

Curtis, John E., Henrietta McCall, Dominique Collon, and Lamia Al-Gailani Werr, eds. *New Light on Nimrud: Proceedings of the*

Nimrud Conference 11–13th March 2002. London: British Institute for the Study of Iraq, in association with the British Museum, 2008.

Dalley, Stephanie. "Foreign Chariotry and Cavalry in the Armies of Tiglath-pileser III and Sargon II." *Iraq* 47 (1985): 31–48.

———. "The Identity of the Princesses in Tomb II and a New Analysis of Events of 701 B.C." In Curtis, et al., *New Light on Nimrud*, 171–75.

———. "Yabâ, Atalya, and the Foreign Policy of Late Assyrian Kings." *State Archives of Assyria Bulletin* 12 (1998): 83–98.

Dalley, Stephanie, and J. N. Postgate. *The Tablets from Fort Shalmaneser*. Cuneiform Texts from Nimrud III. London: British School of Archaeology in Iraq, 1983.

Dan, Roberto. "The Archeological and Geographical Landscape of Urartu." In Matthiae et al., *Proceedings of the 6th International Congress on the Archaeology of the Ancient Near East*, 331–40.

Danti, Michael. "The Rowanduz Archaeological Project: Searching for the Kingdom of Musasir." *Expedition* (Winter 201): 26–33.

De Backer, Fabrice. *L'art du siège néo-assyrien*. Culture and History of the Ancient Near East 61. Leiden: Brill, 2013.

———. "Some Basic Tactics of Neo-Assyrian Warfare." *Ugarit Forschungen* 38 (2007): 69–115.

Deller, K. "Neuassyrische Rituale für den Einsatz der Götterstreitwagen." *Baghdader Mitteilungen* 23 (1992): 341–46.

De Meyer, L. H. Gasche, and F. Vallat, eds. *Fragmenta Historiae Elamicae: Mélanges Offerts à M. J. Steve*. Paris: Éditions Recherche sur les Civilisations, 1986.

De Odorico, Marco. *The Use of Numbers and Quantifications in the Assyrian Royal Inscriptions*. State Archives of Assyria Studies 3. Helsinki: Neo-Assyrian Text Corpus Project, 1995.

Dercksen, J. G., ed. *Trade and Finance in Mesopotamia: Proceedings of the First MOS Symposium (Leiden 1997)*. Publications de l'Institut historique-archéologique néerlandais de Stamboul 84. Leiden: Het Nederlands Instituut voor het Nabije Oosten, 1999.

Dercksen, J. G., ed. *Trade and Finance in Ancient Mesopotamia*. Leiden: Nederlands Historisch-Archeologisch Instituut te Istanbul, 1999.

Deshayes, J., ed. *Le Plateau iranien et l'Asie central des origins á la conquête islamique; leurs relations á la lumière des documents archéologiques [actes du colloque], Paris, 22–24 mars 1976*. Paris: Éditiones de CNRS, 1977.

Dever, William G., and Seymour Gitin, eds. *Symbiosis, Symbolism and the Power of the Past: Canaan, Ancient Israel and their Neighbors from the Late Bronze Age through Roman Palestine*. Proceedings of the Centennial Symposium, W.F. Albright Institute of Archaeological Research and the American Schools of Oriental Research, Jerusalem, May 29–May 31, 2000. Winona Lake, Ind.: Eisenbrauns, 2003.

Dezső, Tamás. *The Assyrian Army I: The Structure of the Neo-Assyrian Army*, vol. 1, *Infantry*. Budapest: Eötvös University Press, 2012.

———. *The Assyrian Army I: The Structure of the Neo-Assyrian Army*, vol. 2: *Cavalry and Chariotry*. Antiqua et Orientalia 3; Assyriologia 8/2. Budapest: Eötvös University Press, 2012.

———. "Neo-Assyrian Military Intelligence." In Neumann et al., *Krieg und Frieden im Alten Vorderasien*, 221–35.

———. "The Reconstruction of the Assyrian Army of Sargon II (721–705 B.C.) based on the Nimrud Horse Lists." *State Archives of Assyria Bulletin* 15 (2006): 93–140.

———. "The Reconstruction of the Neo-Assyrian Army as Depicted on the Assyrian Palace Reliefs, 745–612 B.C." *Acta Archaeologica Academiae Scientarium Hungarica* 57 (2006): 87–130.

———. "Šubria and the Assyrian Empire." *Acta Antiqua* (2006): 33–38.

Dezső, Tamás, and John Curtis, "Assyrian Iron Helmets from Nimrud Now in the British Museum." *Iraq* 53 (1991): 105–26.

Dietrich, Manfried. *The Babylonian Correspondence of Sargon and Sennacherib*. State Archives of Assyria XVII. Helsinki: Helsinki University Press, 2003.

Dietrich, Manfried, and Ingo Kottsieper, eds. *"Und Mose schrieb dieses Lied auf": Studien zum Alten Testament und zum alten Orient: Festschrift für Oswald Loretz zur Vollendurg seines 70. Lebensjahres mit Beiträgen von Freunden, Schülern und Kollegen*. Alter Orient und Altes Testament 250. Münster: Ugarit-Verlag, 1998.

Dietrich, Manfried, and Oswald Loretz, eds. *Mesopotamica—Ugaritica—Biblica: Festschrift K. Bergerhof*. Alter Orient und Altes Testament 232. Kevelaer, Germany: Butzon und Bercker; Neukirchen-Vluyn, Germany: Neukirchener Verlag, 1993.

———, eds. *Vom Alten Orient zum Alten Testament: Festschrift für Wolfram Freiherr von Soden zum 85. Geburtstag am 19. Juni 1933*. Alter Orient und Altes Testament 240. Kevelaer, Germany: Butzon und Bercker, 1995.

Dolce, Rita. "'The Head of the Enemy' in the Sculptures from the Palaces at Nineveh: An Example of 'Cultural Migration'?" In Collon and George, *Nineveh*, 121–32.

Dothan, Moshe. *Ashdod II–III: The Second and Third Seasons of Excavations, 1963, 1965, Soundings in 1967*. 'Atiqot 9–10. Jerusalem: Department of Antiquities and Museums, 1971.

Dubovský, Peter. "The Conquest and Reconquest of Muṣaṣir in the 8th Century B.C." *State Archives of Assyria Bulletin* 15 (2006): 141–46.

———. *Hezekiah and the Assyrian Spies: Reconstruction of the Neo-Assyrian Intelligence Services and Its Significance for 2 Kings 18–19*. Orbis Biblicus et Orientalis 49. Rome: Pontificio Istituto Biblico, 2006.

———. "King's Direct Control: Neo-Assyrian Qēpu Officials." In Wilhelm, *Organization, Representation, and Symbols of Power*, 449–60.

———. "Neo-Assyrian Warfare: Logistics and Weaponry during the Campaigns of Tiglath-pileser III." *Anodos* 4/5 (2004–2005): 61–67.

———. "Tiglath-pileser III's Campaigns in 734–732 B.C.: Historical Background of Isa 7; 2 Kings 15–16 and 2 Chr 27–28." *Biblica* 87 (2006): 153–70.

Düring, Bleda, ed. *Understanding Hegemonic Practices of the Early Assyrian Empire*. Leiden: Peeters, 2014.

Ehrenreich, Barbara. *Blood Rites: Origins and History of the Passions of War*. New York: Holt, 1997.

Engels, Donald W. *Alexander the Great and the Logistics of the Macedonian Army*. Berkeley: University of California Press, 1978.

Eph'al, Israel. *The Ancient Arabs*. Jerusalem: Magnes Press, 1984.

———. "The Bukan Aramaic Inscription: Historical Considerations." *Israel Exploration Journal* 49 (1999): 116–21.

———. *The City Besieged: Siege and its Manifestations in the Ancient Near East*. Culture and History of the Ancient Near East 36. Leiden: Brill, 2009.

———. "'The Samarian(s)' in Assyrian Sources." In Cogan and Eph'al, *Ah, Assyria*, 36–45.

Fagan, Garrett G. "'I Fell upon Him Like a Furious Arrow': Toward a Reconstruction of the Assyrian Tactical System." In Fagan and Trundle, *New Perspectives on Ancient Warfare*, 81–100.

Fagan, Garrett, and Mathew Trundle, eds. *New Perspectives on Ancient Warfare*. History of Warfare 59. Leiden: Brill, 2010.

Fales, F. M. "Art, Performativity, Mimesis, Narrative, Ideology and Audience: Reflections on Assyrian Palace Reliefs in Light of Recent Studies." *KASKAL* 6 (2009): 235–93.

———, ed. *Assyrian Royal Inscriptions: New Horizons in Literary, Historical, and Ideological Analysis*. Rome: Istituto per l'Oriente, Centro per le antichità e la storia dell'arte del vicino Oriente, 1981.

———. "The Assyrian Words for '(Foot) Soldier.'" In Galil, Geller, and Millard, *Homeland and Exile*, 71–94.

———. "Central Syria in the Letters of Sargon II." In Hübner and Knauf, *Kein Land für sich allein*, 134–52.

———. "The Enemy in Assyrian Royal Inscriptions: The 'Moral Judgement.'" In Nissen and Renger, *Mesopotamien und seine Nachbarn*, 425–35.

———. "Evidence for West-East Contacts in the VIIIth Century B.C.: The Bukān Stele." In Lanfranchi, Roaf, and Rollinger, *Continuity of Empire (?)*, 131–48.

———. "Grain Reserves, Daily Rations, and the Size of the Assyrian Army: A Quantitative Study." *State Archives of Assyria Bulletin* IV (1990): 23–34.

———. *Guerre et paix en Assyrie. Religion et imperialisme*. Les conférences de l'Ecole Pratique des Hautes Études 2. Paris: Éditions du Cerf, 2010.

———. *Imperial Administrative Records, part II*. State Archives of Assyria XI. Helsinki: Helsinki University Press, 1995.

———. "Moving around Babylon: On the Aramean and Chaldean Presence in Southern Mesopotamia." In Cancik-Kirschbaum et al., *Babylon*, 91–112.

———. "Narrative and Ideological Variations in the Account of Sargon's 8th Campaign." In Cogan and Eph'al, *Ah, Assyria*, 129–47.

———. "On *Pax Assyriaca* in the 8th and 7th Centuries B.C.E. and Its Implications." In Cohen and Westbrook, *Isaiah's Vision of Peace in Biblical and Modern International Relations*, 17–35.

——. "Preparing for War in Assyria." In Andreau, Briant, and Descat, *Économie antique*, 35–62.

——. "Rivers in Neo-Assyrian Geography." In Liverani, *Neo-Assyrian Geography*, 203–15.

——. "To Speak Kindly to Him/Them" as Item of Assyrian Political Discourse." In Luukko, Svärd, and Mattila, *Of God(s), Trees, Kings, and Scholars*, 27–40.

——. "West Semitic Names in the Assyrian Empire: Diffusion and Social Relevance." *Studi epigrafici e linguistici* 8 (1991): 99–117.

Fales, F. M., and G. B. Lanfranchi. "The Impact of Oracular Material on the Political Utterances and Political Action in the Royal Inscriptions of the Sargonid Dynasty." In Heintz, *Oracles et Prophéties dans l'Antiquité*, 99–114.

Fales, F. M., and J. N. Postgate, *Imperial Administrative Records, Part I*. State Archives of Assyria VII. Helsinki: Helsinki University Press, 1992.

Favaro, Sabrina. *Voyages et Voyageures à l'Époque Néo-Assyrienne*. State Archives of Assyria Studies 18. Helsinki: Neo-Assyrian Text Corpus Project, 2007.

Feliu, L., J. Llop, A. Millet Albà, and J. Sanmartín, eds. *Time and History in the Ancient Near East: Proceedings of the 56th Rencontre Assyriologique Internatinale at Barcelona, 26–30 July, 2010*. Winona Lake, Ind.: Eisenbrauns, 2013.

Finkelstein, Israel, and Lily Singer-Avitz. "Ashdod Revisited." *Tel-Aviv* 28 (2001): 231–59.

Follet, R. "'Deuxième Bureau' et information diplomatique dans l'Assyrie des Sargonides. Quelques notes." *Rivista degli Studi Orientali* 32 (1957) 61–81.

Fortin, Michel, ed. *Tell 'Acharneh 1998–2004*. Subartu 18. Turnhout, Belgium: Brepols, 2006.

Foster, Benjamin R. *Before the Muses: An Anthology of Akkadian Literature*. Bethesda: CDL Press, 2005.

Frahm, Eckart. "Ashurbanipal at Der." In Luukko, Svärd, and Mattila, *Of God(s), Trees, Kings, and Scholars*, 51–64.

——. "Counter-texts, Commentary, and Adaptations: Politically Motivated Responses to the Babylonian Epic of Creation in Mesopotamia, the Biblical World, and Elsewhere." *Orient* 45 (2010): 3–33.

——. *Einleitung in die Sanherib-Inschriften*. Vienna: Institut für Orientalistik der Universität, 1997.

——. "Family Matters: Psychohistorical Reflections on Sennacherib and His Times." In Kalima and Richardson, *Sennacherib at the Gates of Jerusalem*, 163–222.

——. "Nabû-zuqup-kēnu, das Gilgamesch-Epos und der Tod Sargons II." *Journal of Cuneiform Studies* 51 (1999): 73–90.

——. "Nabû-zuqup-kēnu, Gilgamesh XII and the Rites of Du'uzu." *Nouvelles Assyriologiques Bréves et Utilitaires* 2005, no. 1, 4–5.

———. "Observations on the Name and Age of Sargon II, and on Some Patterns of Assyrian Royal Onomastics." *Nouvelles Assyriologiques Bréves et Utilitaires* 2005, no. 2, 46–50.

———. "Rising Suns and Falling Stars: Assyrian Kings and the Cosmos." In Hill and Morales, *Experiencing Power—Generating Authority*, 97–120.

———. "A Sculpted Slab with an Inscription of Sargon II Mentioning the Rebellion of Yau-bi'di of Hamath." *Altorientalishe Forschungen* 40 (2013): 42–54.

Frame, Grant. "Babylon: Assyria's Problem and Assyria's Prize." *Journal of the Canadian Society for Mesopotamian Studies* 3 (2008): 21–31.

———. *Babylonia 689–627 B.C.: A Political History*. Publications de l'Institute historique et archéologique néerlandais de Stamboul 69. Leiden: Nederlands Instituut voor het Nabije Oosten, 1992.

———, ed. *From the Upper Sea to the Lower Sea: Studies on the History of Assyria and Babylonia in Honour of A. K. Grayson*. Leiden: Nederlands Instituut voor het Nabije Oosten, 2004.

———. "A 'New' Cylinder Inscription of Sargon II of Assyria from Melid." In Luukko, Svärd, and Mattila, *Of God(s), Trees, Kings, and Scholars*, 65–82.

———. *Rulers of Babylonia: From the Second Dynasty of Isin to the End of the Assyrian Domination (1157–612 B.C.)*. Royal Inscriptions of Mesopotamia, Babylonian Periods 2. Toronto: University of Toronto Press, 1995.

———. "The Tell 'Acharneh Stela of Sargon II of Assyria." In Fortin, *Tell 'Acharneh 1998–2004*, 49–69.

Frame, Grant, and Andrew R. George. "The Royal Libraries of Nineveh." In Collon and George, *Nineveh*, 265–84.

Franklin, Norma. "The Room V Reliefs at Dur-Sharrukin and Sargon II's Western Campaign." *Tel Aviv* 21 (1994): 255–75.

Friday, Karl F. *Samurai, Warfare and the State in Early Medieval Japan*. Warfare and History. New York: Routledge, 2003.

Fuchs, Andreas. *Die Annalen des Jahres 711 v. CHR*. State Archives of Assyria Studies 8. Helsinki: Neo-Assyrian Text Corpus Project, 1998.

———. "Assyria at War: Strategy and Conduct." In Radner and Robson, *The Oxford Handbook of Cuneiform Culture*, 380–401.

———. *Die Inschriften Sargons II. aus Khorsabad*. Göttingen: Cuvillier, 1994.

———. "Pisiri(s)." In *Prosopography of the Neo-Assyrian Empire*, vol. 3, pt. 1, *P–S*, edited by Heather D. Baker, 997. Helsinki: Neo-Assyrian Text Corpus Project, 2002.

———. "Rusa." *Prosopography of the Neo-Assyrian Empire*, vol. 3, pt. 1, *P–S*, edited by Heather D. Baker, 1054–56. Helsinki: Neo-Assyrian Text Corpus Project, 2002.

———. "Šarru-kēnu, Šarru-kīn, Šarru-ukīn." *Prosopography of the Neo-Assyrian Empire*, vol. 3 pt. 2, *Š–Z*, edited by Heather D. Baker, 1239–47. Helsinki: Neo-Assyrian Text Corpus Project, 2011.

————. "Urartu in der Zeit." In Kroll et al., *Biainili-Urartu*, 135–61.

Fuchs, Andreas, and Simo Parpola. *The Correspondence of Sargon II, Part III.* State Archives of Assyria XV. Helsinki: Helsinki University Press, 2001.

Gadd, C. J. "An Inscribed Prism of Marduk-apla-iddina II." *Iraq* 15 (1953): 123–34.

————. "Inscribed Prisms of Sargon II from Nimrud." *Iraq* 16 (1954): 173–201.

Galil, Gershon, Mark Geller, and Alan Millard, eds. *Homeland and Exile: Biblical and Ancient Near Eastern Studies in Honour of Bustenay Oded.* Supplements to Vetus Testamentum 130. Leiden: Brill, 2009.

Gallagher, William R. "Assyrian Deportation Propaganda." *State Archives of Assyria Bulletin* 8 (1994): 57–65.

Galter, Hans. "Sargon der Zweite: Über die Wiederinszenierung von Geschichte." In Rollinger and Truschnegg, *Altertum und Mittelmeerraum*, 279–302.

Garelli, Paul. "The Achievement of Tiglath-pileser III: Novelty or Continuity?" In Cogan and Eph'al, *Ah, Assyria*, 46–51.

Gaspa, Salvatore, et al., eds. *From Source to History: Studies on Ancient Near Eastern Worlds and Beyond, Dedicated to Giovanni Battista Lanfranchi on the Occasion of His 65th Birthday on June 23, 2014.* Alter Orient und Altes Testament 412. Münster: Ugarit-Verlag, 2014.

George, A. R. *The Babylonian Gilgamesh Epic: Introduction, Critical Edition and Cuneiform Texts*, vol. 1. Oxford: Oxford University Press, 2003.

Ginsberg, H. L. "Reflexes of Sargon in Isaiah after 715 B.C.E." *Journal of the American Oriental Society* 88 (1968): 47–53.

Grayson, Albert Kirk. "Assyria: Tiglath-pileser III to Sargon II." In Boardman et al., *The Cambridge Ancient History*, vol. 2, pt. 1, 71–102.

————. *Assyrian and Babylonian Chronicles.* Winona Lake, Ind.: Eisenbrauns, 2000.

————. "Problematical Battles in Mesopotamian History." In Güterbock and Jacobsen, *Studies in Honor of Benno Landsberger on His Seventy-Fifth Birthday*, 337–42.

Grekyan, Yervand. "The Battle of Uauš Revisited." In Kosyan, Petrosyan, and Grekyan, *Urartu and Its Neighbors*, 83–108.

————. "When the Arrows Are Depleted (Towards the Fall of the Urartian Empire)." *Aramazd* 4 (2009): 98–126.

Gunter, Ann. "Representations of Urartian and Western Iranian Fortress Architecture in the Assyrian Reliefs." *Iran* 20 (1982): 103–12.

Güterbock, Hans, and Thorkild Jacobsen, eds. *Studies in Honor of Benno Landsberger on His Seventy-Fifth Birthday.* Assyriological Studies 16. Chicago: Chicago University Press, 1965.

Hallo, W. W. "The Death of Kings: Traditional Historiography in Contextual Perspective." In Cogan and Eph'al, *Ah, Assyria*, 148–65.

Harmanşah, Ömür. "Beyond Aššur: New Cities and the Assyrian Politics of Landscape." *Bulletin of the American Schools of Oriental Research* 365 (2012): 53–77.

————, ed. *Of Rocks and Water: Towards an Archaeology of Place.* Joukowsky Institute Publications 5. Oxford, England: Oxbow Books, 2014.

Hassanzadeh, Y., and H. Mollasalehi. "New Evidence for Mannean Art: An Assessment of Three Glazed Tiles from Qalaichi (Izirtu)." In Álvarez-Mon and Garrison, *Elam and Persia*, 407–17.

Hawkins, J. D. *Corpus of Hieroglyphic Luwian Inscriptions,* vol. 1, *Inscriptions of the Iron Age, Part 2.* Berlin: De Gruyter, 2000.

————. "Kings of Tabal in the Later 8th Century B.C." *Anatolian Studies* 29 (1979): 162–67.

————. "The Neo-Hittite States in Syria and Anatolia." In Boardman et al., *The Cambridge Ancient History,* vol. 3, pt. 1, 372–441.

————. "The New Sargon Stele from Hama." In Frame, *From the Upper Sea to the Lower Sea,* 151–64.

Hawkins, J. D., and J. N. Postgate. "Tribute from Tabal." *State Archives of Assyria Bulletin* 2 (1988): 31–40.

Hecker, K., and W. Sommerfeld, eds. *Keilschriftliche Literaturen: Ausgewählte Vorträge der XXXII. Rencontre Assyriologique Internationale, Münster, 8.–12.7. 1985.* Berlin: Dietrich Reimer, 1986.

Heidhorn, Lisa A. "The Horses of Kush." *Journal of Near Eastern Studies* 56 (1997): 105–14.

Heintz, Jean-Georges, ed. *Oracles et Prophéties dans l'Antiquité.* Paris: De Boccard, 1997.

Henshaw, Richard A. "The Assyrian Army and Its Soldier, 9th–7th C., B.C." *Paleologia* 16 (1969): 1–24.

Hill, J. A. and A. J. Morales, eds. *Experiencing Power—Generating Authority: Cosmos, Politics, and the Ideology of Kingship in Ancient Egypt and Mesopotamia.* Philadelphia: University of Pennsylvania Press, 2013.

Holloway, Steven W. *Aššur Is King! Aššur Is King! Religion in the Exercise of Power in the Neo-Assyrian Empire.* Culture and History of the Ancient Near East 10. Leiden: Brill, 2002.

Hovhannisyan, K. L. *See* Oganesjan, K. L.

Howarth, Anthony. *People of the Wind.* Carolyn Films, 1976.

Howe, Timothy, ed. *Traders in the Ancient Mediterranean.* Chicago: Ares, 2015.

Hübner, U., and E. A. Knauf, eds. *Kein Land für sich allein: Studien zum Kulturkontakt in Kanaan, Israel/Palästina und Ebirnâri für Manfred Weippert zum 65. Geburstag.* Orbis Biblicus et Orientalis 186. Göttingen: Universitätsverlag, Vandenhoeck and Ruprecht, 2002.

Hurowitz, Victor Avigdor. "'Shutting Up' the Enemy—Literary Gleanings from Sargon's Eighth Campaign." In Cogan and Kahn, *Treasures on Camels' Humps,* 104–120.

Inomata, T., and L. Coben, eds. *Spectacle, Performance, and Power in Premodern Complex Society.* Walnut Creek, Calif.: Altamira, 2006.

Ivantchik, A. I. *Les Cimmeriéns au Proche Orient.* Orbis Biblicus et Orientalis 127. Göttingen: Vandenhoeck and Ruprecht, 1993.

————. "The Current State of the Cimmerian Problem." *Ancient Civilizations* 7 (2001): 307–40.

Izre'el, Shlomo, and Rina Drory, eds. *Language and Culture in the Near East: Diglossia, Bilingualism, Registers.* Israel Oriental Studies 15. Leiden: Brill, 1995.

Jacoby, R. "The Representation and Identification of Cities on Assyrian Reliefs." *Israel Exploration Journal* 41 (1991): 112–31.

Jakubiak, Krzysztof. "Some Remarks on Sargon's Eighth Campaign of 714 B.C." *Iranica Antiqua* 39 (2004): 191–202.

Jean, Cynthia. "Magie et Histoire: les rituels en temps de guerre." In Feliu, Llop, Millet Albà, and Sanmartín, *Time and History in the Ancient Near East*, 107–12.

Jonkers, Gerdien. *The Topography of Remembrance: The Dead, Tradition and Collective Memory in Mesopotamia.* Studies in the History of Religions 68. Leiden: Brill, 1995.

Johnson, Erika Diane. "Stealing the Enemy's Gods: An Exploration of the Phenomenon of Godnap in Ancient Western Asia." PhD diss., University of Birmingham, 2011.

Kagan, Donald. *The Peloponnesian War.* New York: Penguin Books, 2003.

Kahn, D. "The Inscription of Sargon II at Tang-i Var and the Chronology of the 25th Dynasty." *Orientalia* 70 (2001): 1–18.

———. "Was There a Coregency in the 25th Dynasty?" *Mitteilungen der Sudanarchäologischen Gesellschaft zu Berlin* 17 (2006): 135–41.

Kalima, Isaac, and Seth Richardson, eds. *Sennacherib at the Gates of Jerusalem: Story, History and Historiography.* Leiden: Brill, 2014.

Kämmerer, Thomas R., ed. *Studien zur Ritual und Sozialgeschichte im Alten Orient / Studies on Ritual and Society in the Ancient Near East.* Beiheft zur Zeitschrift für die alttestamentliche Wissenschaft, 374. Berlin: Walter de Gruyter, 2007.

Kaplan, J. "The Stronghold of Yamani at Ashdod-Yam." *Israel Exploration Journal* 19 (1969): 137–49.

Kaplan, Yahuda. "Recruitment of Foreign Soldiers into the Neo-Assyrian Army during the Reign of Tiglath-pileser III." In Cogan and Kahn, *Treasures on Camels' Humps*, 135–52.

Kargar, Bahman, and Ali Binandeh. "A Preliminary Report of Excavations at Rabat Tepe, Northwestern Iran." *Iranica Antiqua* 44 (2009): 113–29.

Kataja, Laura, and Robert Whiting. *Grants, Decrees, and Gifts of the Neo-Assyrian Period.* State Archives of Assyria XII. Helsinki: University of Helsinki Press, 1995.

Kealhofer, Lisa, ed. *The Archaeology of Midas and the Phrygians: Recent Work at Gordion.* Philadelphia: University of Pennsylvania Museum, 2005.

Kelle, Brad E., Frank R. Ames, and Jacob L. Wright, eds. *Warfare, Ritual and Symbol in Biblical and Modern Contexts.* Atlanta: Society for Biblical Literature, 2014.

King, L. W. and R. Campbell Thompson. *Cuneiform Texts from Babylonian Tablets in the British Museum,* volume 22. London: Trustees of the British Museum, 1906.

Konakçı, E. and M. B. Baştürk. "Military and Militia in the Urartian State." *Ancient West and East* 8 (2009): 169–201.

König, F. W. *Handbuch der chaldischen Inschriften*. Archiv für Orientforschung Beiheft 8. Graz: Ferdinand Berger & Söhne, 1957.

Köruğlu, Kemalettin, and Erkan Konyar, eds. *Urartu—Transformation in the East / Doğu'da Degisim*. Istanbul: Yapi Kredi Yayinlari, 2011.

Kosyan, Aram, Armen Petrosyan, and Yervand Grekyan, eds. "Urartu and Its Neighbors: Festschrift in Honor of Nicolay Harutyunian in Occasion of his 90th Birthday." Special issue, *Aramazd* 5 (2010).

Kozuh, Michael. "A Hand Anything but Hidden: Institutions and Markets in First Millennium B.C.E. Mesopotamia." In Howe, *Traders in the Ancient Mediterranean*, 73–100.

Kravitz, Kathryn F. "A Last-Minute Revision to Sargon's Letter to the God." *Journal of Near Eastern Studies* 62 (2003): 81–95.

Kristensen, Anne K. G. *Who Were the Cimmerians and Where Did They Come From? Sargon II, the Cimmerians, and Rusa I*. Translated by J. Laessoe. Det Kongelige Danske Videnskabernes Selskab, Historisk-filosofiske Meddelelser 57. Copenhagen: Munksgaard, 1988.

Kroll, Stephan. "Sargon II's 8th Campaign: A New View on Old Constructs." In Muscarella and Elliyoun, *The Eighth Campaign of Sargon II*, 10–16.

———. "The Southern Urmia Basin in the Early Iron Age." *Iranica Antiqua* 40 (2005): 65–85.

Kroll, S. C., et al., eds. *Biainili-Urartu: The Proceedings of the Symposium Held in Munich 12–14. October 2007 / Tagungsbericht des Münchner Symposiums 12.–14. Oktober 2007*. Acta Iranica 51. Leuven: Peeters, 2012.

Kuhrt, A. *The Ancient Near East, 3000–330 B.C.*, vol. 2. London: Routledge, 1995.

Lambert, W. G. "Portion of Inscribed Stela of Sargon II, King of Assyria." In Muscarella, *Ladders to Heaven*, 125.

Lanfranchi, Giovanni B. "The Assyrian Expansion in the Zagros and Local Ruling Elites." In Lanfranchi, Roaf, and Rollinger, *Continuity of Empire (?)*, 79–118.

———. "Assyrian Geography and Neo-Assyrian Letters." In Liverani, *Neo-Assyrian Geography*, 127–37.

———. "Consensus to Empire: Some Aspects of Sargon II's Foreign Policy." In Waetzoldt and Hauptmann, *Assyrien im Wandel der Zeiten*, 81–87.

———. *I Cimmeri: emergenza delle élites militari iraniche nel Vicino Oriente (VIII–VII sec. a.C.)*. Padua: S.A.R.G.O.N., 1990.

———. "The Ideological and Political Impact of the Assyrian Imperial Expansion on the Greek World in the 8th and 7th Centuries B.C." In Aro and Whiting, *The Heirs of Assyria*, 7–34.

———. "Sargon's Letter to Aššur-šarru-uṣur." *State Archives of Assyria Bulletin* 2 (1988): 59–64.

———. "Some New Texts about a Revolt against the Urartian King, Rusa I." *Oriens Antiquus* 22 (1983): 124–35.

Lanfranchi, Giovanni B., and Simo Parpola. *The Correspondence of Sargon II, Part II*. State Archives of Assyria V. Helsinki: Helsinki University Press, 1990.

Lanfranchi, G. B., M. Roaf, and R. Rollinger, eds. *Continuity of Empire (?): Assyria, Media, Persia.* Padua: S.A.R.G.O.N., 2003.

Lanfranchi, G. B., and R. Rollinger, eds. *Concepts of Kingship in Antiquity: Proceedings of the European Science Foundation Exploratory Workshop Held in Padova, November 28th—December 1st, 2007.* History of the Ancient Near East Monographs 11. Padua: S.A.R.G.O.N., 2010.

Lanfranchi, G. B., et al., eds. *Leggo! Studies Presented to Frederick Mario Fales on the Occasion of His 65th Birthday.* Leipziger Altorientalistische Studien 2. Wiesbaden: Harrasowitz, 2012.

Larsen, Mogens Trolle, ed. *Power and Propaganda: A Symposium on Ancient Empires.* Mesopotamia 7. Copenhagen: Akademisk Forlag, 1979.

Lauinger, Jacob, and Stephen Batiuk. "A Stele of Sargon II at Tell Tayinat." *Zeitschrift für Assyriologie* 105 (2015): 54–68.

Lebeau, Marc, and Philippe Talon, eds. *Reflets des deux fleuves: volume de mélanges offerts à André Finet.* Akkadica Supplementum 6. Leuven: Peeters, 1989.

Lee, Wayne E. *Barbarians and Brothers: Anglo-American Warfare, 1500–1865.* Oxford: Oxford University Press, 2011.

Leichty, Erle. *The Royal Inscriptions of Esarhaddon, King of Assyria (680–669 B.C.).* Royal Inscriptions of the Neo-Assyrian Period 4. Winona Lake, Ind.: Eisenbrauns, 2010.

Lemaire, A. "Aššur-šarru-uṣur, governeur de Qué," *Nouvelles Assyriologiques Bréves et Utilitaires,* no. 1 (1987): 5–6.

———. "Une inscription aram   éene du VIIIe siècle av. J.-C. trouvée à Bukân (Azerbaidjan iranïen)." *Studia Iranica* 27 (1998): 15–30.

Levine, Louis D. "East-West Trade in the Late Iron Age: a View from the Zagros." In Deshayes, *Le Plateau iranien et l'Asie central des origins á la conquête islamique,* 171–86.

———. "Geographical Studies in the Neo-Assyrian Zagros: I." *Iran* (1973): 1–27.

———. "Observations on 'Sargon's Letter to the Gods.'" *Eretz Israel* 27 (2003): 111–19.

———. "Sargon's 8th Campaign." In Levine and Young, *Mountains and Lowlands,* 135–51.

———. *Two Neo-Assyrian Stelae from Iran.* Royal Ontario Museum Art and Archaeology Occasional Paper 23. Toronto: Royal Ontario Museum, 1972.

Levine, Louis D., and T. Cuyler Young, eds. *Mountains and Lowlands: Essays in the Archaeology of Greater Mesopotamia.* Malibu, Calif.: Undena Publications, 1977.

Linder, Elisha. "The Khorsabad Wall Relief: A Mediterranean Seascape or River Transport of Timbers?" *Journal of the American Oriental Society* 106 (1986): 273–81.

Lipiński, Edward. *On the Skirts of Canaan in the Iron Age: Historical and Topographical Perspectives.* Orientalia Lovaniensia Analecta. Leuven: Peeters, 2006.

Lipschits, Oded, and Joseph Blenkinsopp, eds. *Judah and the Judeans in the Neo-Babylonian Period*. Winona Lake, Ind.: Eisenbrauns, 2003.

Littauer, M. A., and J. M. Crouwell. *Wheeled Vehicles and Ridden Animals in the Ancient Near East*. Leiden: Brill, 1979.

Liverani, Mario. *The Ancient Near East: History, Society, and Economy*. New York: Routledge, 2014.

———. "The Growth of the Assyrian Empire in the Habur/Middle Euphrates Area: A New Paradigm." *State Archives of Assyria Bulletin* 2 (1988): 81–98.

———. "The Ideology of the Assyrian Empire." In Larsen, *Power and Propaganda*, 297–319.

———. "The King and His Audience." In Gaspa et al., *From Source to History*, 373–85.

———. "Memorandum on the Approach to Historiographic Texts." *Orientalia* 42 (1973): 178–94.

———, ed. *Neo-Assyrian Geography*. Quaderni di Geografia Storica 5. Rome: Università di Roma, "La Sapienza," 1995.

———. *Prestige and Interest: International Relations in the Near East ca. 1600–1100 B.C.* History of the Ancient Near East/Studies 1. Padua: S.A.R.G.O.N., 1990.

Loretz, O., K. A. Metzler, and H. Schaudig, eds. *Ex Mesopotamia et Syria Lux: Festschrift für Manfried Dietrich zu seinem 65. Geburtstag*. Alter Orient und Altes Testament 281. Münster: Ugarit-Verlag, 2002.

Loud, Gordon. *Khorsabad Part I: Excavations in the Palace and at a City Gate*. Oriental Institute Publications 38. Chicago: University of Chicago Press, 1936.

———. *Khorsabad Part II: The Citadel and the Town*. Oriental Institute Publications 40. Chicago: University of Chicago Press, 1938.

Luraghi, Nino. "Traders, Pirates, Warriors: The Proto-History of Greek Mercenary Soldiers in the Eastern Mediterranean." *Phoenix* (2006): 21–47.

Luukko, Mikko. *The Correspondence of Tiglath-Pileser III and Sargon II from Calah/Nimrud*. State Archives of Assyria XIX. Helsinki: Neo-Assyrian Text Corpus Project, 2012.

Luukko, Mikko, Saana Svärd, and Raija Mattila, eds. *Of God(s), Trees, Kings, and Scholars: Neo-Assyrian and Related Studies in Honour of Simo Parpola*. Studia Orientalia 106. Helsinki: Finnish Oriental Society, 2009.

Machinist, Peter. "Assyria and Its Image in the First Isaiah." *Journal of the American Oriental Society* 103 (1983): 719–37.

Malbran-Labat, F. *l'Armée et l'Organisation Militaire de l'Assyrie*. Geneva: Librairie Droz, 1982.

———. "Le texte de l'inscription." In Caubet, *Khorsabad, le palais de Sargon II*, 169–79.

Maniori, Fulvia. *Le campagne babilonesi ed orientali di Sargon II d'Assiria: un'analisi topografica*. Rome: L'Erma di Bretschneider, 2014.

Manitius, W. "Das stehende Heer der Assyrerkönig." *Zeitschrift für Assyriologie* 24 (1910): 97–149, 185–224.

Manning, J. G. and Ian Morris, eds. *The Ancient Economy: Evidence and Models*. Stanford: Stanford University Press, 2005.

Marf, Dlshad A. "The Temple and the City of Muṣaṣir/Ardini: New Aspects in the Light of New Archeological Evidence." *Subartu* 8 (2014): 13–29.

Marriott, John, and Karen Radner. "Sustaining the Assyrian Army among Friends and Enemies in 714 B.C.E." *Journal of Cuneiform Studies* 67 (2015): 127–43.

Mattern, Susan P. *Rome and the Enemy: Imperial Strategy and the Principate*. Berkeley: University of California Press, 1999.

Matthiae, Paolo. "Subject Innovations in the Khorsabad Reliefs and Their Political Meaning." In Lanfranchi et al., *Leggo!*, 477–99.

Matthiae, Paolo, et al., eds. *Proceedings of the 6th International Congress on the Archaeology of the Ancient Near East, 5 May–10 May 2009, "Sapienza," Università di Roma*. Wiesbaden: Harrassowitz, 2010.

Mattila, Raija. *The King's Magnates: A Study of the Highest Officials of the Neo-Assyrian Empire*. State Archives of Assyria Studies 11. Helsinki: Neo-Assyrian Text Corpus Project, 2000.

Mattingly, Gerald L. "An Archaeological Analysis of Sargon's 712 Campaign against Ashdod." *Near East Archaeological Society Bulletin* 17 (1981): 47–64.

Mauss, Marcel. *The Gift: The Form and Reason for Exchange in Archaic Societies*. Translated by W. D. Halls. New York: Norton, 1990.

Maxwell-Hyslop, K. R. "Assyrian Sources of Iron: A Preliminary Survey of the Historical and Geographical Evidence." *Iraq* 36 (1974): 139–54.

May, Natalie Naomi. "ᵐAli-talīmu, or What Can Be Learned from the Destruction of Figurative Complexes?" In May, *Iconoclasm and Text Destruction*, 187–230.

———, ed. *Iconoclasm and Text Destruction in the Ancient Near East and Beyond*. Oriental Institute Seminars 8. Chicago: Oriental Institute of the University of Chicago, 2012.

———. "Triumph as an Aspect of the Neo-Assyrian Decorative Program." In Wilhelm, *Organization, Representation, and Symbols of Power in the Ancient Near East*, 461–88.

Mayer, Walter. "Die chronologische Einordnung der Kimmerier-Briefe aus der Zeit Sargons II." In Dietrich and Loretz, *Mesopotamica— Ugaritica—Biblica*, 145–76.

———. "Die Finanzierung einer Kampagne (TCL 3, 346–410)." *Ugarit Forschungen* 11 (1979): 13–33.

———. "Sargons Feldzug gegen Urartu—714 v. Chr.: Eine militärische Würdigung. *Mitteilungen der Deutschen Orientgesellschaft zu Berlin* 112 (1980): 14–16.

———. "Sargons Feldzug gegen Urartu—714 v. Chr.: Text und Öbersetzung." *Mitteilungen der Deutschen Orientgesellschaft zu Berlin* 115 (1983): 65–132.

———. "Die Stadt Kumme als überregionales religiöses Zentrum." In Loretz, Metzler and Schaudig, *Ex Mesopotamia et Syria Lux*, 329–58.

———. "Der Weg auf den Thron Assurs. Sukzession und Usurpation im assyrischen Königshaus." In Dietrich and Kottsieper, *Und Mose schrieb dieses Lied auf*, 533–55.

Medvedskaya, Inna N. "The Localization of Hubuškia." In Parpola and Whiting, *Assyria '95*, 197–206.

Melchert, Craig H., ed. *The Luwians.* Handbuch der Orientalistik 68. Leiden: Brill, 2003.

Melville, Sarah C. "Ideology, Politics, and the Assyrian Understanding of Defeat." In Clark and Turner, *War Losses in the Ancient World*, forthcoming.

———. "Kings of Tabal: Politics, Competition, and Conflict in a Contested Periphery." In Richardson, *Rebellions and Peripheries in the Mesopotamian World*, 85–107.

———. "Neo-Assyrian Royal Women and Male Identity: Status as a Social Tool." *Journal of the American Oriental Society* 124 (2004): 37–57.

———. "Sargon II." In Chavalas, *The Ancient Near East*, 333–42.

———. "Win, Lose, or Draw? Claiming Victory in Battle." In Neumann et al., *Krieg und Frieden Frieden im Alten Vorderasien*, 221–35.

Melville, Sarah C., and Duncan J. Melville. "Observations on the Diffusion of Military Technology: Siege Warfare in the Ancient Near East and Greece." In Ross, *From the Banks of the Euphrates*, 145–68.

Melville, Sarah C., and Alice L. Slotsky, eds. *Opening the Tablet Box: Near Eastern Studies in Honor of Benjamin R. Foster.* Culture and History of the Ancient Near East 42. Leiden: Brill, 2010.

Menzel, B. *Assyrische Temple.* Studia Pohl, Series Maior, vol. 10, pt. 2. Rome: Biblical Institute Press, 1981.

Miglus, A., and Simone Mühl. *Between the Cultures: The Central Tigris Region from the Third to the First Millennium B.C.* Heidelberg: Heidelberger Orientverlag, 2011.

Millard, Allan. *The Eponyms of the Assyrian Empire 910–612 B.C.* State Archives of Assyria Studies 2. Helsinki: Helsinki University Press, 1994.

Mollazadeh, K. "The Pottery from the Mannean Site of Qallaichi (Bukan), NW Iran." *Iranica Antiqua* 43 (2008): 107–25.

Moorey, P. R. S. *Ancient Mesopotamian Materials and Industries: The Archaeological Evidence.* Winona Lake, Ind.: Eisenbrauns, 1999.

Muscarella, Oscar White, ed. *Ladders to Heaven: Art Treasures from the Lands of the Bible.* Toronto: McClelland and Stewart, 1981.

Muscarella, Oscar White, and Samad Elliyoun, eds. *The Eighth Campaign of Sargon II: Historical Geographical, Literary, and Ideological Aspects.* Iran: Hasanlu Translation Project, 2012.

Mynářová, J., ed. *Egypt and the Near East—the Crossroads: Proceedings of an International Conference on the Relations of Egypt and the Near East in the Bronze Age, Prague, September 1–3, 2010.* Prague: Charles University, 2011.

Na'aman, N. "The Boundary System and Political Status of Gaza under the Assyrian Empire." *Zeitschrift des Deutschen Palästina-Vereins* (1953–) 120 (2004): 55–72.

———. "The Brook of Egypt and Assyrian Policy on the Border of Egypt." *Tel Aviv* 6 (1979): 68–90.

———. "The Conquest of Yadnana according to the Inscriptions of Sargon II." In Abusch et al., *Historiography in the Cuneiform World*, 129–34.

———. "Ekron under the Assyrian and Egyptian Empires." *Bulletin of the American Schools of Oriental Research* 332 (2003): 81–91.

———. "Forced Participation in Alliances in the Course of the Assyrian Campaigns to the West." In Cogan and Eph'al, *Ah, Assyria*, 80–98.

———. "The Historical Background to the Conquest of Samaria (720 B.C.)." *Biblica* 71 (1990): 206–25.

———. "Sargon II and the Rebellion of the Cypriote Kings against Shilṭa of Tyre." *Orientalia* 67 (1998): 239–47.

———. "Sargon II's Second *Palû* according to the Khorsabad Annals." *Tel Aviv* 34 (2007): 165–70.

Nadali, Davide. "Assyrian Open Field Battles: An Attempt at Reconstruction and Analysis." In Vidal, *Studies on War in the Ancient Near East*, 117–52.

———. "Assyrians to War: Positions, Patterns and Canons in the Tactics of the Assyrian Armies in the VII Century B.C." In Nadali and Di Ludovico, *Contributi e Materiali di Archeologia Orientale X*, 167–207.

Nadali, Davide, and Alessandro Di Ludovico, eds. *Contributi e Materiali di Archeologia Orientale X: Studi in onore di Paolo Matthiae presentati in occasione del suo sessantacinquesimo compleanno.* Rome: La Sapienza, 2005.

Neuman, Hans, et al., eds. *Krieg und Frieden im Alten Vorderasien, 52e Rencontre Assyriologique Internationale, Münster, 17.–21. Juli 2006.* Alter Orient und Altes Testament 401. Münster: Ugarit-Verlag, 2014.

New English Bible with Apocrypha. New York: Oxford University Press, 1970.

Niederreiter, Z. "L'insigne de pouvoir et le sceau du grand vizir Sîn-ah-uṣur." *Revue d'Assyriologie* 99 (2005): 57–76.

———. "Le rôle des symboles figurés attribués aux membres de la Cour de Sargon II: Des emblèmes créés par les lettrés du palais au service de l'idéologie royale." *Iraq* 70 (2008): 51–86.

Nissen, Hans, and Johannes Renger, eds. *Mesopotamien und seine Nachbarn: politische und kulturelle Wechselbeziehungen im alten Vorderasien vom 4. bis 1. Jahrtausend v. Chr.* Berliner Beiträge zum Vorderen Orient I. Berlin: Reimer, 1982.

Niven, Bill, and Stefan Berger. *Writing the History of Memory.* London: Bloomsbury Academic, 2014.

Noble, Duncan. "Assyrian Chariotry and Cavalry." *State Archives of Assyria Bulletin* 4 (1990): 61–68.

Novák, M. "Arameans and Luwians—Processes of an Acculturation." In Van Soldt, *Ethnicity in Ancient Mesopotamia*, 252–66.

———. "From Assur to Nineveh: The Assyrian Town Planning Programme." In Collon and George, *Nineveh*, 177–86.

Oates, David, and Joan Oates. *Nimrud: An Assyrian Imperial City Revealed*. London: British Institute for the Study of Iraq, 2001.

Oded, Bustenay. "'The Command of the God' as a Reason for Going to War in the Assyrian Royal Inscriptions." In Cogan and Eph'al, *Ah, Assyria*, 221–30.

———. "Cutting Down Orchards in Assyrian Royal Inscriptions: The Historiographic Aspect." *Journal of Ancient Civilizations* 12 (1997): 93–98.

———. *Mass Deportations and Deportees in the Neo-Assyrian Empire*. Wiesbaden: Dr. Ludwig Reichert Verlag, 1979.

———. "Observations on Methods of Assyrian Rule in Transjordania after the Palestinian Campaign of Tiglath-Pileser III." *Journal of Near Eastern Studies* 29 (1970): 177–86.

———. *War, Peace and Empire: Justifications for War in Assyrian Royal Inscriptions*. Wiesbaden: Dr. Ludwig Reichert Verlag, 1992.

Oganesjan, K. L. "Assiro-urartskoe sraženie na gore Uauš." *Patmabanasirakan Handes* 3 (1966): 107–18.

Oppenheim, A. L. "The City of Assur in 714 B.C." *Journal of Near Eastern Studies* (1960): 133–47.

———. "Neo-Assyrian and Neo-Babylonian Empires." In Oppenheim et al., *Propaganda and Communication in World History I*, 111–44.

Oppenheim, A. Leo, et al., eds. *Propaganda and Communication in World History I: The Symbolic Instrument in Early Times*. Honolulu: University Press of Hawaii, 1979.

Park, Sung Jin. "A New Historical Reconstruction of the Fall of Samaria." *Biblica* 93 (2012): 98–106.

Parker, Bradley J. "Abaliuqunu." In *The Prosopography of the Neo-Assyrian Empire*, vol. 1, pt. 1:A, edited by Karen Radner. Helsinki: Neo-Assyrian Text Corpus Project, 1998.

———. "Ašipâ Again: A Microhistory of an Assyrian Provincial Administrator." In Luukko, Svärd, and Mattila, *Of God(s), Trees, Kings, and Scholars*, 179–92.

———. "At the Edge of Empire: Conceptualizing Assyria's Anatolian Frontier ca. 700 B.C." *Journal of Anthropological Archaeology* 21 (2002): 371–95.

———. "The Construction and Performance of Kingship in the Neo-Assyrian Empire." *Journal of Anthropological Research* 67 (2011): 357–86.

———. "The Earliest Known Reference to the Ionians in the Cuneiform Sources." *Ancient History Bulletin* 14 (2000): 69–77.

———. "Garrisoning the Empire: Aspects of the Construction and Maintenance of Forts on the Assyrian Frontier." *Iraq* 59 (1997): 77–87.

———. "Geographies of Power: Territoriality and Empire during the Mesopotamian Iron Age." *Archaeological Papers of the American Anthropological Association* 22 (2013): 126–44.

———. "Hegemony, Power, and the Use of Force in the Neo Assyrian Empire." In Düring, *Understanding Hegemonic Practices of the Early Assyrian Empire*, 287–99.

————. *The Mechanics of Empire: The Northern Frontier of Assyria as a Case Study in Imperial Dynamics.* Helsinki: Neo-Assyrian Text Corpus Project, 2001.

————. "Toward an Understanding of Borderland Processes." *American Antiquity* 71 (2006): 77–100.

Parpola, Simo, "The Assyrian Cabinet." In Dietrich and Loretz, *Vom Alten Orient zum Alten Testament,* 379–401.

————. "Assyrian Royal Inscriptions and Neo-Assyrian Letters." In Fales, *Assyrian Royal Inscriptions,* 117–42.

————. "Assyria's Expansion in the 8th and 7th Centuries B.C.E. and Its Long-Term Repercussions in the West." In Dever and Gitin, *Symbiosis, Symbolism and the Power of the Past,* 99–111.

————. "The Construction of Dur-Šarrukin in the Assyrian Royal Correspondence." In Caubet, *Khorsabad, le palais de Sargon II,* 49–77.

————. *The Correspondence of Sargon II, Part I.* State Archives of Assyria I. Helsinki: Helsinki University Press, 1987.

————. "Neo-Assyrian Concepts of Kingship and Their Heritage in Mediterranean Antiquity." In Lanfranchi and Rollinger, *Concepts of Kingship in Antiquity,* 35–44.

————. "The Neo-Assyrian Ruling Class." In Kämmerer, *Studien zur Ritual und Sozialgeschichte im Alten Orient,* 257–74.

Parpola, Simo, and Michael Porter. *The Helsinki Atlas of the Near East in the Neo-Assyrian Period.* Chebeague Island, Me.: Casco Bay Assyriological Institute; Helsinki: Neo-Assyrian Text Corpus Project, 2001.

Parpola, Simo and Robert Whiting, eds. *Assyria '95: Proceedings of the 10th Anniversary Symposium of the Neo-Assyrian Text Corpus Project, Helsinki, September 7–11, 1995.* Helsinki: Neo-Assyrian Text Corpus Project, 1997.

Pečírcova, J. "The Administrative Methods of Assyrian Imperialism." *Archiv Orientalni* 55 (1987): 162–75.

————. "The Administrative Organization of the Neo-Assyrian Empire." *Archiv Orientalni* 45 (1977): 217–20.

Pecorella, P. E., and M. Salvini. *Tra lo Zagros e l'Urmia. Ricerche Storiche ed Archeologische nell'Azerbaigian iraniano.* Incunabula Graeca 78. Rome: Edizioni dell'Ateneo, 1984.

Pleiner, Radomír. "The Technology of Three Assyrian Iron Artifacts from Khorsabad." *Journal of Near Eastern Studies* 38 (1979): 83–91.

Ponchia, Simonetta. "Administrators and Administrated in Neo-Assyrian Times." In Wilhelm, *Organization, Representation, and Symbols of Power in the Ancient Near East,* 213–24.

————. "Mountain Routes in Assyrian Royal Inscriptions, Part II." *State Archives of Assyria Bulletin* 15 (2006): 193–271.

Pongratz-Leisten, Beate. "The Interplay of Military Strategy and Cultic Practice in Assyrian Politics." In Parpola and Whiting, *Assyria '95,* 245–52.

Porter, B. N. "Language, Audience and Impact in Imperial Assyria." In Izre'el and Drory, *Language and Culture in the Near East,* 51–72.

Postgate, J. N. "The Assyrian Army at Zamua." *Iraq* 62 (2000): 89–108.
———. "Assyrian Texts and Fragments." *Iraq* 35 (1973): 13–36.
———. "Assyrian Uniforms." In Van Soldt, *Veenhof Anniversary Volume*, 373–88.
———. "Assyria: The Home Provinces." In Liverani, *Neo-Assyrian Geography*, 1–17.
———. *Early Mesopotamia: Society and Economy at the Dawn of History.* New York: Routledge, 1994.
———. "The Economic Structure of the Assyrian Empire." In Larsen, *Power and Propaganda*, 193–221.
———. *The Governor's Palace Archive.* Cuneiform Texts from Nimrud II. London: British School of Archaeology in Iraq, 1973.
———. "The Invisible Hierarchy: Assyrian Military and Civilian Administration in the 8th and 7th Centuries." In Postgate, *The Land of Assur and the Yoke of Assur*, 331–61.
———. "Itu' (Utu', Itu'āya)." *Reallexikon der Assyriologie und Vorderasiatischen Archäologie* 5 (1980): 221–22.
———, ed. *The Land of Assur and the Yoke of Assur: Studies on Assyria 1971–2005.* Oxford: Oxbow Books, 2007.
———. "Mannäer." *Reallexikon der Assyriologie und Vorderasiatischen Archäologie* 8 (1989): 340–42.
———. "The Ownership and Exploitation of Land in Assyria in the First Millennium B.C." In Lebeau and Talon, *Reflets des deux fleuves*, 141–52.
———. *Taxation and Conscription in the Assyrian Empire.* Studia Pohl: Series Maior 3. Rome: Biblical Institute Press, 1974.
———. "The Tombs in the Light of Mesopotamian Funerary Traditions." In Curtis et al., *New Light on Nimrud*, 177–80.
Postgate, J. N., and R. Mattila. "Il-Yada' and Sargon's Southeast Frontier." In Frame, *From the Upper Sea to the Lower Sea*, 235–54.
Potts, Daniel T. *The Archaeology of Elam: Formation and Transformation of an Ancient Iranian State.* Cambridge: Cambridge University Press, 1999.
Powell, Marvin A. "Merodach-Baladan at Dur-Jakin: A Note on the Defense of Babylonian Cities." *Journal of Cuneiform Studies* 34 (1982): 59–61.
Radner, Karen. "Aššur-dūr-pānīya, Statthalter von Til-Barsip unter Sargon II. von Assyrien." *Baghdader Mitteilungen* 37 (2006): 185–95.
———. "The Assur-Nineveh-Arbela Triangle: Central Assyria in the Neo-Assyrian Period." In Miglus and Mühl, *Between the Cultures*, 321–29.
———. "Assyrian and Non-Assyrian Kingship in the First Millennium B.C." In Lanfranchi and Rollinger, *Concepts of Kingship in Antiquity*, 25–34.
———. "Assyrians and Urartians." In Steadman and McMahon, *The Oxford Handbook of Ancient Anatolia*, 734–51.
———. "An Assyrian View on the Medes." In Lanfranchi, Roaf, and Rollinger, *Continuity of Empire (?)*, 37–64.

———. "Between a Rock and a Hard Place: Muṣaṣir, Kumme, Ukku and Šubria—the Buffer States between Assyria and Urartu." In Kroll et al., *Biainili-Urartu*, 243–64.

———. "An Imperial Communication Network: The State Correspondence of the Neo-Assyrian Empire." In Radner, *State Correspondence in the Ancient World from New Kingdom Egypt to the Roman Empire*, 64–93.

———. "Money in the Neo-Assyrian Empire." In Dercksen, *Trade and Finance in Ancient Mesopotamia*, 127–57.

———. "Provinz: Assyrien." *Reallexikon der Assyriologie und Vorderasiatischen Archäologie* 11 (2006): 42–68.

———. "Royal Decision-Making: Kings, Magnates, and Scholars." In Radner and Robson, *The Oxford Handbook of Cuneiform Culture*, 358–79.

———. "Salmanassar V. in den *Nimrud Letters.*" *Archiv für Orientforschung* 50 (2003–2004): 95–104.

———, ed. *State Correspondence in the Ancient World from New Kingdom Egypt to the Roman Empire*. New York: Oxford University Press, 2014.

———. "The Stele of Sargon II of Assyria at Kition: A Focus for an Emerging Cypriot Identity?" In Rollinger et al., *Interkulturalität in der Alten Welt*, 429–47.

———. "Traders in the Neo-Assyrian Period." In Dercksen, *Trade and Finance in Mesopotamia*, 101–26.

Radner, Karen, and Eleanor Robson, eds. *The Oxford Handbook of Cuneiform Culture*. New York: Oxford University Press, 2011.

Reade, J. E. "Campaigning around Musasir." In Çilingiroğlu and French, *Anatolian Iron Ages 3*, 185–88.

———. "Narrative Composition in Assyrian Sculpture." *Baghdader Mitteilungen* 10 (1979): 52–110.

———. "The Neo-Assyrian Court and Army: Evidence from the Sculptures." *Iraq* 34 (1972): 87–112.

———. "Sargon's Campaigns of 720, 716 and 715 B.C.: Evidence from the Sculptures." *Journal of Near Eastern Studies* 35 (1976): 95–104.

Renger, Johannes. "Neuassyrische Königinschriften als Genre der Keilschriftliteratur: Zum Stil und zur Kompositionstechnik der Inschriften Sargons II. Von Assyiren." In Hecker and Sommerfeld, *Keilschriftliche Literaturen*, 109–28.

Richardson, Seth F. C., ed. *Rebellions and Peripheries in the Mesopotamian World*. American Oriental Series 91. Winona Lake, Ind.: Eisenbrauns, 2010.

Rivaroli, M., and L. Verderame, "To Be Non-Assyrian." In Van Soldt, *Ethnicity in Mesopotamia*, 290–305.

Roaf, Michael. "Could Rusa Son of Erimena Have Been King of Urartu during Sargon's Eighth Campaign?" In Kroll et al., *Biainili-Urartu*, 187–216.

———. "Did Rusa Commit Suicide?" In Wilhelm, *Organization, Representation, and Symbols of Power in the Ancient Near East*, 771–80.

Roller, L. E. "The Legend of Midas." *Classical Antiquity* 2 (1983): 299–313.

Rollinger, R., and B. Truschnegg, eds. *Altertum und Mittelmeerraum: Die antike Welt diesseits und jenseits der Levante. Festschrift für Peter W. Haider zum 60. Geburtstag.* Oriens et Occidens 12. Stuttgart: Steiner, 2006.

Rollinger, Robert, et al., eds. *Interkulturalität in der Alten Welt: Vorderasien, Hellas, Ägypten und die vielfältigen Ebenen des Kontakts.* Wiesbaden: Harrassowitz, 2010.

Ross, Micah, ed. *From the Banks of the Euphrates: Studies in Honor of Alice Louise Slotsky.* Winona Lake, Ind.: Eisenbrauns, 2008.

Roth, Jonathan P. *The Logistics of the Roman Army at War (264 B.C.–A.D. 235).* Columbia Studies in the Classical Tradition 23. Leiden: Brill, 2012.

Roth, Martha T., ed. *The Assyrian Dictionary of the University of Chicago.* 26 volumes. Chicago: University of Chicago Press, 1956–2011.

Russell, John M. *The Writing on the Wall: Studies in the Architectural Context of Late Assyrian Palace Inscriptions.* Winona Lake, Ind.: Eisenbrauns, 1999.

Saggs, H. W. F. "Assyrian Warfare in the Sargonid Period." *Iraq* (1963): 145–54.

———. "Historical Texts and Fragments of Sargon II of Assyria, I: The 'Assur Charter.'" *Iraq* 37 (1975): 11–20.

———. *The Nimrud Letters, 1952.* Cuneiform Texts from Nimrud V. London: British School of Archaeology in Iraq, 2001.

———. "The Nimrud Letters, 1952—Part IV, the Urartian Frontier." *Iraq* 20 (1958): 182–212.

Sağlamtimur, Haluk, ed. *Altan Çilingiroğlu'na Armağan: Yukarı Denizin Kıyısında Urartu Krallığına Adanmış bir Hayat. Studies in Honour of Altan Çilingiroğlu: A Life Dedicated to Urartu on the Shores of the Upper Sea.* İstanbul: Arkeoloji ve Sanat Yayınları, 2009.

Sagona, T., ed. *A View from the Highlands: Archaeological Studies in Honour of Charles Burney.* Ancient Near Eastern Studies Supplement 12. Leuven: Peeters, 2004.

Salvini, Mirjo. "La bilingue urarteo-assiri di Rusa I." In Pecorella and Salvini, *Tra lo Zagros e l'Urmia,* 79–96.

———. *Corpus dei testi urartei: Le iscrizioni su pietra e roccia,* vols. 1–3. Documenta Asiana 8. Rome: Ist. di Studi sulle Civilta dell'Egeo e del Vicino Oriente, 2008.

———. "The Eastern Provinces of Urartu and the Beginning of History in Iranian Azerbeijan." In Sağlamtimur, *Altan Çilingiroğlu'na Armağan,* 581–98.

———. "On the Location of Ḫubuškia." *State Archives of Assyria Bulletin* 11 (1997): 109–14.

———. "Sargon et l'Urartu." In Caubet, *Khorsabad, le palais de Sargon II,* 135–57.

———. "Una stele di Rusa III Erimenaḫi dalla zona di Van." *Studi Micenei ed Egeo-Anatolici* 44 (2002): 115–43.

Schwemer, Daniel. "Witchcraft and War: The Ritual Fragment Ki 1904–
10–9, 19 (BM 98989)." *Iraq* 69 (2007): 29–42.

Scurlock, JoAnn. "*Kallāpu:* A New Proposal for a Neo-Assyrian Military
Term." In Neumann et al., *Krieg und Frieden im Alten Vorderasien,*
725–34.

———. "Marduk and His Enemies: City Rivalries in Southern
Mesopotamia." In Wilhelm, *Organization, Representation, and
Symbols of Power in the Ancient Near East,* 369–76.

———. "Neo-Assyrian Battle Tactics." In Young, Chavalas, and Averbeck,
Crossing Boundaries and Linking Horizons, 491–515.

———. Review of Fales, *Guerre et paix en Assyrie: Religion et
imperiélisme. Journal of the American Oriental Society* 132 (2012):
313–15.

Scurlock, JoAnn, and Burton R. Anderson. *Diagnoses in Assyrian and
Babylonian Medicine: Ancient Sources, Translations and Modern
Medical Analyses.* Urbana: University of Illinois Press, 2005.

Sevin, Veli. "The Oldest Highway: Between the Regions of Van and Elazig
in Eastern Anatolia." *Antiquity* 62 (1988): 547–51.

Smith, Adam T. "Archaeologies of Sovereignty." *Annual Review of
Anthropology* 40 (2011): 415–32.

———. "The Making of an Urartian Landscape in Southern Transcaucasia:
A Study of Political Architectonics." *American Journal of
Archaeology* 103 (1999): 45–71.

———. "Rendering the Political Aesthetic: Political Legitimacy in
Urartian Representations of the Built Environment." *Journal of
Anthropological Archaeology* 19 (2000): 131–63.

———. "Urartian Spectacle: Authority, Subjectivity and Aesthetic
Politics." In Inomata and Coben, *Spectacle, Performance, and Power
in Premodern Complex Society,* 103–34.

Smith, Gary V. *Isaiah 1–39: An Exegetical and Theological Exposition
of Holy Scripture.* New American Commentary 15A. Nashville:
Broadman & Holman, 2007.

Sokoloff, M. "The Old Aramaic Inscription from Bukan: A Revised
Interpretation." *Israel Exploration Journal* 49 (1999): 105–15.

Spalinger, Anthony J. *War in Ancient Egypt.* Oxford: Blackwell, 2005.

Steadman, S. R., and G. McMahon, eds. *The Oxford Handbook of Ancient
Anatolia.* Oxford: Oxford University Press, 2011.

Strobel, Karl. "'Kimmeriersturm' und 'Skythenmacht' eine historische
Fiktion?" In Lanfranchi et al., *Leggo!,* 793–842.

Stronach, David. "Notes on the Fall of Nineveh." In Parpola and Whiting,
Assyria '95, 307–24.

Swope, Kenneth M. *A Dragon's Head and a Serpent's Tail: Ming China
and the First Great East Asian War, 1592–1598.* Campaigns and
Commanders 20. Norman: University of Oklahoma Press, 2005.

Tadmor, Hayim. "The Campaigns of Sargon II: A Chronological and
Historical Study." *Journal of Cuneiform Studies* 12 (1958): 23–40.

———. "History and Ideology of the Assyrian Royal Inscriptions." In Fales,
Assyrian Royal Inscriptions, 13–34.

———. *The Inscriptions of Tiglath-Pileser III, King of Assyria.* Jerusalem: Israel Academy of the Sciences, 1994.

———. "Philistia under Assyrian Rule." *Biblical Archaeologist* 29 (1966): 86–102.

———. "Propaganda, Literature, Historiography: Cracking the Code of the Assyrian Royal Inscriptions." In Parpola and Whiting, *Assyria '95,* 325–38.

Tadmor, Hayim, and Shigeo Yamada. *The Royal Inscriptions of Tiglath-pileser III (744–727 B.C.) and Shalmaneser V (726–722 B.C.), Kings of Assyria.* Royal Inscriptions of the Neo-Assyrian Period 1. Winona Lake, Ind.: Eisenbrauns, 2011.

Tadmor, Hayim, Benno Landsberger, and Simo Parpola. "The Sin of Sargon and Sennacherib's Last Will." *State Archives of Assyria Bulletin* 3 (1989): 3–51.

Tappy, R. E. "The Final Years of Israelite Samaria: Toward a Dialogue between Texts and Archaeology." In Crawford et al., *Up to the Gates of Ekron,* 258–80.

Tarhan, Taner M. "The Structure of the Urartian State." *Anadolu Araştırmaları* 9 (1983): 295–310.

Thureau-Dangin, F. *Une relation de la huitième Campagne de Sargon.* Textes cunéiformes du Louvre III. Paris, 1912.

Turner, G. "Tell Nebi Yūnus: The *Ekal Māšarti* of Nineveh." *Iraq* 32 (1970): 68–85.

Unger, E. "Ba'il-gazara." *Reallexikon der Assyriologie und Vorderasiatischen Archäologie* 1 (1993): 392.

———. *Sargon II. Von Assyrien der Sohn Tiglatpilesers III.* Istanbul Asariatika Müzeleri 9. Istanbul: Universum Matbaasi, 1933.

Ussishkin, David. "The Fortifications of Philistine Ekron." *Israel Exploration Journal* 55 (2005): 35–65.

Van Buylaere, G. "I Feared the Snow and Turned Back." In Luukko, Svärd, and Mattila, *Of God(s), Trees, Kings, and Scholars,* 295–306.

Van de Mieroop, M. *The Ancient Mesopotamian City.* Oxford: Oxford University Press, 1997.

———. *Cuneiform Texts and the Writing of History.* Approaching the Ancient World. New York: Routledge, 1999.

———. "The Literature and Political Discourse in Ancient Mesopotamia: Sargon II of Assyria and Sargon of Agade." In Böck, Cancik-Kirschbaum, and Richter, *Munuscula Mesopotamica,* 327–39.

———. "Reading Babylon." *American Journal of Archaeology* 107 (2003): 257–75.

———. "A Study in Contrast: Sargon of Assyria and Rusa of Urartu." In Melville and Slotsky, *Opening the Tablet Box,* 417–34.

Van der Spek, R. J. "The Struggle of King Sargon II of Assyria against the Chaldean Merodach-Baladan (710–708 B.C.). *Jaarbericht van het Vooraziatisch-Egyptisch Geselschap Ex Orient Lux* 25 (1978): 56–66.

Van Lerberghe, K., and Anton Schoors, eds. *Immigration and Emigration within the Ancient Near East: Festschrift E. Lipiński.* Leuven: Peeters, 1995.

Van Soldt, W. H., ed. *Ethnicity in Mesopotamia: Papers Read at the 48th Rencontre Assyriologique Internationale, Leiden, 1–4 July 2002.* Leiden: Nederlands Instituut voor het Nabije Oosten, 2005.

———, ed. *Veenhof Anniversary Volume: Studies Presented to Klaas R. Veenhof on the Occasion of His Sixty-Fifth Birthday.* Publications de l'Institut historique-archéologique néerlandais de Stamboul 89. Leiden: Nederlands Instituut voor het Nabije Oosten, 2001.

Vaughn, A. G., and A. E. Killebrew, eds. *Jerusalem in Bible and Archaeology: The First Temple Period.* Atlanta: Society of Biblical Literature, 2003.

Vera Chamaza, Galo W. "Der VIII. Feldzug Sargon II. Ein Untersuchung der Politik und historischer Geographie des späten 8. Jarhundert v. Chr. (Teil I)." *Archäologische Mitteilungen aus Iran* 27 (1994): 91–103.

———. "Der VIII. Feldzug Sargon II. Ein Untersuchung der Politik und historischer Geographie des späten 8th Jarhundert v. Chr. (Teil II)." *Archäologische Mitteilungen aus Iran* 28 (1995): 235–67.

———. *Die Omnipotenz Aššurs: Entwicklungen in der Aššur-Theologie unter den Sargoniden Sargon II., Sanherib und Asarhaddon.* Alter Orient und Altes Testament 295. Münster: Ugarit-Verlag, 2002.

———. "Sargon's Ascent to the Throne: the Political Situation." *State Archives of Assyria Bulletin* 6 (1992): 21–33.

Vidal, Jordi, ed. *Studies on War in the Ancient Near East: Collected Essays on Military History.* Alter Orient und Altes Testament 372. Münster: Ugarit-Verlag, 2010.

Villard, P. "Barsipitu." *The Prosopography of the Neo-Assyrian Empire* 1, part II, *B–G*, edited by Karen Radner, 273. Helsinki: Neo-Assyrian Text Corpus Project, 1999.

Waetzoldt, H., and H. Hauptmann, eds. *Assyrien im Wandel der Zeiten: XXXIXe Rencontre Assyriologique Internationale, Heidelberg, 6.–10. Juli 1992.* Heidelberger Studien zum Alten Orient 6. Heidelberg: Heidelberger Orientverlag, 1997.

Wäfler, M. *Nicht-Assyrer neuassyrischer Darstellungen.* Alter Orient und Altes Testament 126. Kevelaer, Germany: Butzon und Bercker; Neukirchen-Vluyn, Germany: Neukirchener Verlag, 1975.

Walker, C. B. F. "The Epigraphs." In Albenda, *The Palace of Sargon, King of Assyria,* 106–13.

Waters, Matthew W. *A Survey of Neo-Elamite History.* State Archives of Assyria Studies 12. Helsinki: University of Helsinki Press, 2000.

Weaver, Ann M. "The 'Sin of Sargon' and Esarhaddon's Reconception of Sennacherib: A Study in Divine Will, Human Politics, and Ideology." In Collon and George, *Nineveh,* 61–66.

Weinfeld, M. "The Loyalty Oath in the Ancient Near East." *Ugarit Forschungen* 8 (1976): 379–414.

Wilhelm, Gernot, ed. *Organization, Representation, and Symbols of Power in the Ancient Near East: Proceedings of the 54th Rencontre Assyriologique Internationale at Würzburg, 20–25 July 2008.* Winona Lake, Ind.: Eisenbrauns, 2012.

Wilkinson, T. J., Eleanor Barbanes Wilkinson, Jason Ur, and Mark Altaweel, "Landscape and Settlement in the Neo-Assyrian Empire." *Bulletin of the American Schools of Oriental Research* 340 (2005): 23–56.

Winter, Irene J. *On Art in the Ancient Near East*, vol. 1, *Of the First Millennium B.C.* Culture and History of the Ancient Near East 34. Leiden: Brill, 2010.

Woods, Christopher. "Mutilation of Image and Text in Early Sumerian Sources." In May, *Iconoclasm and Text Destruction in the Ancient Near East and Beyond*, 33–55.

Wright, E. M. "The Eighth Campaign of Sargon II (714 B.C.)." *Journal of Near Eastern Studies* 2 (1943): 173–85.

Wright, Jacob L. "Warfare and Wanton Destruction: A Reexamination of Deuteronomy 20: 19–20 in Relation to Ancient Siegecraft." *Journal of Biblical Literature* 127 (2008): 423–58.

Yakar, Jak. "The Ethnoarchaeology of the Socio-Economic Structure of East Anatolia." In Köroğlu and Konyar, *Urartu—Transformation in the East*, 126–45.

Yamada, Shigeo. *The Construction of the Assyrian Empire: A Historical Study of the Inscriptions of Shalmaneser III (859–824 B.C.) Relating to His Campaigns in the West.* Culture and History of the Ancient Near East 3. Leiden: Brill, 2000.

———. "*Kārus* on the Frontiers of the Neo-Assyrian Empire." *Orient: Report of the Society for Near Eastern Studies in Japan* 40 (2005): 56–90.

Yon, Marguerite. "La découverte de la stele à Larnaca (Chypre)." In Caubet, *Khorsabad, le palais de Sargon II*, 161–68.

Young, G. D., M. W. Chavalas, and R. E. Averbeck, eds. *Crossing Boundaries and Linking Horizons: Studies in Honor of Michael C. Astour on His 80th Birthday.* Bethesda: CDL Press, 1997.

Younger, K. Lawson, "Assyrian Involvement in the Southern Levant at the End of the Eighth Century B.C.E." In Vaughn and Killebrew, *Jerusalem in Bible and Archaeology*, 235–63.

———. "The Fall of Samaria in Light of Recent Research." *Catholic Biblical Quarterly* 61 (1999): 461–82.

———. "Recent Study on Sargon II, King of Assyria: Implications for Biblical Studies." In Chavalas and Younger, *Mesopotamia and the Bible*, 288–329.

Zaccagnini, C. "A Urartian Royal Inscription in the Report of Sargon's 8th Campaign." In Fales, *Assyrian Royal Inscriptions*, 259–95.

Zadok, Ran. "The Ethno-Linguistic Character of Northwestern Iran and Kurdistan in the Neo-Assyrian Period." *Iran* 40 (2002): 89–151.

Zamazalová, S. "Before the Assyrian Conquest in 671 B.C.E.: Relations between Egypt, Kush and Assyria." In Mynářová, *Egypt and the Near East*, 297–328.

Zawadzki, Stefan. "Hostages in Neo-Assyrian Royal Inscriptions." In Van Lerberghe and Schoors, *Immigration and Emigration within the Ancient Near East*, 449–58.

———. "The Revolt of 746 B.C. and the Coming of Tiglath-pileser III to the Throne." *State Archives of Assyria Bulletin* 8 (1994): 53–54.

Zertal, Adam. "The Province of Samaria (Assyrian Samerina) in the Late Iron Age (Iron Age III). In Lipschits and Blenkinsopp, *Judah and the Judeans in the Neo-Babylonian Period*, 377–412.

Zimansky, Paul. "Urartian Geography and Sargon's 8th Campaign." *Journal of Near Eastern Studies* (1990): 1–21.

———. "Urartian Material Culture as State Assemblage: An Anomaly in the Archaeology of Empire." *Bulletin of the American Schools of Oriental Research* 299/300 (1995): 103–15.

Index

References to illustrations and tables appear in italics.